Disease, Mortality and Population in Transition

DISEASE, MORTALITY AND POPULATION IN TRANSITION

*Epidemiological–Demographic Change
in England since the Eighteenth Century
as part of a Global Phenomenon*

ALEX MERCER

Leicester University Press
(a division of Pinter Publishers)
Leicester, London and New York

First published in Great Britain in 1990 by Leicester University Press
(a division of Pinter Publishers Ltd)

Editorial offices
Fielding Johnson Building, University of Leicester,
University Road, Leicester, LE1 7RH

Trade and other enquiries
25 Floral Street, London, WC2E 9DS

British Library Cataloguing in Publication Data

A CIP catalogue recored for this book is available
from the British Library

ISBN 0-7185-1344-4

Typeset by Florencetype Ltd, Kewstoke, Avon
Printed and bound in Great Britain by Biddles Ltd,
Guildford and Kings Lynn

Contents

List of figures and tables

vii

Preface

Since the eighteenth century there has been a decline in mortality in England which has had consequences for population growth as in the rest of Europe, and this has been accompanied by a shift from communicable to non-communicable causes of death in an epidemiological–demographic transition. This study further challenges the idea that advances in the economic standard of living and particularly improved nutritional resistance to infectious diseases have been largely responsible. Preventive and public health measures provided the basis for sustained mortality decline, while changes in transmission rates of infectious diseases as a result of socio-demographic change could still have been more important than individual economic circumstances or nutrition in the final phase of mortality decline from the end of the nineteenth century. Using both local and national records from England, and Europe for comparison, relative trends and turning points in cause-specific death rates can be examined, while taking into account the inter-relationships between different diseases. The major epidemic diseases – plague, smallpox, typhus and cholera – killed a high proportion of the population regardless of socio-economic or nutritional status, and their virtual elimination by the end of the nineteenth century in England constituted a health revolution which could not have occurred without preventive action in view of the continued virulence of the micro-organisms. Plague and typhus had been associated with famine, but more because of the adverse circumstances which accompanied these and other socially disruptive events, while efforts to control the spread of these diseases may have been as important as an increasingly more reliable supply of food. Plague did not reappear in England in the eighteenth century although typhus was still prevalent, but the most regular cause of epidemic mortality at that time was smallpox. There is considerable evidence that the use of immunisation against smallpox based first on inoculation, but more significantly on vaccination after 1800, had a quite dramatic effect on mortality levels and population growth despite the growing health hazards in increasingly crowded towns where people sought a better life. Insanitary living conditions were conducive to the spread of cholera which arrived from Asia in the 1830s, and efforts to avert this threat formed the basis for the control of other water-borne diseases through the tracing of sources of infection and the provision of sewerage and pure water supplies. The final recession of cholera, typhus and smallpox occurred at about the same time in the 1870s, and the removal of smallpox from the series of infections encountered probably had repercussions for mortality from inter-current and secondary diseases including respiratory tuberculosis in the nineteenth century. In the twentieth century preventive measures against tuberculosis and other socio-demographic changes affecting the transmission rates and hence severity of air-borne and respiratory diseases, such as longer birth intervals, smaller families, and less overcrowded housing, probably had as much effect in reducing death rates as any improvements in nutrition that may have occurred in this late phase of the mortality transition. However, improvements in the quality of food and milk probably had an increasing impact on mortality from typhoid, gastro-intestinal diseases and non-respiratory tuberculosis, and monitoring for many infectious diseases became possible from the end of the nineteenth century with the new methods of bacteriology.

Against the background of declining infectious-disease mortality, the growing importance of non-communicable diseases – and particularly circulatory disease and cancer – can be seen as part of a global phenomenon. Many rural populations in developing countries now experience high death rates from these causes, so they can no longer be viewed simplistically as products of an industrial way of life *per se*. Nor are they essentially diseases of affluence, since the lower socio-economic groups in industrial societies have higher than average death rates in middle age. Physical factors, albeit related to life-style in a socio-cultural context, do remain the most established influences on mortality from the major non-communicable diseases, but recognised risks cannot explain all aspects of mortality differentials and trends. Many inter-relationships between non-communicable diseases and the communicable diseases which they have replaced as major causes of death may be significant for an understanding of contemporary disease and mortality patterns. Infectious diseases were in fact the original 'diseases of civilisation', being a consequence of living in settled communities and towns. In the last three centuries, some of the most dramatic changes in mortality and population in human history have occurred largely as a result of preventive health measures and other socio-demographic changes affecting the transmission rates of infectious disease, but obviously supported by a more consistent supply of food. The major epidemic diseases of the seventeenth and eighteenth centuries no longer occur at all in Europe, or indeed in most of the world, and the recession of plague, smallpox, cholera and typhus epidemics constitutes a revolutionary change in the human condition. Even so, many of the micro-organisms which caused high mortality under the poorer conditions of life in the past, are still widely prevalent causing communicable disease of varying significance for mortality patterns throughout the world. In addition, the immune and cellular reactions which certain micro-organisms provoke throughout life may have adverse consequences which are also significant in non-communicable manifestations of disease. Further evidence of the significance of this may have worldwide implications, while disease control and preventive health programmes continue to be effective in improving survival chances in developing countries.

Acknowledgement

I am grateful to all those who have read various earlier drafts of the text, including anonymous publisher's reviewers whose constructive comments have helped me to make many revisions in working towards this final version.

1 Introduction

The decline in importance of infectious diseases as major causes of death in industrial societies has been one of the most significant changes in human history and has resulted in an unprecedented life expectancy. The expectation now is that almost all children grow up to adulthood and that most people will live into their seventies despite the risk of many chronic non-communicable disorders. Diseases such as cancer, stroke and heart disease cause much debility and long-term suffering which detracts from the idea of progress in health that has come with the control of communicable diseases. The epidemic diseases which caused high mortality in the past generally resulted in acute, short-term illness and frequently proved fatal. Particularly high mortality in the early years of life, together with a high death rate from tuberculosis which produced more long-term sickness in adults, meant that average life expectancy was about thirty to forty years until only a hundred years ago. The change to a new pattern of chronic, non-communicable diseases, together with the decline in the overall annual death rate, or mortality transition, has occurred in a period of more rapid population growth since the eighteenth century. The whole phenomenon may be regarded as an epidemiological-demographic transition, and although the level of fertility affected population change it probably also responded to changes in the infectious-disease environment. In some respects this historical process indicates an ecologically successful period for the human species, but today global environmental conditions and deprivation in the Third World constitute problems on an unprecedented scale.

The relationship between health and living standards is complex and two-way, although there is a widespread view that improvements in the 'standard of living' have been the main reason for the declining impact of infectious diseases and the mortality transition. A debate on this issue has focused first on evidence from the eighteenth century on changes in real income, and changes in food consumption per head which might indicate better nutrition and hence improved resistance to disease. Even if the evidence were consistent with some effect on mortality levels, the standard of living is a difficult concept when considering this relationship since diseases themselves interfere with physical growth and human productivity. Inadequate nutrition is a contributing factor in high rates of infectious-disease mortality in developing countries today, as it is likely to have been in Europe until relatively recently, but infectious illnesses themselves cause malnutrition or interfere with the ability of the body to convert food into energy and growth.[1] The relationship between standard of living and non-communicable-disease mortality patterns is even less straightforward, since the more affluent societies of the world have high death rates from such diseases compared with most developing countries. However, the exceptionally high death rates from particular non-communicable diseases in some countries which are not heavily industrialised suggest that it is simplistic to consider them as diseases of the 'industrial way of life'. The higher-than-average death rates among the lower socio-economic groups in most industrialised societies also suggest that the term 'diseases of affluence' is inappropriate.[2]

The changing pattern of disease and mortality in the demographic transition in England will be the focus of attention here, although comparative data from Europe are useful in examining the main diseases involved in mortality change. Historical studies of European populations still have particular relevance for other parts of the world where many of the same infectious diseases which caused high mortality in the past still contribute to unacceptably high child mortality today. A continuing high risk for children in the first few years of life probably inhibits the kind of limitation of family size that can eventually lead to a stable population size in particular areas. The demographic implications of changes in the overall death rate relative to changes in the birth rate have been examined in many studies, although the mortality transition has also been an object of research in itself. There has been a longstanding debate over the importance of various factors which might have affected the vital rates and hence contributed to increased rates of population growth. Recently, historical demographers in England have shifted the emphasis towards fertility as being the more significant variable in the acceleration of population growth from the mid eighteenth century. However, it is widely accepted that there was a decline in mortality from this time, with a further downturn at the beginning of the nineteenth century, and again towards the end of the century as in much of Europe.

An analysis of aggregated data from several hundred parish records in England carried out by the Cambridge Group has broadly confirmed this long-term pattern of mortality change. Although it was acknowledged that this had been a substantial influence in the more rapid population growth, it was thought to have been outweighed in importance by fertility increases throughout the eighteenth century.[3] Hitherto it had generally been thought that fertility did not increase in the second half of the eighteenth century,[4] and birth rates fell in other North-European countries for which national records are available.[5] It is outside the scope of this study of disease and mortality change to critically examine the methods of estimation and evidence on changes in the birth rate. However, even if these recent estimates of vital rates are a reasonable reflection of events in England, the changing impact of infectious diseases should still not be underestimated. For one thing marriage and fertility patterns in England in the eighteenth century may have been affected by the changing impact of some infectious diseases on those at reproductive ages, just as mortality levels were reduced. Also, evidence from all over Europe confirms that mortality decline led to the more rapid growth in population at the beginning of the nineteenth century.

In this study of changing disease patterns in the mortality transition, population growth will be considered as a related phenomenon although it is not an objective to establish the main cause of the demographic transition. The acceleration of population growth in Europe from the mid eighteenth century, and the massive increase in numbers up to the mid twentieth century, has been examined by historians, demographers and medical specialists who have considered the relative importance of changes in the standard of living, advances in medical therapy, and efforts at disease control. Historians have also considered the phenomenon in relation to the 'Industrial Revolution', an 'Agricultural Revolution', and an improved economic standard of living which might have affected population growth through increases in fertility or reductions in mortality. Many studies have concentrated on the role of changes in mortality in population growth and indicated certain aspects of disease patterns that were important. For example, the relationship between food supply and mortality rates in the period leading up to the transition has been taken to suggest that many epidemic diseases had an effect of their own which was independent of the effects of famine or poor harvests.[6] In an even longer historical perspective the changing infectious-disease environment has been shown to be linked with the settlement of human communities and with the great migrations of the past.[7] Changes in disease, immunity, and population can also be viewed in relation to the changing environment and different way of life that has come with increased urbanisation, and there has been debate over whether this has been a cause or a consequence of population growth.

In examining the relative importance of different factors in the epidemiological-demographic transition, consideration must be given to the nature of the diseases and to the way in which human beings have reacted to them, both as biological and social beings. Although human populations in the past were devastated by plague and pestilence there seems to have been an earlier perception that protective measures were possible than was the case in relation to other disasters such as earthquakes, typhoons and floods. There have been many interventions by human beings to counteract the adverse relationship between micro-organisms and man.[8] Preventive health measures together with other advantageous changes affecting the transmission and outcome of infectious diseases could have reduced their impact on the quality and length of life. Something amounting to a 'Health Revolution' has certainly occurred in industrialised societies despite the rise to prominence of other non-infectious diseases, and this process continues with repercussions for the human condition in all parts of the world. The question of whether the mortality transition in Europe occurred because of particular social action and health measures, or as a result of advances in people's own economic standard of living, is not just of academic historical interest since it may be relevant to development issues in the Third World today. Evidence relating to this can be re-examined here, although a case for the argument that improvements in people's standard of living occurred at the significant times in relation to mortality decline was not, in fact, presented by the main supporters of this hypothesis, such as McKeown in England and Omran in the United States.[9]

The main objective of McKeown and his co-workers was to explain the recorded fall in mortality of 22% between 1848–54 and 1901, which in turn was only 30% of the reduction for the whole period 1848–54 to 1971. Cause-specific death rates were used to identify arithmetic components of overall mortality decline, but many qualifications have to be made in evaluating the role of different diseases on the basis of such an analysis. The relative arithmetic contribution to overall mortality decline will be referred to in this study, but in terms of the contribution made by recorded disease categories towards each unit of decline in the overall death rate. In others studies such proportions have been expressed as percentage contributions which is inappropriate because death rates for some cause groups were increasing, so that other groups must have contributed more than 1.0 towards a unit fall in the death rate to offset this. Nevertheless, McKeown was clearly correct to emphasise that infectious diseases accounted for most of the mortality decline in the period 1848–54 to 1901. They contributed 0.92 towards each unit of decline in the overall age-standardised death rate, and most of this was due to the reduction in recorded death rates from tuberculosis, cholera, typhus, typhoid and scarlet fever which together contributed 0.79. McKeown's interpretation of the main reasons for these changes was that about half involved improvements in the standard of living and especially the influence of improved diet on tuberculosis mortality. A further quarter of the decline he attributed to sanitary reforms and hygiene measures affecting the mainly water-borne diseases, and a further quarter to a change in the character of disease and scarlet fever in particular.

McKeown pointed out that there is little indication of a general change in the character of infectious diseases which might account for mortality decline, and even his suggestion that scarlet fever was an exception is open to question.[10] He emphasised that medical therapy had not become widely or significantly effective by the nineteenth century, making it clear that some other changes in the prevailing relationship between micro-organisms and man must have occurred from the mid eighteenth century. Possible influences on the impact of infectious diseases such as changes in virulence, exposure, and genetic susceptibility to micro-organisms were rejected. It remains generally accepted that neither these, nor climatic changes,[11] could account for mortality decline. By a process of elimination, McKeown arrived at the conclusion that the widely accepted role of nutritional deprivation in high mortality from many infectious diseases must hold the key to the mortality transition and hence to the modern rise of population.[12] As a result, his work has met with considerable criticism from historians and demographers, in part because the evidence is by no means clear that diet, nutrition or even the economic standard of living, improved in the second half of the eighteenth century when the transition in mortality and population began. It may be that increases in food supply only kept pace with population growth rather than actually causing it,[13] and there are indications that the standard of living actually deteriorated when population was increasing most rapidly in the early years of the nineteenth century. There were reductions in prices later, but studies of economic indicators have in fact found little consistent association with the phases of more rapid population growth.[14] It has been pointed out that the consensus in the 'standard-of-living debate' now seems to be that conditions in England may even have grown worse for the mass of the new urban labour force in the period of industrialisation up to the mid nineteenth century after which economic conditions improved, at least for those in work.[15]

Despite the lack of a coherent body of evidence being advanced in support of the view that mortality decline has been in large part a result of improvements in the standard of living, the approach and general conclusions of studies which have advanced this view continue to influence contemporary work on the mortality transition in other parts of the world.[16] The idea of the importance of changes in the standard of living was also supported in a study of data from New York in which Omran referred to the change in cause-of-death structure and in mortality as an epidemiological transition. He suggested that the shifts in health and disease patterns in the mortality transition stemmed from socio-economic advances, and concurred with McKeown in suggesting that the main determinants of mortality decline were improvements in living standards, nutrition, housing, personal hygiene and, in the case of scarlet fever, a change in the character of the micro-organism.[17] On the other hand, Kunitz in a recent review of studies of mortality change in North America since the seventeenth century, concluded that the relative contribution to decline made by increased resistance to infectious disease or by decreased exposure was difficult to ascertain, although he agreed with McKeown that the role of medical therapy was very limited.[18] It can also be noted here that smallpox and cholera epidemics were involved in many of the mortality peaks recorded in New York in the second half of the nineteenth century, and these could not have been eliminated without preventive measures. Again, in the case of much more recent mortality decline in many developing countries, the improvement does not appear to be linked with advance in the economic standard of living, but with various health interventions imported from more industrialised countries.[19] Some of these have been therapeutic measures developed largely since World War II, but preventive measures which had proved effective in Europe in the past were also introduced.

The major contribution of the studies by McKeown and his co-workers was to open up a debate over the changing conditions which might have

caused the late phase of the disease and mortality transition from the end
of the nineteenth century. They presented the basic case that medicine in
the sense of medical therapy and institutionalised care is unlikely to have
caused the mortality decline between the mid nineteenth century and the
1940s.[20] Effective treatment for tuberculosis came with the use of strepto-
mycin, but this was not until 1947. Sulphapyridine, useful for treating
respiratory disease, and sulphonamides for whooping cough, were not
available until the 1940s when antibiotics also became available for the
treatment of these and other infectious diseases. Smallpox, typhus and
typhoid could not have been very effectively treated in the eighteenth and
nineteenth centuries, while chloramphenicol was not available for the
treatment of enteric fever until 1950.[21] Such limitations have to be borne in
mind when considering the possible role of institutionalised medicine in
mortality decline. However, a later study of the development of the
voluntary hospitals and dispensaries concluded that they did make a
valuable contribution to the care of the sick poor in towns from the second
half of the eighteenth century. The hospital records available for some
towns indicate that a wide range of diseases and casualties was treated, and
mortality rates among in-patients may have been no higher that 5–10%.[22]
Increases in the nineteenth century possibly reflected changes in case load.
More industrial accidents were being treated and population pressure
probably placed a greater strain on resources. Many cases were probably
not critical – such as those involving certain rheumatic, bronchial and
digestive disorders – but treatment for these and for burns, scalds,
fractures and other injuries saved many of the poor from deteriorating.
However, the evidence seems to suggest that the hospitals did not treat
enough people from rural areas to have made any significant impact on
death rates among those who were still the majority of the population at
the end of the eighteenth century,and in some major towns the death rate
declined even before the hospitals were opened in the 1770s.[23] Also, in the
early years children were not generally admitted and the major infectious
diseases were not tackled on any significant scale in hospitals until the end
of the nineteenth century, by which time more was known about the
mechanisms of transmission and about the need to care for the sick.[24]

It is possible that some treatment measures were beneficial for the
population in a preventive rather than a curative way, since the isolation of
severe cases of infectious disease from the end of the nineteenth century
may have helped to reduce transmission rates. Even so, McKeown's basic
case that effective curative measures were not available for most of the
major infectious diseases until the twentieth century constituted an
important challenge to assumptions about mortality decline being the
result of advances in medicine. Two early studies had suggested that some
medical innovations might have been important, including hospitals,
dispensaries, midwifery services and smallpox inoculation.[25] Subsequent
studies seem to have resulted in a consensus that despite important
advances and efforts to organise health care and the treatment of sickness,
these were not a major factor in the mortality decline of the eighteenth and
nineteenth centuries. On the other hand, Razzell made a comprehensive

study of evidence concerning the introduction of inoculation in the eighteenth century and concluded that this measure had been significant in reducing mortality. He also pointed to other preventive measures which were introduced in the eighteenth century, such as the use of citrus fruit and cod-liver oil to reduce the risk of scurvy and rickets. These two were not among the major killing diseases, but at the beginning of the eighteenth century around 300 deaths a years were recorded as due to rickets in the London Bills of Mortality, and there was a rapid fall to negligible levels by the 1780s. Ideas about hygiene were also being promoted but were more readily applied in institutions amenable to the disciplines required, such as army camps and hospitals.[26] Riley has pointed to the improved cure rate for typhus victims in British naval hospitals after the great epidemic of the 1740s. Ideas which were being expressed about cleanliness and ventilation may have been put into practice, reducing the risk to patients from other concomitant infections.[27]

Even though theories of disease transmission were misconceived until the Germ Theory was accepted much later at the end of the nineteenth century, appropriate ideas for reducing the risk of disease and the spread of infection may have been disseminated through the developing dispensaries and with the growth of the lying-in movement.[28] Riley considered a wide variety of improvements and unwittingly appropriate measures relating to the revival of an environmentalist approach to disease from the mid eighteenth century in much of Europe. He concurred with McKeown and Brown's view that medicine for the individual in the eighteenth century was unlikely to have been very effective in reducing mortality risks,[29] but identified other measures such as the ventilation and cleansing of public places, and drainage in more rural areas, which could have had an impact on the transmission of air-borne and vector-borne infections. He emphasised that a new public-spiritedness was translated into actions to intervene where adverse environmental conditions were seen to be linked with disease, although he acknowledged that in the eighteenth century such measures probably had a rather limited effect on mortality decline.

In this study, major preventive and public-health measures will be discussed in relation to the main phases of mortality decline, since their introduction appears to have coincided with major turning points in a way that economic changes did not. The whole period of the mortality transition should be considered when examining the role of different factors, and this particularly applies to evidence of the dramatic impact of immunisation against smallpox. Clearly some causes of the general mortality decline will be specific to one period or another, but many of the advances affecting particular diseases had cumulative repercussions which are not easily quantified. For example, the more rapid improvements in life expectancy in the last phase of the transition from the end of the nineteenth century may have been contingent on the earlier advances such as the control of cholera and smallpox in particular. Razzell presented comprehensive evidence concerning the use of inoculation in the second half of the eighteenth century in England, and his work – although arousing contention – still provides a plausible explanation for the initial downturn in mortality at that time. However, it did not extend to a consideration of the further impact of immunisation based on the idea of vaccination in the nineteenth century. Records from all over Europe indicate a dramatic decline in mortality levels in the first few decades and a major phase in the mortality transition.

There was clearly a major epidemiological-demographic turning point before this in the eighteenth century, while another phase in the historical pattern of disease and mortality ended with the last significant outbreak of plague recorded in London in 1665.[30] Apart from this important change, the recording of deaths under other categories in the London Bills was similar to that in the seventeenth century, 'Fevers', identified as mainly typhus and typhoid in other sets of records, was still a major category to which deaths were assigned in the eighteenth century. Consumption had become an equivalent category by this time, and tuberculosis flourished as contact with expanding towns increased. Regular epidemics of smallpox continued to be an important feature of the mortality pattern according to different sets of Bills of Mortality,[31] although deaths attributed directly to this one disease were fewer than in the other two categories. In towns, smallpox had become more a disease of childhood being sustained by the larger numbers of the newly susceptible but conveying immunity on those who survived. However, along with other diseases of infancy and childhood it had repercussions for future health, and its importance is also reflected in the fluctuations in total mortality corresponding with epidemics (as shown in Figure 3.6, for example).[32] Despite the control of smallpox during the course of the nineteenth century, the period was still characterised by high mortality from infectious diseases, with tuberculosis and the epidemic diseases of childhood being particularly prominent as recognised infections. Significantly, these diseases remain prevalent, and still cause high death rates among the poor in developing countries today.

In general, the conclusions reached in previous investigations of mortality decline in England have been limited by the period considered, and this in part reflects a division of labour among those prepared to consider evidence of cause-specific mortality in different sets of records. Hitherto, studies of the mortality transition have not brought together evidence of disease and mortality change from the pre-registration records, and the more formalised registration data available for England and Wales as a whole from the 1840s. There has been a fragmented approach with different studies considering one or other of the main phases of mortality decline, and understating the importance of changes in other periods and the health measures that were introduced in them. It has been pointed out for example that McKeown's relegation of insect-borne diseases to a role of little importance in mortality decline was the result of a disassociation of the early period of decline from that which occurred after the eighteenth century.[33] Typhus in particular was a major killer in the pre-registration period. There has also been an underestimation of the revolution in health, disease, and mortality risk that came with the disappearance of major killers such as plague, smallpox and cholera which had arrived from Asia and were destructive of life irrespective of economic standards of living and nutrition.

The recent extensive work by Wrigley and Schofield on the population history of England from the sixteenth century to the end of the nineteenth century, places little emphasis on changing disease patterns. A more recent collection of valuable work on nineteenth-century disease and mortality change relating to particular towns in England contains little reference to changes in the first half of the century, inheriting this deficiency from McKeown's work based on national-registration data alone.[34] Views on the mortality transition are likely to be distorted without a long-term perspective, and in the case of England this should take in the early stages of transition in the mid eighteenth century, changes at the beginning of the nineteenth century, the downturn in mortality in the 1870s, and the rapid decline in the twentieth century in which some major non-communicable causes of death also contributed.

Without a long-term perspective on mortality decline, the cumulative and combined effect of various disease-control, public-health, and hygiene measures may continue to be underestimated. By using different sets of records, for example, the changing pattern of mortality that occurred with the control of smallpox[35] can be compared with a much later downturn in mortality from other air-borne infectious diseases from the end of the nineteenth century. Despite the many limitations of early historical records showing cause of death and the national records of the Registrar-General which started in 1838, they do provide a framework for discussion and a means of considering hypotheses about the causes of mortality decline. Serious doubts about the accuracy of the London Bills of Mortality and other pre-registration records have led to an emphasis on the evidence from the registration period. The Bills originated in the sixteenth century, as a means of monitoring deaths from the plague, and were drawn up and published by the Company of Parish Clerks. The main cause-groups can usefully be compared with those found in the Northampton and Carlisle Bills from the late eighteenth century, and the latter, discussed by Heysham, may be the best reflection of medical diagnosis at that time. Despite the uncertainty about the accuracy of recording of causes of death and their consistency over time,[36] the Bills do confirm the impression of historians of disease, that infectious diseases accounted for most deaths in the period of rapid urbanisation and industrialisation in the eighteenth and early nineteenth centuries. It is possible to identify some major turning points in the trends in death rates, while Glass showed that there was some compatibility between the level of recording of the main groups of infectious disease in the London Bills and the early registration records compiled by the Registrar-General.[37]

In England, attempts were made from the beginning of civil registration to see that the death returns were complete and covered all sections of the population. Each death was to be registered within five days, and Chadwick made a strong case for the appointment of medical people to act as registrars, which many did. At first, the provision for obtaining the information on cause of death was quite lax. A relative, or the person responsible for the burial, could either report the cause given by a physician, or simply offer his own opinion.[38] Farr became the biggest influence on the workings of the General Registry Office and was largely responsible for the evolution of techniques and procedures for gathering and analysing mortality statistics. Lister had asked doctors to provide a written statement on the cause of deaths occurring in their practice, and this could be used by the informant. Farr encouraged the written statement on cause of death, and wrote to practitioners urging them to co-operate in certification. It seems there was considerable support for the new system which was to be an improvement on the recording of cause by non-medically-qualified 'searchers' in the London Bills of Mortality. Later, printed forms were supplied on which certification of cause of death was to be written, and by 1870 92% of all deaths in England, and 98% in London, were in fact medically certified.[39] Nevertheless, considerable caution is required in interpreting data from these early records of the Registrar-General given doubts about the veracity of some certificates and other deficiencies.[40]

McKeown pointed out the difficulty in interpreting trends in death rates because of the uncertainty about certification of causes, especially before the experimental findings by bacteriologists in the last three decades of the nineteenth century. Infectious diseases were still a major cause of death in England at this time and controversy raged over the theory which claimed to explain their causes in some general unified way, but which also identified specific agents. The growing of pure cultures of various disease organisms and demonstrations of their association with particular diseases,[41] helped to form the basis of the Germ Theory and a more scientific understanding of infectious-disease transmission. The work dispelled much of the mystery and irrationality that had always surrounded disease, and bacteria and micro-organisms were established as the source of diseases which for centuries had been major causes of death. The new science of bacteriology, virology and immunology contributed to the development of practical measures for preventing disease at a time when medical statistics were being more effectively used to monitor their impact.

Following the pioneering work on statistical methods by Graunt and Petty who began monitoring historical trends and searching for meaningful associations with changes in living conditions, environmental ideas about disease transmission were investigated in the eighteenth century.[42] However, the misguided view of the causes of environmental correlations of disease with such things as foul air, stagnant water and refuse, still persisted when the harmful organisms which were carried in the air and water became identified at the end of the nineteenth century. The Germ Theory, in following on from the Theory of Evolution, became the subject of bitter and lasting controversy.[43] There were many who found such new scientific ideas incompatible with religious doctrine about an all-wise God, and his relationship with Man in the Universe. Disease was seen by many as the work of God, and a measure such as smallpox vaccination was interpreted as an interference in this. The Royal Commission on Vaccination of 1896 referred to the opposition there had been on religious and 'moral' grounds, rather than on the basis of any well-argued scientific case.[44] Nevertheless, this measure was accepted on a vast scale, especially in Europe, long before the theory of germs and contagion had been accepted or specific agents identified.

In the twentieth century, at least until the problems with HIV infection, there has been a shift in scientific attention away from infectious diseases, towards the manifestations of non-contagious disease which can be monitored with ever more specific, but not necessarily more reliable, statistical data. With the increasing control of infectious diseases in countries such as Britain, a concern has grown over the chronic diseases of middle and later life. New methods and techniques have been evolved to determine the geographical distribution of mortality from these causes. Howe suggested that medical geography had been somewhat usurped after the development of the Germ Theory of disease.[45] Much of epidemiology is now concerned with differential mortality risk from these diseases in middle age and the early retirement years, for those with different behaviour, in different environmental conditions, socio-economic groups and geographical areas. A unity of approach to disease that appeared with the Germ Theory, has become of more limited relevance as the pattern of serious disease and cause of death has changed. However, different populations are in different phases of transition and the population dynamics of infectious diseases still have important implications for their control worldwide.[46] Transmission theory has been developed, linking the sciences of epidemiology and immunology, and important findings will be referred to here concerning the continuing impact and severity of some infectious diseases which were significant in the mortality transition in England.

In considering the proportion of mortality decline that was attributed to particular infectious diseases, McKeown argued that many had been clearly identified on clinical grounds in the nineteenth century, and that practitioners would have been very experienced in all types of infectious disease.[47] However, it is important to emphasise the inter-related nature of the infectious-disease environment. Causes of death are more often than not multiple or inter-related, and this is true of the infectious diseases of the past as well as the non-communicable diseases to which most deaths are now attributed. An emphasis on this hitherto neglected aspect of the disease and mortality transition is considered essential here for an understanding of its main causes. It will help to qualify the impression of changes in the cause-of-death structure given by an analysis of the arithmetic components of overall mortality change which relate to discrete recording categories of disease. It seems essential to bear in mind the combined effects of concurrent diseases, and the cumulative impact of different infections and adverse conditions in the body. This is probably more important than attempting to establish just how accurately deaths might have been attributed to one prime cause or another in the records. The evidence can first be taken at face value, but there has to be some qualitative assessment – particularly as little can be done to quantify any corrections to the data which might seem appropriate. It is probably more important here to examine the relativity of trends for particular recorded causes and develop an overall impression of the main events, than attempt to estimate the completeness of recording under particular categories of disease. Without a broad, albeit impressionistic, view of disease and mortality change in the long-term, more detailed analytical studies or attempts at a theory of the demographic transition, may lack a perspective on the changing impact of disease in the epidemiological-demographic transition.

The inter-related nature of diseases, changes in diagnostic preference and techniques, and accuracy of certification of primary cause, are again important considerations in the assessment of trends in death rates for the non-communicable diseases which have replaced communicable diseases as the main causes of death. Much scepticism is obviously necessary as with the early data on infectious diseases, but this should not preclude the development of an overall impression of changing disease and mortality patterns without which more detailed analysis may be meaningless. Non-communicable diseases such as cancer and circulatory disease initially had to be considered as groups of diseases on the basis of similarities in the form of the different manifestations. This approach is reinforced by considerations of accuracy in recording, and the fact that smaller sub-categories of disease may be subject to greater errors in diagnosis which may be largely cancelled out for the main order groups.[48] The large unit of analysis may also be more than an heuristic device for analysing the more reliable trend in mortality for the group as a whole, inasmuch as it summarises a set of inter-related and competing risks. At a rather simplified level, the main fatalities from circulatory disease involve disorders of the blood, such as embolism and thrombosis, and of the arteries because of the process of atherosclerosis. Although these under-lying disorders may be linked with certain exogenous factors in different ways, changes in the total circulatory-disease death rate could reflect changes in the predominant risks and in any common influences.

Processes occurring at the individual, 'biological' level, have to be related to the findings of many epidemiological enquiries which have contributed to a better understanding of environmental and behavioural risks in non-communicable disease. Such variables as cigarette-smoking, diet and air pollution have been studied, along with climatic, geophysical and carcinogenic influences on mortality. Nevertheless, there is a possibil-ity that all these factors may operate through common underlying cellular processes. Although no comprehensive general theory has linked external variables with internal processes in non-communicable disease, some kind of synthesis might be necessary for an understanding of certain historical aspects of disease and mortality patterns. Fragmentation of cause-of-death statistics, and an emphasis on trends in mortality for different forms of circulatory disease – such as cerebrovascular disease, ischaemic heart disease and hypertension – might obscure the effects of some underlying influence on these disorders. Similarly, too much emphasis on trends in mortality for cancer at different sites, might obscure a pattern of mortality for all forms of disease in the group which may involve similar underlying cellular-immunological processes.

With the growing importance of non-communicable diseases, many questions have been raised about aetiology which have not been fully answered, and nothing like the unity of the Germ Theory has emerged to explain them. Nevertheless, it will be suggested that there is probably more of a relationship between past and present patterns of disease than classification of causes implies. The peculiar aetiology of non-communicable diseases which distinguishes them from communicable diseases can be viewed in a historical perspective which takes account of the changing 'infectious-disease environment', with which the underlying disorders may be linked in significant ways through adverse cellular and immunological reactions. Recently, immunological research has been concerned with mechanisms at the cellular level by which unwanted foreign bodies are expelled from the human body, while such cellular processes may also be linked with the impact of the external environment and with immune reactions affecting whole populations.

Links between immunological and epidemiological aspects of disease are possibly clearer when infectious micro-organisms are considered in relation to manifestations of communicable disease. For example, many studies have investigated the role of nutrition in resistance to disease, and have referred to the efficiency of the antigen-antibody reaction in expelling viruses from the body under different nutritional circumstances.[49] However, Burnet has emphasised that evolution probably involved a moulding of immune mechanisms for other purposes than defence against invading micro-organisms.[50] Invertebrates require an effective means of countering infection, just as vertebrates do, but they produce no antibodies. Thus vertebrates required some additional mechanism beyond that which developed to fight bacterial infection, and this may have been developed at an early stage in their evolution. Immune mechanisms in vertebrates such as mammals, seem to suggest that they are basically concerned with the control of tissue integrity and reaction to recognised anomaly. Burnet suggested that, armed with this mechanism, more effective defences were developed to counteract infection, and the two systems developed in some inter-related way thereafter. He developed the hypothesis of immune surveillance against cellular anomalies, which may be significant in the development of certain forms of cancer since the process may be subject to failure.[51] It is possible that environmental and behavioural factors which have been found to be associated with the development of cancers, may not only promote the cellular anomalies themselves, but also interfere with immune defence against them.

Certain circulatory diseases are also known to involve important immunological reactions, such as the reaction to scarlet fever which has been implicated in rheumatic heart disease. This particular category of circulatory disease does not account for many deaths, but there are possibly more general links between infectious micro-organisms and circulatory disease. The underlying processes involved in many circulatory disorders, atherosclerosis and embolism, have been linked with antigen-antibody reactions to common viruses. The work of Mustard and his co-workers has been based on laboratory studies of the effects on blood of contamination with viruses.[52] These results, and those of other work along these lines, seem to have received far less attention than studies of behavioural and environmental correlates of heart disease and stroke, important though these are for an understanding of aetiology. It will be suggested

here that the immunological dimension of disease could still be as
important as it was when nearly all deaths were attributed to infectious
diseases.

Many studies in the history of medical science have considered the
impact of various exogenous and endogenous changes on specific diseases,
while major writers on the changing pattern of infectious diseases such
as Cockburn, Burnet and McNeill have provided the kind of long-term
perspective which is a necessary background for understanding the relatively recent disease and mortality transition to be considered here. The
inter-related nature of the infectious-disease environment may have been
largely ignored in studies of mortality decline or historical demography,
although historians of disease have recognised elements of competition
among micro-organisms seeking human hosts in which to replicate. For
example, Cockburn suggested that tuberculosis may have replaced leprosy,
which had been common in the Middle Ages.[53] A certain degree of cross-
immunity between the two diseases may have meant that tuberculosis
began to convey some immunity from leprosy, among those who survived
infection. Tuberculosis may have become predominant because it spread
more easily at the time of growing contact with the expanding towns. Such
a change in disease patterns falls within the field of what might be called
social immunology, being related to immune reactions in the individual
and the changing immune status of whole populations. This dimension has
been emphasised by immunologists, including Greenwood who referred to
an 'ever varying state of the immunological constitution of the herd'.[54]
McNeill emphasised the processes of migration and human contact which
ensured the global transmission of infectious diseases before the eighteenth
century, and the role of changing immune status in associated mortality
crises.[55] The importance of the changing immune status of the population
will be considered throughout this study, with regard to both the decline
in infectious-disease death rates and the pattern on non-communicable
disease which now predominates in industrialised populations. In considering the modern transition in disease and mortality since the eighteenth
century, more emphasis can be placed on series of statistics of disease
and mortality which were not available to those studying the earlier
changes in disease patterns.

The events in England during the last three centuries since the disappearance of the plague will be placed within a long-term and global
context of changing patterns of disease, mortality and population in earlier
periods, which owes much to the work of McNeill and Burnet. The
objective, then, is to provide a broad picture of changing disease patterns
based on local pre-registration data and national registration statistics,
which has not previously been presented for the whole period of the
mortality transition. Comparison will also be made with trends recorded in
other European countries, particularly to test the universality of interpret-
ations of events based on the data from England. It is intended to examine
the plausibility of hypotheses which might explain the main events, within
the general context of inter-related disease patterns and mortality change.
In particular the eradication of smallpox during the course of the nineteenth

century, which has been underestimated in many previous studies of the mortality and population transitions, will be given appropriate emphasis. A perspective on the inter-related nature of diseases as they affect mortality risk, will also provide much-needed qualification of the possibly distorted picture of the mechanisms of mortality decline that has come with the reliance on discrete categories of recorded causes of death which do not take into account intercurrent infection, debilitating effects of diseases, or the possible links between infectious and non-infectious diseases. The emergence of a new pattern of cause of death in which non-communicable diseases predominate will also be outlined, and aetiological aspects will be related to this overall perspective on disease and mortality change since the eighteenth century.

After a brief historical introduction to infectious diseases in Europe in Chapter 2, based on the evolutionary ecological picture developed by McNeill and Burnet,[56] changes in food supply and standard of living are considered as concomitants of mortality and population change. The main questions to be considered are whether standard of living and food supplies were a major influence on mortality levels before the transition from the mid eighteenth century, or whether the nature of the prevalent diseases was such that fluctuations were largely independent of general economic conditions. This study will not be concerned primarily with the question of whether changes in economic conditions allowed certain health interventions to proceed, although the measures that are discussed in later chapters can be considered as occurring within a context of changing socio-economic conditions outlined in Chapter 2. The main purpose there will be to consider whether any significant increase in food consumption per head, or even general economic standard of living, occurred in association with the main turning points in the death rate. Certain aspects of the relative changes in fertility and mortality levels will also be considered in relation to population change, particularly as both variables may have responded to similar improvements, not in the economic standard of living, but in the impact of infectious diseases.

An outline of the relationships between recorded causes of death and overall mortality in the eighteenth century is given in Chapter 3. This emphasises the association between smallpox epidemics and mortality fluctuations, which were largely independent of changing economic or agricultural circumstances. There follows a more comprehensive discussion of the role of smallpox in causing high mortality, and the effect of immunisation in virtually eliminating the disease before the twentieth century in England and most of Europe. The case that inoculation was instrumental in eighteenth-century decline is considered, together with a greater amount of evidence that the widespread use of immunisation based on the idea of vaccination, brought rapid changes in mortality and population all over Europe. The control of the disease – even before its aetiology or cause was really understood – is thought to warrant more consideration than other diseases since its importance has probably been underestimated in most previous studies of nineteenth-century mortality change. McNeill has shown the importance of earlier changes in immunity and disease patterns, but immunisation against smallpox was unique, being a positive and calculated measure aimed successfully at protecting people against possibly the most-feared disease of the last three hundred years.

The pre-registration records will be used to show the importance, and the decline, of other major killers such as tuberculosis and the 'fevers', typhus and typhoid. These became less important during the course of the nineteenth century, while registration data reveal that by contrast childhood diseases assumed a greater role in the overall cause-of-death structure. These changes are examined in Chapters 4 and 5, mainly with registration data from the second half of the nineteenth century. The threat of cholera after the 1830s, and the importance of efforts to improve water supplies and sanitation, are considered in Chapter 4, along with trends in death rates from other water-borne diseases. The downturn, and final long-term decline in the death rate from typhoid came at the end of the century. The possible reasons for this, and for the decline in death rates from childhood epidemic diseases – such as scarlet fever, measles, whooping cough and diphtheria – are also considered. Reductions in child mortality in the second half of the nineteenth century in fact reflect the experience of children over the age of one year, and the failure of infant mortality to decline in this period will be considered against the background of a fall in the second half of the eighteenth century. Such a detailed re-examination was considered necessary in view of the many differences between cause- and age-specific mortality trends, and inconsistencies in previous explan- ations of the decline in infectious-disease death rates. The death rate from measles, for example, is often taken as an indicator of poor nutrition among children in developing countries, as in Europe in the past. Similarly, diarrhoeal disease has often been the main component of infant mortality, and such death rates have been considered as indicators of the relative standard of living in different countries and populations. Death rates from both these cause groups were high throughout the Victorian period in England. The infant-mortality rate of 150 – 200 per 1,000 live births also implies a far greater death rate among the poorest sections of the urban population. Both the infant-mortality rate and the high death rate from measles, for which the final long-term decline did not really begin until the twentieth century, reflect an appalling standard of living for a large proportion of the population of the whole country. In the light of this, it has to be explained why tuberculosis mortality among adults had been falling for decades.

The decline in tuberculosis mortality outlined in Chapter 5 has been a major feature of improved adult survival, although primary infection probably usually occurred in childhood with repercussions later in life. Dubos and Dubos suggested that knowledge of how the disease spread in crowded conditions, became influential after the casual agent was identified, so that the ventilation of buildings and the isolation of the sick may have reduced the dosage of bacillus contracted by others, and hence the proportion of people developing clinical infection.[57] The earlier decline in the death rate in the nineteenth century will also be considered in the light of the evidence concerning economic standard of living and nutrition, which McKeown suggested had improved resistance to the disease.[58] It can again be emphasised that general explanations of the decline in infectious-disease mortality in terms of improvements in nutrition, have not satisfactorily taken into account the variety of trends for cause-specific death rates, and the timing of the decline for different infectious diseases in relation to known changes in the standard of living. The recorded death rates for each of the main diseases can be compared, but many infectious diseases are likely to have been operating concurrently or in succession, with a whole series of infections being contracted throughout life. Survival from an infectious disease, such as smallpox, would have left many of those infected severely debilitated with a higher risk of mortality from other infections that came along, and this should be borne in mind when considering cause-specific mortality trends.

The possible involvement of infectious diseases other than those recognised or recorded as being the main cause of death, will be considered with regard to both respiratory tuberculosis and other respiratory diseases. The possibility of an underlying role of air-borne infections in respiratory disease within the context of contributing environmental hazards, will also be considered in Chapter 5. Trends in death rates from respiratory disease for both adults and children will be compared with the very different pattern of decline for respiratory tuberculosis in the nineteenth century in England. The group of diseases,bronchitis, pneumonia and influenza, still accounts for about 15% of all deaths in England and Wales, despite the decline in death rates from the end of the nineteenth century. Reductions in the death rate occurred along with those for the many childhood infectious diseases which involve respiratory complications, such as measles, whooping cough and diphtheria. The possible role of viral, bacterial and immunological reactions in respiratory causes of death will be referred to, along with other correlates of high mortality risk whose involvement is sometimes considered to be more substantiated.[59]

The continuing decline in respiratory death rates in the twentieth century will be shown in Chapter 6 to contrast with the trend in the death rate from circulatory disease, which declined from about the same time only to increase again in the 1920s reaching a second peak in the early 1950s. This resurgence was in fact unique to this category of causes, which might not be expected if changes in the standard of living were involved. Increases in death rates in the nineteenth century occurred along with those for cancer and respiratory diseases, but are not readily explained in terms of risk factors established in the twentieth century. The emergence of these non-communicable diseases will be outlined in Chapter 6, and trends in death rates examined on the basis of the longest series of data available from England and Wales. This phenomenon will be viewed as part of a global process, although the comparative data referred to are mainly from Europe because of doubts about the completeness of records for other less industrialised countries. In the last two chapters, the major non-communicable causes of death – circulatory disease, cancer and bronchitis – for which death rates increased in the second half of the nineteenth century, are examined against the background of declining overall mortality and the reduced impact of the infectious diseases.

It will be shown that death rates from cancer analysed by year of birth, suggest that there were important influences on mortality affecting cohorts. Such indications have not previously been noted in relation to any long-term turning point in cancer mortality, although this has been reported for peptic-ulcer death rates.[60] Changes in childhood experience may have been involved, such as nutrition or the impact of infectious diseases, but many external variables operate throughout life. Cigarette-smoking, diet, air pollution and industrial hazards have been found to affect period death rates and the relative risk to different groups in the population. Nevertheless, important questions remain concerning the trends in death rates in relation to year of birth. There also remains the problem of why only a proportion of those exposed to irritants in fact develop cancer, and why it is only in some cases that the presence of micro-cancers leads to clinical disease. The immunological dimension in cancer may be relevant to these questions, and to a long-standing debate over the possibility of some association between tubercular infection and cancer.[61] Whether or not cancer and tuberculosis involve common immune mechanisms, as suggested by Burnet, his hypothesis of immune surveillance against aberrant cells may be important.[62] To date, such mechanisms have only been implicated in certain rare forms of cancer, so that behavioural and environmental factors remain the more established influences on general cancer-mortality risk. However, these risk factors are not easily linked with the long-term changes in death rates outlined in Chapter 6.

After outlining the trends in cause-specific death rates and the main established risk factors in the major non-communicable diseases, specific evidence will be referred to which suggests that immune and cellular reactions to common micro-organisms may be significantly involved in the underlying disorders. Aggregate manifestations of non-communicable disease – such as mortality trends – have to be explained as well as the experience of the individual case. Any change in the 'mortality environment' that might be perceived as being concomitant with increasing industrialisation, should also be considered as taking place within a changing 'infectious-disease environment' with repercussions for individuals and their immunological cellular processes. Such a perspective necessarily complements the approach which seeks ever more specific definition of aetiological features of non-communicable disease patterns relating to other environmental and behavioural risks. Culturally determined aetio ogical features that may be relevant to long-term changes in mortality will be considered in relation to this general concept of chronic non-infectious diseases, which emphasises that the distinctive underlying disorders involve cellular-immunological aberrations.

In the case of circulatory disease, some aspects of the trends in death rates may not be satisfactorily explained in terms of changes in behaviour, while again there is the question of why only a proportion of the population dies from these disorders, when atherosclerosis is usually present in all autopsies.[63] The evidence that infectious diseases and circulatory diseases may be linked, through damage done in the blood and arteries during immune reactions to viruses, will be referred to briefly in Chapter 6 as possibly relevant to these problems. The kind of trigger mechanism through embolism and thrombosis which was suggested by Mustard, could form part of an explanation of temporal associations found between infectious-disease and circulatory-disease mortality trends.[64] Cumulative consequences may be involved in atheroma which could be exacerbated by behavioural factors such as cigarette-smoking. However, a more feasible influence on increasing female death rates in the nineteenth century might have been increased air pollution.

In view of possible links with adult disease and mortality, the continuing prevalence of many of the common epidemic diseases may require more attention than appears to be warranted in view of the negligible mortality from them in Western populations. Immune reactions involved in these and other infectious diseases such as tuberculosis could be an important link between the diseases which in the past caused high mortality in Europe, and the non-communicable diseases which cause most deaths today. Certain international aspects of the transition from communicable to non-communicable disease mortality provide an important perspective on changes in England. However, it is possibly easier to link differences in mortality between populations, and between socio-economic groups, with behaviour and exposure to risk factors, than it is trends in death rates. Even so, there seem to be some grounds for regarding the changing 'infectious-disease environment' as highly significant, not only for mortality levels in developing countries, but in relation to non-communicable diseases which now cause most adult deaths in the more industrialised countries. This is only put forward as a general working hypothesis on the basis of some tangible evidence in the case of circulatory disease and bronchitis, and the growing body of evidence of the possible role of viruses in certain forms of cancer. It may prove useful to consider global problems with both communicable and non-communicable diseases in the context of a transition from infectious to non-infectious causes of death, which will be outlined with data from England since the eighteenth century. Many aspects of the social and health interventions that are linked with these changes in the past, may also be relevant in other parts of the world today, despite very different economic, social and climatic conditions. The inter-relationship between diseases, and the relative patterns of mortality they caused in England and Europe in the epidemiological-demographic transition, could still have implications for future health programmes worldwide.

2 Disease patterns, standard of living and population change after the plague

Some evolutionary aspects of the relationship between man and micro-organisms causing infectious disease will be outlined in this chapter, giving an introductory background to the patterns of disease prevailing in the eighteenth century. Different phases in the changing pattern of cause of death can be identified, but there tends to be an overlap of the main diseases which characterise different periods. The recession of plague epidemics which had terrorised Europe for three centuries, and their disappearance from England after the seventeenth century can be taken as the beginning of a new era for disease and population change. The last outbreak of the disease in London, for example, was in 1665 when 97,000 deaths were recorded in the Bills of Mortality.[1] This probably represented a mortality of between one in six and one in five of the population, and at least two-thirds of the deaths were directly attributed to the disease. England as a whole was free from any significant outbreak in the eighteenth century, but apart from this rather dramatic change the main cause-groups to which death was attributed were similar to those recorded in the seventeenth century. The London Bills of Mortality show that although plague had been devastating, smallpox epidemics which occurred more regularly were closely associated with fluctuations in overall mortality, and had come to be a more consistent check on population growth. (See Appendix 2a).

Different sets of Bills of Mortality will be referred to which confirm that smallpox epidemics were prominent in the fluctuations in overall mortality, although consumption, and 'fevers' were the other main categories of disease under which deaths were recorded in the eighteenth century. Apart from the Northampton Bills, and those from Carlisle which were compiled by a medical practitioner, many parish records of burials provide useful sources of information since deaths attributed to smallpox were often signified. In the context of this prevailing pattern of the disease, the changing pattern of mortality crises and the onset of mortality decline will be considered along with the population growth which occurred from the mid eighteenth century in England and much of Europe. This clearly put additional pressure on food supplies which had to be increased rapidly even to maintain existing levels of nutrition.

Certain aspects of the economic context in which the long-term decline in mortality began, will be considered in the later sections of this chapter. The question of whether improvements in the standard of living could actually have caused more rapid population growth has been examined in different studies. McKeown, for example, proposed that an improvement in resistance to disease could have occurred with improved standards of living, and particularly with increases in food supply.[2] Possibly the crucial questions are whether mortality fluctuations before the long-term decline were associated with changes in the availability of food, and whether any significant increase in food consumption per head occurred at the main turning points for mortality. More recently, Wrigley and Schofield estimated that fertility levels were increasing from the mid seventeenth century until the beginning of the nineteenth century, and suggested this was linked with changes in marriage patterns and the economic standard of living.[3] The relationship between fertility and mortality changes will be given some consideration here with regard to population changes which in turn put pressure on food supplies and prices. However, the main concern is with mortality decline, and with the changing impact of the infectious-disease environment which appears to have been largely independent of changes in the economic standard of living. Evidence from all over Europe also indicates that the recession of mortality crises was the change in circumstances which allowed more rapid and sustained population growth in the nineteenth century.

Historical patterns of infectious disease from early times to the eighteenth century

The history of infectious disease has been reviewed by Burnet, who emphasised the social process of 'civilisation', characterised by the aggregation of greater numbers of human beings into limited areas of land.[4] Human history has been marked by important migrations and adaptations to new methods of survival. These changes have probably had consequences for health and longevity as well as the size of human settlement. Nomadic tribes from the steppes and mountains of Eastern Europe and Central Asia moved into the areas of early settlement and towns emerged in China, India, Mesopotamia, the Nile Valley, and around the Mediterranean and in Western Europe. The nomadic life may have been relatively healthy, with infectious diseases being truly 'diseases of civilisation'. Population probably grew steadily until the land could not support all the children of such human groups. Obviously only imaginative guesses are possible, but it seems likely that our ancestors were troubled by a great variety of parasites, as well as by the need to find a variety of foods. Many of the parasites would not necessarily have produced symptoms which we would recognise as illness, and as long as the biological evolution of early humans kept pace with the evolution of their parasites, predators and prey, no very important alteration in the ecological balance would have occurred.

The change in way of life brought about by hunting and nomadic food-gathering itself, with a need to walk and run, must have involved changes in the type of infection and infestation prevalent among human groups. If such a way of life had resulted from a movement out of the rain forest into the savanna, the change of habitat would have brought contact with new micro-organisms. Life in the rain forest probably gave rise to infestations which were dependent on moist conditions, but new infections were probably contracted by following herds of animals for various purposes. Worms and other parasites, such as trypanosomes, seem likely to have affected man. Many of the micro-organisms contracted by hunter-gatherers would not have provoked immune reactions, or the formation of antibodies. Human groups had to learn to live in a micro-environment, adapting to different climatic conditions in different parts of the world, and domination in temperate zones may have been enhanced by a lack of predators and natural parasites. Migration of humans to such areas was probably very disruptive ecologically, but was sustained by an ability to adapt behaviour as difficulties were encountered, or in fact created. The colder the climate, the more survival seems likely to have depended on the ability to find suitable large-bodied plants and animals, while a balance with parasitic organisms may have been less important than in the tropics. McNeill suggested that disease organisms had been important outside the tropics, but parasites spreading from host to host directly – such as spirochetes, and those in yaws infection – would have survived in small migratory hunting communities.[5] The advantage for humans living this way of life, was probably a smaller diversity of such infections compared with those found in the tropics. As long as the infections acted slowly, and incapacity was not too severe and sudden, survival would not have been threatened.

The retreat of the most recent ice-cap about 20,000 BC, probably contributed to an increasing exploitation of the resources of the sea, through the use of boats and fishing. The gathering of edible seeds probably preceded the more settled life based on agriculture, and with regular food production came the concentration of human beings into larger settlements, and the rise of cities and whole civilisations. This new way of life made human beings the prey of disease organisms which found an 'environment' in which to proliferate and feed, and man became as dependent on immune mechanisms for survival as on agriculture. Some communities became so dense that bacterial and viral infections were sustained without intermediate non-human hosts. Immune reactions ensured that when death did not occur, and there was recovery following the expulsion of the invading organism from the host's tissues by antibodies, these would be effective in preventing re-infection for a period of months or years.

The main infections causing high mortality in the period for which records are first available on cause of death, were air-borne infectious diseases, which convey some immunity on survivors, and water-borne infections. Diseases such as typhoid, cholera, dysentery and diarrhoeal disease are often transmitted by faecal contamination of hands and food. It seems likely that they became important in human history as a consequence of people living in large settled communities, where it was more difficult to avoid contamination of water by human and other forms of waste, which was possible in a nomadic way of life. McNeill suggests that most, and possibly all, the distinctive diseases of civilisation, whether water-borne or air-borne, transferred to human populations as a price that was paid for close contact with animal herds. Even closer contacts were developed with the domestication of animals, and many parallels with animal infectious diseases can be recognised. Measles, for example, may be related to canine distemper; smallpox is related to cowpox; influenza is shared by humans and hogs. Human beings also became affected by disease cycles among wild animals, such as bubonic plague among burrowing rodents, yellow fever among monkeys, and rabies among bats.

The cycle of some diseases became independent of the original source, and one of these, measles, is usually taken as the classic example of air-borne, density-dependent, infectious disease. It became basically a child-hood disease in a large enough population, because of the immunity conveyed on survivors. Statistical studies of the way the disease propagates in modern urban communities, have shown that there is a pattern of regularly occurring epidemics linked with the proportion of 'new suscept-ibles' in the population.[6] The disease probably requires a population of at least 7,000 individuals, and a critical threshold below which the virus cannot result in endemic disease may be a population of 250,000. Smaller populations can be, and have been, devastated by infection brought in from outside, when a community has had little previous contact with the disease.[7] Until quite recently many cities experienced in-migration which probably contributed to urban-health hazards and high mortality, so that deaths exceeded births. Nevertheless, their populations grew, and some cities became large enough to sustain diseases such as smallpox – which was endemic in London, for example, in the eighteenth century. In addition to air-borne infectious diseases and water-borne epidemics, insect-borne diseases such as typhus and malaria probably made life in crowded towns less healthy than for hunter-gatherers, at least when the latter had little contact with settled communities.

Air-borne, density-dependent infectious diseases – such as smallpox and measles – were a major cause of marked fluctuations in mortality in North America, and Kunitz distinguished these from diseases which became endemic from the seventeenth century.[8] Among the latter he found dysentery and malaria to have been the most significant of the named diseases between the time of the first settlement and the end of the colonial period. Yellow fever also became endemic in urban populations, where it was maintained without the animal reservoir that existed in its homeland, Africa. Cholera was a further major disease which does not convey lasting immunity, so that people were repeatedly vulnerable in several epidemic waves during the nineteenth century. Among these diseases which became endemic, yellow fever and typhoid were more significant contributors to overall mortality in New Orleans compared with New York, contributing additional peaks in overall mortality to those caused by cholera.[9] However, their significance for overall mortality fluctuations was shown with data from New York in the nineteenth century.[10] Cholera and smallpox were involved in most of the regular mortality peaks, with a few significant outbreaks of yellow fever and typhus. Smallpox had been a severe epidemic disease affecting the mid-Atlantic colonies most, followed by the South, and then New England.[11] Together with the endemic diseases, it may have been the cause of higher overall mortality in the South in the eighteenth century. The wide fluctuations in mortality due to air-borne, density-dependent, infectious diseases – such as smallpox – became less significant from the end of the eighteenth century at the time of more rapid population growth. This may have led to an increasing similarity of crude death rates between the northern and southern parts of the North-American continent. It may be, as Kunitz suggested, that the endemic diseases became more demographically significant after air-borne, density-dependent, infectious diseases became childhood infections as a result of immunity. However, it seems unlikely that any such change in the predominant causes of mortality crises actually resulted in the beginning of mortality decline in North America, and the role of immunisation in controlling the density-dependent disease, smallpox, was probably crucial – as in Europe. In New York, the air-borne disease smallpox continued to produce mortality peaks until vaccination was more widely used. A different type of air-borne disease, respiratory tuberculosis, was endemic in North America as a whole, and seems likely to have been the most important killer in the nineteenth century, as in England. Much of the mortality pattern of North America was affected by migration, and Kunitz referred to the high transient populations of both New York and New Orleans which were ports of entry. He pointed out that the consequence of a more rapid population growth than elsewhere, probably contributed to a higher mortality because of disruption to existing facilities, inadequate quarantine measures for shipping, explosive growth of poor housing, and improper disposal of untreated sewage.

Migration from areas of high incidence of infectious diseases also affected mortality rates in Europe, as did the problems of rapidly expanding urban areas in which people sought a better life. Many studies have considered other disruptive factors affecting mortality levels and the broad social, economic, political and military framework within which disease and population change can be examined. The broad social context of change in the period 1500 to 1820 has been summarised by Flinn in terms of various factors.[12] First, the diminution of military activity and the re-organisation of armies, which in the past had been responsible for the spreading of epidemics. Second, a shift to naval warfare and efforts to improve hygiene may also have been significant, along with greater military discipline and restraint concerning the destruction of civilian populations. Improvements in agriculture, including the settlement of new land, the use of crop rotation and new crops from the Americas, all seem likely to have contributed to increasing production. The question of whether this merely kept pace with increasing population will be considered in relation to other evidence later. Improved transportation, commercial organisation and social administration may also have been relevant changes concomitant with the 'Industrial Revolution'. Any beneficial aspects of change were at least partially offset by the disastrous consequences of industrialisation and urbanisation for large sections of the population of England.

Some of the agricultural changes were considered by McNeill, such as the 'new husbandry' of the period 1650–1750 which had important consequences for disease patterns. New crops provided feed for cattle on a scale which hitherto had been impossible, and this led to an expansion of meat and dairy production. Ecological consequences may have included the transfer of mosquitoes from man to this larger population of cattle, whose blood they preferred.[13] Although malaria does not feature separately in all the records of mortality in the eighteenth century, it was still an important cause of death in Sweden, while major outbreaks were noted in some English records. It seems likely that it was a major cause of death in pre-industrial England, both directly and through its debilitating effects. Drainage and agricultural changes probably contributed to its declining impact which seems likely to have been before the downturn in overall mortality from the mid eighteenth century.[14] The decline of the disease in Northern Europe contrasted with its continuing prevalence in warmer Mediterranean countries and in France where it was still endemic in the eighteenth century. The administrative records begun in France in 1775, indicated a whole battery of infections, including grippe, dysentery, pneumonia and a fever, 'military sweats'. These continued to plague the French peasantry in the late eighteenth century, while tuberculosis was endemic.[15]

An association has been found between high mortality and areas of Europe with large estates worked by an impoverished peasantry, and also in relation to the deleterious consequences of the exploitation of female labour.[16] Mothers were required to work long hours, and being unable to breast-feed properly they often used unhygienic 'pacifiers' which could have contributed to gastro-intestinal infection. Both regional and social-class differences in mortality in Europe were examined in relation to the decline in mortality after the seventeenth century by Kunitz. He found there was a divergence in the life expectancy of aristocrats and commoners in the eighteenth century, and a difference in death rates between north-western and southern or eastern countries.[17] Living conditions may have been worse in these areas, and a higher infant mortality has been found for Germany and Spain – compared with England, France and Sweden – in the second half of the eighteenth century.[18] Many areas of Europe, where mortality declined to lower levels, were characterised by mixed arable and dairy farming. Medium-sized holdings were more common compared with the large estates and tiny land holdings of southern and eastern Europe. Epidemics caused by many enteric pathogens, by bacterial and viral diseases, may well have been less common in north-western Europe, because of the isolation of farms. A hotter climate could also have contributed to water-borne and gastro-intestinal infections in southern and eastern Europe, although dysentery was devastating in some northern countries as well. Data from Akerhus for the period 1801–15 suggest that about half of all deaths were due to dysentery, which together with smallpox was the main disease in years when deaths exceeded births.[19] Data from one small port-town, Larvik in Norway, for the period 1785–1807, show that 15.6% of deaths were specified as due to dysentery, fever and epidemics other than smallpox and tuberculosis which were referred to in a further 15% of deaths.[20] Records from Brittany for the eighteenth century also reveal regular epidemics of typhus or typhoid and dysentery, as well as smallpox.[21] Most records of cause of death in the eighteenth century are in fact from north-western Europe, although some sources have too many ill-defined causes to be useful. The main features of the records are the presence of smallpox, tuberculosis, fevers, childhood infectious epidemics, water-borne diseases and the absence of plague.

The period of plague epidemics and their absence in the eighteenth century

Plague had devastated the population of Europe for three centuries, but was absent from England and much of the Continent during the eighteenth century. Changes affecting the transmission processes remain plausible explanations, along with the possible role of immunological factors. Recent mutations of viruses have suggested that some form of bacillus related to that responsible for the plague, might have become prevalent in the eighteenth century, giving cross-immunity to the disease.[22] A further suggestion is that there may have been a build-up of immunity in the human population as a result of centuries of contact. However, this would not explain the continuing outbreaks of plague in areas which had always been major foci of the disease, and it has also been pointed out that the hypothesis of some transformation of micro-organisms would be impossible to test.[23] The alternative hypotheses which are likely to remain the main contenders for bringing about the change, relate to the role of the animal vector, or to human intervention to control the transmission of the disease. Changes in the rodent population responsible for carrying fleas infested with *Pasteurella pestis* might have been significant, but the idea that the black rat was displaced by the brown rat, or killed off by it, has been discounted.[24] The black rat has been identified as the main carrier of fleas which could carry the micro-organism, and if necessary they would transfer to man for feeding. However, the brown rat probably did not appear in England until the 1720s, while the black rat was still predominant in London at the end of the eighteenth century.[25] A further consideration is whether the susceptible rat population might itself have been continually reduced by the disease, so that the only sources of infection were certain species of wild rodent in more remote areas. This assumes that the latter were not destroyed by the disease otherwise it could not have persisted in Asia for so long.

In Europe, climatic advantage may have meant that in cold winters the rat fleas which carried the plague bacillus, died off, so that there had to be a re-introduction of the disease from the Middle East for epidemics to occur. A further precondition was probably that people were living in overcrowded conditions in close proximity to rats near to the port of entry or along trade routes from the east. Changes in trade patterns might have had some effect on contacts between east and west, but authorities had also seen that it was possible to break the chain of transmission by quarantine and isolation measures. There had been a change in attitude to the disease which was known to come from outside Europe, since not everyone was resigned to plague as a manifestation of the anger of God over the sins of Man.[26] Civil-intelligence reports on plague incidence in the east were used in deploying soldiers to areas particularly at risk, and routine border patrols were instituted. The procedures took a long time to develop, but increasing knowledge about the spread of infection from east to west did lead to the establishment of a permanent 'cordon sanitaire' along the border between the Hapsburg Empire and the Ottoman Empire. Other measures were introduced to protect towns against the spread of infection, including quarantine for ships from infected areas, and watches at the gates of towns to screen travellers from areas where plague had been reported. Enforced isolation of households where cases occurred was certainly attempted in England, but may have been the least effective preventive measure because rats could still move from house to house in search of food.

It seems likely that the widespread adoption of quarantine against shipping was a most significant factor in reducing the risk of plague entering European ports from foci of infection overseas. Slack has pointed out that once plague reached north-western Europe it was likely to reach England because of the frequent trade and shipping contacts. Orders were issued against ships coming to Britain from several infected areas after the 1660s outbreak, and particularly during the disastrous outbreak in Marseilles in 1720 in which as many as 50,000 people may have died.[27] Later outbreaks occurred in Moscow in 1771, when about 56,000 people were reported to have died, and as late as 1894 when probably 90,000 people died of plague in Canton and Hong Kong. The use of steamships which could bypass quarantined ports in Europe en route to England meant that plague did reach Britain at the beginning of the twentieth century after being absent during the previous two centuries. There was considerable concern that plague or cholera might spread from such sources, but in the last three decades of the nineteenth century the port sanitary authorities had become increasingly active and effective in inspecting ships and were empowered to remove the infected to hospital.[28] It seems unlikely that changes in living conditions with respect to over-crowding near the ports and close proximity to rats could account for the absence of plague from England in the eighteenth century, and typhus, with a similar mode of transmission, continued to be destructive of life on a massive scale in the overcrowded impoverished conditions in English towns in the nineteenth century. The other explanations for the recession of plague in England and Western Europe are not mutually exclusive, but it does seem plausible that early quarantine measures and other preventive interventions could have been largely responsible. Slack emphasised the monitoring and control of shipping and that the protection of Britain against plague was probably also contingent on measures introduced elsewhere in Europe.[29]

After the 1660s England was free from any significant outbreak of the disease which had 'haunted' Europe for three centuries. The reduction in frequency and size of plague epidemics in Europe, and their disappearance from England after the seventeenth century, can be taken to mark the beginning of a new era for disease and population change. The Black Death of 1348 caused a dramatic reduction in population which lasted for over a hundred years, and although the disease flourished in the dreadful, overcrowded living conditions which existed in Europe at that time, the epidemic was probably not an inevitable consequence of population pressure alone. Hatcher found that the death rate in England between the thirteenth and seventeenth centuries showed little association with an index of economic standard of living, and concluded that the prime determinant of population change in this pre-industrial period in England was mortality change.[30] Following the Black Death there may have been little recovery from the decline in population it caused it Europe until the fifteenth century, but population was probably growing quite steadily again in the sixteenth century. In England the period 1565–85 was particularly free of epidemic peaks in mortality and population growth was quite rapid until the setback caused by plague in the 1660s. However, most of the growth was only a recovery from the severest period of plague pandemic in Europe in the fourteenth century.

The absence of plague after the epidemics of the seventeenth century might have produced a more dramatic effect on population growth had it not been for the regularly occurring epidemics of smallpox. McNeill pointed out that smallpox had probably spread to Europe by the sixteenth century – with the expansion of sea trade and with the development of commerce which led to regular contact between all the principal centres of population worldwide[31] – and by the eighteenth century it was probably universally contracted throughout Europe. Although plague had been periodically devastating, and caused 28.5% of all deaths in London in the 1660s for example, the Bills of Mortality generally indicate that other diseases were important as regular causes of high mortality which restrained population growth. A consistently high proportion of 25–50% of all deaths was attributed to three groups of infectious disease: smallpox, consumption and 'fevers', as shown in Appendix 2a. Diarrhoeal diseases and dysentery were probably also significant causes of death as in other parts of Europe, and Creighton suggested that such deaths were classified as 'griping of the guts', 'bloody flux' and 'surfeit' at the end of the seventeenth century.[32] Deaths in these categories represented 5.5% of all deaths in the Bills for the 1650s, but the proportion rose to 17.0% and 13.8% in the two decades after the plague. The decline of recording to a level of 1.4% of total deaths by the 1730s probably reflected a transfer to other cause-groups, and

Table 2.1 Deaths from different causes as a percentage of all burials in the Bills of Mortality for nine years between 1779 and all 1787†

Cause	Carlisle	London	Northampton
'Fevers'	9.5	12.5	9.7
Smallpox	14.7	9.4	8.2
Convulsions	0.6	24.9	17.9‡
Weakness of infancy	12.6		
Measles	1.9	1.1	3.3
Whooping cough	1.2	1.4	0.8
Scarlet fever	2.4	*	*
Thrush	4.0	*	0.4
Worm fever	1.7	*	0.6
Consumption	13.3	24.0	19.8
Dropsy	3.0	4.6	7.6
Asthma	1.7	1.5	1.1
Apoplexy	2.0	1.2	1.0
Palsy	0.9	0.3	1.0
Old age	14.0	6.5	9.8
Accidents	1.8	0.6	1.0
TOTAL (above)	85.3	88.0	82.2
Other causes	7.1	12.0	17.8
and unknown	7.6		
(Total number of deaths)	(10,000)	(175,143)	(828)

* Cause not specified until later Bills.
† Data for 1780 missing for Carlisle and excluded from London; 1787 missing from Northampton series.
‡ Fits included in Northampton figure. Fevers approximately comparable.

Sources: Carlisle Bills from H. Lonsdale (1870) *The Life of John Heysham MD*. London Bills of Mortality: J. Marshall (1832) *Mortality in the Metropolis*. Northampton Bills of Mortality: Bills of Mortality for All Saints Parish (British Library, London).

Creighton suggested that there had been many deaths among infants which were transferred to the growing 'convulsions' category.

The main cause-groups to which a large proportion of deaths was regularly assigned in the London Bills are compared with similar categories in the Northampton and Carlisle Bills of Mortality in Table 2.1. The recording of deaths under different causes in Carlisle is shown in more detail in Appendix 2b, since this may be the best guide to cause-specific mortality in England at the end of the eighteenth century. The Bills for eight years between 1779 and 1987 might be a good indication of medically recognised causes of death at the time, given Heysham's interest in health demography and his medical practice in the town.[33] Most of the causes he recorded were infectious diseases, with only 7.6% of deaths not being attributed to some category of causes, or to old age and infancy diseases. Heysham assigned over 50% of all deaths in the town to particular infectious diseases which typically occurred in records from north-western Europe, including smallpox, consumption, measles, whooping cough, thrush and jaundice. The broad category of 'fevers' was subdivided into inflammatory, nervous, putrid, worm and jail fever (i.e. typhus). Where the proportion of deaths under different causes differs from that in the Northampton and London Bills it is difficult to assess whether this is a genuine reflection of cause-specific mortality differences. For example, the proportion of deaths attributed to consumption in Carlisle (12.6%) was almost half that recorded in the London Bills for an equivalent period, but recording did vary between 10% and 25% in London over the eighteenth century. The higher proportion of about 15% of all deaths attributed to smallpox by Heysham might reflect an awareness of the less obvious forms of the disease, although different living conditions and epidemic variation might also account for this difference.

Data from Geneva for the periods 1730–39 and 1775–86 reveal similar major cause-groups, and smallpox was in fact endemic, with up to 10% of deaths being regularly attributed to the disease in successive decades, as in London.[34] Data for the national population of Sweden give some indication of the disease and mortality pattern in both rural areas and towns, and about half the deaths were attributed to specific causes. In the period 1779–82 about 10% of deaths were directly attributed to smallpox, while 10–11% were classified as due to tuberculosis.[35] Data from South Sweden confirm the importance of these causes over a longer period, 1749–1801.[36] Data from Finland show that over 40% of deaths were attributed to specified infectious diseases in national records for the eighteenth century.[37] For the decade 1751–60, the proportion of all deaths attributed to the six main specified diseases was: smallpox or measles, 12.8%; whooping cough, 6.9%; pulmonary tuberculosis, 8.4%; typhus, 9.5%; dysentery, 2.8%; and malaria, 2.1%. There are many limitations of these records and qualifications will have to be made when cause-specific death rates are discussed in later chapters. However, at this stage it is sufficient to consider these data as an indication of the main diseases which were recognised as important killers in the eighteenth century, even if the actual level of mortality attributed to each is highly suspect.

Mortality decline and changes in food availability

Despite the many limitations of the records and qualifications about the level of mortality attributed to different categories of disease, they do indicate the prevailing pattern of infectious diseases causing high mortality in England and Europe in the eighteenth century. Consideration can now be given to the cause of the sustained decline in the death rate from mid-century, which affected population growth and thus the demand for food. The interpretation of the modern rise of population proposed by McKeown, for example, was based on the view that a reduction in the death rate resulted in large part from improved resistance to infectious diseases which occurred because of an improved standard of living and increased food availability in particular.[38] His thesis has been summarised as follows:

Population growth was not influenced by improved sanitation before about 1870 or by specific medical measures before the introduction of sulphonamides in 1935 . . . the rise of population in the eighteenth and early nineteenth centuries [was due] to a decline of mortality which resulted from improvement of diet . . . [through] a large increase in food production . . .[39]

There have been many criticisms of this hypothesis, and recently Wrigley and Schofield placed much more emphasis on fertility levels, although acknowledging that mortality decline had played a significant part in population growth.[40] Much of the relevant evidence from several studies contributing to a 'standard-of-living debate' will be reviewed here. However, the primary concern is with the changing pattern of mortality and the recession of mortality crises which had been such a check on population growth.

Many of the problems with the broad thesis on mortality and population change proposed by McKeown stem from the fact that he did not consider in any detail evidence of disease and mortality patterns in the eighteenth century, nor that relating to the decline in mortality which took place in the first half of the nineteenth century. A later review of evidence by Flinn confirmed that there had been a downturn in the overall death rate in the eighteenth century. He also compared family reconstitution evidence from Scandinavia, Germany and Spain which suggested that infant mortality was falling. He compared similar evidence from England, France and Switzerland, which indicated that improvements in child survival also occurred towards the end of the eighteenth century.[41] Flinn emphasised that the decline in mortality was linked with the attenuation and wider spacing of mortality crises, which had become less severe from the mid eighteenth century. Aggregate data from several hundred parishes taken from the study by Wrigley and Schofield support this view of mortality change in England. Years in which the annual crude death rate was more than 10% above a 25-year moving average were classed as mortality crises. These were further subdivided into three categories, and the eleven most severe crises in which mortality was more than 30% above the trend occurred before 1750. The last of the secondary crises, involving mortality which was 20–30% above the expected level, occurred in 1762/3. After 1802/3 there were only two years in which mortality was more than 10% above the trend level, in 1846/7 and 1848/9.[42] The data in Figure 2.1 can be interpreted as showing that the pattern of mortality fluctuation had changed dramatically from the 1740s. The nineteenth century was relatively free of the extreme fluctuations in annual mortality that had been a feature of the previous mortality pattern.

In general there is little evidence to suggest that mortality crises in England had been associated with higher food prices in the period leading up to the change in mortality pattern. From the mid sixteenth century to the mid seventeenth century, poverty may have been exacerbated by increases in the price of food under pressure from growing demand. Even

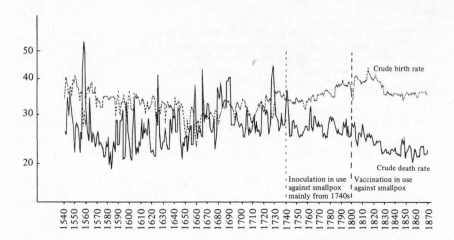

Figure 2.1 Estimates of annual birth and death rates per 1,000 in England 1540–1870.

Sources: E.A. Wrigley and R. Schofield (1981) *The Population History of England, 1541–1871: A Reconstruction* (London: Edward Arnold), pp. 531–535.

so, an index of real wages among building craftsmen referred to by Wrigley and Schofield and shown in Figure 2.2, suggests a higher economic standard of living in the mid eighteenth century than at the beginning of the seventeenth, when average expectation of life had if anything been somewhat higher. The lower expectation of life at times in the period between the mid seventeenth and the mid eighteenth century, when prices do not appear to have been increasing, was probably more related to the transmission processes of air-borne diseases. Tuberculosis had probably become more widespread and endemic in the population through contact with towns and migration from rural areas. By this time more towns were probably also reaching the size necessary to maintain as endemic air-borne epidemic diseases such as smallpox. However, Wrigley and Schofield pointed out that the process of urbanisation itself is likely to have been affected by socio-economic factors,[43] which therefore indirectly affected disease and mortality patterns.

Wrigley and Schofield also suggested that local food shortages might have been reflected in local mortality crises, and epidemics of some diseases could have spread from such situations.[44] This may have been the case with the lice-borne disease typhus, although the risk of mortality may not have depended on the malnutrition prevalent in periods of food shortage or war, but rather on the social disruption and deterioration in the conditions of life and personal hygiene.[45] There is some evidence of correlation between bread prices and mortality from typhus as indicated by deaths attributed to 'spotted fever' in the London Bills. After 1729, the typhus categories in the London Bills were merged with 'ague and fevers',

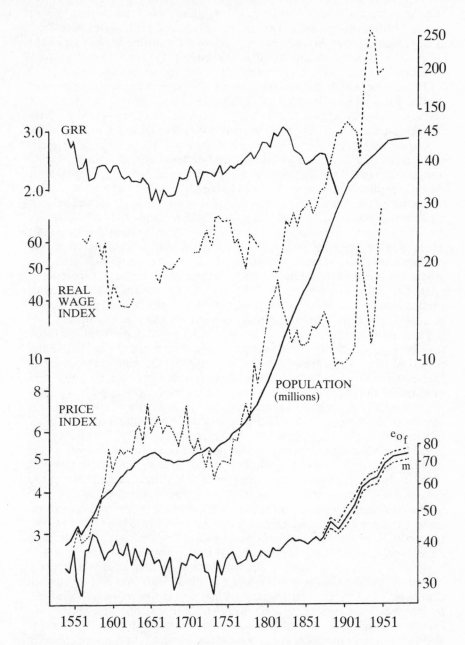

Figure 2.2 Quinquennial indices of economic and demographic change in England, 1541–1951.

Sources: E.A. Wrigley and R. Schofield (1981); E.H. Phelps-Brown and S.V. Hopkins: see note 82.

and Appleby again found some correspondence between fluctuations in mortality from this group and changes in bread prices. It seems plausible, as he suggested, that the body lice capable of transmitting the disease could have been more prevalent because scavenging for food brought closer contact with the rat population from which infection was transferred.[46]

On the other hand, little correlation was found between bread prices and deaths from plague which had a similar mode of transmission, but epidemics usually arrived from sources outside the country. Also, little correlation was found between smallpox mortality and bread prices, and it is known that even the well-nourished had a high risk of dying from smallpox or plague. Shortages of food and under-nutrition would certainly have contributed to a high risk of dying from some infectious diseases in the eighteenth century, as in developing countries today.[47] There were also the dietary-deficiency diseases such as scurvy and rickets. However, it is unlikely that nutritional status was the major determinant of high mortality risk from many of the major diseases, including typhoid for example. There is also likely to have been high case fatality from many of the predominant diseases among all social classes regardless of their ability to obtain adequate food, while the onset of infection would not have been related to nutritional status.[48] This was almost certainly the case with *variola major*, and there is evidence of the particular independence of smallpox epidemics from fluctuations in harvest yields, for example.[49]

There must also be some doubt as to whether food supplies did any more than keep pace with population growth in the nineteenth century and in the period of most rapid growth at the beginning of the nineteenth century. McKeown in fact acknowledged that there is little direct evidence that diet or nutrition did improve.[50] The capacity to improve food supplies is clearly of great importance for any expanding population whether undernourished already or not. Among other factors, climatic changes affect the variability of harvests, so that periodic subsistence crises occur where it has not been possible to build up any surplus. The peasant economy of Europe in the eighteenth century probably gave little scope for any excess production of food, so that in a bad year cash crops grown to pay the rent probably had to be consumed, or even next year's seed crop.[51] Subdivision of small holdings may have provided no answer to the demands of excess population, since yield per acre would probably not have increased.[52] Other opportunities to increase food supplies by cultivating new land, for example, may have involved the use of poor land locally, or migration. Flinn also suggested that the settlement and cultivation of new land was more a feature of eastern than western Europe in the seventeenth and eighteenth centuries.[53] In England, enclosures did increase in the eighteenth century, as did the development of agricultural techniques, but the consequent increase in agricultural yields through fatter stock and heavier crops, should be seen in the context of social disruption and rural poverty among those dispossessed of land.

Scarcity of food was probably localised in some years, so that distribution was a further important aspect of maintaining food supplies. Transport developments, including canals, harbours, navigation aids, roads and bridges, could all have contributed to the alleviation of the problem as the beginnings of a 'famine relief' attitude became manifest.[54] It is plausible that famine crises were also reduced with the introduction of new crops, such as the potato, corn and buckwheat. The value of these crops may not necessarily have been related to increased yields from the land available, but because of their lower susceptibility to damage under weather conditions which could destroy traditional crops.[55] However, even if food supplies became more regular there is little direct evidence concerning any increase in food consumption per head in the eighteenth century, although some estimates are available for the nineteenth century. These suggest that although there were increases in wheat yields in England and Wales in the first forty years, they did not match population growth, and wheat consumption per person may have fallen between the 1770s and the 1830s. There was an increase in potato-growing in the first forty years of the nineteenth century,[56] but whether this constituted anything significantly more than a substitution for other types of food, is difficult to assess.

Other indications of variation in the economic standard of living

Many studies have considered food supplies, and other indicators of standard of living, such as real wages, in relation to mortality and population chance. One early study suggested that the standard of living may in fact have deteriorated between 1720 and 1821 when population began to increase very rapidly.[57] In the Vale of Trent, the relationship between food supply and death rates suggested that epidemics had an effect which was independent of the results of famine.[58] A similar conclusion was reached after a study of data from Exeter, where a period of rising standard of living, between 1838 and 1875, was one of fairly constant mortality.[59] It might be argued that any improvements in living standards would tend to benefit the next generation, but even allowing for a 'lag' between trends and for inconsistencies between indices compiled for the same period, studies have not been able to show any consistent relationship between standards of living and mortality change. Significantly, recent work on changing living standards in the Industrial Revolution has indicated that the second half of the eighteenth century – when mortality decline began – was a period of wage stagnation.[60] Other inconsistencies in the evidence concerning the importance of changes in the economic standard of living have been pointed out. For example, there were increases in real wages for London and Lancashire building labourers in the first half of the eighteenth century, but not in the second half when mortality was falling and population growing faster.[61] There is certainly firmer evidence of improved real wages in the period 1820 to 1850, but this was one hundred years after the initial onset of mortality decline and the modern phase of population growth. It can also be noted that the doubling of real wages in the period 1820–50 was probably not the result of actual increases, but a reflection of deflation after the Napoleonic Wars.[62] Also the real wages of farm labourers only increased by about

25% in this period, compared with a 400% increase for white-collar workers.[63]

Data have been reported which, if reliable, reflect a possible improvement in health among boys from poor backgrounds in London in the first half of the nineteenth century, as indicated by an increase in their average height.[64] However, other studies on height have pointed out that this is a net, rather than a gross measure of nutritional status. Increases in height do not necessarily reflect a greater consumption of food per person or improved nutritional value of food. Past nutritional experience of the mother has to be taken into account, and a low birth-weight can reflect the health of the mother and have adverse consequences for the health and growth of the child. Maternal care has also been found to be an associated variable affecting the impact of infectious diseases on health, in addition to predetermining factors such as length of gestation and low birth-weight.[65] A further important influence on physical growth is the efficiency of the body in utilising nutrients. Of most relevance for the discussion here is the effect of infectious disease and consequent severe illness on both the ability to ingest food and to convert nutrients into energy and growth. Smallpox vaccination, in preventing the debilitating effects of the severest of the childhood diseases, removed what may have been an important inhibiting factor in physical growth. There are many exogenous and environmental variables likely to have been involved in this complex interaction including climate, clothing, shelter, work, sanitation, and the quality of the food itself. Many aspects of poor living and working conditions in the Industrial Revolution of the nineteenth century were probably as significant as nutrition for physical growth and survival chances.

Evidence on survival chances for different social groups in this period, from the 1840s, suggests that about 90% of the children of the gentry would have lived to their first birthday, but only 80% among tradespeople, and 68% among operatives. Survival rates to age five years for these social groups were 82.4%, 61.8%, and 44.6% respectively. An estimated 63.4% of the gentry would have lived to the age of forty years, compared with only about 20% of the children of the operatives.[66] Clearly survival chances of those without regular work would have been even worse, but Rickman argued that the poor were too large a proportion of the population to have been excluded from economic advances.[67] By contrast, Engels suggested that the appalling living conditions of most people in the towns in the 1840s were known to the entrepreneurial classes, which he accused of 'social murder' for failing to do anything.[68] The so-called 'Golden Age' of Victorian prosperity, from 1850–73,[69] was a period of economic boom which affected those in work through wage increases. However, the benefits for some of the working class have to be seen in the context of the dreadful environmental and living conditions which continued to exist in most industrial towns.

The disclosure of poverty by Booth and Rowntree around the turn of the century had little effect on government attitudes.[70] Investigations just prior to the First World War began to reveal the still deplorably low standards of nutrition among women, children and large sections of the working class.[71] By contrast, the wealthy and upper classes had probably been well-fed throughout the nineteenth and eighteenth centuries when their expectation of life increased. Estimates of average expectation of life at birth (e_o) among females of the British peerage have suggested a steady level of about 33 years from the fourteenth to the seventeenth century. After this, survival chances improved and e_o increased from 36.7 for 1725–49, to 45.7 for 1750–74. A further rapid increase appears to have taken place in the nineteenth century, from 51.7 for 1800–24, to 58.4 for 1825–49.[72] It is clear that any explanation of mortality decline from the mid eighteenth century, has to account for changes among the peerage which were probably not the result of a change in economic circumstances or food availability. On the other hand, for the majority of the population in England it is far from certain that there was the kind of improvement in economic standard of living that might have consistently contributed to the first hundred years of the mortality transition.

Mortality, fertility and population change: a vital revolution

Estimates by Wrigley and Schofield of changes in the average expectation of life at birth for the general population of England, suggests that e_o was about 40 years in some quinquennial periods around 1600, but declined during the seventeenth century.[73] It may not have increased again until the second half of the eighteenth century, when it rose to levels of between 35 and 40 years. After 1800, there were none of the rapid fluctuations in quinquennial values that had occurred in previous centuries, and there was a more sustained increase throughout the nineteenth century as shown in Figure 2.2. Such estimates concur with the widely accepted view of the overall trend in the death rate in England, but a shift in emphasis from previous studies of vital rates has come with the estimate of a 'fertility bulge' in the period 1751–1830. Previous studies have suggested that if fertility did return to sixteenth-century levels in eighteenth century England, the increase took place in the first half of the century.[74] The estimates presented by Wrigley and Schofield suggest increases in the second half of the eighteenth century up to a level of about 40 per 1,000 in the 1810s. On the other hand, evidence from other north-European countries with national registration records shows that if anything fertility was declining in the second half of the eighteenth century, in which case it could not have contributed to any increase in the rate of growth of population. It can also be noted that the birth-rate levels of 30–35 per 1,000 found around the turn of the century in Sweden, Denmark, Norway and France were nothing like as high as the estimates for England shown in Figure 2.1. The long-term trend estimated for England suggests there was an increase in the gross reproduction rate (GRR) from a low of about 1.8 in 1661, with a levelling-off at 2.2–2.3 in the period 1701–56, followed by a quite consistent increase over successive quinquennial periods up to a peak of about 3.0 in 1816 as shown in Figure 2.2. It was estimated that

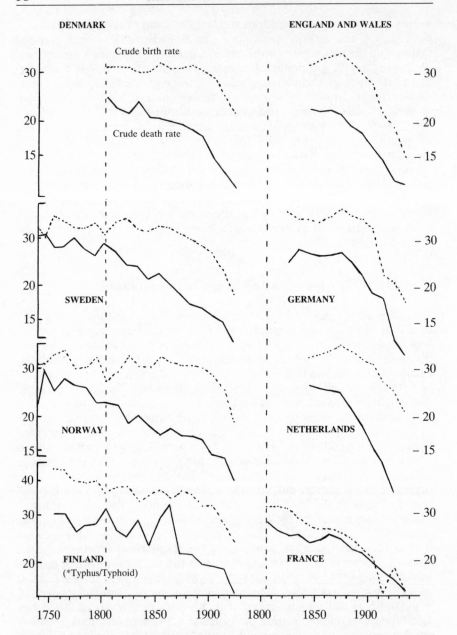

Figure 2.3 A comparison of European populations with long registration series of birth and death rates: the widening gap in the 19th century. (Average annual rates per 1,000 population for each decade).

Source: Data from national records given in B.R. Mitchell (1971) *European Historical Statistics, 1750–1970* (London: MacMillan).

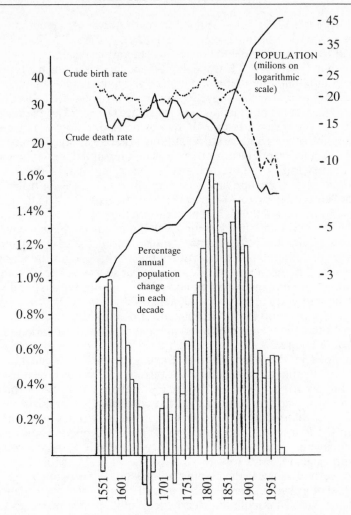

Figure 2.4 Estimates and indicators of decennial population growth in England, 1541–1981.

* Registrar-General (*Annual Reports* and *Statistical Reviews*) probably understated the birth rate by about 3 per 1,000: see D.V. Glass (1973) *Numbering the People* (Farnborough: Saxon House), p. 182.

Source: E.A. Wrigley and R. Schofield (1981) *The Population History of England, 1541–1871: A Reconstruction* (London: Edward Arnold), pp. 531–535.

GRR declined until the mid nineteenth century, while registration data reveal the well-recognised downturn in the birth rate from the 1870s.

Wrigley and Schofield emphasised the role of fertility levels in population growth in England on the basis of these estimates. The recovery of GRR to levels prevailing before the Great Plague occurred by the end of the seventeenth century, with a subsequent increase over a hundred-year period from the 1710s to the 1810s. However, it was also pointed out that there was a period of quite rapid population growth in England between 1540 and 1640, when the death rate fell well below the declining birth rate, as illustrated in Figure 2.4.[75] Europe at this time may once again have neared the limits of population that could be fed, given the land available and the state of agricultural technology. However, Flinn noted that this does not appear to have led to any increase in subsistence crises.[76] The evidence from Europe generally suggests that there was a slowing down of population growth in the seventeenth century, although there was much divergence of rates. In the eighteenth century there was uninterrupted growth in virtually every country in Europe, particularly in the second half of the century.[77] The population of Europe has been estimated as increasing from around 120,000,000 in 1700, by 16.7% up to 1750, and then by 28.6% in the next half century. By the end of the eighteenth century, the population of Europe was probably greater than it had been in 1500, but it may not have recovered to the levels of the early fourteenth century before the plague pandemic. However, the uninterrupted growth continued throughout the nineteenth century when the birth rate was declining – but so was the death rate – and population probably increased by about 47% in both the first and second half of the century to reach about 390,000,000 by 1900.

Rates of population growth in England appear to have been higher in all decades of the nineteenth century than those estimated for earlier periods, as shown in Figure 2.4. There seems little reason to doubt that the highest growth rates in the population of England occurred in the first three decades of the nineteenth century. At this time a further downturn in the death rate occurred following the decline in the second half of the eighteenth century, and this coincided with a continuingly high birth rate or a possible peak of around 40 per 1,000 according to Wrigley and Schofield's data. In the first few decades after 1800, many European countries were experiencing growth rates over 1% per year and in some countries, including England, rates rose to 1.5% as shown in Appendix 2c. Growth rates in recent decades in developing countries have been much higher, but the period of growth in nineteenth century Europe was unprecedented.

Such increases in population clearly necessitated rapid increases in food supply, and imports probably could not provide a major proportion of food consumed in the early periods of rapidly increasing demand.[78] There appears to have been a close correspondence between population change and movements in a price index based mainly on food consumables.[79] Malthus had suggested that food prices would increase with the pressure of population growth, and this generally appears to have been the case except in the nineteenth century. It seems likely that the increasing demand for food in the period of rapid population growth from the mid sixteenth to the mid seventeenth century led to higher food prices. After this, prices appear to have remained stable in a period of little population growth up to the mid eighteenth century, as shown by the actual indices for quinquennial periods in Figure 2.2. From this time, the price index increased again with the renewed rapid growth in population, and inflation became even more marked under the pressure of prolonged war. At the beginning of the nineteenth century, after the Napoleonic Wars, prices probably fell back again but rose between 1851 and 1873, and then rose more consistently in line with population growth after the 1890s. In some periods rapid price inflation was accompanied by a fall in real wages, at least on the basis of the index of real wages for building craftsmen. This evidence is consistent with the idea that the economic standard of living may have declined in some periods of rapid population growth, such as in the second half of the sixteenth century and the second half of the eighteenth century.

Wrigley and Schofield found no evidence of a long-term association between a 25-year moving average of their wage index and average expectation of life, although it was suggested that there was a close relationship with fertility changes.[80] The pattern of change in GRR referred to earlier can be summarised in terms of three main phases, the first of which was a period of declining fertility from 1541 until the turning point around 1661, which was followed by increasing fertility up to a second turning point and downturn in GRR around 1816. These turning points occurred about fifty and sixty-five years after comparable long-term turning points in the 25-year moving average of the real-wage index. Wrigley and Schofield pointed out that there was in fact a closer long-term correlation with GRR for cohorts, since the lag was only about twenty years. This was held to be consistent with a causal relationship between economic standard of living and fertility.[81] Such a relationship seems plausible for the period of declining GRR between the mid sixteenth and the mid seventeenth century, since food prices appear to have increased rapidly while real wages if anything declined. The rapid population growth occurred mainly in the absence of mortality crises in several decades, when the birth rate – although declining – was much higher than the death rate. Over the next hundred years up to the mid eighteenth century, GRR was estimated to have risen, and this was still consistent with an association with economic standard of living since the real-wage index was increasing and prices if anything were falling.

The estimated increase in fertility did not lead to much population growth until the middle of the eighteenth century when the death rate began to fall. It is from this point that the association between fertility levels and indices of the economic standard of living ceases, suggesting that some important change in the conditions of life occurred to sustain increasing fertility in a period of rapid price inflation. The indices presented by Wrigley and Schofield show price inflation and a fall in real wages,[82] while other data indicate that at best there was stagnation of real wages between 1751 and 1816. Thus, in the 'take off' period of the vital revolution in England, there may have been increasing fertility as well as the more established downturn in the death rate, but neither of these changes appears to have been the immediate consequence of changes in the economic standard of living.

Wrigley and Schofield suggested that the increase in fertility during the course of the eighteenth century was linked with changing marriage patterns.[83] A later study has suggested a lag of fifteen to twenty years after long-run changes in real wages relating to the period of prime earnings and saving for marriage.[84] For cohorts born before 1700, changes in real wages appear to have been matched by changes in the proportion ever married, but this may have remained steady in the eighteenth century. The rise in fertility, and particularly that after 1750, was found to have been associated more with a fall in the age of marriage of about three years. It was suggested that this was linked with the increasing availability of industrial work for a proportion of the population. Wrigley and Schofield also found evidence of a more immediate response to economic circumstances, since short-term variations in both fertility and marriage rates were more closely associated with short-term variations in real wages. Changes in the marriage rate appeared to be associated with movements in this economic index in the current and previous year.[85]

It may, however, be significant that birth rates were also negatively associated with short-term fluctuations in death rates. 'Fertility crises' became less frequent from about the same time – in the mid eighteenth century – that the change in frequency of mortality crises occurred. Thirteen of the fifteen years in which the birth rate fell more than 10% below a 25-year moving average were before the 1740s.[86] After 1800/1 and 1801/2, the birth rate did not fall this sharply in any year, so that the pattern of annual levels of fertility and mortality became more steady from about the same time. The reduction in numbers of baptisms during and after a mortality crisis is a recognised feature of the demography of pre-industrial Europe and epidemics as well as famine affected those of reproductive age.[87] Wrigley and Schofield pointed out that in the absence of any link between economic change and change in mortality levels, this relationship emphasised the independent and double importance of disease as a factor behind short-term demographic variation in the past.[88]

The more long-term changes in fertility and mortality could also have been linked with changes in the impact of infectious diseases. Increases in fertility, if they did occur in the second half of the eighteenth century, were exceptional in that food prices appear to have been increasing rapidly. It could be that some quite dramatic change in the relationship between fertility and mortality occurred in the period 1751–1816 because of a change in the impact of infectious diseases which was independent of changing economic circumstances. Such a hypothesis might also be more relevant to the question of why changes in vital rates occurred among the aristocracy whose standard of living seems unlikely to have been affected by economic circumstances or changes in food prices, but who would have been subject to common air-borne infectious diseases.

Razzell suggested that the introduction of smallpox inoculation in England in the mid eighteenth century could have affected marriage and fertility patterns in the population generally, as well as reducing mortality levels. It was used among all sections of society,[89] and there is some evidence that any reduced incidence of smallpox as a result of this may have tended to increase fertility levels because of a reduction in the incidence of associated male sterility.[90] Studies in India found a much higher incidence of azoospermia – or absence of viable sperm – among those known to have had smallpox, and lesions at the lower end of the epididymis were thought to have resulted from this infection. There is also evidence of increased childlessness during periods when smallpox mortality was increasing in Britain. For example, the rate increased from about 14% among the British peerage in the seventeenth century, to 23% by the 1740s, after which it declined to about 18–19% by the end of the eighteenth century. The increasing impact of smallpox epidemics does appear to correspond with reduced fertility among the peerage, and in the period 1550–1724 the average number of children per married female fell from about 5 to 3.5. The downward trend from about 1590 was arrested in the mid eighteenth century, and mean family size rose again to almost 5 by 1815.[91] As with improvements in life expectancy among the peerage, such changes are unlikely to have been the result of a better economic standard of living for this group of the population.

It does seem plausible that inoculation introduced around the 1740s could have resulted in less sterility than arose from 'natural' smallpox infection. However, it might be questioned whether this caused significant changes in childlessness in the general population. It is outside the scope of this study to consider the relative importance of reduced male sterility and reductions in the age of marriage. However, there are further grounds for supposing that changes in fertility were not independent of changes in the disease and mortality environment. In rural areas where smallpox epidemics were less frequent so that the disease was often contracted for the first time in adolescence, inoculation in reducing morbidity as well as mortality could have significantly improved chances for earlier marriage or pregnancy. Conversely, at a later time when vaccination brought a reduction in the high child death rate in towns, longer survival and extended periods of infertility associated with suckling,[92] could have contributed to the decline in fertility rather than tending to increase it. It also seems feasible that the recognised success of smallpox vaccination in securing a greater chance of survival among young children, could have helped boost confidence and bring about a change in attitudes, as well as in any strategy to produce as many children as possible to allow for losses.[93] Thus there are many reasons why changes in fertility levels should not be considered as independent of the changes in the disease and mortality environment which are the main concern in this study.

It may be that fertility increased in England in the eighteenth century and then fell again after 1816 as Wrigley and Schofield's evidence suggests. For the second half of the eighteenth century there have been different estimates of change in birth rates, age at marriage, and proportion marrying.[94] Also, the estimate of increasing fertility in the period 1751–1816 differs from earlier estimates – by Brownlee, for example. However, these later estimates do raise the possibility that in England an increase in fertility, and the circumstances which brought this about, made a particularly significant contribution to the demographic transition, compared with the experience of other north-European countries. The relative trends in the two vital rates recorded under national-registration systems in European countries are shown in Figure 2.3. All these data indicate the important role of the recession of mortality crises in the increased rate of population growth in the nineteenth century – and even in the second half of the eighteenth century – for the countries with registration data available: Sweden, Norway and Finland. Estimates for France indicate the consistently important contribution of the declining death rate to the maintenance of the rate of population growth as the birth rate declined.[95] Flinn also pointed out that birth rates in France, Scandinavia, Spain, Switzerland and Hungary have all been estimated as falling in the nineteenth century, so that the factors involved in mortality decline were probably most important for the rapid population growth experienced in the demographic transition in Europe generally.[96]

If increases in fertility levels did play a major part in the initial stages of the vital revolution in England, it seems plausible that changes in marriage and fertility patterns – like those in mortality – were significantly affected by the changing impact of infectious diseases independently of changes in the economic standard of living. However, the main concern here is with the relationship between the infectious-disease environment and mortality change. The general trend in the crude death rate in England presented by Wrigley and Schofield is more consistent with evidence from other European countries than the estimated trend in the birth rate, although the decline from the mid eighteenth century to the mid nineteenth century is somewhat less than some previous estimates have suggested.[97] An important advance is that the series provides an illustration of the changing pattern of short-term annual fluctuations in mortality over four centuries. The trend in the annual crude death rate in Figure 2.1 indicates regular peaks in the period 1541–1741, which reached levels of between 35 and 40 per 1,000 population, but after the 1740s the annual crude death rate only reached 30 per 1,000 in three years, all in the 1760s. This relaxation of the mortality crises of the previous two centuries was reflected in more rapid and sustained population growth.

Summary

In this chapter it has been suggested that with the virtual disappearance of plague epidemics after the seventeenth century in Europe, the biggest epidemic threat to lives was smallpox. The disease had become widespread in Europe by this time and a more regular cause of high mortality, while other diseases – such as tuberculosis which was endemic, and fevers which included typhoid and typhus – were significant among the causes of death noted in early records in different parts of Europe. The pressure of population growth in the eighteenth century, meant that food supplies had to be increased, but there is little evidence to support the view that more food became available per person in a way that could have increased nutritional resistance to infectious disease.[98] Many of the significant diseases causing regularly high mortality, and particularly *variola major*, would have resulted in high case-fatality rates in well-fed populations anyway. Certainly high grain prices following harvest failure caused serious survival problems among the poor of pre-industrial Europe, bringing conditions which favoured the spread of 'fevers' such as typhus, as well as starvation and malnutrition with a lowered resistance to other diseases. Both mortality and fertility responded in the short-term to harvest failure in Europe, and this 'positive' and 'preventive' check on population growth continued into the nineteenth century in the poorer regions such as Austria and Tuscany.[99] A reduced incidence of harvest failure and famine linked with various changes in the more developed areas, may have meant fewer mortality crises involving typhus, but this may not have actually initiated the downturn in overall mortality. In France, for example, there is evidence of close correlation between years of great scarcity and exceptionally high mortality – but only until the eighteenth century. Epidemics of infectious disease which acted independently of harvest failure seem to have become the main cause of periodic fluctuations in mortality by this time. This also appears to have been the case in Sweden and Finland and, although serious harvest failure may have contributed to peaks in mortality in Sweden until the 1740s,[100] smallpox epidemics had come to predominate.

In England, economic change and urbanisation were more advanced than elsewhere in Europe, but long-term changes in mortality do not appear to have been linked with changes in the economic standard of living as measured by real wages, for example. Short-term fluctuations in mortality may have been determined less by changes in grain prices than elsewhere,[101] and harvest failure does not appear to have been a significant factor in Britain just before the mortality transition in the first half of the eighteenth century. Even before this, trends in burial rates do not indicate a close association with levels of food output.[102] There was a national food crisis in the 1690s,[103] after which such problems may have become more localised. In London,for example, mortality attributed to 'fevers', which was more likely to be associated with such crises, does appear to have levelled off just before the long-term decline in overall mortality. However, the annual death rate was still peaking at over 35 per 1,000 in the first half of the eighteenth century in England, and typhus was recognised as a major contributor. During the course of the century a more regular supply and better distribution of food may have gradually restricted the famine conditions which gave rise to foci of infection. Certainly there had come to be a closer association between smallpox epidemics and fluctuations in overall mortality as in other parts of northern Europe. There is little to suggest that the virulence of *variola major* declined in a way that might explain the downturn in mortality, nor evidence to support the view that the resistance of the population increased through long exposure.[104] However, there is evidence that the introduction of inoculation – which coincided with the changed pattern of mortality crises after the 1740s – could also have contributed significantly in the initial stages of mortality decline in the second half of the eighteenth century in England. After this, immunisation based on the idea of *vaccination* became more widespread and the effects of this preventive measure will be considered in the next chapter. Its introduction coincided with the dramatic phase of mortality decline in the first few decades of the nineteenth century in much of Europe and in England, where the conditions of life in the expanding towns may have actually deteriorated at this time.

3 Smallpox epidemics and mortality in the eighteenth century: the impact of immunisation measures

The beginning of the sustained mortality decline in Europe in the mid eighteenth century does not appear to have been associated with any improvement in the economic standard of living, and there is little to suggest that any major improvement in nutrition could have taken place which might have led to better resistance to infectious diseases. The pattern of mortality in Europe in the eighteenth century was characterised by various infectious diseases, and particularly smallpox, tuberculosis, typhus, typhoid and dysentery, which appear to have been of varying significance in different countries. It was pointed out in Chapter 2 that the recession of plague epidemics at the end of the seventeenth century did not lead to rapid population growth at that time, although the disease had periodically caused extremely high mortality and even reduced the size of the population at the beginning of the pandemic in the fourteenth century. By the eighteenth century, smallpox had become more significant as a regular cause of the epidemic mortality crises which constituted a major check on population growth. The predominance of smallpox in patterns of fluctuating mortality in the eighteenth century and the introduction of inoculation have been examined in previous studies, but the effect of preventive measures based on vaccination has often been underestimated in connection with epidemiological-demographic change in England. Changes in the immune status of the population may have been significant for earlier disease and mortality patterns – with the recession of leprosy for example – but the intervention by man with immunisation against smallpox was unprecedented.

The relationship between epidemics of smallpox and fluctuations in overall mortality will be illustrated here with data from several sources. First, evidence from European countries will be examined, since national as well as local records provide data which can be used to illustrate the impact of vaccination on mortality. Studies of data from Scandinavia have been particularly valuable,while further data will be presented here from the reports of the Royal Commission on Vaccination which considered a great deal of evidence relating to the possible impact of this measure on mortality levels. The pattern of disease and mortality in England in the eighteenth century will then be examined with reference to different sets of Bills of Mortality and some of the parish registers which contain references to smallpox deaths. The role of immunisation, and particularly vaccination, in the virtual elimination of smallpox mortality in England during the course of the nineteenth century, will be viewed in the context of epidemiological-demographic change in Europe as a whole. The issue of the role of inoculation in mortality decline has been contentious, perhaps largely because of the possible dangers that accompanied this crude immunisation method. It is important to distinguish between inoculation involving the use of smallpox matter from an infected person, and vaccination in which cowpox matter was intended to be used to produce temporary immunity against the related disease of smallpox. Razzell presented evidence concerning the use of inoculation in England from the 1720s and suggested it may have been the most important factor in the downturn in overall mortality in the second half of the eighteenth century.[1] This will be considered here together with evidence of the impact of immunisation measures based on the practice of vaccination, and of later preventive measures which helped control the spread of the disease.

There were probably various types of smallpox virus which varied in virulence, but survival from infection usually resulted in life-long immunity. This was perhaps the main reason that smallpox had become more of a childhood disease by the eighteenth century when populations were reaching the size that could sustain the disease, while the life-long immunity also provided the basis for the practice of inoculation. No matter how crude and dangerous the method was by today's standards, if it gave people an attack of the disease with a mild enough strain, they would be likely to survive with an induced immunity to protect them in 'natural' epidemics. The argument that inoculation was more likely to have increased the spread of the disease,[2] may be less important if case-fatality can be shown to have been lower among the inoculated than among the rest of the population. In this regard the Royal Commission on vaccination referred to any doubts about inoculation, and the report stated:

That inoculation might have the effect of diminishing very largely the mortality from smallpox is shown by the records from Boston, USA. . . . The diminution both in the whole mortality from smallpox and in the cases of natural smallpox is very great indeed. Making allowance for greater care being taken in Boston than in London on for instance that cases of inoculation should not serve as causes of infection, these records afford very strong evidence in support of the view that on the whole inoculation did not, at least materially, increase the mortality from smallpox.[3]

In fact there was a dramatic reduction in mortality in smallpox epidemics when large numbers of people in Boston, USA, had been inoculated in the mid eighteenth century, as shown by the data in Table 3.1. Razzell pointed out that the decline in the death rate from smallpox is unlikely to have been

Table 3.1 Smallpox deaths and numbers inoculated in smallpox epidemics in Boston (USA) before vaccination came into use

Year	Smallpox Deaths		Death rate per 1,000	Natural cases of smallpox	Case-fatality %	Numbers inoculated	Case-fatality %
1702	213	*	31.5	Not available		Not available	
1721	850	(6)	77.3	5759	14.7	247	2.4
1730	500	(12)	33.3	3600	13.6	400	3.0
1752	569	(30)	36.2	5545	9.7	2124	1.4
1764	170	(46)	10.9	669	18.5	4977	0.9
1776	57	(28)	10.0	304	9.5	4988	0.6
1778	61	(19)	6.1	122	34.4	2121	0.9
1792	198	(165)	9.9	232	14.2	8114	2.0

* Smallpox deaths among the inoculated in parentheses, excluded in calculation of case-fatality among natural cases.

Source: Royal Commission on Vaccination (1889–96) *Third Report*, Appendix, p. 200.

due to any reduction in the virulence of the disease, since case-fatality among the 'naturally' infected remained high.[4]

The Royal Commission on Vaccination in 1896 pointed out that vaccination was probably in use in the last few decades of the eighteenth century in England, long before Jenner heard of this 'folk practice' in Gloucestershire. One example mentioned was that of a Dorset farmer, Jesty, who introduced matter from cowpox infection into his wife and sons to protect them against the smallpox in 1774. In a review of nationwide evidence, the Commission concluded that the practice spread rapidly after the publication in 1798 of the results of research by Jenner in his *Inquiry into the Causes and Effects of Variolae Vaccinae*. Within a few weeks the practice had spread, with perhaps remarkable rapidity compared with the delay in implementing BCG vaccination against tuberculosis in the twentieth century. Smallpox vaccination found acceptance within a decade in Europe and the United States, and even became compulsory in some Scandinavian countries as early as 1810 although legal penalties were not always enforced. It may be that the cowpox matter used as a basis for much of the immunisation performed in the early years of the nineteenth century, had been adulterated with smallpox matter.[5] The evidence that at first it was not genuine vaccination based on cross-immunity to cowpox, but a continuation of the practice of inoculation, seems unlikely to detract from the value of what was thought to be a new and tested measure. Although it was not Jenner's discovery, his work was influential in convincing the medical profession to take the evidence of success seriously. This produced a worldwide acceptance of the 'new' type of immunisation which, together with other preventive control measures, eventually led to eradication of the disease.

Smallpox epidemics and mortality change in Europe: the impact of immunisation

Smallpox inoculation appears to have been used in Tibet from at least the eleventh century,[6] but was probably not used on a wide scale in England until the 1740s, after the practice had been tried by royalty in the 1720s. It is possible that, on the continent of Europe, opposition to inoculation lasted longer than in England, where the argument that it was an interference with 'God's Will' was countered by the pioneering statistical studies of the Royal Society and the Smallpox Censuses. The widespread use of the practice in rural areas and small towns in particular, has been compared with the experience in France where organised resistance continued until the death of Louis XV from smallpox, in 1774.[7] McNeill referred to a boost to the credibility of immunisation at the beginning of the nineteenth century that came with the work of Jenner, and suggested that the extraordinary population growth in Europe in that century might have been largely a consequence of this and the ensuing curtailment of smallpox. In fact, estimates for France indicate that the death rate had already fallen in the second half of the eighteenth century compared with the 1740s, with a further sharp fall in the crude rate of 5 per 1,000 in the 1790s. The crude death rate then fell sharply again between 1810–14 and 1820–4. Other estimates of female mortality for the period 1740–1829 suggest an improvement in survival chances in the 1790s, but an even greater improvement in the decade 1800–9, which was maintained over the first three decades of the nineteenth century.[8] However, of more importance here is evidence from other countries, which enables such changes in mortality to be compared with the changing pattern of smallpox epidemics as immunisation was introduced.

Data from Copenhagen, extracted from the report by the Royal Commission on Vaccination, enable consideration to be given to different phases in the introduction of immunisation against smallpox. Inoculation was introduced into Denmark in the 1750s, and the Vaccination Commission in that country suggested some important events in the history of the decline in death rates, such as the opening of an inoculation establishment in 1770 on the outskirts of Copenhagen.[9] Other evidence – presented as a graph in Figure 3.1 – suggests that this event was followed soon after by a definite change in the pattern of smallpox epidemics, which became less severe. Peaks in overall mortality which had usually been associated with epidemics of the disease also became less extreme. In this period of inoculation (ii), between 1770 and 1801 when vaccination was introduced, the peaks in total mortality were probably due to other causes and demographically there appears to have been more of a balance between recorded births and deaths. There was therefore little natural population growth in the town, but this compares with the earlier phase of natural population decline in period (i) prior to the opening of the inoculation establishment. A third phase (iii) is distinct, after vaccination was made compulsory in 1810, with the forty years after this being relatively free from smallpox deaths. None at all were recorded in many years, and the

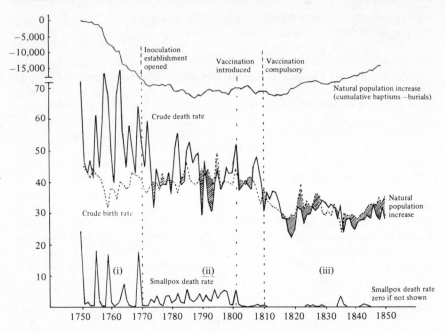

Figure 3.1 Comparison of smallpox death rate with annual crude birth and death rates per 1,000 population in Copenhagen (Denmark), 1750–1850.

Source: Data from Royal Commission on Vaccination (1889–96) *First Report* (London), pp. 107–108.

overall death rate was markedly lower after 1810. It is clear from these data that the long-term natural increase in population in the capital began around 1814, soon after the introduction of compulsory vaccination when smallpox deaths were reduced to negligible levels.

The fact that the birth rate does not appear to have increased in the first half of the nineteenth century in Copenhagen, indicates the greater importance of mortality decline in this exceptional population growth accompanying the introduction of vaccination. The extent to which there was a significant level of vaccination in Copenhagen was considered by the Royal Commission, which reported a ratio of 0.7 vaccinations to births for 1808, and it remained over this for the next two decades. The number of annual vaccinations in Iceland rose to about the level of births by 1817, and there was no major outbreak of smallpox in the nineteenth century except in 1839 when it was contained by isolation measures. This compares with the experience in the eighteenth century when devastating outbreaks were recorded, for example in 1785–7 when 1,425 deaths from the disease were reported. An earlier record suggested that in 1707 as many as 18,000 deaths had occurred in a smallpox epidemic when the population was around 50,000.[10] These changes in the epidemic pattern of smallpox in Copenhagen and Iceland can be viewed in relation to census data shown in

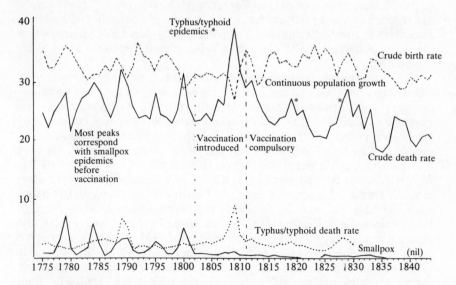

Figure 3.2 A comparison of the smallpox death rate with crude birth and death rates per 1,000 in Sweden, 1775–1845.

Source: Data from Royal Commission on Vaccination (1889–96) *First Report, Appendix* (London), pp. 112–113.

Appendix 2c. Population growth in the first half of the nineteenth century was considerably higher than that at the end of the eighteenth century.[11] For Copenhagen, the divergent birth-rate and death-rate trends shown in Figure 3.1,[12] also indicate that the more rapid population growth in the first half of the nineteenth century was the result of a decline in the death rate while the birth rate remained high. It did not decline until the second half of the century.

This well-known pattern of demographic transition can also be seen in the birth-rate and death-rate trends for Sweden, where statistics are also available for the second half of the eighteenth century together with data on smallpox deaths which can be used to assess the impact of vaccination measures at a national level.[13] Data presented in Figure 3.2 give some indication of the way in which fluctuations in the overall crude death rate in the second half of the eighteenth century were frequently associated with smallpox epidemics. It is also clear that there was a reduction in the death rate after the introduction of compulsory vaccination, so that smallpox mortality was rapidly reduced to almost negligible levels. It has been questioned whether vaccination was sufficiently effective to have caused the decline in mortality and whether inoculation – introduced earlier, in the 1780s – was sufficiently widely used to have had a major impact. The decline in mortality from smallpox in Sweden has also been attributed to an increase in natural immunity among the population after long exposure to the disease, or to a change in virulence of the organism.[14] However, in the absence of supporting evidence and in view of the timing of observed reductions in the death rate in relation to the introduction of immunisation measures in many parts of Europe, this intervention seems a more likely explanation.

The immediate impact of vaccination measures in Sweden was somewhat obscured by the very high mortality in the period 1804–13, when there was an exceptional epidemic of typhus in the Finnish Wars. However, the evidence suggests that the decline in smallpox mortality was not offset by increases for other infectious diseases. Death rates for the group, smallpox, measles, diphtheria and scarlet fever, have been estimated to have declined from 2,633 per 1,000,000 for 1790–1800, to 1,373 for 1801–11, with reductions for the separate causes, but with smallpox contributing most as shown in Appendix 3a (i).[15] Diphtheria mortality did increase later, possibly because of the epidemic which affected other parts of Europe including England. There was also a tenfold increase in the recorded scarlet-fever death rate for the period 1861–71, but this probably resulted from improved recognition and the transfer of deaths previously classified under the 'fevers' category. Despite these changes, the death rate for the four diseases was still only 1,804 per 1,000,000 in 1861–71. Other work has indicated that there was no increase in whooping-cough mortality when smallpox mortality declined rapidly, and vaccination was considered to have resulted in a postponement of mortality, such that the decline in the crude death rate in Sweden was largely attributed to the practice.[16] A further study referred to the fact that 10% of deaths were recognised as directly attributable to smallpox before vaccination was introduced, and that not only was this mortality reduced to negligible levels, but lives were also saved because smallpox had previously caused many other deaths from its severe sequelae.[17]

Further evidence confirms the predominance of smallpox in eighteenth-century mortality patterns in Sweden, since fifteen of the twenty peaks in infant mortality in the period 1752–1801 involved smallpox epidemics.[18] In contrast, the ten peaks in the period 1806–30, when vaccination was in use, were mainly due to dysentery cases and whooping cough (four cases). Measles epidemics featured largely in the other two peaks, such that small-pox was no longer an important cause of death. There was also little consistent relationship between severe smallpox epidemics and poor harvests, which in earlier times might have been a more significant deter-minant of mortality crises. Prior to vaccination other diseases had combined with smallpox to produce peaks in mortality, but the diseases had epidemic cycles of their own.[19] The cycle of smallpox was predominant in a competitive environment for micro-organisms seeking human hosts in which to replicate, Variola major would probably have pursued its independent cycle of destruction even without underlying malnutrition: many poor harvests were not accompanied by or immediately followed by smallpox epidemics, and the worst-ever outbreak followed the good harvest in 1778–9.[20]

In Finland also there was a clear relationship between peaks in the crude death rate and smallpox epidemics in the second half of the eighteenth

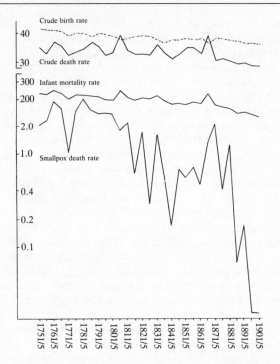

Figure 3.3   Crude birth and death rates per 1,000 population, infant mortality and smallpox death rates in Finland, 1751–1906.

Sources: O. Turpeinen (1979) Fertility and mortality in Finland since 1750. *Population Studies* **33**(i), pp. 101–114; K.J. Pitkanen, J.H. Mielke and L.B. Jorde (1989) Smallpox and its eradicaion in Finland: implications for disease control. *Population Studies* **43**, pp. 95–111.

century, and again no association with poor harvests. In fact, ten out of twelve peaks in the period 1750–1810, have been shown to correspond with smallpox-mortality peaks, as illustrated in Appendix 3b (i).[21] Data from Finland also indicate the universality of contact with the disease since, in the period 1749–73, 14.4% of the 18,920 deaths in rural parishes were attributed to smallpox or measles and 13.2% of the 12,390 deaths in town parishes, while about 9% of all deaths in the second half of the eighteenth century were attributed to smallpox alone.[22] The trend in the smallpox death rate shown in Figure 3.3 again indicates the marked change that occurred as vaccination was introduced in the first half of the nineteenth century. However, the average annual overall death rate remained at over 25 per 1,000 population in most quinquennial periods and other epidemics – particularly of 'fevers' – contributed to the peaks of 60 per 1,000 in 1808 and 1809 during the Russian War, 46 per 1,000 in the famine of 1838, and 77 per 1,000 in the famine of 1868.[23] The average annual death rates for adults and older children were in fact higher in the first half of the nineteenth century than they were in the second half of the eighteenth century. Despite this, the average annual overall death rate was slightly lower,[24] which was almost entirely due to declining infant mortality. Together with a high birth rate by European standards, this ensured that population growth continued in the nineteenth century.

The relationship between the changing death rate from smallpox and infant mortality is illustrated in Figure 3.3. The pattern of change is consistent with the idea that the recession of smallpox was significant and that immunisation played a major role, while other data indicate that the infant death rate from smallpox alone fell from 17.1 per 1,000 births for 1776–1800, to 9.4 per 1,000 for 1801–25. On the other hand in the second half of the eighteenth century when infant mortality as a whole declined, the death rate from smallpox or measles was no lower in 1776–1800 than in 1751–75. It has been suggested that the decline in the overall infant death rate at this stage could have reflected the beneficial effects of changes in breast-feeding practices, and the use of breast-feeding certainly appears to be highly significant in relation to the risk of diarrhoeal disease.[25] Even so, in the second half of the eighteenth century, fluctuations in smallpox mortality appear to have been the main determinants of peaks in mortality, including those of infants. As mentioned, other epidemics contributed to the maintenance of child-mortality levels in the particularly adverse circumstances in Finland, where – despite the high levels of vaccination coverage in the nineteenth century – the death rate at ages 1–4 did not fall consistently until after the 1870s, when monitoring and control of the spread of infectious diseases also became more effective.[26] By contrast, the trends in mortality quotients at ages 1–4 years for Geneva in Switzerland, shown in Appendix 3b (ii), clearly indicate both an association with smallpox and a decline in mortality levels over a period of two centuries between 1580 and 1760. At least 7% of all deaths in the town were attributed to the disease and one in five of the deaths among children under 5 years of age. Epidemics of smallpox have also been shown to correspond with peaks in total annual mortality and their control appears to have brought a dramatic change in overall mortality levels.[27]

Although data on smallpox mortality are not available for Norway, there was a similar pattern of change in the crude death rate to that in Sweden, as indicated in Figure 3.4. The vital rates show that peaks in overall mortality occurred regularly in the eighteenth century as a check on population growth. However, after the adoption of compulsory vaccination in 1810, the birth rate exceeded the death rate uninterruptedly, such that population growth became more rapid and continuous. One study gave evidence of the widespread use of vaccination as well as changes in food supply concomitant with population growth, but the practice was not considered to have been the main cause of the dramatic change in vital events.[28] Without data on smallpox mortality change, the evidence does not carry the same weight, but there does seem little reason to doubt that the virtual elimination of smallpox as a killer was highly significant, even if the disease had only accounted for the 10% of deaths attributed to it in Sweden – almost certainly an underestimate. Evidence from other countries again lacks the support of data on smallpox deaths, but that for the region of Lombardy in Italy is certainly consistent with the idea that vaccination had

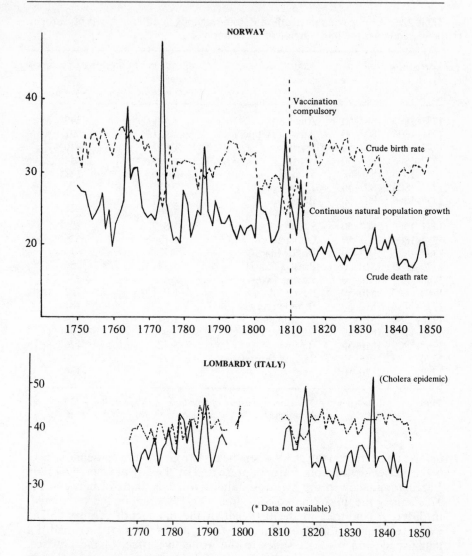

Figure 3.4 Crude birth and death rates per 1,000 population in Norway, 1750–1850, and in Lombardy (Italy), 1770–1850.

Sources: Data from B.R. Mitchell (1971) *European Historical Statistics, 1750–1970* (London: MacMillan); C.M. Cipolla (1965) Four centuries of Italian demographic development. In *Population in History: Essays in Historical Demography*, D.V. Glass and D.E.C. Eversley eds (London: Edward Arnold).

a dramatic impact. The estimates produced by Cipolla,[29] and illustrated in Figure 3.4, indicate a widening gap between annual birth rates and the declining death rate after the 1810s when vaccination was introduced. Again, the consequent population growth was uninterrupted as never

Table 3.2 Average annual death rate from smallpox in different parts of Europe, before and after the introduction of vaccination

Years compared	Place	Death rate per million from smallpox	
		before vaccination	after vaccination
1777–1806 : 1807–50	Austria (Lower)	2,481	340
1777–1806 : 1807–50	Austria (Upper)	1,421	501
1777–1806 : 1807–50	Styria	1,052	446
1777–1806 : 1807–50	Illyria	518	244
1777–1806 : 1838–50	Trieste	14,046	182
1777–1803 : 1807–50	Tyrol/Voralberg	911	170
1777–1806 : 1807–50	Bohemia	2,174	215
1777–1806 : 1807–50	Moravia	5,402	255
1777–1806 : 1807–50	Silesia (Austria)	5,812	198
1777–1806 : 1807–50	Gallicia	1,194	676
1787–1806 : 1807–50	Bukowina	3,527	516
1776–1780 : 1810–50	Prussia (East)	321	56
1780 : 1810–50	Prussia (West)	2,272	356
1780 : 1816–50	Posen	1,911	743
1776–1780 : 1810–50	Brandenberg	2,181	181
1776–1780 : 1816–50	Westphalia	2,643	114
1776–1780 : 1816–50	Rhenish Province	908	90
1781–1805 : 1810–50	Berlin	3,422	176
1776–1780 : 1816–50	Saxony (Prussian)	719	170
1780 : 1810–50	Pomerania	1,774	130

Sources: E.J. Edwardes (1902) *A Concise History of Smallpox and Vaccination in Europe*, pp. 18–19, 48–50, 180–182. Royal Commission on Vaccination (1889–96) *First Report*, p. 72.

before, apart from in the 1830s when the disastrous cholera epidemic struck.

Further evidence from Europe, presented by the Royal Commission on Vaccination, showed the high case-fatality from smallpox of between 16–47% among the unvaccinated compared with 1.8% among the vaccinated, in different countries in the first half of the nineteenth century.[30] The evidence suggests that the virulence of the disease at that time had not diminished, and it also testifies to the protective effect of the practice. Further data from the report, shown in Table 3.2, indicate a contrast between smallpox mortality in periods of about thirty years before vaccination, and rates after the measure was introduced in several countries. In may provinces, such as Moravia and Silesia, the decline in mortality from smallpox contributed a very considerable reduction in the overall death rate of about 5 per 1,000 population. In some provinces, the recorded smallpox death rate was much lower at the end of the eighteenth century, but in most areas there would have been a reduction of between one and five in the overall crude death rate as a result of the control of smallpox at the beginning of the nineteenth century, even before allowing for any further reductions in secondary mortality associated with the

Table 3.3 Average annual death rate from smallpox in Stuttgart and Berlin, before and after the introduction of vaccination

Average annual deaths from smallpox Stuttgart		Berlin		Percentage of all deaths Berlin	
1772–1796	224	1782–1791	4,453	1775–1799	6.5
1797–1801	274	1792–1801	4,999	1800–1804	7.5
1802–1806	154	1802–1811	2,955	1803–1809	6.4
1807–1811	2	1812–1822	555	1810–1814	0.7
1812–1816	0			1815–1819	1.3
1817–1821	10			1820–1824	0.2
1822–1826	0				

Sources: E.J. Edwardes (1902) *A Concise History of Smallpox and Vaccination in Europe*, pp. 18–19, 48–50, 180–182. Royal Commission on Vaccination (1889–96) *First Report*, p. 72.

Table 3.4 Smallpox deaths per 1,000,000 population in Germany in the 1870s

Year	Prussia	Bavaria	Württemberg
1868	620	120	133
1869	432	250	63
1870	188	190	19
1871	194	101	74
1872	175	75	293
1873	2,432	1,045	1,130
1874	2,624	611	637
1875	356	176	30
1876	95	47	3
1877	36	17	1
1878	31	13	2
1879	3	17	0
1880	7	13	0

Source: E.J. Edwardes (1902) *A Concise History of Smallpox and Vaccination in Europe*, pp. 181–182.

disease. The decline in the death rate of about 14 per 1,000 in Trieste indicates that a very large constraint on population growth was removed by the control of just one disease.

Dramatic reductions in smallpox mortality in Germany were recorded in parish records from Stuttgart and Berlin, as shown in Table 3.3. In 1810 there was a very high ratio of vaccinations to births in Berlin, and a fall in mortality to negligible levels quickly ensued, as it did in Stuttgart.[31] Edwardes pointed out that in Europe generally there were two major epidemics of smallpox after vaccination became available, one in 1838 and one in 1870–5. It seems plausible that the practice had lapsed somewhat after the initial enthusiasm at the beginning of the century, and with the apparent disappearance of epidemics for several years. In Bavaria, the epidemic of the 1870s attacked even the vaccinated, which was the main reason for the introduction of re-vaccination, while in England the coverage of primary vaccination was far from complete despite legislation. The German Vaccination Law of 1874, following the epidemic of 1871–2 appears to have had a considerable effect, as implied by the data in Table 3.4. The death rate from smallpox in three states, Prussia, Bavaria and Württemberg, after this law, rapidly declined to almost negligible levels.[32] There were no further major epidemics in the three provinces, and the death rate for the disease was below 5 per 1,000,000 after 1886. The long-term and continuous decline in the overall crude death rate in Germany occurred from the 1870s, with a downturn similar to that in England and Wales and the Netherlands.

Smallpox immunisation and mortality decline in England

Studies of the mortality transition in England have generally under-estimated the role of smallpox control in the nineteenth century, because of a concentration on the downturn in crude death rates from the 1870s discernible from national registration data. For example, McKeown and his co-workers implied that immunisation did not play much part in mortality decline,[33] but made little reference to data on mortality change in the pre-registration period. The use of inoculation by royalty in the 1720s probably aroused considerable interest among the general population, and there is certainly a great deal of evidence that inoculation was effectively and extensively used among the general population of England after the 1740s, particularly in rural areas.[34] Evidence from the Bills of Mortality for London indicates a levelling off in the rising death rate from smallpox, between the 1720s and the 1770s, a period which coincided with the extensive use of the improved Suttonian method of inoculation.[35] There have been suggestions that, anyway, smallpox might not have been universally contracted or have caused particularly high mortality in the first half of the eighteenth century. However, the evidence from the smallpox censuses in the 1720s compiled by Jurin, although based on selected epidemics reported by local medical practitioners, indicates the destructive-ness of the disease in different areas, with a case-fatality rate of 16.5% overall and 24.1% in the six rural areas included. Razzell pointed out that the age pattern of mortality for the disease was also consistent with universal contact,[36] while the data from Finland provide the strongest evidence of universal contact in town and country. There can be little doubt that the level of mortality in the population was high before inoculation came into use, and the data from Britain, Ireland and Scandinavia shown in Appendix 3c, much of which was presented by Razzell in his comprehensive study of inoculation, indicates that the disease made a very significant contribution to mortality in the first half of the eighteenth century, with between 8% and 20% of deaths being attributed to it directly.

The London Bills of Mortality indicate that smallpox was recognised as the direct cause in about 10% of deaths and was endemic in the eighteenth century with no gaps between major outbreaks. Data from the burial registers of the London Quakers have been presented showing that a substantial proportion of deaths from smallpox were above the age of 10 years in the period 1650–1800,[37] although it seems likely that individuals born in the capital had all contracted smallpox earlier than this. Older fatalities were probably among in-migrants from less populous areas where there were long intervals between epidemics.[38] Epidemics occurred at less frequent intervals in small rural towns and villages, and Creighton pointed to the case of Banbury,[39] where a larger proportion of deaths from small-pox occurred in early adulthood. He attributed this to the fact that people could grow up without experiencing an epidemic, not contracting the disease until adolescence or early adulthood unless they had cause to visit a nearby town where a larger population meant that epidemics were more frequent. The combination of smaller population size and less frequent travel contacts, would have made epidemics less likely than in a town such as Northampton where they occurred once or twice a decade, or cities like Glasgow, London and Edinburgh, where the disease was endemic.[40]

McNeill pointed out that the later age-incidence of the disease in rural areas compared with towns in England, might actually have encouraged the use of inoculation. Deaths of young people may have caused greater distress than the expected 'die off' of infants who were more regularly at risk where the disease was endemic or epidemics more frequent.[41] Smallpox may have been controlled to a greater extent through a wider use of inoculation in rural areas, where there may also have been less opposition on the grounds of interfering with 'nature'. The epidemiological-demographic pattern in rural England in the second half of the eighteenth century may, as a result, have been very different from that in towns for which more records on smallpox deaths were kept. A regular excess of baptisms over burials[42] could have been a common consequence of the greater use of inoculation compared with that in towns.

Most evidence on cause-specific mortality in the eighteenth century in England comes from towns, and Figure 3.5 illustrates one of the longest series of data, from All Saints parish in Northampton. This clearly shows the pattern of change in deaths from smallpox and in natural population growth from the time that vaccination was introduced, although inoculation may have had some impact in the 1790s. The evidence is particularly useful since it indicates the clear association between epidemics of smallpox and peaks in overall mortality. Nearly all the 'extra' burials registered in peak years in Northampton could be attributed to smallpox, and two other features of the pattern of mortality are especially worth noting. First, there is a contrast in the level of recorded smallpox deaths in the second half of the eighteenth century compared with the first half of the nineteenth century. Second, it is clear that a natural increase in the population only occurred when smallpox deaths were very few, or when none at all were

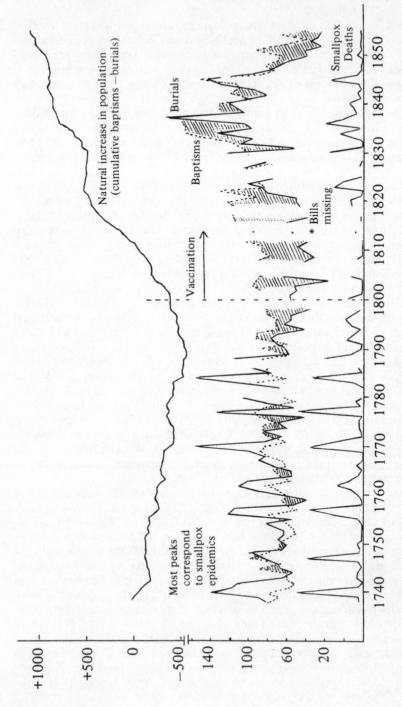

Figure 3.5 Annual smallpox deaths, all burials and baptisms recorded in the Bills of Mortality for All Saints Parish, Northampton.

Source: Bills of Mortality, All Saints Parish, Northampton (British Library, London).

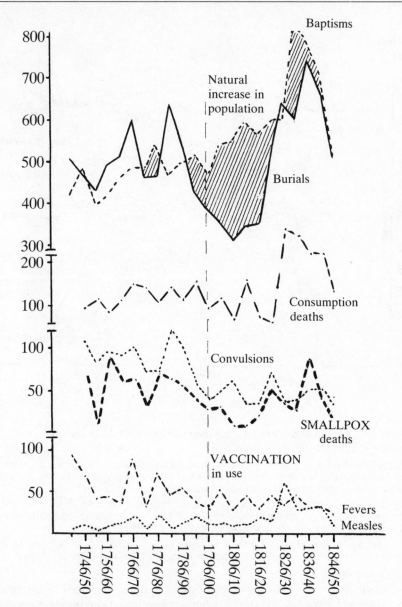

Figure 3.6 Quinquennial deaths recorded as due to specific causes in the Northampton Bills of Mortality, 1746–1850, in relation to changes in natural population growth.

Source: Bills of Mortality, All Saints Parish, Northampton (British Library, London).

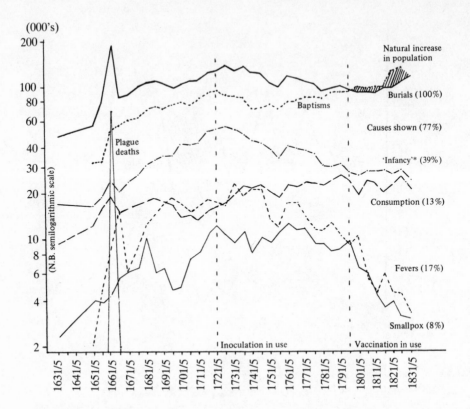

(000's)

Figure 3.7 Quinquennial burials from the main causes of death recorded in the London Bills of Mortality, 1631–1835.

* Infancy death ratio is the number of deaths from infancy divided by baptisms in the current and previous year, since deaths include infants and those in first year of life. The category includes mainly deaths involving convulsions and teething.

N.B. The semi-logarithmic scale, used to enable the large numbers to be shown, does mean that the contribution of different causes to overall mortality cannot be inferred from the relative levels, but the contribution in the peak period 1726–30 has been shown.

Sources: Data on annual deaths from a summary in J. Marshall (1832) Mortality in the Metropolis (London); London Bills of Mortality from 1830 (Guildhall Library, London).

recorded. It is not necessary to know actual population sizes to establish this, since the cumulative difference between baptisms and burials provides a useful indicator of natural increase, as with the data from Copenhagen. The long-term trend became continuously upward when smallpox epidemics receded from the end of the eighteenth century following the introduction of vaccination.

Even without information on population levels, such data provide a useful indication of disease and population change, while Figure 3.6 shows the pattern of change in quinquennial deaths attributed to some of the other main disease groups under which death was recorded in Northampton. Early studies of the possible impact of vaccination stressed the importance of considering changes in mortality attributed to other causes, as smallpox receded.[43] It was noted that the decline in smallpox mortality was not offset by increases among competing causes of death, such as measles and whooping cough. In Glasgow, measles appears to have been the first epidemic that came along after a dramatic fall in smallpox deaths in the first few years of the nineteenth century. This is shown in Appendix 3a (ii) and, along with the data from Sweden referred to earlier (Appendix 3a (i)), also supports the view that the reduction in smallpox mortality far outweighed the dangers attendant on young children from other infections which were around to take over from smallpox as the major killers.

Apart from the problems of accuracy of certification referred to briefly in the introduction, the main difficulty in interpreting changes for particular causes of death relates to the calculation of death rates. Despite this, much can be revealed by graphs of burials and baptisms such as this, without using often rather dubious estimates of population for pre-census years. A broad outline of the changes in the pattern of recorded cause of death from the seventeenth century to the nineteenth century is illustrated in Figure 3.7, with quinquennial numbers of deaths from the London Bills of Mortality.[44] Broadly there appears to be a correspondence between changes in total mortality and those for smallpox mortality. Apart from the plague years in the 1660s, the main turning points in the long-term trends coincide, at 1681–5, 1721–5 and after 1791–5, although natural population growth after this was rapid enough to produce an actual increase in the number of deaths.

Given some assumptions about the population of London, death rates for smallpox did decline rapidly after 1800 when vaccination was introduced. There is nothing to suggest that there had been a sudden large out-migration from the area of the Bills, or a dramatic change in recording accuracy. Similarly, assuming that the population of London did not decline in the eighteenth century, but was at least maintained by in-migration,[45] there were also significant changes in mortality from the mid eighteenth century. There appear to have been important changes in mortality for most cause-groups after the 1720s, and overall mortality declined in the second half of the eighteenth century. Some indication of the trends in death rate for the main cause-groups has been given in Appendix 3d, but this material must be of limited value because of the assumptions about a population base before the census of 1801. However, some idea of the *relative* changes for different disease groups is given, and the pattern of change in the overall burial rate most closely reflects changes in smallpox and 'fevers' mortality. A summary of the relationship between changes in smallpox mortality and the overall recorded burial rate, is given in Figure 3.8, which is based on two possible extreme population assumptions for 1700.

Smallpox mortality was almost certainly much higher than that recorded in the London Bills, since many forms of smallpox in infants are likely to have gone unrecognised. Fulminating smallpox, or *purpura major*, did not give

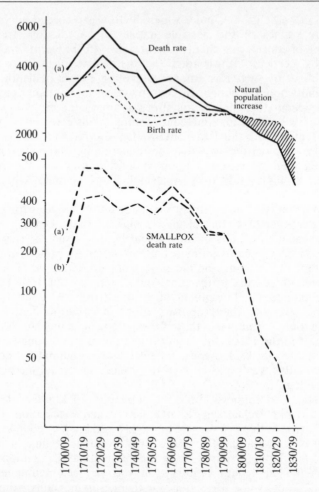

Figure 3.8 Average annual crude baptism and burial rates per 100,000 population and smallpox death rates in London, 1700/9–1830/9.
(a) Population in 1700 taken as 400,000. (See Chapter 3, note 45).
(b) Population in 1700 taken as 600,000.

Source: Data from J. Marshall (1832) *Mortality in the Metropolis* (London).

rise to the eruption of lesions, but often resulted in convulsions in infants whose deaths may have been recorded under this category. This may have been particularly the case in London where the disease was endemic, and outbreaks less clear-cut than in smaller towns and villages.[46] However, the trends for Northampton shown in Figure 3.6 also indicate some similarity between fluctuations in burials recorded in the 'convulsions' and smallpox categories. Obviously, these early records have to be treated with a great deal of scepticism and caution when it comes to the interpretation of trends over time. Trends may be affected by changes in the level of recording of

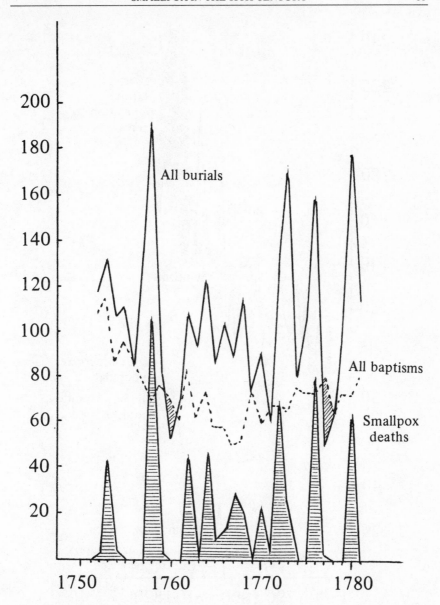

Figure 3.9 Smallpox deaths, burials and baptisms in Holy Trinity Parish, Whitehaven, 1752–1780.

Source: Parish Register of Holy Trinity, Whitehaven (County Records Office, Carlisle).

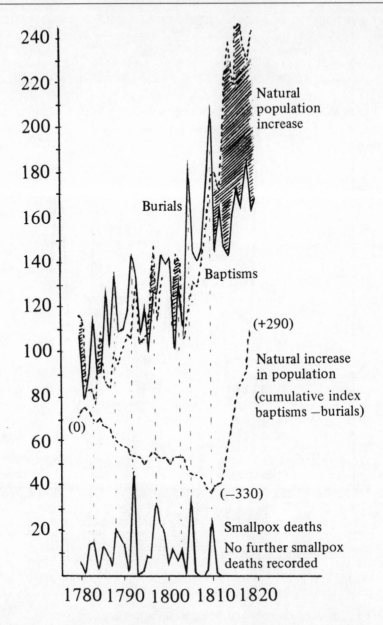

Figure 3.10 Smallpox epidemics, overall mortality and population growth in St John's Parish, Chester, 1780–1820.

Source: Parish Register of St John's, Chester (County Records Office, Chester).

burials, as well as inaccuracies in even the broadest categories of cause of death. Even so, it seems plausible that many 'infancy deaths' involved smallpox infection as an underlying cause. This category of deaths in infancy, together with those attributed directly to smallpox, to consumption and various fevers, accounted for about three-quarters of deaths in London in most years in the eighteenth century. Whatever the effects of deficiencies in the data, and uncertainties about a population base for establishing trends in death rates, those for smallpox, fevers and diseases of infancy, declined after the 1720s, contributing significantly to a decline in the overall number of burials from the mid eighteenth century.

Apart from these long series of data, other Bills of Mortality and parish registers provide useful evidence of the relationship between smallpox epidemics and overall mortality and of the dramatic impact of vaccination in the early years. It is not practicable to present here all the sets of data from parish registers in which smallpox deaths were recorded, but the disease caused 19% of deaths in Whitehaven in the second half of the eighteenth century, for example, and Figure 3.9 illustrates the clear association between smallpox epidemics and fluctuations in overall mortality. The data from the Bills of Mortality for Carlisle covering the years between 1779 and 1787 indicate that about 14.7% of deaths were attributed to smallpox, with the actual numbers recorded being 90, 3, 19, 30, 19, 10, 39, 1 and 30. Lonsdale, in a biography of Heysham, the compiler, pointed out that vaccination was introduced in the town in 1800, and twelve years elapsed before a single death from smallpox occurred.[47] There is evidence from Chester that it was not until vaccination was introduced that smallpox epidemics came under any kind of control in that town. The restrictive prejudice against inoculation, among other doctors and clergy, which Heysham had encountered in Carlisle, had also dis-illusioned Haygarth in his efforts to introduce the measure in Chester.[48] Haygarth began his work with inoculation in 1779, and Figure 3.10 indicates the kind of peaks in smallpox mortality that were prevalent there in the second half of the eighteenth century. Epidemics of smallpox in Chester appear to have ceased altogether in 1811, or at least they were no longer considered to be worth noting in the parish records of St John's. After this time there was also a continuous natural increase in the population of the parish, suggesting some major change had occurred.[49]

The decline in death rates in some industrial towns began before vaccination was introduced, but inoculation was used on a large scale in the Leeds epidemic of 1781, for example. This was too late to prevent a high mortality from smallpox which accounted for one-quarter of the deaths in that year,[50] but inoculation may have been effectively used in many towns in the 1790s. However, it was probably not until the enthusiasm for vaccination that the disease came under the kind of control that might significantly affect population growth. Data from other towns in England suggest that there was considerable urban population growth when vaccination was first introduced, as in other north-European towns. A study of Carlisle found that the most rapid population growth occurred there in the decades 1811–21 and 1821–31. It was pointed out that this unprecedented growth, before the development of adequate sewerage or clean water supplies, must have been highly conducive to the transmission of disease, although a resurgence in mortality may not have been as great as the crude death rates indicate.[51] The data from Northampton, shown in Figure 3.6, also indicate a resurgence of smallpox after a downturn in mortality at the beginning of the nineteenth century, while there was a severe smallpox epidemic in Norwich in 1819 in which 39% of all deaths were attributed to the disease. Edwardes suggested that a lapse in vaccination coverage after the initial gains could account for this resurgence and others,[52] so that enthusiasm for having children immunised may not have been sustained in the relative absence of severe epidemics. Smallpox epidemics once again returned to cause high mortality, and possibly to trigger other sequelae such as consumption, but the evidence does not suggest any increase in 'fevers' mortality in the 1820s and 1830s.

Data from the burial registers for three other towns, Leeds, Norwich and Leicester, are shown in Figure 3.11. Together with data from Glasgow, these indicate a much lower crude death rate in the early decades of the nineteenth century, when vaccination was introduced.[53] The resurgence in the death rate did not mean a return to the much higher levels of the eighteenth century, and might be viewed as only a setback in a long-term decline. The Bills of Mortality for Warrington are useful because of the additional data on deaths attributed to smallpox,[54] and the seven Bills available for the period 1791–1800 suggest a crude death rate of 31.4 per 1,000 population. About 15% of deaths were attributed to smallpox, which contributed 4.6 per 1,000 to the overall death rate. Compared with these high death rates at the end of the eighteenth century, the fairly complete set of Bills between 1818 and 1829 suggests that the crude death rate was down to 27.4 per 1,000. The death rate for smallpox was down to 1.3 per 1,000, so that most of the decline in overall mortality was probably attributable to smallpox mortality decline. In nearby Manchester over 15% of all deaths had been attributable to smallpox in the 1760s, and 13% in the 1780s,[55] and there seems little reason to doubt that the decline in mortality, which followed a similar pattern occurred for the same reason.

The element of compulsion eventually made vaccination measures more effective in towns in England, but also led to controversy. The decline in mortality at times before the measure was made compulsory in 1853 has been shown, but the law was not fully enforced until the epidemic of 1870. This probably had a critical effect in renewing efforts to control the disease, and led to a greater coverage being achieved by vaccination officers. It has been pointed out that although vaccination measures greatly reduced the number of susceptibles and provided the basis for preventive organisation to limit the spread of smallpox, it was not entirely responsible for the final elimination of the disease in England. It had been recognised in the eighteenth century that the isolation of the infected would help to prevent the spread of the disease, and the idea was re-introduced in the 1860s.[56] It was recognised that it would be essential to develop effective notification of cases, while the staff of hospitals would have to be vaccinated. These proposals were taken up by local sanitary departments

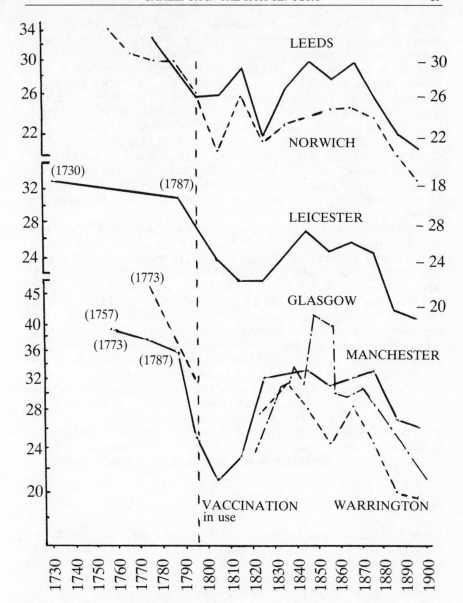

Figure 3.11 Crude burial and death rates per 1,000 population for selected towns in Britain (annual averages for decades unless year is specified).

Sources: S. Cherry (1979) The hospitals and population growth: Part I. *Population Studies* **34**, pp. 64–5; Royal Commission on Vaccination (1889–96) *Final Report, Appendix IV* (London), p. 41; M. Flinn (1977) *Scottish Population History from the 17th Century to the 1920s* (Cambridge: Cambridge University Press), p. 377, p. 383.

whose efforts began to focus on tracing the infected, isolating them in their homes or removing them to hospital, and cleansing the possibly contaminated home environment. The longer continuance of major epidemics of smallpox in London in the last three decades of the nineteenth century appears to have been due in part to the lack of co-ordination of sanitary administration for the whole city, compared with the provinces where local councils took over responsibility and where notification was more effective. Even so, between 1800 and 1870, smallpox mortality in London declined from 3,000–4,000 deaths per 1,000,000, to about 300 per 1,000,000, as shown in Figure 3.12. Possibly half the children born in British towns were vaccinated in this period.[57] However, the major epidemic of 1871 was Europe-wide, and it was recognised that ports were vulnerable as sources of epidemics brought in from overseas, and London in particular was threatened.

The final decline of smallpox epidemics in England probably owed much to tighter preventive controls including the inspection of ships and the monitoring of outbreaks of the disease both in the country and in areas abroad from which it might be imported. The death rate from smallpox was down to 89 per 1,000,000 after the 1870 epidemic in the period 1872–91, and was then reduced to only 13 per 1,000,000 in the 1890s. The last outbreak of smallpox in London, in 1901, revealed the effectiveness of preventive organisation in limiting the disease to certain areas of the capital from which it did not spread to the rest of the city or to other parts of the country. A disease such as smallpox, and particularly *variola major*, would not have been inhibited from spreading without the preventive measures, even when the population became better fed and better housed. The importance of the recent worldwide eradication of the disease is illustrated by considering the effect of an outbreak in England in 1962. The fact that the population was well-fed did not prevent either the spread of smallpox, or fatality from it, since 26 of the 66 confirmed cases, that is 39.4%, died before the outbreak was controlled with isolation measures.[58]

Summary

There is evidence from the main sources of data available that, by the eighteenth century, smallpox epidemics had come to predominate in the pattern of fluctuations in overall mortality in Europe. Excess burials over baptisms associated with smallpox epidemics, represented a more regularly occurring check on the growth of population than plague had been. This cycle of epidemics was, for aetiological reasons, largely independent of influences such as poor harvests which may have brought higher mortality from other diseases. They were probably a significant influence on mortality fluctuations before the eighteenth century in many parts of Europe and later than this in the poorer regions. Increasing contact with towns, and their growth in these times, seems likely to have been involved in the creation of 'pools of new susceptibles', and populations of the size and density required to sustain such an air-borne epidemic disease. Although

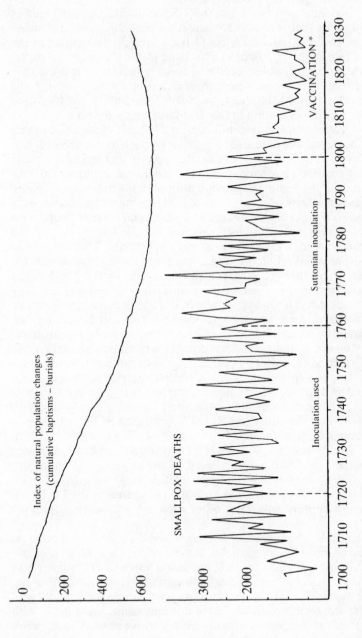

Figure 3.12 Annual numbers of deaths attributed to smallpox in London, 1700–1830.

* Only about 25% of births were vaccinated by 1820, according to the Royal Commission on Vaccination (1889–96). Parish suggested that by 1840 about 70% were vaccinated in some parishes, but there was still much apathy: H.J. Parish (1968) *Victory with vaccines* (Edinburgh: Livingstone).

Source: Data taken from a summary of annual deaths recorded in the London Bills of Mortality, to be found in: J. Marshall (1832) *Mortality in the Metropolis* (London).

undernutrition seems likely to have contributed to a higher case-fatality
from smallpox and other diseases, the destructive *variola major* could have
come to predominate in this way even in a well-fed population, and both
the aristocratic and the royal succumbed to it.

Evidence from England, Boston in the USA, and from Copenhagen in
particular, suggests that the use of inoculation probably protected many
from smallpox to an extent which could have brought reductions in the
overall death rate in the population. This issue may have been controver-
sial because the practice was so crude by today's standards, but the case
seems very strong that *vaccination* introduced after 1800 had a dramatic
epidemiological-demographic effect. In many European populations,the
most rapid growth in population in the demographic transition occurred in
the first few decades of the nineteenth century. The use of vaccination was
becoming widespread and data from England, Copenhagen and Sweden in
particular, as well as from all parts of Europe, indicate that this intervention
began to bring smallpox under control in the nineteenth century. This was
not only crucial for the health of the population, but instrumental in a more
rapid and sustained growth. It was made all the more important as a
preventive measure because of the increasing concentration of people into
crowded urban areas, where industrialisation and the factory system had
disastrous consequences for perhaps a majority there. The towns had
inherent environmental problems, and as yet there had been no concerted
effort to solve them through public-health measures or the provision of
sewerage and water supply. The final drive towards eradication of smallpox
was delayed until the 1870s in many parts of Europe, when a resurgence of
the disease and a major epidemic was probably taken as a warning that
something could, and should, be done to prevent such catastrophes.
Something of an epidemiological-demographic turning point is discernible
in the 1870s, such as that which occurred at the beginning of the century
when vaccination was first introduced. A further sharp downturn in death
rates occurred in England, Germany and the Netherlands, for example.
In Germany, the specific measures introduced following the Vaccination
Law of 1874 were reported by the Royal Commission as having ensured
the virtual elimination of deaths from smallpox within a few years in
that country. In England, the Vaccination Laws of 1863, and of 1853 which
had made infant vaccination compulsory, were more widely enforced.
In the period 1800–70 vaccination reduced the death rate from smallpox by tenfold, and the disease was virtually eradicated at the beginning
of the twentieth century following other effective measures to prevent
its spread.

The timing of the introduction of inoculation and vaccination measures,
and patterns of change in smallpox mortality in the eighteenth and
nineteenth centuries, suggest that immunisation was a major influence in
the initial phase of the epidemiological-demographic transition in Europe.
Three major turning points in the mortality transition correspond with
phases in the implementation of immunisation against smallpox, with
inoculation, then vaccination, and finally with the drive towards eradication
at the end of the nineteenth century, when monitoring of the disease and

isolation of cases also became important. The impact of inoculation on mortality in the second half of the eighteenth century probably varied greatly, both between countries and within them, and there may have been other important influences on 'fevers' and infant mortality which will be considered in the next chapter. There are also important differences between countries with regard to the widening gap between birth rates and death rates, and some evidence of a possibly exceptional contribution to eighteenth-century population growth by fertility increases in England. Even so, the decline in mortality in the early decades of the nineteenth century at least, seems likely to be attributable in large part to the use of immunisation against smallpox, based on the idea of vaccination. A dramatic phase of mortality decline also occurred throughout Europe regardless of variation in standards of living. By the end of the century, deaths from smallpox were negligible compared with the 8–20% of all deaths attributed directly to the disease in records from many different parts of Europe in the eighteenth century, when a further unquantifiable proportion of deaths must also have resulted from secondary complications and potentially fatal illnesses. In the early decades of the nineteenth century the introduction of vaccination measures seems likely to have been the main cause of the unprecedented population growth, and the further control of the disease with this and other preventive measures during the course of the century was uniquely beneficial for the health of the population of Europe.

4 Changes in infant mortality, gastro-intestinal disease, typhus, typhoid and cholera

The preventive-health measure of immunisation against smallpox may have been the most important factor in the early phase of the mortality transition in Europe in the period from the mid eighteenth century to the 1820s for which there is no firm evidence of a consistent improvement in the economic standard of living. The pattern of mortality fluctuation in the eighteenth century was characterised by the predominant cycle of smallpox epidemics, which was independent of changes in food supply. However, the pre-registration records of cause of death reviewed here, indicate that many deaths were classified as due to unspecified diseases among children in the first two years of life, and to 'fevers' affecting adults as well as children. In the eighteenth-century records, many infant deaths were ascribed to the vague category 'convulsions', which really referred to a set of symptoms probably brought on by viral infections, and by bacterial infections attributable to contamination of food and water and to poor standards of personal hygiene. Gastro-intestinal disorders also affected adults, with deaths being recorded under many categories in the London Bills of Mortality in the seventeenth and eighteenth centuries, and distinguished as a major component of adult mortality in the nineteenth-century registration records.

The possible impact of health and hygiene measures and other advantageous changes affecting the transmission of infectious diseases, will be further considered here along with trends in mortality attributed to convulsions, infancy diseases and fevers. Two of the main fevers, typhus and typhoid, became separated in the registration data after 1869, and the distinction was particularly important in view of the different modes of transmission. Hospital statistics and earlier medical writings suggest that the lice-borne disease typhus was probably the greater killer. Trends in mortality from typhoid and other water-borne diseases will also be considered here, and particularly the relatively brief but highly significant appearance of cholera for a few decades in the mid nineteenth century.

The threat of cholera becoming a regular and terrifying epidemic disease in England seems to have induced a greater sense of urgency to implement public-health measures to counteract poor sanitation and contaminated water supplies. However, the advances from the mid nineteenth century in respect of all these causes of death have to be viewed against the background of declining death rates from 'fevers' and 'infancy' in the second half of the eighteenth century before any concerted efforts at sanitary reform. Other factors were probably involved from the mid eighteenth century, particularly as typhus would not have been inhibited from spreading even with good sewerage and pure water supplies. The 'fevers' probably also included scarlet fever which did not become properly distinguished in records until the registration period, and will be considered in the next chapter with other major epidemic diseases of childhood.

The vagueness in classification before the mid nineteenth century and changes in recognition of specific diseases, mean that any estimate of their role in overall mortality decline in straightforward arithmetic terms, is likely to require considerable qualification. A component analysis of mortality change based on pre-registration data must be treated with extreme caution, and even the approach used in previous studies of registration data has been too simplistic in not allowing for the inter-relationship between diseases causing mortality. The arithmetic components of the decline in death rates in London between the 1720s and the 1820s implied by the data in the London Bills of Mortality are shown in Appendix 4a. In arithmetic terms the reduction in recognised smallpox deaths resulted in a fall of 6% in overall burial rates in this period, although the actual impact of the control of smallpox may have been far greater, as suggested in the previous chapter. Reductions in 'fevers' and 'infancy' deaths brought a further decline of 11% and 24%, and overall the burial rate fell by 60%. The contribution made by different cause-groups towards a unit change in the overall death rate should only be seen as a very crude indicator of the relative importance of different diseases at different stages in the mortality transition. In the period from the 1720s to the 1820s in London, a fall in deaths recorded under these three main categories contributed 0.69 towards each unit of decline in the overall burial rate. The decline in recognised smallpox deaths contributed 0.10, fevers 0.19 and infancy (which included one-year olds) 0.4. In the 1720s the vague category of convulsions accounted for about 28% of all deaths in the London Bills, and other infancy deaths a further 10%. The decline in mortality classified under the term convulsions itself contributed about 0.33 towards each unit of decline in the overall burial rate in the period up to the 1820s.

Changes in infant mortality

In the eighteenth century there was probably a great deal of fatalism about illness in the early months of life, and infancy itself may have been regarded as sufficient reason for death occurring. There may have been little attempt to distinguish any specific underlying infection or cause that was responsible. Convulsions were probably linked with the onset of some infectious disease and with dietary-deficiency diseases, or they could have been present in the terminal stages of most untreated infant diseases.[1] Fatal diarrhoea in infants often terminates in convulsions, and many deaths classified under the term were probably of the kind observed in Third-World countries today, where improper food administered on weaning leads to gastro-intestinal disorders.[2] The summer peaks in convulsion deaths might also be a reflection of a large gastro-intestinal disease component, since problems with contaminated food- and fly-borne infection would have been exacerbated.[3] It has also been suggested that teething could have lowered resistance to gastro-intestinal diseases resulting from unsuitable food on weaning, as well as to infectious diseases. The large number of deaths attributed to the vague category of 'teething' in the London Bills, and many convulsions deaths, may have been associated with weaning and its attendant dangers.[4]

As emphasised, a great deal of scepticism is required in considering these early records in which 'cause of death' was assigned by people who were not medically qualified. Two women 'searchers' were given a financial incentive to trace burials and ascertain the cause of death. Medical writers such as Black and Heberden recorded their comments on the Bills, since they were interested in them as a means of monitoring disease and mortality.[5] Black consulted several parish clerks who were responsible for the records because of doubts about the completeness of coverage, and pointed out that deaths were only recorded when the body was buried in the parochial churchyard. This may not always have been the case, particularly during severe epidemics, while deaths among certain religious sects and in mad-houses would have been excluded. Heberden also referred to such problems and to the vagueness of many of the categories of cause of death. The two major categories of 'convulsions' and 'fevers' could, for example, have included many infant deaths from smallpox which had not produced visible symptoms associated with the disease at older ages, although a febrile stage or convulsions were manifest.[6]

Some combination of infections, including smallpox, fevers and gastro-intestinal infections, might have occurred in the living conditions which prevailed in the eighteenth century. It is not therefore surprising that the death rates for 'fevers' and 'infancy' both declined markedly after 1800 along with that for smallpox. All kinds of fevers could have taken a greater toll of children who were infected with smallpox, or just recovering from illness. The correlation between mortality in different disease-groups, after removing the underlying trend from the series of quinquennial deaths recorded in the London Bills in the period after the plague (1671/5–1831/5), was +0.59 between smallpox and 'infancy', +0.64 between smallpox and fevers, and +0.49 between smallpox and burials. All these values were statistically significant,[7] while an index of mortality in the first two years of life based on the ratio of infancy deaths to baptisms, showed an even stronger association of +0.65 with smallpox deaths, and +0.71 with total burials. The close association between major turning points in the trends in these death rates is also illustrated in Figure 3.7.

Changing levels of infant mortality to some extent reflect the prospects for health, growth and longevity for a population and the experience of different cohorts with regard to 'disease trauma' in early life. Registration data for England and Wales indicate a continuingly high infant mortality rate in the second half of the nineteenth century, but this should be viewed against the background of changes that occurred before this. Wrigley and Schofield estimated an infant mortality rate of 170 per 1,000 births for England as a whole in the second half of the seventeenth century, on the basis of aggregated data from several hundred parishes. A higher rate of 195 per 1,000 was estimated for the first half of the eighteenth century, after which it was estimated to have fallen to 165 per 1,000 in the second half of that century.[8] This is close to the level recorded under national registration in the mid nineteenth century, as shown in Figure 4.1. Several sets of data, with some exceptions, have also indicated a noticeably lower infant mortality rate in the 1780s compared with the 1730s and earlier.[9] Estimates for London based on the Bills of Mortality suggest that the rate may have been as high as 380 per 1,000 births in the 1740s, and about 337 in the 1750s, double the rate for England as a whole. The rates were down to 258 in the 1780s and 205 by the 1810s, which was closer to the rate of 170 per 1,000 births recorded under national registration in the mid nineteenth century, as shown in Figure 4.2.[10] Data for the British peerage also indicate a reduction in the infant mortality rate for the first half of the eighteenth century compared with the previous three half-centuries. The rate was lower than that for the population as a whole at 167 per 1,000 births in the period 1700–49, and there was a further sharp reduction to a level of 93 per 1,000 births for the second half of the eighteenth century,[11] well below the estimated 165 per 1,000 for the whole population of England.

A study of data from North Shropshire also indicated a sharp drop in the infant burial rate in the eighteenth century, and the decline over the period 1711–60 reflected reduced mortality in the first three months of life in particular. There was little information on causes of infant death in parish records, but higher rates in towns were thought to reflect a higher incidence of infectious diseases and diarrhoeal illness.[12] Evidence from the Warrington Bills of Mortality and from Chester indicates that more deaths from smallpox were recorded between the sixth and twelfth months of infancy than in the first six months of life.[13] However, this may again have been a reflection of the inability, or lack of concern, to distinguish a specific cause of death in a very young infant. Certainly by the end of the nineteenth century when such data became available in the registration records, infant deaths from smallpox were nearly all in the first six months of life. Inoculation, if given at this early stage of infancy, might have been responsible for improved survival chances in the eighteenth century. There is also evidence that the death rate among infants in the first month of life may have fallen more rapidly than for infants as a whole between the 1680s and the mid nineteenth century when it levelled off. Neo-natal

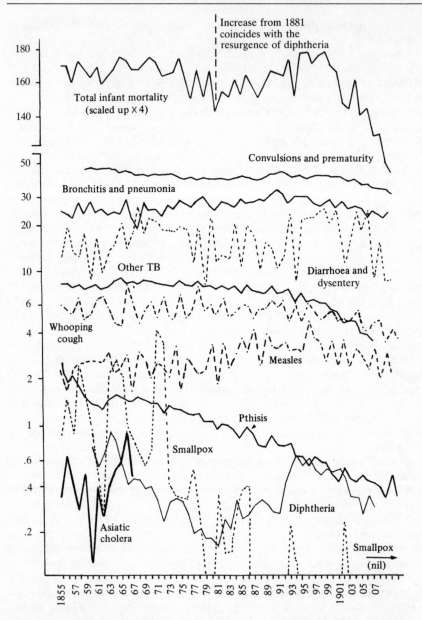

Figure 4.1   Annual male infant mortality rates per 1,000 live births for the main causes in England and Wales, 1855–1907.

Source: Registrar-General (1838–   ) *Annual Reports for England and Wales* (London: HMSO).

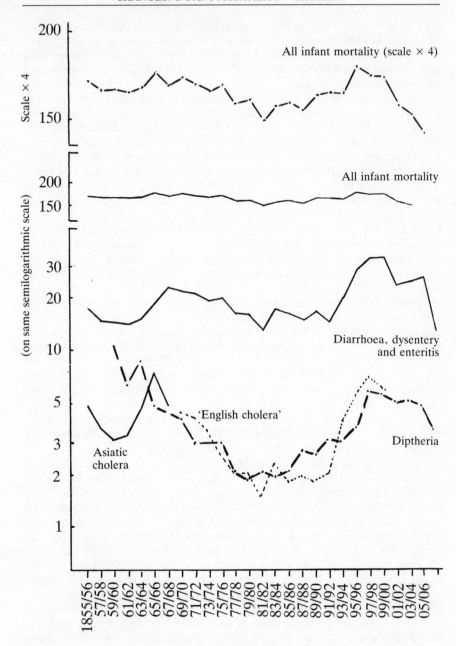

Figure 4.2 Average annual male infant mortality rates per 1,000 live births, for cholera, diphtheria and diarrhoeal diseases in England and Wales, 1885–1906.

Source: Registrar-General (1838–) *Annual Reports for England and Wales* (London: HMSO).

feeding practices would be important at this stage of life, since the mother's first milk, colostrum, contains protective antibodies and other proteins.[14] The maternal death rate probably also fell in the eighteenth century, and any improvement in the health of women could also have increased survival chances for babies.[15]

The feeding and care of infants, particularly on weaning, would have affected the risk of gastro-intestinal disease. There may also have been many other deaths from these causes which were recorded under 'atrophy' and 'debility', since the practice of purging often led to a rejection of food, to emaciation, thirst and fever.[16] A lack of improvement in these practices and continually poor living conditions exacerbating respiratory problems, were probably major factors in the failure of infant mortality to decline much in the second half of the nineteenth century. Registration records reveal some of the specific causes of death that were involved as shown in Figures 4.1 and 4.2 and Appendix 4b. Diarrhoeal disease, respiratory disease and prematurity were the largest categories of causes in this period accounting for about half of all infant deaths. Among the specified infectious diseases, measles and whooping cough were the most significant, and about 13% of all deaths were attributed directly to them. Mortality attributed to diarrhoeal disease was a major factor in the continuingly high infant mortality rate as shown in Figure 4.2, and increases occurred in the last two decades before the final long-term decline. In contrast, the decline in the total death rate for gastro-intestinal causes at all ages, shown in Figure 4.3, contributed significantly to the overall mortality decline in the second half of the nineteenth century. The way that infants were treated and fed probably contributed most to this difference between adult and infant mortality change.

Apart from a lack of good food among the town poor, much of the problem of gastro-intestinal disease would have been due to contamination by micro-organisms carried by flies, and to poor personal hygiene. Fly-borne disease would have been a great problem because of exposed human excreta and animal droppings in the streets. The contamination of food by flies carrying infection from such sources, may have been alleviated later by the use of water closets, but this did not extend to many working-class dwellings in the nineteenth century. Improvements in refuse removal and the conveyance of human waste away from inhabited areas, probably contributed to a reduction in fatalities associated with fly-borne infection. Cleaner streets probably did not become a significant factor until the twentieth century when the horse-drawn carriage disappeared, which would have helped to reduce a further source of fly-borne gastro-intestinal disease. Such problems would have affected all age groups, but food given to infants may have been particularly unhygienic and damaging to health.[17] Diarrhoea and dysentery and other gastro-intestinal disorders seem likely to have produced much higher mortality among the poorer sections of society. Infant death rates in parts of Bradford, for example, were almost certainly higher than the national average.[18] People in such areas would also have been the last to benefit from greater knowledge about the spread of infection that came at the end of the century.

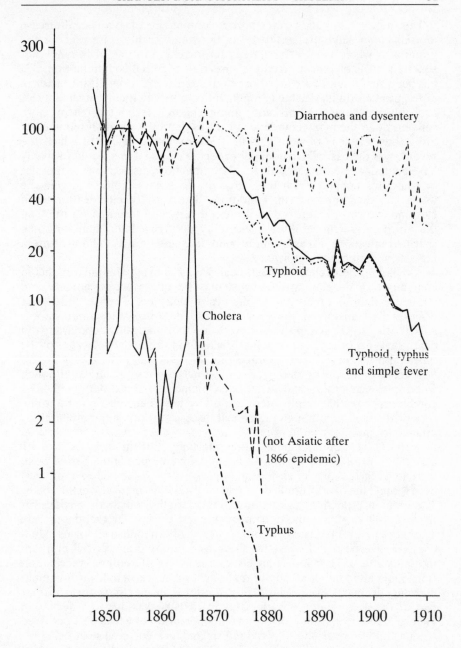

Figure 4.3 Crude death rates per 100,000 population for typhus/typhoid, cholera and diarrhoeal disease in England and Wales, 1850–1910.

Source: Registrar-General (1838–) *Annual Reports for England and Wales* (London: HMSO).

The food-borne and water-borne component of diarrhoeal-disease mortality may have predominated in the trend in the death rate for the group as a whole, which fluctuated and increased in the 1890s when hot summers probably encouraged the spread of bacterial contamination.[19] It has been suggested that water-borne infections were a significant factor in differential mortality decline in nineteenth-century France.[20] Such illnesses probably weakened infants and young children, rendering them more susceptible to the many epidemic infections that they encountered in early life. However, it is obviously difficult to know the extent to which the reverse was the case. Diarrhoeal disorders in many infants would probably have been due to earlier or unrecognised infectious disease such as measles or whooping cough, which both give rise to such symptoms among the undernourished in poor living conditions. The cause-specific death rates in England shown in Figure 4.1 indicate a diversity of trends, with the final downturn in diarrhoeal-disease mortality occurring later than for some specified infectious diseases, but around the same time as the downturn in measles and diphtheria mortality.

A delay in the decline of diarrhoeal-disease mortality among infants in contemporary developing countries, may be due more to poverty and ignorance than to a failure of public-health measures to control infectious diseases.[21] A historical study of Bradford described the circumstances contributing to the lag in the downturn in infant mortality compared with death rates for other children which declined in the last few decades of the nineteenth century. It was pointed out that this was not entirely due to negligence or apathy on the part of individuals or the community, although working-class mothers had often been blamed by those better-off. The conditions of female employment could also have been detrimental to the care of the young, although diarrhoeal disease was as commonly fatal for infants in mining communities as in areas where women worked in factories.[22] The quinquennial infant mortality rate in fact declined by about 16% in 1876–80, but this decline did not continue in the period up to the end of the century in either the poorest or the most exclusive districts even though the overall crude death rate fell quite dramatically in the 1880s. There was no reduction in gastro-intestinal mortality, which was responsible for over 40% of all infant deaths, and no decline in the death rate attributed to 'prematurity'. In some other northern industrial towns, Manchester, Liverpool and Glasgow, there was a quite dramatic fall in infant mortality after 1871,[23] and it may be that the impact of smallpox-vaccination campaigns after the epidemic in that year was more significant for infant mortality decline than elsewhere. For Bradford, the data show that a further part of the decline in infant mortality in 1876–80 was due to a decline in the death rate from other air-borne epidemic diseases which also occurred among children over one-year old in England and Wales as a whole.

The trend in infant mortality for England and Wales in the second half of the nineteenth century might be seen as a levelling-off in a long-term decline since the mid eighteenth century. The differential that this represents in comparison with trends for other childhood death rates, probably reflects greater dangers for infants being artificially fed in circumstances of continuingly inadequate domestic sanitation and personal hygiene. Peak levels of infant mortality were associated significantly with domestic sanitation in a local-government survey of sixteen towns at the beginning of the twentieth century.[24] Apart from deficiencies in protein and vitamins in the kind of food administered, such as bread and milk, there was probably little attempt made to wash the equipment used, let alone sterilise it before use.[25] It may also have been possible for the better-off to prepare hot water, but some bottles used by working-class mothers may not even have been fully washable. The initial impact of the sale of sterilised milk in stoppered bottles seems likely to have been limited by such poor hygiene practices among many of the less well-off families who did start buying it. Evidence from the district in St Helens, where the first milk depot opened in 1899, does suggest that infant mortality was lower than for the urban district as a whole, but obviously many other character-istics of the population might have been involved.[26]

Some reduction in non-respiratory tuberculosis, gastro-intestinal diseases and infant mortality associated with diarrhoeal symptoms probably occurred in the twentieth century as a result of purer milk being available. However, the effect on the incidence of diarrhoeal disorders would also have depended on the extent to which breast-feeding was practised anyway, and whether it was abandoned in favour of such convenience food. The ability to breast-feed would have depended on the mother's state of health and time available. Where possible it ought to have been preferred on the grounds of cost, while there may have been some idea of the partial protection against pregnancy that comes with suckling.[27] It seems feasible that differentials in infant mortality, and the lack of resurgence in the 1890s in some districts, might at least in part have been due to differences in the extent of breast-feeding. Many aspects of breast-feeding practice including the extent of early neo-natal feeding and age at weaning, could have varied within the population and affected the risk of dying in infancy and early childhood from air-borne and intestinal infections in particular.[28]

Apart from poor food hygiene and the use of substitutes for breast milk, dangerous passifiers probably also contributed to ill health among working-class infants. Factory work may have contributed to a deterioration in the standard of care and in the relationship between mother and infant which has physiological and emotional repercussions.[29] Even before birth, circumstances during pregnancy would have contributed to the risk of low birth weight which is associated with a higher risk of infant mortality. Prematurity was given as the cause in about 10% of infant deaths in the second half of the nineteenth century, and the death rate increased markedly in the 1880s and 1890s. This contributed to the lack of decline in the overall infant death rate when that for other children continued to decline. In the period 1895–9, there was also exceptionally high gastro-intestinal-disease mortality among infants, while the higher infant mortality in 1865–9 had also been a result of deaths attributed to these causes as shown in Appendix 4c.

It should not be overlooked that in England and Wales as a whole the infant mortality rate fell in the 1870s, as in the towns mentioned earlier.

The reduction was about 9% between 1865–9 and 1880–4, and all specified causes of death apart from prematurity, measles and respiratory disease, contributed to this. The trend in the death rate for infants in the second half of the nineteenth century really only differed markedly from that for two-, three-, and four-year olds in the 1880s and 1890s. These other children were subject to the adverse trends in measles, diphtheria and respiratory-disease mortality which affected infants, but this was more than offset by the dramatic decline in the death rate from scarlet fever to which one- to four-year olds were particularly prone. In addition, infants were subject to the increasing death rate associated with prematurity, while their greater vulnerability to gastro-intestinal disease meant that unlike other children they suffered a dramatic increase in mortality when the climatic conditions exacerbated the problems of infection at the end of the century.

A recent study has shown that the increase in the national infant mortality rate at the end of the nineteenth century largely reflected increases in urban districts, and over half the variation in infant mortality was associated with differences in population density.[30] The subsequent decline in infant mortality also reflected changes in urban areas, while there was a greater association with declining fertility than had been found in studies of regional and county data. Declining marital fertility could have had some effect on infant mortality from the 1870s, if there were longer birth intervals leading to less neglect and less disruption of breast-feeding.[31] The evidence does not suggest a very significant effect for the population as a whole, but an analysis of changes in infant mortality and fertility by father's occupation found some evidence over the period 1895–1910 for the group with relatively high rates of fertility decline.[32] There may have been an interactive effect with other factors, and it was concluded that environmental improvements were important in the timing and rate of decline in infant mortality. Again, the most dramatic reductions were among urban rather than rural occupational groups. Rural and semi-rural occupations also had lower reductions in infant mortality irrespective of income. In fact, income and social class did not appear to have been of critical importance in relation to the timing or the rate of decline, although they were found to be have been significant in different levels of infant mortality.[33] Improvements in housing, sanitation and refuse removal seem more likely determinants of change and, as suggested, they would have been more important for the urban occupational groups which had generally been more deprived in these respects.

A study of retrospective data from the 1911 Census of England and Wales also showed that among the variables tested for any relationship with the proportional fall in infant mortality, there was a strong link only with increased density of houses per acre.[34] However, it seems likely that this reflected new construction, as suggested, and hence a reduction in the damp overcrowded living conditions which had probably increased respiratory problems as well as the transmission rates and severity of related air-borne infectious diseases. It was also pointed out that there was a greater decline in infant and child mortality from diarrhoeal and respiratory diseases than from diseases of nutritional deficiency which might be expected to have been more responsive to any changes in nutritional standards, had these occurred.

It was gastro-intestinal and respiratory diseases that were in fact the main groups of causes involved in the final phase of infant mortality decline in the twentieth century. They contributed 0.20 and 0.18 towards each unit of decline in the infant mortality rate, while the vaguer categories – prematurity, atrophy, debility and convulsions – contributed 0.43 in the period 1901–10 to 1971, as shown in Appendix 4b. As mentioned, these arithmetic components should be considered with some regard for the inter-related nature of childhood diseases and secondary complications of epidemic infections such as measles, whooping cough and diphtheria. In arithmetic terms, these epidemic diseases contributed only 0.07 towards each unit of decline in the infant mortality rate in this period. However, some unquantifiable proportion of the decline in deaths attributed to diarrhoeal and respiratory symptoms may have been a consequence of reduced transmission rates and hence reduced severity of common air-borne epidemic infections. A reduction in the actual numbers of births each year from the first decade of this century, could in particular have increased the age at infection with measles, thereby reducing the severity of illness and the incidence of secondary complications such as diarrhoea and broncho-pneumonia.[35] This will be considered further in the next chapter, since changes in the death rate at ages one to four years may have been more closely associated with changes in the birth rate than infant mortality on which water-borne and fly-borne gastro-intestinal disease was the major influence.

Changes in fertility patterns from the end of the nineteenth century probably reflected quite dramatic changes in attitudes towards having children. A more secular outlook and the spread of education and of infor-mation about family planning contributed to a change in public opinion and a legitimisation of the whole idea of limiting family size. The continuing decline in the birth rate probably reflected both voluntaristic changes and deterministic effects of longer child survival and the consequent extension of periods of infertility associated with suckling. Other changes in attitudes towards children and intended family size were probably contingent on a perceived improvement in their survival chances. It became a viable and more economic option to deliberately limit the number of children, and invest more care and attention in their development,[36] encouraged by more organised education and advice for young mothers. The final phase of decline in infant mortality, from the beginning of the twentieth century, also coincided with the development and professionalisation of the health-visiting movement.[37] In the 1890s, concern about high infant mortality became widespread in England, and voluntary organisations for health visiting were developed by municipal corporations and training courses were formalised. Visits to every home with a mother and young child were instituted, and nurseries were established where mothers could be instructed in infant care and feeding,[38] and such changes probably had a significant impact on infant mortality after the turn of the century.

The decline in mortality from fevers

The circumstances in which the final downturn in infant mortality occurred were far different from those in the second half of the eighteenth century when the decline in 'infancy' deaths recorded in the London Bills was accompanied by a fall in mortality attributed to 'fevers' which pre-dated any concerted efforts to promote health care and sanitary reform. The Bills indicate a fall in recorded deaths from 'fevers' from the 1750s, but unfortunately there are not many other sets of records giving causes other than smallpox over long periods. However, the Northampton Bills show some categories of disease and allow a consideration of changes between the mid eighteenth and the mid nineteenth century. The lack of data to use as a reliable population base does not invalidate conclusions drawn from the trends illustrated in Figure 3.6. There does appear to have been a reduction in fevers mortality over this period, and certainly a diminution of the large peaks in quinquennial mortality. Fevers mortality peaked in the 1740s on the evidence from the London Bills, and this reflects the great epidemic of 1741–2 referred to by Creighton. He pointed out that one in five deaths in London in these years were recorded as due to fevers, while in Tiverton, for example, one in twelve deaths were attributed to fevers and particularly to 'spotted fever'. Creighton suggested that typhus was the disease mainly responsible for this high fevers mortality in London and in the weaving towns of the West Country. Mortality was also very high in towns such as Norwich, Newcastle and Edinburgh, where about 16% of deaths were attributed to fevers, 22% to consumption, 16% to smallpox and about 12% to measles and whooping cough. Although Creighton was not certain whether typhus was the disease involved in the northern towns, he was convinced that some diminution of fevers mortality occurred after the 1740s epidemic in the second half of the eighteenth century.[39]

Differentiation of specific infectious diseases causing fever was difficult even when distinguishing symptoms were known, since not all the definitive manifestations of the major diseases were always present. Zinsser pointed out that when a rash with red spots, together with fever, headache, delirium and extreme weakness, was observed, there could be little doubt that the disease was typhus. However, the red spots may not always have been distinctive, particularly among children, such that the disease could often have been categorised as measles, or later scarlet fever. Typhus fever among adults may often have been indistinguishable from typhoid or even malaria.[40] This latter disease probably accounted for some deaths as well as debilitating illness, but the proportion of deaths attributed to it in other European countries in the eighteenth century suggests that it could not have been a major component of the declining death rate, except perhaps in East Anglia where marshland was common.

The discovery of the louse transmission of typhus removed the mystery of the otherwise correct association of the disease with famine, war, prisons, ships and other places where living conditions were overcrowded and filthy. The disease had probably transferred to man in the same way that plague had done, via the rat flea. Under the conditions in army camps and famine areas, the close proximity to rats carrying typhus-infected fleas would have provided a source of human contagion, which from then on only required the human louse or flea as vector.[41] The first unmistakable appearance of the disease in England was in gaols, but in the seventeenth century the disease accompanied plague in its ravages throughout Europe. At this time typhus may in fact have been the only 'famine fever' capable of producing subsistence-related mortality crises, and then only because of the continued existence of really backward areas.[42] As mentioned, a deterioration in standards of hygiene during periods of social and economic disruption – including war – could have been as important for mortality risk as the effects of undernutrition itself. Being a lice- or flea-borne disease, typhus spread from particular foci of infection into the crowded areas of towns. The London Bills of Mortality show a huge outbreak of fevers in the years just after the Great Plague in the 1660s, and typhus appears to have been widespread in Europe with major outbreaks occurring in conjunction with disruptive social and military events.

The downturn in fevers mortality, indicated by the London Bills, came after typhus or 'spotted fever' had become re-incorporated into the general 'fevers' category. Zinsser could see no reflection of the age of enlightenment in any greater cleanliness, although he pointed out that medical writers may have had some influence in disseminating knowledge about transmission. Experience of the disease in ships had given rise to the idea that it might be transmitted through the clothes of the infected. Towards the end of the eighteenth century, the relationship between fever and gaols became recognised, which led to action to reform conditions and reduce the risk from these foci of infection in England.[43] Changes were advocated in the writings and practice of medical people who had gained experience of disease in army camps. Creighton pointed out that it was well know that armies, fleets and gaols were sources of contagion which could lead to terrible epidemics in the appalling living conditions prevalent in towns in mid eighteenth-century England.[44] It was known that better hygiene was important in preventing outbreaks of dysentery in army camps, and that typhus might be prevented by hygiene measures in ships and naval hospitals. It was also known that, in general, slums, overcrowding, urban filth and ignorance fostered fevers epidemics, but such revelations did not lead to parliamentary action and initiatives were essentially at the parish level. Ventilation of meeting halls, ships, hospitals and prisons, and the clearing of stinking refuse and puddles in towns were proposed, but effective powers to control environmental hazards were not granted until the mid nineteenth century.[45]

The dissemination of ideas about cleanliness among ordinary people may have become increasingly significant, and was possibly encouraged by the dispensary movement in the second half of the eighteenth century. The first dispensary opened in London in 1773 and outpatient services were provided for the sick poor, where it was possible to educate them about the need to care for sick relatives and infants. Physicians learned from home visits about the dreadful sanitation and housing conditions that fostered disease among the poor.[46] Two major types of disease could have been affected by any changes in personal hygiene that resulted from the more widespread acceptance of such ideas: on the one hand, diseases such as gastro-enteritis, typhoid and dysentery, which were caused by infections of the intestinal tract; on the other hand, diseases transmitted from person to person by lice, such as typhus, relapsing fever and trench fever. Hygiene is important in relation to intestinal infection because pathogenic micro-organisms in faeces can be transmitted via the hands to food, or directly to the mouth. Cleanliness of the body, clothes and bedding, would be more important in relation to lice-borne infection. Razzell noted the reductions in fevers, as well as infant mortality, in London in the second half of the eighteenth century, and pointed out that contemporaries had expressed the view that it was due to greater cleanliness. He referred to the evidence of greater soap consumption, although this does not specifically indicate increased domestic consumption.[47]

Any alleviation of famine conditions which lessened the risk of a major outbreak of typhus, would have been at least partially offset by the adverse living conditions associated with the growing towns, and Luckin drew attention to both aspects of the transmission of the disease. Evidence from hospital records in London suggested that typhus was far more destructive of life than typhoid, although the latter was probably endemic. He pointed out that typhoid was likely to have been linked with more continual problems of contaminated water, milk and food, while outbreaks of typhus in the 1850s and 1860s might be traced to immigration from famine-stricken Ireland, and to soldiers returning from the Crimea. The typhoid death rate in London, as in England and Wales as a whole, declined from 1870 when separate statistics became available, although there appears to have been an increase in the annual death rate in the 1890s. This may have been associated with the hot summers in some of those years, and mortality declined continuously after the turn of the century. The public-health reforms and monitoring of sources of infection which removed the threat of cholera after the 1860s, were almost certainly more important in this than in the decline in the typhus death rate, although a readily available supply of water would have been necessary for the washing of clothes. There is evidence that water did become more available between the 1850s and 1870s in typhus-prone areas, though it was not until the 1890s that permanent access to piped water reached half of the population.[48]

Typhus had really ceased to be a major killer in most towns in England after the 1860s outbreak, and death rates in even the poorest boroughs of London were down to under 10 per 100,000 population from the 1870s. There was no indication of case-fatality falling after the 1860s epidemic of typhus, so *Rickettsia prowazeki* had probably not become less virulent. Luckin pointed out that the major towns probably became increasingly isolated from foci of infection outside the country, such as the urban centres in Ireland from which lice-infested people could import the disease. Immigration from Ireland peaked in the 1850s and the proportion of Irish-born in London declined after the 1860s. Also, the drainage project completed in London in this decade involved the removal of large quantities of refuse away from the inner city, and this may have reduced the risk of close contact with rats carrying the disease. With no further influx of carriers from abroad the epidemic probably just ran its course and could not be maintained. The death rate from typhus declined less rapidly in towns which were centres of trade and traffic from Ireland. It was 58 per 100,000 in Liverpool in the 1870s, while rates were still 100 per 100,000 in Dublin and Belfast.[49] In contrast with Ireland,which suffered dreadful famines in the mid nineteenth century, there had probably been an increasingly more consistent food supply in England since the eighteenth century. This reduction in 'famine crises' with their concomitant adverse living conditions was probably more significant for typhus mortality decline than any improvement in 'normal' levels of nutrition.[50] The reduction in typhus mortality at the end of the nineteenth century should be seen in the context of long-term decline in the death rate from fevers from the mid eighteenth century. The high mortality in the 1850s and 1860s probably reflected the introduction of infection from overseas, with internal sources having been increasingly limited over the previous hundred years. The subsequent downturn in the death rate affected both adult and child survival, and the recession of typhus and smallpox from the 1870s coincided with the final downturn in child mortality to be considered in the next chapter.

Cholera and public-health reforms

The 1870s marked a turning point for disease and mortality patterns for many reasons, not least of which was the absence of cholera in that decade. In the 1830s Asiatic cholera threatened to join typhus and smallpox as the most regularly destructive epidemic causes of death in England. The micro-organism involved, *Vibro cholerae*, is highly pathogenic to man and spreads rapidly where sanitation is bad and water supplies polluted. People become infected by consuming water, milk and food contaminated by faecal matter, or by other direct contact with faeces and material infected by those suffering from the symptoms of diarrhoea and vomiting. The case-fatality is usually higher than that for smallpox,[51] and the arrival of the disease in Britain in 1831 not surprisingly caused great consternation. In the years between 1831 and 1835, deaths recorded as due to cholera in the London Bills were 48, 3,200, 1,150, 630 and 5. In the peak year of 1832, 11.2% of all deaths were attributed directly to the disease. This was probably an underestimate, since many more deaths than usual were recorded in the categories of 'aged' and 'unknown causes'.

Data from New York also show that major epidemics of cholera occurred in 1832, 1834, 1849, 1854 and 1866, with deaths attributed to the disease being 3,513, 971, 5,071, 2,509 and 1,137. Slightly smaller epidemic mortality from smallpox occurred in 1824, 1851, 1872, 1875 and 1881, but these two diseases accounted for most of the regular mortality peaks. Cholera was not mentioned as a major killer after 1866 although there were nine deaths recorded in 1892, while smallpox mortality was not significant after 1902. The absence of epidemic peaks caused by these diseases was probably the most significant factor in the reduction of overall mortality from the mid nineteenth century in New York. This phase of the mortality transition cannot be ascribed to socio-economic changes,[52] since it is unlikely that cholera and smallpox epidemics would have receded without preventive-health measures such as immunisation, isolation of cases, or improvements in water supplies, sewage disposal, hygiene and the monitoring for possible outbreaks of disease.

It was probably fear of cholera that encouraged the authorities in many towns and rural districts in England to set up local Boards of Health, and this was later done in New York, in 1866.[53] The epidemic of 1831–2 left much apprehension that slum areas in town and country could form breeding grounds for social unrest as well as disease, and Chadwick's revelations in 1842 probably shocked the middle classes into an awareness of the conditions in industrial slums.[54] However, those in power and their supporters among the landowners were not generally moved by humanitarian instincts and although a Royal Commission was set up to enquire into the workings of the Poor Law, this was to find a cheaper system of relief. Chadwick outlined a scheme, but only his repressive measures were adopted by the government, which did not act on his proposals for free education and sanitation. The sanitary maps which he later produced showed a higher incidence of disease in the most overcrowded areas, although his conclusions about higher mortality did not allow for differences in age distribution.[55] The General Board of Health on which he served was set up in 1848, not because of such evidence of deprivation, but because of the alarm among government politicians about the possibility of another epidemic of cholera. Medical Officers of Health were appointed whose work involved house-to-house visiting in search of infectious diseases, removal of sick people in overcrowded tenements, and the vaccination of smallpox contacts. They were also to pursue enquiries into outbreaks of disease in schools and factories, and carry out other public-health duties.

Although investigation following the cholera epidemics of 1849 and 1853 led to a theory of the water-borne transmission of the disease, and a decision to introduce improved water and sewage systems, there was a considerable delay before completion of the engineering.[56] It may not have been until the municipalisation of separate water companies that necessary improvements were effective in reducing the death rate from the gastro-intestinal diseases in general at the end of the century. Sewers were nothing new, but until the 1840s they may have consisted of little more than elongated cesspools with a overflow at one end. Chadwick's proposals included the important consideration of being able to deposit the waste matter away from human habitation, but McNeill pointed out that not everyone agreed that filth and ill-health went together.[57] There was much opposition to social legislation, and particularly that relating to public health, and Chadwick's idea of sewers constructed out of smooth ceramic pipes, which could be flushed with water, was not always enthusiastically received.[58] The objectives of the public-health movement ran counter to ideas about a 'law of nature' by which the weak died off. Some argued that mutual aid was in opposition to the tide of 'progress' seen in the process of natural selection and survival of the fittest.[59] Much of the *laissez-faire* opposition to public intervention had to be overcome by high compensation payments, for example where pipes were laid beneath the land. The requirements of public health also necessitated powers for the Boards of Health to act on polluted water supplied by private companies.

Rosen pointed out the influence of the philosophical radicals in the extensive changes enacted in Parliament between the 1820s and 1870s.[60] The social and political philosophy of the reformers trying to implement preventive-health measures, did not extend to a questioning of the structural inequalities and injustices of the social and economic order which gave rise to so much poverty and ill-health. Working people themselves had probably come to accept even the industrial diseases as part of working life, while the poor did not share equally in the sanitary improvements that reformers eventually did manage to implement.[61] The champions of public health were not usually medical people, and anyway the important changes required health engineering and preventive organis- ation, not medicine. Chadwick advocated prevention in preference to cure,and this necessitated environmental action to cope with the hazards of polluted water, sewage, and animal and industrial waste. Legislation was often required, such as the Nuisance Removal Acts in the 1850s and 1860s which gave the newly created Medical Officers of Health the powers necessary to control environmental hazards.[62]

A major extension of powers by which infectious diseases could be controlled came with the Sanitary Act passed in 1866 under threat of a major cholera epidemic. Riverside sanitary authorities were given respons- ibility for the condition of ships and the London authority appointed an officer to inspect them.[63] It required further legislation in the Public Health Act of 1872 to establish port sanitary authorities, and new urban and rural sanitary authorities in the provinces. Medical inspection of vessels and personnel quickly became extensive and seems likely to have played an important part in preventing the introduction of cholera from overseas. The Sanitary Acts of 1866 and 1872 divided the country into sanitary districts and provided a basis for the organisation of public-health programmes. Local authorities were compelled to provide drainage, sewerage and an adequate water supply, and further re-organisation was implemented following the Local Government Act of 1888. The British Isles only suffered a few cases of cholera after 1866, with infected people arriving from abroad, although there was a minor outbreak in 1892 in the Midlands and the North.[64]

The precise timing of the impact of particular physical measures on the death rate from cholera and other water-borne diseases is difficult to determine with national data. After the last epidemic of Asiatic cholera in England and Wales, in 1866, the registration records refer to 'English cholera', but this later became incorporated into the total diarrhoeal-disease category. Apart from this, the death rate from typhoid declined, and also that associated with a whole series of water-borne infections and diseases linked with faecal contamination of food as well as water. However, as mentioned, mortality from 'fevers' which included such causes of death, had been falling in the period between the mid eighteenth and the mid nineteenth century. Many studies of the events in particular towns in the second half of the nineteenth century have contributed to a more detailed understanding of the role of various changes in declining death rates from particular diseases. Changes in living standards have been examined, along with the introduction of public-health measures, and much evidence of social-class differentials in mortality change has come from such work.[65]

The cycle of structural poverty probably meant that the health of working-class people in Manchester, for example, may not have fundamentally improved in the second half of the nineteenth century. Many of the social-reform porgrammes for certain small areas of the large industrial towns appear to have been totally inadequate, while some public-health measures were based on false assumptions before the Germ Theory of disease gained acceptance.[66] Real wages may have increased in the 1870s for those who had work, but evidence from different towns suggests that a significant proportion of their populations still lived in conditions in which the spread of water-borne infectious diseases was a major hazard. After considering reports from different towns, Howe concluded that even the late Victorian period was a time of pauperism and fearful mortality.[67] There was a contrast with the affluence of the few, who were benefiting directly from industrial developments, and to some extent were able to move away from the filthy and neglected parts of the big cities where their wealth was created. These towns were described by Engels and Dickens, who characterised them as having damp, crowded and poorly ventilated living conditions, pools of stagnant water, and piles of stinking refuse.[68] In Manchester, areas of generally poor living conditions became the focus of attention for sanitary reform at the end of the nineteenth century. However, Local Acts of the Borough Council had only been selectively used, and direct responsibility for housing was not assumed until the 1890s. It was probably not until this time that a water-borne sewage disposal and treatment system was put into operation which could bring down water-borne disease mortality more rapidly, while water closets were still a feature of only a minority of houses.[69]

The role of improvements in sanitation and water supply in London before the end of the century has also been called into question, since it was only by the 1890s that access to a constant water supply reached half the population.[70] There had been some improvements in filtration by some of the privately-owned water companies by the 1870s, so that supplies were no longer suspected of being unsafe. Working-class areas were not always covered by these advances even by the 1890s, and there were district differentials in mortality from typhoid. The role of the new public fever hospitals, and co-operation between many different specialists, may also have become important in combating the disease, together with bacteriological laboratory services which identified local outbreaks and monitored food and milk as well as water supplies.[71]

In Birmingham there was found to have been less association than might have been expected between domestic sanitary provision and mortality variables, and poor housing was more closely correlated with high mortality, even that from typhoid.[72] However, contamination of the water and food might have differed between areas and accounted for differential typhoid mortality, as it was thought to have done in London. A study of Bradford indicated the importance of epidemics of typhoid in the second half of the nineteenth century, and the vulnerability of the middle classes as well as those living in filthy, overcrowded and poverty-stricken conditions.[73] Milk supplies which were more likely to be used by the better-off, were found to be contaminated when a public analyst was appointed in 1874. Also, faecal contamination of water supplies was probably occurring because of bad connections in the plumbing for water closets in the relatively affluent households which could afford them. The risk of typhoid mortality among the better-off may have been reduced when the Sanitary Association was formed and surveyors were employed to inspect sanitation in the 1880s.[74]

For working people, even if real-wage increases in the 1870s brought a better economic standard of living, the conditions in many towns were still conducive to the spread of water- and fly-borne infectious diseases. It was probably only through specific preventive measures that an uninterrupted fall in the death rate from these diseases could occur. The national registration data illustrated in Figure 4.3 do show that the death rate attributed to typhoid was declining from 1870 when separate recording began. The death rate fell for two decades along with that for diarrhoea and dysentery, but at the end of the century the decline in the gastro-intestinal disease death rate was interrupted in the succession of hot summers referred to earlier. Although restrictions affecting the possibility of cholera entering the country may have been a crucial factor in controlling the disease, it would not be surprising if other efforts to prevent its spread were effective, and brought some reduction in the incidence and death rates for diseases which had a similar mode of transmission. By the end of the century, probably over half the urban sanitary authorities were running their waterworks for the benefit of the majority. The death rate attributed to typhoid declined more sharply after this, as did that from diarrhoea and dysentery (as shown in Figure 4.3). It has also been shown that a dramatic decline in the typhoid death rate occurred in Philadelphia when filtered water was provided in 1906, and became available for all in 1909.[75]

Studies of particular industrial towns in England have pointed out that poverty and crowded housing conditions were closely associated with differential mortality from infectious diseases at the end of the nineteenth century. There is some doubt as to whether major improvements in these living conditions occurred before the twentieth century to an extent that could have affected water-borne disease death rates. A combination of preventive-health measures seems likely to have been involved in the last three decades of the nineteenth century, with improvements in sewerage and water supplies, and then with purer milk and the monitoring of food for contamination. Future research might reveal the extent to which the later more rapid decline in the twentieth century reflected the benefits of rehousing and related improvements in living conditions including sanitation and water supply.

Summary

In the last few decades of the nineteenth century the major diseases typhus and cholera – which arrived from Asia in the 1830s – were practically eliminated in England. Such a change was of major importance in reducing the death rate among adults as well as children, while the virtual elimination of smallpox between the mid eighteenth century and the end of the nineteenth century was probably the most important factor in reducing infant mortality in this period. It seems certain that the prevention of deaths which would otherwise have been directly attributed to smallpox contributed a minimum of 0.1 towards each unit of decline in the overall death rate in London between the 1720s and 1820s. The summary of arithmetic components of mortality change recorded in the London Bills shown in Appendix 4a, suggests that a further contribution of 0.4 towards each unit of decline in the death rate involved reductions in deaths among infants and one-year olds. Many of these deaths had probably been due to unrecognised forms of infectious disease including smallpox, and to diarrhoeal disorders. A decline in mortality recorded under the fevers category contributed a further 0.19 towards each unit of decline in the overall burial rate in London between the 1720s and the 1820s. The gradual elimination of famine crises within the country probably contributed, not so much through improved nutritional resistance but because associated living conditions had been breeding grounds for typhus epidemics. In addition there may have been some beneficial application of knowledge about the need for cleanliness of the body and clothes to prevent the spread of the disease from foci of infection such as prisons, ships and hospitals.

The epidemics of cholera in England in the mid nineteenth century were part of a worldwide pandemic exacerbated by increased trade and travel, but within four decades of the disease arriving in the country in the 1830s it had been prevented from becoming a regular epidemic cause of death. Important in this were the epidemiological findings on possible water-borne transmission, although bacteriological identification of the bacillus was not achieved until the epidemics of 1883–4 in Egypt and India.[76] Containment was probably mainly due to the development and gradual acceptance of the water-borne germ theory of the disease, the progress in sanitary reforms, and measures to prevent the introduction of infection from overseas. The monitoring of water supplies and sewerage that was important in the prevention of cholera almost certainly had some impact on other water-borne diseases, and provided the impetus for a sustained control of such causes of death in the twentieth century. However, the role of other public-health and hygiene measures was probably very important, and in London efforts to monitor for contamination of food and milk as well as water seem likely to have been significant in the control of typhoid. Improvements in sewerage and a safer water supply meant that these other sources of infection could be more readily traced.[77] This may have made some contribution to the decline in the typhoid death rate after 1870, which was discernible with separate recording of the disease, and occurred along with that for diarrhoea and dysentery.

Before distinction of typhus and typhoid, the two combined contributed 0.17 towards each unit of decline in the age-standardised death rate in the second half of the nineteenth century, of which 0.043 was attributable to the decline in the typhoid death rate from 1871–1901 and 0.025 to the final recession of typhus in this period. Cholera, diarrhoea and dysentery contributed 0.12 towards each unit of decline in the overall death rate in the second half of the nineteenth century, which fell by 2.7% as a result of reductions in mortality from this group of causes. The epidemics of the 1830s had warned that cholera alone was capable of becoming a regular cause of at least 10% of annual mortality, and simplified arithmetic analysis of component causes of mortality decline underestimates the impact of measures to control the disease. It has been pointed out that, in his early analysis, McKeown oversimplified in stating that changes introduced by sanitary reformers were responsible for a quarter of the decline in the overall death rate in the second half of the nineteenth century.[78] However, much of the 0.29 contribution to a unit of decline made by this whole group of causes probably involved the kind of public-health and hygiene measures referred to here. The poor in the towns may not have benefited so much from improvements in sanitation and water supply until the twentieth century, when community action on new housing may have become significant for them. However, typhus had been a major killer among the impoverished in crowded living conditions and had virtually receded by the end of the century.

After the turn of the century, with cholera and typhus virtually eradicated, gastro-intestinal diseases remained, but contributed 0.10 towards each unit of decline in the overall death rate up to 1971, while typhoid only contributed a further 0.01. Further advances in preventive control, together with purer food and milk, contributed to what was a more rapid fall in the death rate from these diseases in the twentieth century. Even so, the broad group of diseases which had contributed 0.29 towards each unit of decline in the death rate in the second half of the nineteenth century, was much less of a component of overall mortality decline in the period 1901–71, despite the downturn in infant mortality involving diarrhoeal disease. Gastro-intestinal and respiratory diseases, whooping cough, measles and tuberculosis were the main diseases involved in infant mortality decline between the 1910s and 1971, and contributed 0.5 towards each unit of decline. However, many deaths assigned to the vaguer categories, such as convulsions, debility and atrophy, were probably also linked with infectious and diarrhoeal diseases.

The infant mortality rate which had been 155 per 1,000 births in 1848–54 was still 151 in 1901, but it then fell rapidly to 18 per 1,000 by 1971. This final phase of infant mortality decline from the beginning of the twentieth century probably reflected the benefits of specific measures to control sources of water-borne and food-borne infectious diseases, and efforts to promote better hygiene and care for young children. Some reduction in transmission rates and hence severity of air-borne epidemic infections seems likely to have occurred with the trend to smaller families and through reduced overcrowding.[79] The resumed fall of infant mortality from the turn of the century contributed to the more rapid improvement in average life expectancy in the twentieth century, along with the downturn in adult mortality. These important changes in part reflect the decline in respiratory-disease death rates which occurred among adults as well as children in the twentieth century, and the possible role of reduced transmission rates from related air-borne infectious diseases will be considered in the next chapter.

5 Respiratory and air-borne infectious diseases

The 1870s was a major turning point in the mortality transition for several reasons, including the rapid recession of typhus and of smallpox – following renewed efforts to prevent the disease – and because of the absence of cholera as preventive control measures became more effective. All three diseases had caused periodically high epidemic mortality in the mid nineteenth century, while smallpox and typhus had been even more significant as major killers in the eighteenth century along with tuberculosis. If smallpox had been the most feared disease of the eighteenth century, and plague the scourge of Europe in the previous three centuries, it was tuberculosis – the endemic 'white plague' – that came to be seen as characteristic of life in industrialising England in the nineteenth century. By then there were many more deaths attributed to consumption, although there are indications that the death rate was in fact falling in the nineteenth century. Little was known about effective treatment before the mid twentieth century, while the virulence of the bacillus does not appear to have diminished. In view of this McKeown, for example, suggested that there must have been an improvement in nutrition and hence resistance to respiratory tuberculosis to account for the declining death rate in the second half of the nineteenth century.[1] However, the relative trends in death rates for specific diseases, and the inter-relationship between infections involved in a series of diseases which made life so hazardous, suggest that other factors may have been involved.

Consumption was given as the cause in about 15–20% of deaths in the eighteenth century in the London Bills of Mortality. It may be that 'consumption' and 'phthisis' simply referred to 'wasting',[2] and at the end of the eighteenth century Black noted that the term was 'lax and indefinite' with many emaciations from infancy to old age being classified as consumption. Even so, in his experience and in that of his contemporary physicians, a very large proportion of cases were genuine pulmonary phthisis, that is respiratory tuberculosis.[3] Many lung diseases were probably also classified as consumption, including lung cancer, certain forms of pneumonia, and bronchitis, although the term 'asthma' probably also covered these and many other respiratory diseases in the eighteenth century.[4] The Royal Commission on Tuberculosis was aware of the rise in the respiratory-disease death rate as that from tuberculosis fell in the second half of the nineteenth century, and there was probably some transfer of classification.[5]

Changes in mortality from consumption were not particularly significant in the early phase of the mortality transition as indicated by data from the London Bills for the eighteenth century shown in Appendix 4a. However, the decline in the death rate from respiratory tuberculosis in the second half of the nineteenth century in England and Wales contributed 0.33 towards each unit of decline in the overall age-standardised death rate, and this reduction may have been too dramatic to be entirely due to changes in classification. The disease has been virtually eliminated in Western populations, whereas bronchitis remains as a major cause of death, particularly in England. Both diseases are chronic and long-term rather than acute and short-term like epidemic infections, although there are important links with air-borne epidemic diseases. Comparison will be made here between turning points and trends in death rates for respiratory tuberculosis, bronchitis, other respiratory diseases and the air-borne epidemic diseases of childhood which can give rise to respiratory complications.

Many of the air-borne infectious diseases, still common today among children in Western populations, were frequently fatal in the nineteenth century. Both whooping cough and measles had epidemic cycles of their own which reflected the fact that immunity was conferred on survivors.[6] The streptococcal disease, scarlet fever, usually occurred later in childhood between the ages of one and ten,[7] and probably followed infections of early life. As in developing countries today, children in large families with inadequate nutrition and poor living conditions must have been at great risk from an inter-related series of air-borne and respiratory diseases. The adverse effect of malnutrition on mortality risk from infectious diseases is well known, although it may itself result from serious infection which can interrupt the growth and development of a child. A clear case is that of malaria infection, which results in an inability to retain food during attacks, although malnutrition may also result from the more general restrictions on food intake which accompany serious infectious illness. The association of malnutrition with over half the cases of measles and diarrhoeal disease in some developing countries probably reflects this two-way relationship.[8]

The importance of under-nutrition in high infectious-disease mortality in the nineteenth century, was rightly emphasised by McKeown and his co-workers,and tuberculosis is particularly lethal in poorly fed and crowded communities. However,there are several objections to the view that an improvement in general levels of nutrition must have occurred to bring about the reduction in death rates from the major air-borne infectious diseases. A re-examination of details of the annual trends in death rates reveals important differences between patterns of decline for different diseases, even within this group. There is a marked contrast between diseases for which death rates declined from the eighteenth century – as indicated by the London Bills – and increasing death rates at different times in the second half of the nineteenth century for measles, diphtheria and croup, as well as diarrhoeal disease among infants. Smallpox and consumption death rates appear to have declined throughout the nineteenth century in contrast with the continuing high death rate for measles, which could be taken to indicate continuingly inadequate nutrition and adverse living conditions among large sections of the population.

The decline in tuberculosis mortality

In early times tuberculosis was probably not a disease of rural areas, and Cockburn suggested that human beings must have developed the disease when the introduction of agriculture encouraged a more settled life and eventually the growth of towns.[9] It has not been a disease of hunter-gatherers, except in recent times where there has been contact with infected people from other civilisations living in densely populated and settled areas. As indicated,there was an increase in recorded mortality from consumption in the London Bills of Mortality for example, in the seventeenth century. Although a majority of people at that time still lived in rural areas, there was probably an increasing contact with towns and hence with a disease to which many people may not previously have been exposed.[10] There were increasing death rates from tuberculosis in the nineteenth century in some Western populations, and in the twentieth century in England where the death rate rose rapidly in the First World War. In the mid nineteenth century the tuberculosis death rate was increasing in some southern states of America and in New York, and these changes may have been linked with the Civil War and with immigration from areas of high incidence of the disease,such as famine-stricken Ireland.[11] In Ireland, the crude death rate from tuberculosis increased in the second half of the nineteenth century,and this may also reflect a later process of development of urban contact.

In considering periods of increasing tuberculosis mortality in the past, Dubos and Dubos emphasised the social aspects of the disease and its association with the process of urbanisation and increasing social contacts with crowded towns.[12] Populations without previous exposure to the disease were more susceptible, although it is not clear to what extent partial resistance is conveyed genetically. It might be thought that high mortality eventually selected out the most susceptible, so that the general level of resistance to the disease improved over generations. However, the impact of adverse living conditions, such as in times of war, appears to predominate, with the death rate falling only when conditions improve. It seems unlikely that an immuno-genetic explanation can account for the decline in the tuberculosis death rate, particularly in view of the differential between trends for respiratory and other forms of tuberculosis for which the death rate did not fall much in the second half of the nineteenth century. The importance of genetic factors in tuberculosis may have been overemphasised anyway, and there is evidence that the predominant influences are exogenous.

Hereditary influences on mortality risk from tuberculosis had been found in studies of rabbits, but differences between various families were obliterated when the degree of exposure to infection was high.[13] Studies on humans have found that the degree of exposure to infection is the predominant factor in the development of the disease, and it was only when this was high that incidence of tuberculosis among those who showed no sign of previous contact with the disease, exceeded that of those who were tuberculin-positive.[14] The degree of infectivity, and closeness of contact with cases, appears to be more important than blood relationship *per se*. In a further study of tuberculosis in blood relatives, spouses and non-relatives, death rates were compared after age-standardisation and no hereditary influence was found.[15] It may be that an apparent association found in earlier studies of twins,[16] between the risk of tuberculosis and the degree of relatedness to someone with clinical disease, was due to more frequent and closer contacts between people the more related they were.

The findings on the environmental and transmission aspects of respiratory tuberculosis suggest that the risk of inhaling and the level of dosage of bacillus are important. The agent of tuberculosis, *tubercle bacillus* (*Mycobacterium tuberculosis*), enters the body via the nose or mouth. In bovine tuberculosis, the main non-respiratory form, it is usually spread via contaminated milk, while respiratory disease is transmitted in droplets from the coughing of infected people. As with other air-borne infections, the initial attack may be 'over' within a few weeks, if indeed any clinical disease becomes manifest at all. However, with tubercular infection, the living bacilli can survive in the body for many years. In the primary infection the body becomes sensitised to the products of the bacillus, in a type of allergy, particularly to the toxic product, tuberculin. In a case of clinical tuberculosis, many cells are destroyed on contact with these products, while new cells are produced rapidly in order to maintain the integrity of tissues and, indeed, preserve the lung itself. This process of containment of 'galloping consumption', involves a reaction to 'wall off' the bacilli with fibrous tissue.[17] Failure of the process may be linked with the dosage of bacillus received as well as undernutrition and other factors, and it is likely to result in the destruction of the lung. Even if successfully contained within a caseous mass, or hard nodule, the bacilli can remain virulent inside for years, and an internal source of infection if disrupted. Recent studies have shown that the appearance of pulmonary and other forms of tuberculosis in previously healthy older people, is usually the result of re-activation of a primary infection which itself did not necessarily produce clinical symptoms of disease.[18]

People in towns in the eighteenth and nineteenth centuries seem likely to have contracted some primary infection at an early age, as with other air-borne infectious diseases.[19] The destructiveness of tuberculosis at the beginning of the nineteenth century should be seen in the context of a series of epidemic diseases to which everyone was exposed in overcrowded living conditions. Many exanthamata, infectious diseases which produce a rash, give rise to respiratory complications in which there is disruption of the lungs and coughing. Studies on measles have suggested that such infections with micro-organisms conveying immunity, might also temporarily depress the immune response to tuberculin.[20] There may not be enough evidence yet that this in itself can lead to clinical tuberculosis, but such studies indicate the inter-relationship between air-borne infectious diseases as they produce immune reactions and give rise to physical complications. Suppression of tuberculin reaction has in fact been found during scarlet fever, glandular fever and measles infection, and smallpox probably produced such an effect. However, the actual physical disruption produced by respiratory complications of such infections may have been even more important. For example,the constant coughing in attacks of whooping cough among both children and young adults, could well have been significant in the re-activation of latent tubercular infection.[21] The respiratory complications and coughing induced by diseases such as measles and smallpox could also have impaired the defences at the time of primary tubercular infection, and led to a greater risk of actual clinical or latent disease rather than just subclinical infection.

Connections between smallpox and consumption were recognised in the eighteenth century, and Black gave some idea of the medical view of different groups of causes of death in the London Bills of Mortality in 1778, when he referred to smallpox in the following terms:

It attacks the same person but once in life, had this not been the case, the human race must long since have been extinct. On a promiscuous [sic] average one of every seven infected die of natural disease; but under inoculation only 1 in 500. Besides to the former deadly catelogue may be supperadded a frightful train of mangled constitutions and countenances, of consumptions, abscesses, ulcers, ophthalmics, blindness.[22]

Black clearly considered there was a link between the destructive smallpox and consumption, and many other medical writers at that time referred to this.[23] The impressions of eighteenth-century medical writers have been largely borne out by later studies indicating the secondary complications of smallpox, including bronchitis and broncho-pneumonia, as well as the exacerbation of tubercular infection into potentially fatal clinical disease.

The Royal Commission on Vaccination referred to the secondary effects of smallpox among those who survived, and particularly to typhoid and tuberculosis, for which the term scrofula was used to include both respiratory and non-respiratory forms of the disease.

It would be difficult therefore to conceive against vaccination a charge more ludicrously inapplicable than that it has tended to aggravate diseases which are essentially the diseases of debility. For if you compare the extreme degree in which natural smallpox weakens and exhausts those whom it refrains from killing, with the contrary and entire absence of such results among the ordinary effects of vaccination you have in this comparison a measure of the important influence which Jenner's discovery has exerted – not in aggravating but in mitigating the diseases in question . . . all writers on smallpox attest the frequency with which scrofulous affections [sic] follow in its [smallpox's] train and that in such measure as vaccination is less impoverishing and less depressing than smallpox, in just such measure does its substitution for smallpox act in prevention of scrofula.[24]

More recent authorities on smallpox, such as Dixon, have attested to the disruption of the lungs that could occur,[25] and the control of the disease could therefore have brought a significant reduction in mortality attributed to consumption.

The evidence of a decline in mortality from consumption in London at the beginning of the nineteenth century, when vaccination against smallpox was introduced, is certainly consistent with the idea of some secondary benefit. The trends in death rates shown in Appendix 3d indicate that there may have been at least a levelling-off in the increase after the mid eighteenth century. However, as emphasised, changes in mortality recorded under the term consumption in the London Bills and other records cannot be taken as firm evidence of changes in the death rate from respiratory tuberculosis. No great weight should be attached to the early trends, not least because of doubts about the validity of the population base. However, the reduction in the death rate from consumption after 1800 is based on the firmer denominators of census population figures, and this downturn at the time of the most rapid fall in the smallpox death rate is reflected in a correlation coefficient of + 0.62 between the trends in quinequennial rates for the two disease groups over the period 1701/6 to 1831/6.

It is likely that if the tuberculosis death rate did fall as a result of protection against the exacerbating disease smallpox, death rates among children and adolescents would have been the first to be affected. This is borne out by the correlation coefficients for quinquennial smallpox death rates and those for consumption five, ten, fifteen, twenty and twenty-five years later which were + 0.66, + 0.81, + 0.86, + 0.76 and + 0.79 – all statistically significant at the 95% level – while the coefficient for a lag of thirty years was just + 0.49. If these associations involve a causal link there may have been an immediate effect on total consumption mortality through reduced risks among young children just protected against small-pox, but a possibly more significant benefit through reduced risk later in life, at ages 10–19, and at the peak ages for adult tuberculosis mortality, 20–29 years. Data from Sweden show that child mortality from tuberculosis at ages 0–9 years, fell in the first three decades of the nineteenth century as smallpox vaccination was introduced, while the period death rate among adults continued to increase. Data from Paris also suggest that the death rate from tuberculosis declined for the 0–19 age group between the 1810s and 1880s, when again the period death rates among adults continued to increase. A more continuous series of annual data for the second half of the century, indicates that the overall crude death rate for tuberculosis was falling from at least 1872 as it was in London.[26] None of the differentials in age-specific death rates are inconsistent with the idea that mortality might have been falling over successive cohorts with a lag between the decline in period death rates at older compared with younger ages. Age-specific death rates from registration data for England and Wales, presented by year of birth in Figure 5.1, suggest that tuberculosis death rates among

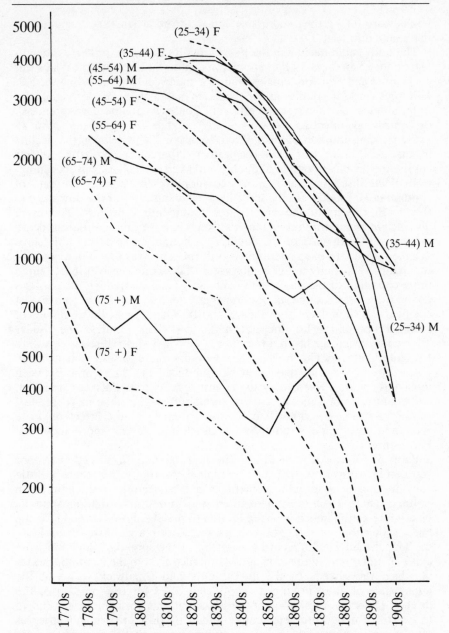

Figure 5.1 Average annual death rates per 100,000 population for respiratory tuberculosis in England and Wales among cohorts born between the 1770s and the 1900s.

Source: Registrar-General *Decennial Supplements for England and Wales, 1850–61* to *1900–10*, and subsequent annual data.

adults were falling over successive cohorts from at least the beginning of the nineteenth century.

The quite rapid decline in the period death rate for respiratory tuberculosis in the second half of the nineteenth century in England and Wales was even more marked for females than for males, as shown in Figure 5.2. Different working conditions for the sexes may have been involved in this differential, while men frequented public houses where there was great risk of contracting infection as well as any greater risk associated with an excessive consumption of alcohol and tobacco.[27] The delay in the decline in the death rate from non-respiratory tuberculosis probably reflects continuing problems with food quality and hygiene. The growing consumption of sterilised milk,and efforts to monitor and control the sale of contaminated food, seem the most likely explanations for the downturn in the death rate from the end of the nineteenth century.[28] The more destructive respiratory tuberculosis appears to have caused different death rates in different parts of the country, although generally the pattern of decline appears to have been fairly uniform. This was found in a study of tuberculosis mortality in five major areas of economic growth in Britain in the second half of the nineteenth century.[29] Particularly high tuberculosis death rates were found in the northern textile towns, the north-east coalfields, Birmingham, the Black Country, Glamorgan, the coalfields of South Wales, and in London and the metropolitan counties. The disease affected all social classes, but the poor in heavily industrialised towns were particularly at risk. The movement of workers to the towns and back again when they became ill, may even have reduced the differential between town and country. Even so, at the county level differentials were marked, and death rates in Lancashire were about 50% higher than in Worcestershire, for example, while there is also evidence of the effect of acute economic crisis on the tuberculosis death rate in the more industrial Lancashire.[30]

Poor diet, crowded conditions in housing and at work, and poor ventilation, contribute to high tuberculosis mortality, but there is little convincing evidence of improvements from the beginning of the nineteenth century. There was a movement to encourage better ventilation of public places, but action may have been limited to prisons, hospitals and meeting halls, rather than affecting tenements and work places. As early as 1796, the Manchester Health Board was aware of the spread of infection from children and others in the crowded cotton factories, to the neighbourhoods in which they lived. In the 1840s, Guy and Chadwick wrote of the importance of close proximity to infected cases for transmission of the disease. Defective ventilation of houses, shops and work places was known to be still a major problem, compounded by dust in such industries as textiles and clothes-making.[31] Factory legislation might have led to some improvements at the end of the nineteenth century which were reflected in the tuberculosis death rate. Before this, however, warnings probably had little effect on those so intent on making money that they ignored the physiological effects,and the misery of crowded conditions among machine operatives, which promoted diseases which in turn affected them.[32] The

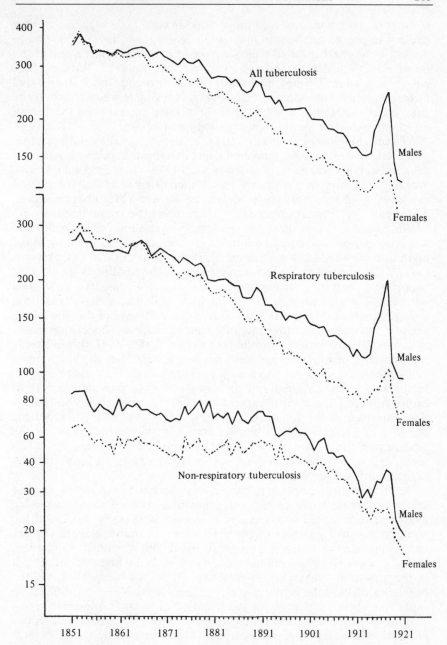

Figure 5.2   Age-standardised annual death rate for tuberculosis in England and Wales, 1851–1921.

Note: Death rates per 100,000 age-standardised to 1901 civilian population.

Sources: Registrar-General (1838–) *Annual Reports for England and Wales* (London: HMSO), and *Annual Statistical Reviews for England and Wales* (London: HMSO).

writings of those who observed these working conditions suggest that they had not improved by the mid nineteenth century, and Engels referred to 'hollow-eyed ghosts,riddled with scrofula and rickets, which haunted the factories of Manchester and the manufacturing towns'.[33] Working-class people with clinical symptoms had to continue to go to work in crowded factories ideal for the spread of the disease. Inevitable contacts with those from other social classes meant that the disease spread from the foci of infection created by the ruthless exploitation of labour.

At work, employees generally had no influence over the conditions that prevailed, while the undernourished living in unheated rooms, would have been unlikely to add to their misery with cold air from an open window. Working conditions in many towns contributed to a miserable and exploited existence,which was probably the only alternative to a life of begging,theft, pauperism, and thus constant fear. There was little commitment to the health regulations that did exist concerning sweatshops, even in the late Victorian period, and living conditions in slums or on the street provided no respite from the 'dark satanic mills', Dicken's description of Coketown in *Hard Times* conveys a general impression of the conditions for working people who lived in 'an ugly citadel,where nature was as strongly bricked out as killing air and gases were bricked in'.[34] There may have been improvements in the provision of housing from the end of the nineteenth century, but municipal authorities often had to overcome opposition to this as an interference with the workings of a 'free market'.[35] Nutrition among working-class people may not have improved even after the 1870s when real wages increased,since there do not appear to have been major shifts in food-consumption patterns and diet may still have consisted largely of carbohydrates.[36] It may be that there were periods in which food consumption improved in the nineteenth century along with a better economic standard of living generally, but the consistent long-term decline in the tuberculosis death rate is not easily accounted for, particularly when contrasted with trends in death rates for other diseases which might be expected to have responded in a similar way.

Death rates from respiratory tuberculosis declined most rapidly at ages 15–25 years and it has been pointed out that reduced stress and rising living standards could have been responsible, particularly in view of the correlation with rising real wages.[37] However, in the nineteenth century there were almost certainly periods in which the economic standard of living for working people did not improve, such as the first two decades. It is the possibility that the tuberculosis death rate declined from the beginning of the nineteenth century in England that is most difficult to explain in terms of changes in the standard of living. Changes in transmission of the disease seem rather unlikely to have been beneficial in this phase of mortality decline when population growth in towns was at its most rapid and conditions became increasingly overcrowded from in-migration and from natural increase. The association between high tuberculosis mortality and the process of industrialisation is seen in developing countries today, while Japan's tuberculosis death rate peaked in the second decade of the twentieth century.[38] The first countries to industrialise were also the first to experience the downturn in the tuberculosis death rate, but the early reduction in England and Wales has to be seen in the context of the whole infectious-disease environment, and at that time smallpox was still rampant. There are many indications that reduced exposure to concurrent, exacerbating,air-borne infectious diseases could have occurred in the twentieth century, as numbers of births declined and overcrowding was reduced for some people. However, in the early part of the nineteenth century the control of smallpox epidemics may have been the only beneficial change in the infectious-disease environment.

During the course of the nineteenth century, contact with the tubercle bacillus was probably universal, and there is nothing to suggest any decline in virulence or reduction in the long-term prognosis. A study of case-fatality from tuberculosis as late as 1923–40 suggested that it remained at about 50% in this period.[39] McKeown emphasised that there was no effective cure for the disease until sulphonamides were introduced in the mid twentieth century.[40] Rest in sanatoria was only available for a small minority even when they did become more widespread from the end of the nineteenth century. Isolation of the infected, and efforts to improve ventilation and overcrowded housing conditions, could eventually have led to a reduction in the dosage of bacillus contracted and hence to a lower risk of clinical infection despite the continuing universality of contact in the first half of the twentieth century.[41] The scientific basis of these preventive measures to control the spread of infection became more widely recognised with the bacteriological discoveries at the end of the nineteenth century. Dubos and Dubos pointed out that anti-tuberculosis movements and education programmes started in the 1890s after the discovery of the causative agent had confirmed the contagion theory of transmission of the disease. Public-health work had certainly predated this, as had a growing awareness that early diagnosis was important to ensure that some care was taken of sufferers, but there were conflicting views on how best to care for the sick in the nineteenth century.[42] Even for the twentieth century, it is not clear whether changes in living conditions, nutrition, or cause-specific preventive measures to curb the spread of the disease have been more important for the reduction in the tuberculosis death rate. However, long before the direct health measure of BCG and chemotherapy were introduced in the mid twentieth century, preventive interventions, together with changes in housing and working conditions with regard to overcrowding and ventilation, seem likely to have reduced the risk of infection and the dosage of bacillus contracted.

Respiratory diseases

The continuous decline in the respiratory tuberculosis death rate in the nineteenth century, may be compared with a much later downturn for the group of respiratory causes of death, bronchitis, pneumonia and influenza. The death rate at different ages for respiratory diseases as a whole increased up to a peak at the end of the nineteenth century, as did that for

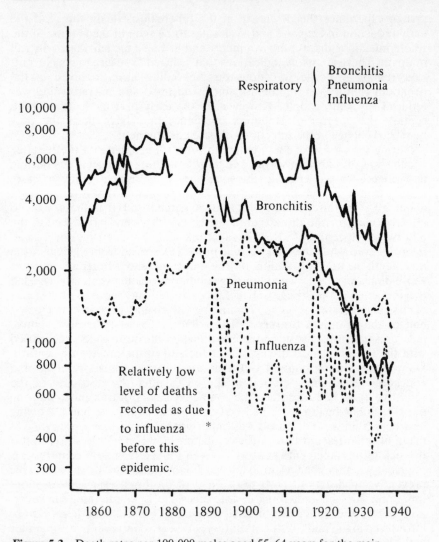

Figure 5.3 Death rates per 100,000 males aged 55–64 years for the main respiratory diseases in England and Wales, 1860–1940.

Sources: Registrar-General (1838–) *Annual Reports and Statistical Reviews* (London: HMSO).

the predominant group of bronchitis. The trend in death rate for adults in the age group 55–64, which would have been relatively free from transfers of the 'old age' and ill-defined causes, is shown in Figure 5.3. There had in fact been some levelling-off in the death rate from bronchitis among adults after about 1870, before the impact of the major influenza epidemic of 1889–91. Death rates for males and females, shown separately in Appendix 5a, reveal a differential in the rate of decline in the twentieth century, but rates for males alone are sufficient here to compare the trends for the main component causes of respiratory disease. There is no 'cohort influence' detectable in the trends for the main component disease, bronchitis. Many factors affect mortality risk throughout life, although considerable attention will be given here to the importance of childhood experience, since there is evidence of its effect on the risk of later adult disease given other exacerbating irritant conditions. The death rate for respiratory disease among children aged 0–4 years, did not begin to decline continuously until after the influenza epidemic of 1891. The trend shown in Figure 5.4 reflects changes in mortality recorded as due to bronchitis, for which the death rate also levelled off in the 1880s. The beginning of the long-term decline in the death rate for pneumonia appears to have occurred later for children, from the 1900s, and the trend was different for adult death rates in the 1860s and 1870s. However, the inter-related nature of the component forms of respiratory disease, and the difficulties of identifying the primary cause of death, mean that the separate trends for pneumonia must be considered with caution.

The death rates from respiratory diseases for all age groups declined consistently in the twentieth century apart from a resurgence among older males after World War II, which seems likely to have been due to increased cigarette-smoking. Nevertheless, this group of diseases still accounted for over 14% of all deaths in the country in 1981. The contribution of the decline in the respiratory-disease death rate to overall mortality decline has been found to be less significant in other countries than in England and Wales. Clearly many of the adverse living conditions referred to already, such as overcrowding, poor housing and under-nutrition, would have contributed to high mortality. Relatively high death rates from these causes in England and Wales may also reflect climatic conditions. Severe winters are known to affect mortality,[43] but other countries have worse conditions in terms of temperature,[44] so further factors such as dampness of housing seem likely to be involved. Apart from the adverse conditions referred to, high mortality from chronic bronchitis is correlated with heavily indistrialised and polluted areas,and there is a marked urban-rural differential in mortality.[45] There was certainly an awareness of the need to control the emission of smoke in industrial areas in the second half of the nineteenth century, but comprehensive measures on a nationwide basis, were not implemented until the second half of the twentieth century.[46] Pollution from factories and the use of certain types of domestic coal would have contributed to high mortality long after the peak in the death rate, although better housing may have alleviated some of the problems of ventilation and smoke as well as dampness.

For many people the effects of poor living conditions persisted even if there was some improvement in the quantity as well as the quality of food available at the end of the nineteenth century, and influences in early life may have been particularly important. Contemporary evidence suggests that children who develop lower respiratory tract infection, who live in polluted areas, or belong to lower socio-economic groups, have an increased liability to develop productive cough and have a worse lung function.[47] Differences in childhood experience, including nutrition, might

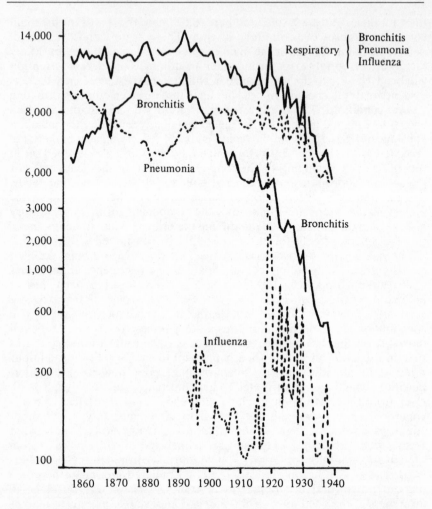

Figure 5.4 Death rates per 100,000 males aged 0–4 years for the main respiratory diseases in England and Wales, 1860–1940.

Sources: Registrar-General (1838–) *Annual Reports and Statistical Reviews* (London: HMSO).

also have repercussions for adult mortality risk given other exacerbating influences. There is evidence that cigarette-smoking and dusty working conditions have probably been the dominant factors in adult bronchitis mortality, although other conditions which vary locally might determine the onset or evolution of the disease among both young and old.[48] Social-class differentials in bronchitis mortality among children in the mainly pre-smoking age groups have been found, with increased symptoms being recorded in relation to higher levels of air pollution. A longitudinal study has found that at twenty years of age cigarette-smoking had the greatest effect on the prevalence of symptoms, and then a history of respiratory-tract illness under the age of two years.[49]

Bronchitis does not involve any known immunity being conferred, which contrasts with influenza in which many varieties of virus are involved, and also with lobar pneumonia in which there is an import immune response.[50] Different antigenic types of influenza have been implicated in major epidemics, such as in 1918–19 when there was probably a sudden mutation of the Type A virus.[51] Another massively destructive outbreak had occurred in 1889–91, and there were several recognised epidemics in the eighteenth century including that in 1743 when the disease was given the Italian name. The contributing causes in bronchitis include different infections, as well as cigarette-smoking, atmospheric pollution, and dusty working conditions.[52] The irritant effects of these produce damage to the lungs which can eventually lead to chronic and deteriorating symptoms, and finally to disabling cough and breathlessness. In some respects a link with infective agents has not been formally substantiated,[53] but infectious diseases produce many secondary effects including bronchial disorders. Common infections such as the various types of influenza, common cold and other viral respiratory infections can damage the lungs.[54]

The risk of contracting common respiratory infections depends on contacts within the household as well as those in the community. It has been found that the incidence of common respiratory diseases, in terms of episodes of illness per person-year, increases with family size.[55] The incidence rate of bronchitis and pneumonia among a cohort of children born in north London in the period 1963–5 and followed up for five years, was almost twice as high for those with three or more siblings than for those with one. Although rates of infection were lower among breast-fed children, they still increased with the number of siblings as they did among those not breast-fed.[56] Numbers of children in a household may also have implications for adult respiratory illness, since children appear to be the main introducers of influenza into households. In one prospective study the risk of infection with influenza was found to be about three times as high in households with five serologically-defined susceptibles compared with those with only one.[57] The number of children in a family appears to be more important than different levels of crowding,either in the household itself, as measured by persons per room for example, or in the community.[58] The school child may also be the most frequently exposed to extrafamilial infection with streptococci and pneumonococci, and therefore the most likely to spread these infections among the family, and this was found even where families lived in congested working-class areas. Much of the association of high infectious-disease death rates with poor housing may in fact be explained by larger family sizes. In view of these findings, declining fertility levels might account for a significant proportion of the decline in respiratory-disease death rates in the twentieth century.[59]

The common air-borne epidemic diseases of childhood are also well known for producing secondary respiratory complications in large families with inadequate food and poor living conditions. Diseases such as measles, whooping cough and diphtheria are in a sense respiratory, and can damage that system in children, and measles virus for example causes a specific inflammatory reaction in the tracheo-bronchial tree. Broncho-pneumonia was mentioned as a complication of smallpox in the past, and the proneness of very young children with whooping cough to pneumonia and mechanical damage to the lungs is well known.[60] One of the bacilli involved in whooping cough, *Bordetella pertussis*, produces an acute tracheo-bronchial inflammatory reaction, and can therefore be a specific primary cause of bronchitis or pertussis in adults which is categorised as such.[61] Different studies have shown that immunity gained by whooping-cough infection or immunisation probably wanes after some years. Symptomatic disease has been identified among adults working in hospitals, which otherwise would probably have been regarded as bronchitis.[62] In view of these and other connections between common air-borne infections and respiratory diseases, it is not surprising that the historical decline in death rates occurred from about the same time for bronchitis and whooping cough. The latter could not have been the result of disease-specific measures or therapy which was not available until the 1930s.[63]

Damage to the lungs among children as a result of whooping cough is more substantiated than for adults who contract the bacillus, and secondary respiratory complications of other childhood infectious diseases have been found in several studies. A review of fifty cases of collapsed lung in children for whom there had been radiological follow-up after hospitalis-ation was carried out in the 1940s,[64] and the mode of onset of symptoms was through whooping cough in seven cases, through measles in four, and diphtheria in one case. Another study of 956 cases of pertussis, and 897 cases of measles, hospitalised between 1948 and 1955, considered the chest radiographs and cases were classified according to severity of the fever and the other common complications of pertussis, broncho-pneumonia and gastro-enteritis.[65] Fifty-two children had detectable damage to the lungs on follow-up in 1954–5, and twenty-five of these cases involved bronchitis and recurrent cough. Both studies suggested that in the past, measles and whooping cough had given rise to much chronic pulmonary infection and collapse and possibly permanent damage before the use of sulphonamides from the 1940s. The extent of the problem remaining when these studies were conducted, indicates that both diseases could have been associated with high respiratory-disease mortality among children in earlier times.

Secondary complications of measles in particular have long been documented, and data from Glasgow for the period 1893–1902 show that bronchitis, pneumonia, and broncho-pneumonia were recorded in 54.2% of deaths from the disease.[66] There were relatively few hospitalised cases of measles in England by the 1970s, but about half the deaths were the result of respiratory complications.[67] A study of hospitalised cases in Uganda showed that about 10% resulted in death, and half of these involved broncho-pneumonia, while a further 18% of deaths involved associated diarrhoea and vomiting, and 13% died with bronchitis or pulmonary tuberculosis.[68] A study of 1,283 hospitalised cases of measles in Nigeria showed that 604 involved broncho-pneumonia, and 169 children died.[69] A separate study in the same country concluded that the role of protein-calorie malnutrition was very important, since immunity was impaired, and the virus could not be completely expelled from the body.[70] Thus many studies indicate that secondary complications of common childhood infectious diseases are frequently respiratory. Historically this may have been significant in both the high levels of mortality from bronchitis and broncho-pneumonia, and in the downturn in death rates from respiratory disease among children from the end of the nineteenth century.

Air-borne epidemic diseases of childhood

Clearly respiratory diseases did not contribute to the overall decline in mortality before the twentieth century, but the contribution to each unit of decline in the overall death rate was 0.19 in the period 1901–71. Similarly it has been emphasised that infant mortality did not contribute to overall mortality decline over the whole of the second half of the nineteenth century, although there was some improvement in the 1870s. Much of the decline in the death rate in this period was due to a reduction in the child death rate,[71] which was mainly among the 1–4 year age group, and about 60% of deaths at these ages were caused by air-borne and respiratory diseases in mid nineteenth-century England and Wales. The changing impact of air-borne infectious diseases is illustrated in Figure 5.5 with death rates for the age group 0–9 since most deaths from the epidemic diseases of childhood occurred in this age range. The involvement of diseases such as measles and whooping cough in respiratory and diarrhoeal diseases, means that their arithmetic contribution of 0.03–0.05 to each unit of decline in the overall death rate after the mid nineteenth century probably underestimates their real contribution. Similarly, the final recession of smallpox and typhus epidemics from the 1870s predated the fall in mortality from some childhood epidemic diseases, and probably contributed more to the decline in child mortality from this time than is suggested by the arithmetic component of mortality. Among the childhood diseases, scarlet fever accounted for the biggest arithmetic component of mortality decline in the second half of the nineteenth century, and contributed 0.12 towards each unit of decline in the overall death rate. However, this may be an oversimplification because of the inter-related pattern of infectious diseases and the difficulty there may have been in distinguishing between diseases in young children or identifying the prime cause of death.

Scarlet fever is one manifestation of infection with *Haemolytic strepto-coccus* which was identified as the agent in 1924. It is probably carried by a large proportion of the population, although there may be several types which have the toxin-producing capacity to cause the disease.[72] Clinical disease results in variable symptoms of sore throat, fever and rash. Rosen suggested that clinicians were reasonably clear about childhood diseases and could identify scarlet fever, and McKeown considered that they would have been experienced in all types of childhood infectious disease.[73] Even so, there may have been confusion between scarlet fever and other

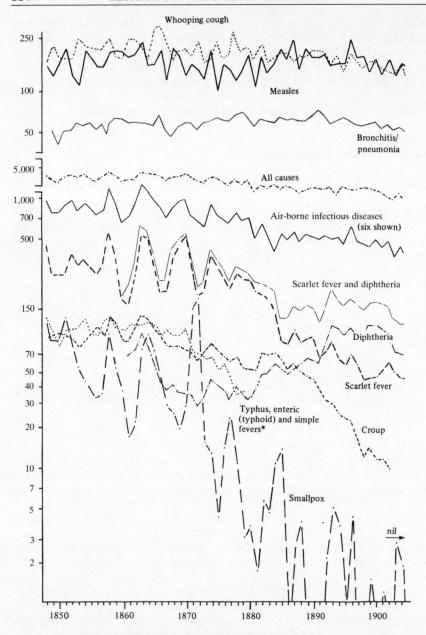

Figure 5.5 Annual death rates per 100,000 children aged 0–9 years for the main infectious diseases in England and Wales, 1848–1905.

* Typhus, enteric (typhoid) and simple fevers. This group was the only major category of causes of death at ages 0–9 which was not air-borne disease. Recording on this basis ceased in the 1870s when the diseases were distinguished.

Source: Registrar-General (1838–) *Annual Reports* (London: HMSO).

infectious diseases during concurrent epidemics since both symptoms and severity vary. Factors which may have affected the manifestation of the disease include dosage of streptococcus and the particular strain involved, modes of infection such as by inhalation of droplets or through infected milk, and the general state of health and hence resistance in the child. It has been suggested that the severity of the disease has varied over time, so that in the seventeenth century for example, it was known as a mild disease.[74] In the eighteenth century, Creighton referred to destructive epidemics of scarlet fever, and by the end of the century it seems to have been regarded as the leading epidemic disease.[75] Although it had been well described by then, deaths were classified in the 'fevers' group and some may have been confused with measles and even with milder manifestations of typhus.[76]

At the beginning of the nineteenth century, records kept by a physician at the Public Dispensary and Fever Institution in London for the period 1804–16, have been taken to indicate that scarlatina was a mild disease at this time, although still common.[77] Any phase of low mortality attributed to scarlet fever certainly ended in the 1830s, and in the first few years of registration from 1836–9 many deaths were attributed to the disease and the number doubled by 1840. Major epidemics of scarlet fever were reported in all parts of England in the 1840s, but the most destructive epidemics were in the 1850s and 1860s when it was the leading cause of death among children. One suggestion is that the increased death rate from scarlet fever could have been due to a more virulent form of *H. streptococcus*, perhaps having come from Ireland with the influx of immigrants affected by famine. There is some indication of a universal influence such as this in the similar death rate from scarlet fever recorded in different districts in Manchester in 1840–2, when rates for other causes and for total mortality differed by as much as 100%. The introduction of a new organism might have obliterated mortality differentials that would be expected in view of different living conditions and economic status. On the other hand, the better-off may have made more use of milk supplies which were also a source of severe infection offsetting any other advantages their children might have had.[78]

Whether or not a new strain of *H. streptococcus* was introduced into England in the mid nineteenth century, it is equally uncertain whether the declining death rate from scarlet fever from the 1870s was the result of a milder strain. The death rate from the disease also declined in a similar way in Ireland as shown in Appendix 5, and it seems likely that a reduced incidence of severe illness occurred in both countries for the same reasons. There was an increase in the death rate from diphtheria in both countries, but any transfer of recording could only explain part of the decline. Apart from the possibility that a different strain of *H. streptococcus* might have become prevalent, it may be that resistance was affected by health status and general well-being, and particularly by the influence of recent and concurrent infections. Given that many children harbour *H. streptococcus* in their throats, infection may have been triggered off in particularly adverse circumstances. Disruption in the household during other major epidemics,and even concurrent infection, might have provoked more severe manifestations of scarlet fever. Typhus epidemics receded rapidly in

Table 5.1   The ratio of deaths to cases of scarlet fever in Sweden in relation to the control of smallpox

| Years | Number of cases | | Deaths : Cases |
	Smallpox	Scarlet fever	Scarlet fever
1861–1870	3,992	7,172	0.40
1871–1880	3,823	8,159	0.42
1881–1890	358	10,334	0.23
1891–1900	63	8,623	0.10
1901–1910	11	8,321	0.05

Source: Historisk Statistik för Sverige I, Befolkung: 1720–1950 (Stockholm: Statistiska Centralbyran, 1955).

most parts of England after 1870, and the recession and resurgence of both smallpox and typhus in the nineteenth century, which occurred for different reasons, roughly coincided with the changing level of scarlet-fever mortality.

The pattern of decline in the death rate from scarlet fever in both England and Wales and Ireland, does show some similarity with the decline in the death rate from smallpox, but there is no consistent association between peaks in mortality for the two diseases which did not have the same epidemic cycle. Case numbers for the two diseases were recorded in Sweden and the data in Table 5.1 indicate a dramatic reduction in the incidence of smallpox in the 1880s, and a rapid decline in the death rate from scarlet fever despite the undiminished level of incidence. The ratio of deaths to cases gives some indication of case-fatality even if records were incomplete, and this was 0.23 in the 1880s, compared with about 0.4 in the 1860s and 1870s. The rapid decline in the death rate attributed to the disease in England and Wales from the 1880s, probably reflected a genuine fall in case-fatality in view of this evidence from Sweden. At this time in England more children with severe infections were being placed in isolation fever hospitals. In Birmingham, for example, 70% of reported cases of infectious disease were treated in such establishments in 1886–9, compared with only 14% in 1882–5, when these were mainly scarlet fever and smallpox cases. The proportion reached 83% by 1890–3, and even though case-fatality may have been only slightly lower among the hospitalised, the increasing use of isolation hospitals might have reduced the rate of infection from severe cases.[79]

The decline in the death rate recorded as due to diphtheria after 1863 lessens the possibility that 'transfer' of deaths from the scarlet fever category occurred at that time, although the diseases may have been confused earlier because of the common symptom of sore throat.[80] The difficulty of attributing too much credibility to the trends in death rates for these separate causes is further compounded by the fact that membranous croup was probably also confused with diphtheria until after the identification of the diphtheria bacillus in 1882. Croup was a general term for obstruction of the breathing from which many children undoubtedly died, but when diphtheria was prevalent this was probably the commonest cause of croup. When it was not, parainfluenza viruses seem likely to have been responsible as they are today.[81] Until the 1890s the annual death rates for the two diseases fluctuated in a similar way, although diphtheria itself may have been less prevalent than in France before the severe epidemic which reached many parts of England in 1855. In view of the confusion between all three of these diseases they should probably be considered as a group before the 1890s. However, it can be noted that the increase in the death rate from diphtheria alone in the 1880s and early 1890s, did not offset the very considerable decline in the death rate attributed to scarlet fever, together with that attributed to croup.

Antitoxin for use in diphtheria infection was developed in the 1880s and became widely used in the mid 1890s, being unique as a successful treatment measure against infectious disease. This was noted by McKeown in his study of the possible role of curative medicine in mortality decline before the mid twentieth century.[82] It has also been pointed out that the death rate from diphtheria in London fever hospitals declined from 63% in 1894 to 12% by 1910.[83] There are also indications of a change in case-fatality in the general population of Italy and Norway, and data given in Table 5.2 suggest that the proportion of infected children dying from diphtheria probably declined rapidly from the mid 1890s. The death rate among the most affected 0–14 year age group does appear to have followed the epidemic pattern of incidence in both countries, so that some reduction in mortality might have occurred anyway at this time with the passing of a major epidemic wave. However, the most important factor in the long-term decline in the diphtheria death rate appears to have been antitoxin, which reduced the risk of dying among the infected.

Table 5.2 The ratio of deaths to cases for measles and diphtheria in Norway and Italy*

| | *Italy* | | | *Norway* | |
Years	Measles	Diphtheria	Years	Measles	Diphtheria
			1874–1876	0.034	0.144
1888–1890	0.10	0.55	1882	0.037	0.195
1891–1893	0.11	0.54	1890–1892	0.042	0.230
1894–1896	0.09	0.49	1893–1895	0.036	0.211
1897–1899	0.05	0.37	1896–1898	0.029	0.152
1900–1902	0.06	0.29	1899–1901	0.034	0.113
1903–1905	0.06	0.23	1902–1904	0.026	0.084
1906–1908	0.06	0.24	1905–1907	0.020	0.075
1909–1911	0.07	0.24	1908–1910	0.020	0.078
1912–1914	0.05	0.22	1911–1913	0.020	0.073

* These are only an indication of changes in case-fatality being based on separate records of deaths and cases. It is of course possible that an under-recording of cases may have contributed to the higher 'case-fatality' in Italy.

Sources: Central Bureau of Statistics (1880–) *Health Statistics* (Oslo); Central Institute of Statistics (1956–) *Cause di Morte, 1887–1955, Annuaria di Statistiche Sanitarie* (Rome).

There is some similarity in the trends in death rates for measles and diphtheria, with the long-term decline beginning for both diseases in the 1890s, although for measles it was not very rapid or continuous until after 1910. (See, for example, the data for London in Appendix 5c.) The ratios of deaths to cases in Italy and Norway shown in Table 5.2 indicate a decline for both diseases from the same time in the 1890s. Although such early data on incidence should be treated with caution, case-fatality might initially have been reduced because of hospitalised care for those infected, while this could also have reduced the risk of infection spreading. However, there are many epidemiological and socio-demographic factors that affect the rate of transmission and outcome of the childhood infectious diseases. Like diphtheria, measles had an independent cycle of epidemics which is now known to respond to changes in the proportion of new susceptibles in the population,[84] and to changing patterns of social contact.[85] The rise in measles mortality in Paris in the second half of the nineteenth century was thought to have been linked with growing school attendance.[86] In England, the Education Act of 1870 certainly led to a rapid increase in both school places and school attendance which could have speeded up the spread of infection.[87]

Conditions of overcrowding and poverty persisted for large numbers of people in many towns, and any improvements – such as higher wages for those in work, and new housing – did not result in sustained decline in the measles death rate before the twentieth century. An association of high infectious-disease mortality with crowded living conditions could be due to increased rates of intercurrent infection, as well as to a greater dosage of virus which might be significant in some diseases. Data from Birmingham indicate an association between poor housing conditions and high death rates from measles and scarlet fever, and even for typhoid there was more of an association than with sanitary provision for example.[88] There were local Housing Acts for some towns in the 1860s which linked housing with sanitary policy, and later Acts extended the objective of slum clearance to other cities including London.[89] In Manchester there was no direct municipal involvement in house building until the 1890s as mentioned, which probably meant that overcrowding was not alleviated until the twentieth century.[90] The Royal Commission on Housing of the Poor in 1885 recognised that the major housing problem was overcrowding rather than sanitation, and this was exacerbated because population growth increased the demand for housing in the inner-city areas which led to high rents and the need for people to share accommodation. The period 1891–1911 does appear to be one in which there was house building at a rate that was more in line with population growth.[91] However, it has been questioned whether changes in crowding – as indicated by census data for England and Wales on numbers of persons per room – would have had any significant effect on the transmission of air-borne infectious diseases independently of changes in household composition and family size.[92]

The large families and crowded living conditions which were a feature of Victorian England would have exacerbated the infectious-disease environment, particularly among the poorer sections of society already at greater risk because of inadequate nutrition. The relationship between the risk of mortality from measles and living conditions, family size, age at infection and nutritional status has been considered in studies conducted in Guinea–Bissau. Measles virus does not appear to change or vary in virulence, but the severity of the illness varies considerably and evidence from the 1979 measles epidemic in one urban district showed that case-fatality was higher in households where several children caught the disease.[93] It was also found that fatality risk was inversely related to age at infection, such that if contact with measles were delayed, mortality could be reduced even if nutrition was not improved.[94] Such findings on the incidence and severity of measles in malnourished and crowded communities may have important implications for immunisation programmes in developing countries. They also contribute to an understanding of how the long-term decline in the death rate from measles occurred in the industralised countries before this preventive measure became available.

Historical data from Sunderland for 1885 have also revealed that measles mortality was higher in households with multiple cases, while severe complications were associated with greater number of siblings.[95] Therefore any reduction in family size that is implied by a falling birth rate from the 1870s, might have had an important effect on the rate of transmission of air-borne infections, and reduced the risk of contracting micro-organisms at an early, more vulnerable age. A further study of data from England and Wales investigated the hypothesis that the decline in the birth rate, inasmuch as it reflected reduced family size, led to an increase in the median age at infection for most childhood diseases. Case-fatality was much higher at ages 1–2 than at ages 3–4 years so that a shift in the age at infection could have appreciably reduced the risk of dying. Measles mortality at ages 5–9 years was found to have increased over the first two decades of the twentieth century, and it was suggested that there had been a major shift in the age distribution of measles infections associated with the decline in measles mortality in infancy.[96] For measles it may not have been until after the turn of the century, when even the absolute number of births declined,that these changes predominated over other factors affecting the transmission of the disease.[97]

Recent work on the population biology of infectious diseases has emphasised the important factor, Ro, the transmission rate, and the significance of demographic variables such as population size and density, and family size as reflected in the birth rate, which may affect the number of new cases arising from one infected individual.[98] Thus demographic changes can have deterministic implications for the impact of infectious disease, and in turn these can have deterministic effects on fertility levels. However, the relative role of such changes compared with voluntaristic changes which may have been linked with the economic standard of living and education, has not been established. A significant correlation has been found between child-mortality and fertility levels in the counties of England for the years around the final downturn in the 1870s. The immediate association between short-term changes in child mortality and fertility has been taken to be consistent with the idea that socio-economic changes were a common cause.[99] However, this might also reflect some deterministic interaction between these variables. As well as the possible effect of socio-demographic changes on the severity of infection, increased child survival could in turn have had some effect on periods of infertility associated with breast-feeding, and hence would have tended to increase birth intervals.[100] The inter-relationship between child-mortality and fertility levels is likely to be complex and two-way. Further investigation might concentrate on the 1–4 age group, since infant mortality was not found to be correlated with marital fertility in the period 1901–31.[101]

The contemporary evidence from Guinea–Bissau suggests that changes in the severity of air-borne infections can occur independently of changes in the economic standard of living, for epidemiological-demographic reasons. From the end of the nineteenth century any synergistic relationship between declining child mortality and fertility may have been enhanced by voluntaristic changes, in attitudes towards having children, and in attitudes to the children themselves as their prospects for survival were seen to improve, particularly between the ages of one and four. Improvements in general education and more specific knowledge about basic child care were also becoming more widely available, and the nature of contagious diseases was more widely understood following the acceptance of the Germ Theory, so there was probably increasingly better care, and more food available for a deliberately smaller number of children. Reductions in family size together with other efforts to alleviate overcrowded housing conditions, would have helped to reduce the transmission rate and raise the age at infection, hence reducing the severity of many infectious diseases, and all these advances could have been important in sustaining the decline in child mortality in the twentieth century.

Summary

It has often been suggested that changes in the standard of living, and particularly in nutrition, were a major contributing factor in the decline in infectious-disease mortality. Apart from the lack of convincing evidence relating to the early phase of mortality decline from the mid eighteenth century, the nineteenth century saw the recession of the particularly virulent epidemic diseases – smallpox, typhus and cholera – which would kill a large proportion of those infected whatever their economic circumstances. There is also the problem of accounting for a variety of trends in cause- and age-specific death rates in the second half of the nineteenth century, before the more consistent decline for all infectious diseases in the twentieth century. For this final phase of the mortality transition there is considerable evidence that there was an increase in the height of children which is an indication of improved nutritional status. However, it is not clear whether improved nutrition played an important role in this change, since many endogenous and exogenous constraints affect the relative success of the body in converting food into growth. Data from other countries confirm the trend and suggest improvements from the 1870s onwards, with a more rapid increase for adults as well in the twentieth century. The fact that the increase for adults has not been as great has been taken to suggest that the increase in child height has probably been the result of earlier maturation, and records on age at menarche show that girls have indeed reached this stage of life progressively earlier.[102] Clearly the trend towards smaller families should have improved the chances of children receiving adequate food whether or not there were improvements in real family incomes for particular sections of society. However, children in smaller families could also have had advantages through a reduced risk of infectious diseases leading to severe illness which interfered with growth. Also, death rates declined for all infectious diseases in England in the twentieth century, regardless of the extent to which undernutrition is known to contribute to the risk of dying,[103] and other factors seem likely to have been involved.

The decline in infectious-disease mortality in the period from the mid nineteenth century to 1971 accounted for at least three-quarters of the decline in the overall death rate, but no convincing case has yet been presented to support the view that improved nutrition was the most important factor in reducing death rates. In his early work, McKeown (with Record) argued that improvements in the standard of living and particularly in diet were responsible for about half of the decline in the overall age-standardised death rate between 1848–54 and 1901, particularly through improved resistance to respiratory tuberculosis.[104] In England and Wales, falling death rates from endemic tuberculosis did contribute most to the decline in the overall death rate in the second half of the nineteenth century, but in this period death rates for some infectious diseases actually increased, indicating the importance of factors other than the standard of living. The declining death rate from respiratory tuberculosis in fact contributed 0.33 towards each unit of decline in the overall death rate, but even this may have been exaggerated because of increasingly more accurate certification. Changes in the quality of food were probably involved in the further contribution of 0.04 towards each unit of decline in the overall death rate made by non-respiratory tuberculosis in both the periods 1848–54 to 1901, and 1901 to 1971. The introduction of pasteurised milk and the monitoring of food were manifestations of the growing awareness of the disease-transmission process that came in the last two decades of the nineteenth century, following the new bacteriological discoveries and acceptance of the Germ Theory. However, for respiratory tuberculosis the dosage of bacillus contracted in an initial infection may have been a more important variable than improvements in nutrition *per se*. Any improvements in ventilation could have been beneficial, while isolation of the sick could also have reduced transmission rates. Even so, concerted efforts to control the spread of the disease were not made until the 1890s after the causal agent had been identified and the contagion theory confirmed. The decline in the death rate before this may in part have reflected more accurate diagnosis of respiratory diseases, but some of the decline in cohort death rates could have been linked with the prevention of a different disease, smallpox, which had probably exacerbated the outcome of tubercular infection. Children may have benefited initially but postponement of clinical tubercular infection until later in life may have been significant in the falling adult mortality observed over successive cohorts.

The virtual elimination of such a serious disease as smallpox at the end of the nineteenth century probably brought some general improvement in the health and physical development of children. The decline in the overall death rate and that among children aged 1–4 years from the 1870s, also reflected the final recession of typhus epidemics which probably involved factors affecting the transmission of the disease. The end of immigration from famine-stricken Ireland may have been significant in this, while conditions there might also have affected the severity of scarlet fever introduced into England. The further drop in child mortality in the 1880s may have reflected some additional benefit from the use of isolation hospitals for severe cases of childhood infectious diseases such as scarlet fever, which could have reduced case-fatality and further interrupted transmission from severe cases. In view of these possibilities, McKeown and Records' suggestion that changes in the nature of micro-organisms, and scarlet fever in particular, were involved in a quarter of the decline in the crude death rate in the second half of the nineteenth century,[105] seems likely to be exaggerated. Recorded scarlet-fever mortality in fact contributed 0.12 towards each unit of decline in the death rate, and many other factors could have been involved including changing rates of intercurrent infection and mis-diagnosis.

Any combination of intercurrent infections would have been more likely to result in a child dying, but some diseases such as diphtheria and measles were more consistently killers in their own right in the prevailing conditions of the nineteenth century. The use of antitoxin was exceptional as a treatment measure which contributed to a reduction in death rates, while treatment of children in isolation hospitals can also be viewed as a preventive intervention. The lower birth rate from the 1870s, and more particularly the lower numbers of new susceptibles after the turn of the century, could also have reduced transmission rates, raised the age at infection, and hence reduced severity and the risk of fatality from air-borne infectious diseases such as measles. Bronchitis and broncho-pneumonia are also frequent secondary complications of measles and whooping cough, for example, in crowded, poverty-stricken living conditions. The transmission of other air-borne epidemic diseases also appears to be linked significantly with the presence of child susceptibles in the household, so that a fall in family size could have been significant for adult as well as child mortality. The risk to adults from whooping cough may have been affected, but the overall pattern of change in respiratory-disease mortality may have been more closely linked with the risk of infection with influenza and phneumonococci in which children appear to play a major role. Demographic changes from the end of the nineteenth century, together with new housing schemes,could have contributed to a reduced impact of many infectious and respiratory diseases even if nutritional resistance was not improving significantly among the poorer sections of society.

The possibility of inter current infections affecting mortality risk, has highlighted again the general problem in attempting to quantify the contribution to total mortality decline made by separate diseases, since indirect causes of death, and indeed mis-recording, are not allowed for in rigid accounting terms.[106] The decline in recorded smallpox mortality only contributed about 0.05 towards each unit of decline in the overall death rate in the second half of the nineteenth century. However, secondary effects of the disease are not allowed for in such an unqualified component analysis and this is also the case for the earlier period of the mortality transition. For the period 1901–71, the contribution to each unit of decline in the overall death rate made by falling death rates from measles and whooping cough was probably much greater than the 0.05 suggested by the registration data. Simple quantitative analysis is also misleading because of the links between respiratory causes of death and the air-borne infectious-disease environment. Again, changes in transmission rates as a result of socio-demographic changes, and any improvements in housing which alleviated overcrowded and damp living conditions, may have been more important for mortality decline from air-borne infectious and respiratory diseases in the first half of the twentieth century, than improved economic circumstances and nutrition. Clearly changes in attitudes to family size may have been in part a function of changes in social and economic circumstances, but the will to take action at the community level is likely to have been important for housing improvements, given the economic insecurity of a large section of the population in a free-market economy subject to the kind of recession that occurred in the 1930s.

The downturn in respiratory-disease mortality from the end of the nineteenth century seems more likely to have been a product of socio-demographic changes affecting the air-borne infectious-disease environment rather than a direct result of any improvement in people's own economic standard of living or nutrition. This change in mortality recorded as due to respiratory diseases – including bronchitis, pneumonia and influenza – contributed 0.19 towards each unit of decline in the overall death rate in the period 1901–71, and the group had taken over from the water-, food- and insect-borne diseases as a major component of mortality change since typhus and cholera had been virtually eliminated. The initiation of anti-tuberculosis programmes from this time, as well as the last significant smallpox outbreak and the final downturn in infant mortality, make the turn of the century a natural point at which to split the mortality decline for the whole period from 1848–54 to 1971. The change in the pattern of cause-specific mortality decline after 1900 in England, with mortality from many more diseases contributing,[107] is reflected in the more rapid improvement in average life expectancy shown in Figure 2.2. The downturn in infant mortality was a major contributing factor as indicated in Appendix 6a, but improvements in the expectation of life occurred at all ages, and among adults, in spite of the adverse trends in mortality from some non-communicable causes of death which will be considered in the next chapter.

6 The transition to non-communicable disease mortality patterns

The decline in infectious-disease mortality described in previous chapters has been accompanied by an increasing expectation that children should survive to adulthood, and that human intervention can be effective in preventing mortality from such causes. There has been a shift in the age pattern of mortality as shown in Appendix 6a, with an increasingly higher proportion of deaths in adulthood compared with the high proportion of infant and child mortality in the nineteenth century and in developing countries today. Even so, survival chances for adolescents and young adults also improved in the second half of the nineteenth century as shown in Appendix 6b, particularly with the decline in the death rate from respiratory tuberculosis, and this continued in the twentieth century with mortality from other respiratory diseases contributing. After the turn of the century, survival rates for infants improved dramatically and average life expectancy increased at all ages as death rates from many more causes, including some non-communicable diseases, declined. Increases in average expectation of life, and expectations of a longer lifespan, have focused attention on the various manifestations of 'premature' mortality among adults in the middle age groups. Non-communicable diseases have become the predominant cause of death as death rates from infectious diseases have declined, and they now account for most mortality in industrialised countries.

The growing proportion of deaths in the twentieth century attributed to heart disease, stroke, cancer and other non-communicable diseases, such as diabetes, cirrhosis of the liver and ulcers, was described by Omran as a transition to a 'new age of man-made or degenerative diseases' in a study of data from New York.[1] Adult males have been more at risk, as found in a study of heart disease and lung cancer in the Netherlands and other countries but it was pointed out that aetiology had not been fully understood.[2] Different aspects of life style and environment have been linked with the major non-communicable diseases for which increasing mortality has been observed, and such changes might be seen as detracting from the idea of improving health and quality of life resulting from the success of human intervention in the infectious-disease processes. Something of a 'preventive health revolution' has occurred, and contributed to improving human productivity and standard of living, as well as increasing survival chances at all ages. However, there are great inequalities in health and in the risk of dying at an 'early' age among different socio-economic groups and populations, as well as between the sexes.

The trend towards excess male mortality has accompanied economic modernisation, and reflected higher death rates from circulatory disease in particular. Changes in non-agricultural employment and the concentration of population accompanying urbanisation have been associated with this sex differential in mortality, but other related variables have clearly also been involved.[3] Preston considered whether genetic or socio-cultural factors – such as occupational stress – could have borne more heavily on males, but found these difficult to link with the trends in death rates that had occurred. Physical factors were thought to be more significant and almost all the sex differences in cancer death-rate trends in the twentieth century were found to be attributable to cigarette-smoking through lung cancer. The habit was also implicated in higher mortality risk from heart disease, emphysema, and bronchitis,[4] but it would not have been significant in the increasing death rates in England and Wales in the second half of the nineteenth century. Certain aspects of long-term trends in mortality from the major non-communicable diseases in England and Wales will be referred to here, which together with differentials in mortality between socio-economic groups in Western populations, and known levels of mortality in the less industrial populations of the South, further indicate that the major non-communicable diseases cannot be understood in generalised terms as products of 'affluence' or the 'modern way of life'.

Many studies have contributed to a growing understanding of behavioural and environmental-risk factors identified as contributing to mortality from the major non-communicable diseases in 'middle age', and reference will be made here to some of the main findings. However, the risk factors that have been identified still only explain part of the differentials in mortality between sections of the population, while it is difficult to link long-term trends in mortality with the main established contemporary risks. In reviewing epidemiological aspects of the major non-communicable causes of death against a historical background of declining general mortality, the changing impact of the infectious-disease environment will be considered here as a possible influence in itself. Among environmental-risk factors, micro-organisms and adverse effects of cellular and immune reactions to them may be significant for an understanding of both underlying aetiology and trends in mortality from the non-communicable diseases which have replaced communicable diseases as the major causes of death.

Long-term trends in mortality from non-communicable diseases will be examined using registration data from England and Wales available from the mid nineteenth century onwards. Increasing death rates for circulatory disease and cancer in the second half of the nineteenth century added 1.4

to the overall death rate per 1,000. While this was offset by the contribution to decline made by reductions in mortality classified as due to unknown causes and 'old age', the increases for some specified causes may not be entirely explicable in terms of such transfers,[5] or survival to older ages at which non-communicable diseases more usually occur. Undoubtedly some of the increase in non-communicable disease death rates in the second half of the nineteenth century resulted from improved recognition and specification. Nevertheless, major turning points in the long-term trends for non-communicable diseases contributing significantly to overall mortality in England and Wales probably have some genuine significance and will be examined here. In addition to circulatory disease and cancer, a third group of rather heterogenous non-communicable diseases – including diabetes, nephritis, cirrhosis of the liver and peptic ulcers – will also be referred to briefly, although they have been less significant for overall mortality and accounted for about 3% of all deaths· in England and Wales in 1981. Of deaths due to disease in 1981, 90% were attributed to circulatory disease, cancer and respiratory diseases; and of the remaining 10%, the main causes were digestive diseases, rheumatic diseases and diseases of the genito-urinary and nervous systems.[6]

In all discussion of twentieth century trends, changes in the international methods of classification of diseases need to be borne in mind. (See Appendix 6c.) Diagnostic change may mean that very long-term trends are misleading, such as the increases in death rates for minor non-communicable diseases shown in Appendix 6d. There has been both 'inter-group' and 'intra-group' diagnostic error, but recent evidence suggests that for the major order groups such as circulatory disease and cancer, errors tend to have cancelled each other out. A study of both ante-mortem and post-mortem diagnoses carried out in 1975–6, using a sample of 1,200 patients in England and Wales, found that the three main cause groups, circulatory disease, cancer and respiratory disease, accounted for 73.2% of deaths before autopsy, and 73.8% on re-classification after autopsy. About 40.8% of deaths were attributed to circulatory disease before autopsy, and about 44.0% on re-classification after autopsy, while for cancer the proportions were even closer, at 21.7% and 21.3%. In fact the proportion of diagnoses that had changed to another International Classification of Diseases (ICD) order group was 16.3% for circulatory disease and 23.8% for cancer, with less than half the deaths in the three main order groups being attributed to the correct subcategory before autopsy. However, the significant figure here is the percentage error after 'transfers in' and 'transfers out', which was only +0.4 for cancer, −3.2 for circulatory disease, and +2.1 for respiratory disease.[7]

A review of studies carried out between 1917 and 1970, concluded that there was no evidence that the proportion of errors had changed over this period, although the types of disease and mistakes in diagnosis had altered.[8] In the nineteenth century many deaths at ages 65 and over were assigned to the 'ill-defined' and 'old age' categories, although at ages 45–64 the proportion among male deaths in 1848–72 was only 1.8%, so that the fall to negligible levels by the 1950s would not have distorted cause-specific mortality trends.[9] However, there is a further problem concerning multiple cause of death, since certification of the underlying cause is obviously difficult when any of the competing risks might have eventually proved fatal.[10] Recording of circulatory-disease mortality in particular may have been affected, with variations in the practice of giving respiratory disorders as a secondary cause of death. Nevertheless, a consideration of relative trends for the broad categories of disease should mean that errors lie within the limitations discussed, and major turning points can be detected.

Circulatory-disease mortality trends in England and Wales

An early indication of the known mortality from stroke and circulatory diseases can be found in the London Bills of Mortality under such categories as 'apoplexy' and 'palsy'. Black pointed out that these terms often 'alternated' in the records, and he took them to be basically a reflection of the same cause of death.[11] He noted that palsy – including paralysis, hemiplegia and paraplegia – accounted for about one-third as many deaths as apoplexy which he thought included 'polypi' or coagulations of the blood, internal aneurysm or distension and weakness of the arteries, and palpitation of the heart. He concluded that these types of disorder, together with syncope and asphyxy, were part of the category denoted by the crude terms, 'apoplexy' and 'sudden death'. There was an increase in apoplexy mortality in the first few decades of the nineteenth century, along with increases in measles and whooping-cough burial rates, as indicated in Appendix 3d. Heberden noted the increase in deaths at the turn of the century, but rejected the explanation that increased consumption of alcohol and tea was responsible.[12]

Recent studies of trends in circulatory-disease mortality have tended to trace back death rates on a comparable basis for major component subcategories, such as ischaemic heart disease, and cerebrovascular disease. However, as suggested, the death rate for the groups as a whole may be the only reliable unit for analysis, and an 'M-shaped' trend for total circulatory-disease mortality is indicated in Figure 6.1. The two peaks in the trend belie the idea of a 'modern epidemic' of circulatory disease, and it seems likely that the age-standardised death rate was at least as high at the end of the nineteenth century as after World War II, particularly when allowance is made for distortion because of possible transfers of 'old age' deaths. Further illustration of the major turning points in age-specific death rates in Figure 6.2 confirms the peak at the end of the nineteenth century among the middle age groups. A divergence of death rates in middle age for males and females is also apparent for the interwar period, and a decline in death rates has certainly occurred this century for females. At older ages death rates appear to have increased in the twentieth century from levels recorded in the second half of the nineteenth century, but this reflects a more significant transfer of 'old age' deaths. A mistaken idea of the trend in circulatory-disease mortality may have come from early studies of crude death rates for the population as a whole, which indicated increases from

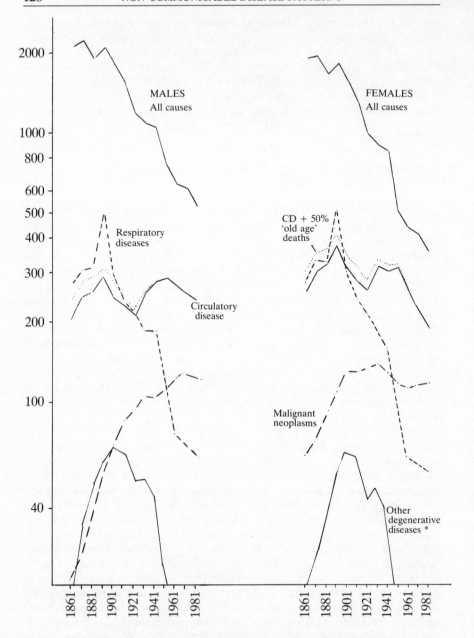

Figure 6.1   Age-standardised death rates per 100,000 population for cancer, circulatory disease and respiratory diseases in England and Wales, 1861–1981 (age-standardised to 1901 population).

* Peptic ulcer, nephritis, nephrosis, diabetes mellitus and cirrhosis of the liver.

Sources: S.H. Preston, N. Keyfitz and R. Schoen (1972) *Causes of Death, Life Tables for National Populations* (New York: Seminar Press), pp. 224–270; OPCS (1984) *Mortality Statistics, Cause, Series DH2* (London: HMSO).

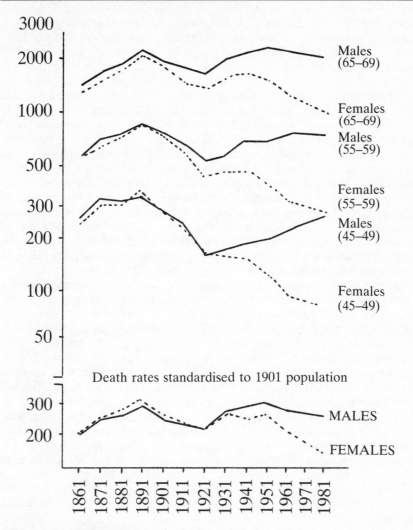

Figure 6.2 Age-specific death rates per 100,000 population for circulatory disease in England and Wales, 1861–1981.
Source: S.H. Preston, N. Keyfitz and R. Schoen (1972) *Causes of Death, Life Tables for Nationl Populations* (New York: Seminar Press), pp. 224–270.

the 1920s. The attempt to link these with increased survival to middle age was confused because changes in the age structure were not allowed for.[13] Such misinterpretation has since been avoided by examining age-specific death rates, but there are further difficulties because of increasingly more specific definition of primary cause.

A 'modern epidemic' of heart disease was observed when records specifying ischaemic heart-disease mortality became available for several years, but this increase must be considered in relation to other trends in circulatory-disease mortality since intergroup transfers seem likely to have occurred. Death rates for the age group 45–74 years revealed increasing ischaemic heart-disease mortality in the United States,[14] which was confirmed in a study of the period 1920 to 1940.[15] Original death certificates were examined in Ontario, and these suggested that a genuine increase in ischaemic heart-disease mortality had occurred between 1931 and 1951.[16] Even so, as mortality attributed to ischaemic heart disease or arteriosclerotic heart disease increased rapidly in the postwar period in England, that attributed to myocardial insufficiency or degeneration, and to hypertension, declined.[17] The decline ascribed to hypertension was most noticeable for females, and it seems likely that with the greater awareness of the role of this in ischaemic heart disease, there was some transfer of diagnosis.[18] There has been a recent decline in adult death rates for ischaemic heart disease reported for the United States,[19] although a review of data from England and Wales found no comparable decline by the 1970s.[20] In contrast, age-adjusted death rates for cerebrovascular disease have been falling from at least 1910, as in the United States.[21]

Death rates for cerebrovasuclar disease declined even more rapidly after World War II, and cerebral haemorrhage was the main component in this decline in England and Wales between 1932 and 1965.[22] Again, transfer of recording to other categories of circulatory disease was probably partly responsible, and at the turn of the century many deaths may have been recorded as 'apoplexy', which more recently came to be specified as coronary occlusion. Also, studies in the United States showed that the decline in the death rate from cerebral haemorrhage between 1920 and 1960 was partly offset by an increasing death rate for cerebral thrombosis,[23] which probably involved transfers. Nevertheless, the decline in cerebral-haemorrhage mortality outweighed other increases, and the total death rate for cerebrovascular disease declined even before the use of specific anti-hypertension medication. There were indications that an acceleration occurred with their introduction, but a review of specific medical interventions in relation to total circulatory-disease mortality concluded that factors other than these have played a major role in mortality decline.[24]

For circulatory disease as a whole, there was a decline in death rates for different adult age groups after World War II in the United States, with a more dramatic fall after 1968.[25] Death rates for total circulatory disease have also been reported as declining in Switzerland.[26] The decline in the total circulatory-disease death rate in England and Wales since the peak in 1950–1 is shown in Figure 6.3, which also illusrates the importance of changes in cerebrovascular-disease mortality in this trend. For other Western populations, trends in the circulatory-disease death rate reveal a downturn in recent decades in several countries.[27] Data from Italy from the 1880s in fact indicate a more consistent decline in circulatory-disease death rates this century,[28] although again there was some resurgence up to a second peak in the early 1950s, as in England and Wales. Such long-term trends in circulatory-disease mortality, including the 'M-shaped' trend for

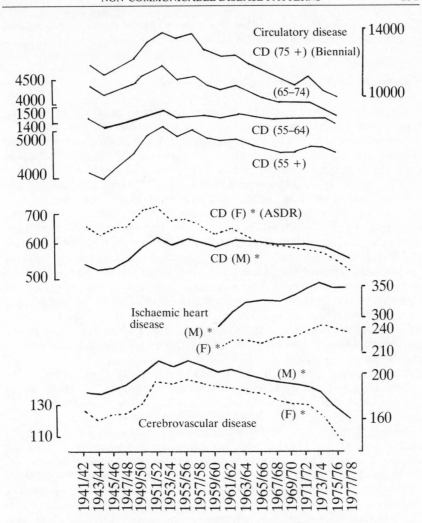

Figure 6.3 Age-specific and age-standardised death rates per 100,000 population for circulatory disease in England and Wales, 1941/2 to 1977/8.

* Rates are age- and sex-standardised using SMRs, which are ratios of observed to expected mortality if 1968 age-specific rates are applied to the population of each year, with 1968 = 100. Ratios have been converted to rates by taking the actual death rate for the base year, 1968. ICD group VII includes 390–458 (8th revision); 330–334, 400–468 (6th, 7th); 58, 83, 90–103 (4th); 51, 74, 75, 83, 87–90, 91b, c (3rd); 47, 64–66, 77–85, 142 (2nd).

Source: Data published by Registrar-General and OPCS.

England and Wales, suggest that risk factors are not continuously related to increasing industrialisation for example.

Cancer mortality trends in England and Wales

There were early references to cancer as another form of 'tubercle' at the end of the eighteenth century, and cancer did not in fact appear as prominently in pre-registration records of cause of death as did heart disease and stroke under their crude classification terms. There was probably confusion between cancer and consumption until reference was made specifically to malignant tumours in 1837, and 'carcinoma' and 'genuine crude tubercle' were distinguished in 1855.[29] For many years pathologists were interested in the definition of differences in these disorders. However, discussion arose about the possibility of some kind of special inverse relationship between the diseases and the mortality attributed to them. One suggestion was that there was some kind of 'antagonism' between the two diseases, although examples had been found of both at the same time.[30] The idea of a link between the death rates was reported with data from New South Wales, Australia, for the second half of the nineteenth century.[31] The work of Cherry in the 1920s and 1930s, and several studies in the 1960s, drew attention to both statistical and pathological associations between the two disease groups, but no theory of pathogenesis has been developed which might link tuberculosis and cancer.[32] Other aspects of the trends in mortality from cancer over different cohorts will be examined here, and these raise questions about the nature of this group of diseases which like other non-communicable diseases have been thought of as diseases of industrialisation.

Trends in death rates from cancer among females appear to belie the idea of a simple relationship between this group of diseases and increasing industrialisation. There appears to have been an actual peak in age-specific death rates among cohorts of females born in mid nineteenth-century England and Wales, as shown in Figure 6.4, although this is not a feature of other long-series data, for example for Italy and New Zealand.[33] Annual death rates confirm this 'cohort turning point' in mortality, but important period influences are also suggested in an analysis by year of death.[34] For males, mortality attributed to cancer has generally been increasing since at least the mid nineteenth century, independently of changes in the age structure of the population, although trends in age-specific mortality in relation to year of birth reveal a reduction in rates of increase for cohorts born after the 1860s. The period trends in age-specific death rates at ages over 35 years again show a difference between the sexes, with male mortality increasing more rapidly after World War II in an earlier resurgence than that for females around 1961. The different pattern of increase in lung-cancer mortality after the war for males and females, shown in Figure 6.5, underlies this, and probably reflects the greater influence of increased cigarette-smoking among males during the war,[35] with a later increase among females. Increases for both sexes were more

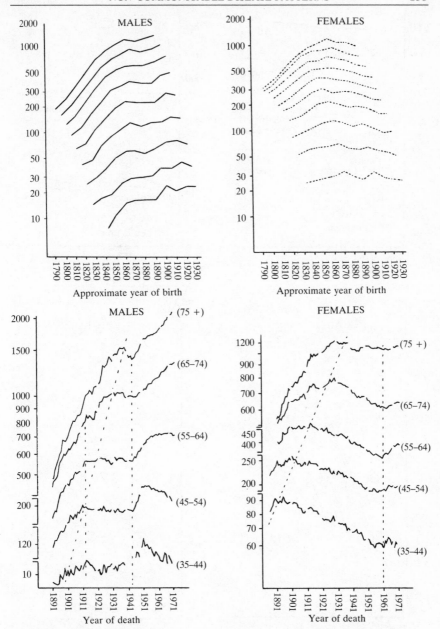

Figure 6.4 Death rates per 100,000 population at different adult ages for all malignant neoplasms in England and Wales, by year of birth and annually by year of death, 1790–1930.

Sources: S.H. Preston, N. Keyfitz and R. Schoen (1972) *Causes of Death, Life Tables for National Populations* (New York: Seminar Press), pp. 224–272; Registrar-General (1880–) *Annual Reports* (London: HMSO).

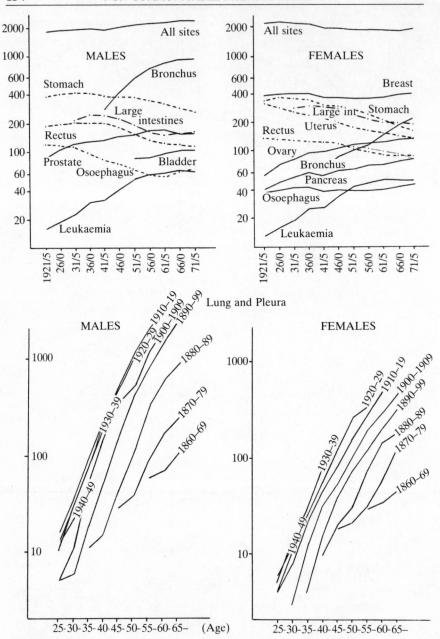

Figure 6.5 Age-standardised and age-specific death rates per 100,000 population for cancer in England and Wales, by site, and by cohort for lung and pleura, 1921/5 to 1971/5.

Source: Institute of Cancer Research (1976) *Serial Mortality Tables* (London). Quinquennial rates standardised directly using average population for 1951–5.

apparent for cohorts born before the 1920s, while the largest rise in cancer mortality was from lung cancer occurring among males. This was emphasised in the first cohort study of death rates for all twenty-one cancer sites,[36] in which death rates for the period 1911–54 were analysed by year of birth. These showed rising cancer mortality among males, but reductions for females, and only a few sites showed death rates that were still increasing over successive cohorts: the kidneys, the pharynx, the lung, the pancreas, the male urinary bladder, and the female genital organs.

Age-standardised death rates for the main sites appear to group into two main categories with regard to period trends in the first half of this century. Death rates for both males and females increased throughout for lung and bronchus, but rates for the alimentary-canal sites – including mouth, oesophagus, intestine, stomach, rectum and anus – increased in the first three or four decades and then declined thereafter, as did mortality from cancer of the breast.[37] These changes are probably the product of period-related factors, but the long-term pattern of female cancer mortality in England and Wales might reflect changes related to childhood experience, such that each generation has to some extent carried its own risk of cancer mortality into later life.

Differential mortality and risk factors in the main non-communicable diseases

The long-term trends in mortality for the major groups of non-communicable disease in England and Wales outlined here, could have been significantly different from those in other countries with regard to major turning points. However, because few sets of data exist for the second half of the nineteenth century, comparisons with the experience of other countries may be more meaningful when confined to twentieth-century data. For this period circulatory disease, for example, made some contribution to overall mortality decline in England and Wales, reflecting a fairly continuous decline in female death rates. This experience is consistent with a model based on international data indicating that female mortality from circulatory disease has fallen with overall mortality levels except at very old ages at which transfers from the 'old age' category had occurred.[38] However, the resurgence of circulatory-disease mortality in England and Wales reflected a rapid increase in the death rate from heart disease among males between the wars, which contrasts with trends for most other diseases as shown in Appendix 6d. Any reduction in the death rate from circulatory disease since the peak in the 1890s has been less than that for all causes, so that the group has continued to be an increasing component in the cause-of-death structure as it was in the nineteenth century. Circulatory disease and cancer alone now cause about 70% of all deaths in England and Wales, compared with only about one in ten in the mid nineteenth century. Age-standardised death rates by cause confirm that the 'aging' of the population alone has not been responsible, and the shift in disease patterns has occurred at different ages throughout

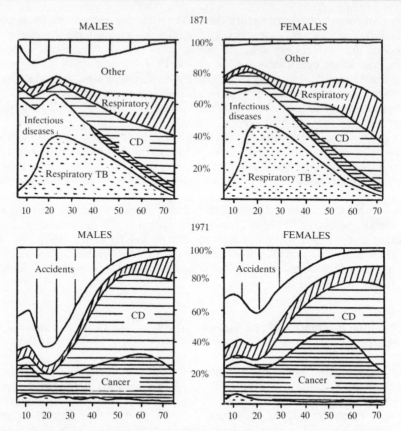

Figure 6.6   Proportion dying from the main cause-groups at different ages in England and Wales, in 1871 and 1971.
Sources: Registrar-General (1838–   ) *Annual Reports*, and (1900–   ) *Annual Statistical Reviews* (London: HMSO).

life, as illustrated in Figure 6.6. This also indicates the higher proportion of cancer deaths among young adult and middle-aged females compared with males who had higher death rates for heart disease.

In Western populations generally, about 60–70% of deaths are attributed to circulatory disease and cancer when there is almost complete recording of causes, and a similar proportion is recorded in data from the USSR and Eastern Europe.[39] In a recent study it was pointed out that in Hungary in 1980, for example, 49.8% of deaths among males were attributed to circulatory disease and 57.6% among females, while 20.0% and 18.3% of deaths were attributed to cancer. These diseases together with respiratory diseases had all made significant contributions to recent increases in age-standardised death rates for both sexes in that country.[40] The direction of trends in death rates for major non-communicable diseases differs between countries which have different economic circumstances, but there appears to be little consistent correlation between standard of living and levels of mortality from circulatory disease and cancer among Western populations. Gross domestic product (GDP) per head of population may be taken as a very crude indication of relative standard of living, and Western populations with estimates available showed a range of 4,000–14,000 US dollars in 1981.[41] Correlation coefficients for this indicator and cancer mortality at ages 45–54 years are −0.17 for males and +0.12 for females; circulatory-disease mortality among females at these ages is in fact negatively correlated with GDP per head; while that for males is positively correlated, and the coefficients are again very low at +0.19 and −0.33, and not statistically significant. All the nineteen countries included in this analysis, and shown in Appendix 6f, can be seen as 'affluent' anyway, and the transition to non-communicable causes of death should certainly be viewed in a global context.

Data for less industrially developed countries, while available, are generally less reliable because of bias in the coverage of recording towards the better-off and urban sections of the population. Nevertheless, the data from some countries, such as Trinidad, belie the notion of circulatory disease as a disease of affluence or the industrial way of life. In 1977, the death rates at ages 45–54, for example, were 660.7 per 100,000 for males and 216.4 for females,[42] which were almost double those in England and Wales and other Western populations. The very high death rate from cancer in middle age in Hong Kong may also genuinely indicate a population that is more at risk than in countries with larger concentrations of heavy industry. For males, at ages 45–54, there were 262.4 deaths per 100,000 population attributed to cancer in 1981, which was a higher rate than for most Western populations, while the rate for females was 145.4. The proportion of deaths that these rates represented was 42.7% for males and 43.5% for females, which again was exceptionally high. A study of mortality in Japan indicated that even by the 1950s the problem there, as in England and Wales, was mortality in middle age and disease among the elderly, rather than childhood infections which had been such a problem even in the interwar period in Japan.[43]

Despite the obvious association of the emergence of a new cause-of-death structure with increasing industrial development, it is significant that rural populations in developing countries are also affected by a high proportion of mortality attributed to non-communicable causes. The Khanna study of a rural area of Punjab in the 1950s showed that cancer exceeded even tuberculosis and heart disease as a cause of death in middle age.[44] In Asia generally deaths from circulatory disease now account for over 25% of deaths in areas where average life expectancy is over 60 years, while cancer is recorded in 5% of deaths.[45] Many developing countries now have a high proportion of adult deaths recorded as due to circulatory disease and cancer while still having high mortality from infectious diseases. In the Philippines in 1977, for example, 30% of deaths at ages 45–54 years were recorded as due to circulatory disease and cancer, and 30% to respiratory tuberculosis. Death rates at ages 45–54 for registration areas in mainland China in a recent 30-year period were between 110 and

145 per 100,000 for heart disease, cerebrovascular disease and cancer, such that about 55% of all deaths at these ages were attributed these causes – even in rural areas.[46]

In a general perspective on non-communicable disease patterns, social changes associated with urbanisation have been considered in many studies,[47] and there is now a vast literature on urban-rural variations in cancer mortality and morbidity, for example. A review of several studies emphasised that cancer occurs frequently in the less developed parts of the world as well, but cancer of specific sites shows larger international variation than mortality for the group as a whole.[48] Stocks was the first to examine cause-specific death rates for evidence of urban-rural differences, allowing for the age and sex distribution of the population.[49] His studies of cancer mortality showed a high correlation between environmental indices, such as persons per room, and death rates in middle age for cancer of the stomach and for bronchitis. This was also found to be the case for infectious diseases and respiratory tuberculosis, but not for lung cancer. 'All cancer' and bronchitis now appear to be most susceptible to urban-rural differences in mortality,[50] which may be linked with various forms of inhaled pollution, such as tobacco smoke, dust particles and the products of industrial and domestic fuel consumption.[51] The much higher death rates found in heavily industrialised areas may also be linked with both occupational and behavioural risks. For circulatory disease, regional differences in stroke and heart-disease mortality are highly correlated, which has been attributed to the role of atherosclerosis and high blood pressure in both.[52] Generally though, the influence of factors linked with urbanisation has been found to be relatively weak for circulatory disease as a whole, so that more favourable death rates in the south of England extend to the cities in that region. In the past, and in developing countries today, it may be wealthy urban dwellers who have been thought of as more at risk from coronary disease, but if hazardous behaviour is more readily adopted, avoidance of risks may be more quickly learned by them.[53]

Although area differentials in mortality have been found to be correlated with environmental factors such as hardness of water,[54] they may largely reflect economic, socio-cultural and occupational factors. In 1970–2 in England and Wales, adult death rates were higher for social classes IV–V than for classes I–II, in all but four minor categories of disease out of a total of ninety-two. In a recent study it was found that mortality from heart disease had been more common among women in classes IV–V over the whole period 1931–71. On the other hand, heart-disease mortality among men had been more common in social classes I–II in 1931 and 1951, but in 1961 it was more common in social classes IV–V than in classes I–II.[55] Again, lung cancer and duodenal ulcer, for example, showed no social-class gradient in adult mortality in 1931, but there is now a higher death rate from these causes in social classes IV–V than in classes I–II.[56] Certainly heart disease came to be thought of as a disease of affluence with the higher death rate observed in industrial societies and among higher socio-economic groups. Clearly this is no longer the case, even though changes in occupational composition of social-class groups mean that these do not represent comparable populations at different points in time.[57]

It has been suggested that changing social structure and the effects of health selection have resulted in an artificial widening of social-class differentials in mortality.[58] However, the use of alternatives to socio-economic classes based on occupation, suggests that observed differences are not just a product of one particular method of classification which at any time is related to the structure of the male labour force. By using mortality data linked with information collected at census, it has been found that other indicators of socio-economic status such as household tenure and access to a car can be used to identify other groups of men and women whose death rates are as different as those recorded for classes I and V,[59] Consideration of differentials in mortality in terms of these groups has the advantage that they consist of a larger proportion of the population, so that the level of excess-mortality risk associated with disadvantage does not relate only to a small and diminishing group.[60] The trend towards wider social-class differences in death rates between 1931 and 1981 might anyway relate to changing disease patterns as much as to changes in the occupational structure of the male labour force. Respiratory tuberculosis and pneumonia have been replaced as the major killers at working ages by lung cancer and ischaemic heart disease, which are more associated with life-long health-related behaviour known to vary with socio-economic circumstances. Although social differentiation of mortality varies with age and sex for different cause-groups, in general it is thought to have been a consequence of past changes at working ages involving this shift from communicable to the major non-communicable diseases.[61]

For lung cancer, death rates for each social class increased in the first half of the twentieth century, but then levelled off for higher socio-economic groups while only rising less rapidly for lower groups. This resulted in a clear social-class gradient of mortality after 1961 and it has been attributed to differential changes in cigarette-smoking among different cohorts. Increasing death rates from ischaemic heart disease, although affected by classification changes, brought a reversal of social-class gradient which probably involved differential changes in cigarette-smoking, and possibly diet and leisure activity as well.[62] Cigarette-smoking is also likely to be a major influence in current social-class differentials in mortality from many non-communicable diseases, while it has also been implicated in changing sex differentials in mortality from cancer, bronchitis and circulatory disease.[63] Preston found that mortality in the twentieth century varied in the expected manner with daily consumption of cigarettes, age at which smoking began, and length of time since discontinuing, if this had occurred.[64] Trends in consumption for several countries including England and Wales, revealed rapid increases since the 1930s,[65] which reflected the adoption of the habit on a much larger scale after World War I, initially among young men. A further study of changes in the United States concluded that about 75% of the increase in the male-female difference in life expectancy at ages over 50 years, between 1910 and 1962, could be accounted for by cigarette-smoking.[66]

Apart from cigarette-smoking, the role of diet, exercise and body weight in relation to height, has been investigated in relation to differentials in mortality among different groups in the population. There is a significant effect on mortality risk from circulatory disease when persons are over-weight by 50 pounds or more in relation to height, but the proportion that is so excessively overweight is quite small.[67] Obesity may be a common cause of hypercholesterolaemia and hypertension which are precursors of ischaemic heart disease, and few cases occur in the absence of both these largely independent conditions, as found in the Framingham study in the United States.[68] The hypothesis that a lack of physical exercise might be linked with a greater risk of ischaemic heart disease has been examined in occupational studies,[69] but an inclination to obesity might have been brought into a sedentary job. This was suggested as a possible reason for the higher incidence of coronary heart disease and hypertension found among busdrivers compared with busconductors and other occupational groups.[70] A study of British male doctors found a decline in the incidence of coronary heart disease over a recent twenty-year period and it was suggested that it might have been due to changes in health-related behaviour among this occupational group.[71] However, despite a large body of evidence linking increased risk with lack of physical exercise, fatty diet and smoking, these variables can only explain part of the occurrence.[72] A study of British civil servants showed that less than half the social-class differentials could be attributed to smoking, obesity, high blood pressure and plasma cholesterol.[73]

Risk factors and circulatory-disease mortality trends

The relationship between *changes* in coronary heart-disease mortality and consumption of dietary nutrients and cigarettes in different countries, has only recently been studied. The conflicting nature of the evidence is indicated by trends in circulatory-disease death rates which were negatively associated with changes in the consumption of animal fats, but also positively associated with milk intake which had declined.[74] Furthermore, dietary fibre may be important as a protective agent, as much as fat being an adverse factor. Another problem arises when changes over time are considered, in that changes in causally-related variables may not have an immediate effect in relation to mortality from circulatory disease. Consumption of dairy products and cigarettes increased in several countries between the 1950s and the mid 1970s, but coronary heart-disease death rates did not increase between 1969 and 1975, for example.[75] Significant correlations have also been found between consumption of nutrients, tobacco and other commodities for the period 1954–65, and the coronary heart-disease death rate, but only when the latter was considered for a later period 1969–75.[76] A lag between time series has also raised doubts concerning a possible stress-related link between ciculatory-disease mortality trends and unemployment.[77] It has been argued that some data can actually be presented in a way that indicates that high circulatory-disease mortality risk follows periods of prosperity and low unemployment.[78] Both work-related stress, and relative deprivation during unemployment could affect health, but stress is difficult to measure or even define.[79] Preston earlier found inconsistencies in this connection, such as the low death rates from circulatory disease among highly mobile, high-level professionals and administrators. Geographical mobility or changes in urban-rural residence might also involve stress, but it was found that time-series data on circulatory-disease mortality could not be linked with these variables.[80]

The overall 'M-shaped' trend for the ciculatory-disease death rate in England and Wales is not easily linked with even combinations of well-established risk factors, many of which undoubtedly correlate with higher adult death rates among different groups in the population. In view of this, it is necessary to consider the possibility that other risk factors have been influential in the fluctuations in mortality and particularly with regard to the recent fall in the circulatory-disease death rate. Evidence of a possibly important underlying feature of circulatory disorders has come from studies of the effect of viruses on blood, but this work seems to have received much less attention than studies of behavioural and environmental factors. Several studies since 1958 have tested the action of mumps and influenza viruses on human and animal blood, and indicated that agglutination of platelets occurs in their presence.[81] Mustard viewed such a formation of platelets which occludes the lumen of a blood vessel, as a similar process to that whereby blood responds to a cut vessel to form a haemolytic plug. Embolism and thrombosis may result from this clotting of the blood during antigen-antibody reactions, which could be a 'trigger mechanism' in cardiovascular accidents. The underlying process of atheroma may in part be a cumulative product of responses to viruses which will be regularly contracted by adults, with resulting arteriosclerosis increasing the risk from embolism when it occurs.[82] Other studies have suggested that the monoclonal nature of the arteriosclerotic plaque is consistent with the view that it could be the result of cell mutations caused by infectious micro-organisms.[83]

Statistically-based studies have also suggested temporal associations between specific air-borne infections, which precipitate immune reactions in adults, and circulatory-disease mortality. For example, influenza has been linked with ischaemic heart-disease mortality risk,[84] while measles incidence and total circulatory-disease death rates appear to be related over long periods in most Western populations for which both sets of data are available for at least twenty years.[85] Although several factors such as climate in the short-term, and the delayed effects of war and nutritional deprivation, could have combined to influence in similar ways the trends for two diseases manifest at opposite ends of the life cycle, a coincidence seems unlikely, as the association is generally upheld in a variety of trends for several populations and correlation coefficients are usually high and significant as shown in Appendices 6g (i) and (ii). A 'trigger' mechanism involving immune reactions in the formation of emboli would be a plausible explanation of the statistical associations, which suggest that if there is such a link between viral infection and cardiovascular disorders, measles might have been the predominant influence in many European countries. Such a working hypothesis is also consistent with the association between circulatory-disease and general mortality levels in the twentieth century, and with the possibility that transmission rates of air-borne infectious diseases were reduced with declining family size and reduced overcrowding.[86]

Risk factors and cancer mortality trends

Like circulatory disease, cancer has a multifactorial aetiology, with many identified risk factors and agents including viruses. The association of these with particular sites and types of cancer inevitably creates difficulties for any explanation of trends in death rates for the group as a whole, which may be the only reliable unit for analysis of data in the long-term. There were fewer data on cancer mortality by site in the nineteenth century, and in the past it tended to be considered as one disease, with one suggestion being that the overall susceptibility to cancer in a population might be relatively constant such that reductions in incidence of one form would be offset by increased incidence of another. It was thought that this might account for the widely different site incidence of cancer among populations with similar total cancer death rates.[87] It is now usual to treat cancer as a group of diseases differing widely in aetiology, frequency of occurrence and type of manifestation. The common underlying processes are usually viewed as the cumulative product of various irritants and carcinogens. Burnet proposed that error proneness in the repair of DNA might be the only process needed to explain substantiated associations, such as those between radiation and skin cancer, cigarette-smoking and lung cancer, naphylamines and bladder cancer, radium salts in paints and bone sarcoma, and many others. A sufficient hypothesis for 'environmental' cancer might be that an agent enters the cell and in a certain proportion of cases produces damage to DNA that can be repaired, but with an increased risk of informational error, and hence abnormal cells which can replicate beyond control. It is only in certain special circumstances that a virus can insert itself into the DNA of certain cells, and final proof of viral aetiology remains elusive for some known examples, such as Burkitt's lymphoma and nasopharyngeal carcinoma. However, improved methods of detecting viruses might establish links with many more types of cancer, and there is growing evidence of their possible importance.[88]

Cigarette-smoking is by far the biggest of the known risk factors in cancer, and Doll and Peto estimated that it was responsible for about 30% of male deaths from this group of causes in the United States for example.[89] A somewhat lower proportion of 7–8% of female deaths from cancer probably reflects different smoking habits in the past and present. Epstein emphasised the multifactorial aetiology, suggesting that occupational risks probably interact with the adverse effects of cigarette-smoking to produce an even greater risk of the disease.[90] He contested the very low proportion of 5% of deaths which had been regarded as due to occupational exposure.[91] A further consideration was that 20% of lung-cancer deaths in the United States were among non-smokers, and the risk in certain occupational groups was almost the same for smokers and non-smokers. Among the major risks are contact with asbestos dust, radon daughters, nickel ores, chromium, and the products of other industries, and pollution generally. Many of these factors could have affected mortality risk for males more than females, even before cigarette-smoking began in the mid nineteenth century.

Nutritional factors are of major importance in the risk of gastro-intestinal, epithelial and breast cancer which accounted for 20% of female cancer mortality in England and Wales in 1981. Both experimental and human observations provide indications of this, although international correlations between consumption of total fat and rates of cancer of the breast and colon, may reflect the effects of over-nutrition rather than any direct causal link.[92] The main role of other dietary factors in cancer may be to act by modifying the incidence of tumours induced by carcinogens, or to act as vehicles for these, and many aspects of diet, vitamins, trace elements and other micro-nutrients could be involved, acting to enhance carcino-genesis or to inhibit the process by some protective effect. Much of the evidence does not allow firm conclusions even about contemporary risks, but Doll and Peto pointed out that nutritional rather than carcinogenic influences have been emphasised.[93] One study suggested that the decline in death rates from gastric cancer in certain countries might be linked with a reduction in consumption of carbohydrates. However, it was also pointed out that increased consumption of foods with a protective effect might cause part of any reduction that was not due to improved methods of detection and treatment.[94] Reductions in age-specific death rates for cancer of the stomach, intestines and rectum might all reflect this and other improvements in diet and the quality of food, but the role of specific factors is difficult to identify or link with trends.

The main contributors to cancer mortality apart from diet, tobacco, industrial products and pollution, are probably alcohol, sexually-related causes and infections. There is a growing body of evidence of association between viruses and human cancer, and indications of a close aetiological relationship in some cases, such as between Epstein–Barr virus and Burkitt's lymphoma and nasopharyngeal carcinoma; hepatitis B virus and hepatocellular carcinoma; and between human papillomavirus and cervical, penile and vulval carcinoma. There is also now preliminary evidence suggesting the presence of a retrovirus in patients with breast cancer, which might be disabling the macrophage and allowing the development of potentially malignant cells into frank tumours, as is thought to in some tumours associated with human immuno-deficiency virus infection.[95] Some of these viruses, if capable of transmission, may be widespread – such as Epstein–Barr virus, which is the cause of glandular fever (infectious mononucleosis).[96] Thus other factors affecting immunological-cellular processes are likely to determine whether exposure leads to cancer in an individual. It has been suggested that immune surveillance against aberrant cells may fail, increasing the risk of cancer, but excess mortality following disorders and suppression of the immune system is predominantly due to a few rare types which are mostly those for which the evidence of viral aetiology is strongest.[97] This may not mean that immune surveillance and failure of the function have no general significance in relation to common cancers, but other factors must be important in determining the site and circumstances necessary for development. Recent research has indicated that a process related to platelet aggregation might determine whether aberrant cells actually proliferate as a malignancy.[98]

'Microcancers' appear to be a common occurrence – in relation to old tubercular scars, for example, although as Doll pointed out they could not all be precursors of cancer.[99] The historical hypothesis that cancer has in a sense replaced tuberculosis remains interesting, because of a suggested common immune defence mechanism,[100] although there is a lack of evidence or theory of pathogenesis linking the two disease groups. Certainly cancer has taken over from tuberculosis as a group of causes of death with manifestations in many sites in the body, which is not a characteristic of any other group of diseases, while in a statistical way cancer mortality has taken over from tuberculosis mortality in accounting for about one in five deaths in each generation. A growing proportion of the population survived with only some manifestation of subclinical tuberculosis, as the 'tuberculosis environment' improved in the nineteenth and twentieth centuries. Whether or not this has meant the survival to ages at which cancer is more likely, of individuals who would previously have been susceptible to clinical tuberculosis, remains speculative and a difficult hypothesis to test. Causal agents linked with behaviour and environment remain the most established risk factors relevant to an understanding of trends in cancer death rates.

Other non-communicable disease mortality patterns

Changes in risk factors affecting successive cohorts may also have been significant in relation to mortality from peptic ulcer, although increasing period death rates and incidence in the twentieth century have sometimes been taken to indicate that it is another 'disease of civilisation'. Death rates at ages over 65 years, for both gastric and duodenal ulcer, continued to increase even in mid-century when there were reductions in the death rates at younger ages. These reflected reduced sickness rates, suggesting that they were probably not the result of better treatment.[101] Serial mortality records illustrated in Appendix 6h show a decline in the age-standardised death rate for stomach ulcer in the postwar period, and before the war for females.[102] Peptic ulcers are not in fact killers in themselves, but the risk of fatality is from perforation and haemorrhage. There may have been improvements in medical care and through treatment becoming more available, which could have reduced these risks. However, in consideration of long-term changes in mortality, a study of death rates for peptic ulcer analysed by year of birth, found clear cohort turning points. Death rates at different adult ages had fallen for cohorts born after the 1880s, and while dietary changes might be suspected there is no clear indication of the role of different risk factors in causing the disease.[103] As the study suggested, falling death rates over successive cohorts are unlikely to have been the result of changes in diagnosis or treatment which would be reflected more in period changes, and this argument would also apply to the similar but earlier cohort turning point in cancer death rates.

Like ulcers, diabetes need not be a killing disease, and the use of insulin since 1922 has probably had a considerable impact on this group of illnesses resulting from deficiency of the substance. The indices of diabetes mortality reveal reductions in the age-standardised death rates for both sexes between the 1930s and the 1960s,[104] but rates have subsequently increased again. In the very long-term, changes in recording practice and in the identification of prime cause of death, have probably been a significant factor in the earlier rise and fall of diabetes death rates since the mid nineteenth century. A study of the more recent reductions in death rates considered the possibility that they were genuine, and could have been linked with changes in diet and type of food available, as well as better treatment.[105] For younger age groups of diabetics, insulin and improved medical care did seem to be the two principal factors involved in declining death rates. Among older adults, death rates may have stopped falling at the end of the 1940s because of the effect of increases in the consumption of fibre-free energy foods, sugar and fat. For those susceptible to diabetes and obesity, fibre-depleted, starchy, carbohydrate foods are thought to be a risk, while fibre-rich foods might give some protection. The relative importance of various aspects of aetiology is not clear, and there are probably genetic, auto-immune, and toxic or viral factors which contribute as underlying causes of the disease.[106] Some features of trends in the incidence of certain types of diabetic case appear to match changes in the incidence of aseptic meningitis, but not consistently.[107] There are also indications from the seasonal pattern of incidence that viral infection might be initiating the underlying process, but evidence is far from conclusive.[108]

Among the other major non-communicable diseases, cirrhosis of the liver has resulted in increasing death rates since the 1930s in England and Wales, particularly among females.[109] Studies of increases in other Western countries have linked them with trends in alcohol consumption, since a history of heavy drinking is a known risk factor. However, in developing countries links with infectious disease may again be significant as non-alcoholic cirrhosis and cancer of the liver are frequent sequelae of viral hepatitus for which an effective and safe vaccine is available.[110] Death rates for nephritis, the fourth in the group of degenerative diseases considered here, have contributed to the decline in mortality for the group as a whole throughout this century.[111] A study of trends in death rates for acute and chronic nephritis found a sharp decline in many countries in the postwar period.[112] As was suggested, changes in diagnostic habits and the effect of competing mortality risk from arteriosclerosis, were probably involved in the decline in certification of renal disease as the underlying cause of death. However, some genuine reduction was not ruled out as deaths may have been due to infection with streptococcus, and a similar decline has been observed for rheumatic-fever mortality before the anti-biotic era.

The recent epidemic of acquired-immune-deficiency syndrome is a further case in which degenerative disorders appear to be associated in some way with viral infection, while adverse effects of immune responses to micro-organisms may indeed be a general phenomenon. The role of viral agents in cancer may appear at the moment to be of relatively minor importance, but knowledge about the true extent of such influences on cancer incidence may require more sensitive techniques of immunological investigation. The role of viral infections and immune reactions in respiratory disorders may be more straightforward, but requires further substantiation as discussed earlier. Damage to the tracheo-bronchial system is known to occur with the immune reaction to many air-borne viruses, including common childhood infections such as measles and whooping cough in particular. The important viral hypothesis of circulatory disease could be the subject of further research with different organisms being tested, and particularly measles virus in view of the temporal association between incidence of the disease and mortality from circulatory disease. Any evidence of raised antibody levels among stroke patients, for example, might also indicate specific infectious micro-organisms that could have provoked an immune response involving platelet aggregation and embolism.

There are many links between communicable diseases and the non-communicable forms of disease which have replaced them as the predom-inant causes of death. Many forms of circulatory disease prominent at earlier times, and among younger age groups, were infectious in origin, such as the bacterial forms of endocarditis, and rheumatic fever linked with scarlet fever.[113] Even where heart disease is not known to involve infectious causes in themselves, infectious diseases – and particularly those with respiratory complications – can precipitate cardiovascular accidents. Behavioural factors inter-relate with the underlying processes in non-communicable disease, which may also be the product of other environmental agents including micro-organisms. For example, substances in cigarette smoke may render the blood more readily susceptible to adverse effects of immune reactions to common air-borne viruses, which have been implicated in embolism, thrombosis, and the cumulative under-lying circulatory disorder, atherosclerosis.[114] Cigarette smokers may also be more prone to lung cancer because bacterial infections associated with chronic bronchitis lead to impairment of the ability to clear the bronchi.[115] Also, as mentioned, secondary complications of air-borne epidemic diseases may have consequences for the risk of respiratory disease itself,[116] and this may affect adults, too, given other exacerbating influences such as cigarette-smoking and air pollution.

As well as being linked with infectious diseases, many non-communicable diseases are themselves inter-related through multifactorial risks of incidence, while similarities in the underlying processes of some non-communicable diseases have been suggested, for example by age-incidence patterns of mortality. The rates of increase in mortality with age have been shown to be similar for cerebral haemorrhage, cancer and gastric ulcer.[117] Various aspects of the aging process have been suspected of being involved, such as generations of body cells concerned with growth,[118] or those concerned with the repair of DNA.[119] Also, the cumulative impact of irritants and other contributing agents, including micro-organisms, might be related to length of exposure and hence to age. Mutation theory suggests that most of the chronic non-infectious diseases may be mutation-induced with such diverse manifestations as atherosclerosis, diabetes and cancer being aetiologically related since they might all be the result of single-cell mutation. For example, the initial stage in atherosclerotic plaque formation appears to be the proliferation of muscle cells in the arteries which are monoclonal in origin and therefore probably the result of single-cell mutation which could be caused by viruses. Diabetes involves dysfunction relating either to the production of insulin or responses to it, which again might be the result of single-cell mutation such that both diabetes and atherosclerosis might be viewed as non-malignant forms of neoplasia defined in terms of the unnatural proliferation of aberrant host cells.[120]

The internal processes whereby micro-organisms produce the symptoms of infectious illness have been linked with mechanisms of cell destruction and immune defence against the presence and proliferation of such foreign cells which threaten the integrity of the body. In chronic non-infectious diseases it is the proliferation of aberrant host cells which often character-ises the underlying disorder, although again the causal agent may be some foreign substance or virus which has a mutagenic effect. The actual causal agents in these diseases are likely to operate within a culturally determined nexus of risks of incidence of disease and mortality, but may be subject to other biological restraints within the internal host environment such as repair of genomic damage and immunosurveillance. Cellular-immuno-logical processes may be crucial for an understanding of the underlying nature of many chronic non-infectious diseases, while adverse effects of micro-organisms or immune reactions to them may underly disorders as varied as circulatory disease, cancer, diabetes, nephritis and cirrhosis of the liver. In these respects there are aetiological similarities between chronic non-infectious diseases, based on the concept of environmental mutagenic causes including viruses, and a conceptual similarity with the Germ Theory of infectious disease which holds out the possibility of a unifed theory of disease.[121]

Summary

In the twentieth century an increasing proportion of deaths has been attributed to chronic non-infectious diseases, while increases in age-specific death rates were found from the second half of the nineteenth century with the new registration data on cause of death. The long-term trend for the main contemporary cause of death – circulatory disease – is distinctive, but in the second half of the nineteenth century there were increases in age-standardised death rates for bronchitis, cancer, and the group of degenerative diseases – diabetes, nephritis, cirrhosis of the liver and ulcers – as well as for circulatory disease. In the first half of the twentieth century there was a fairly continuous decline in the age-standardised death rate reflecting reduced death rates from most causes. These included respiratory disease which declined from the end of the nineteenth century along with death rates for many childhood infectious diseases. There was a decline in circulatory-disease death rates among adults around this time, but it was followed by a unique resurgence from the 1920s until the 1950s, while cancer death rates for males continued to increase into the twentieth century in an equally distinctive way. Neither longer survival from diseases of young adulthood and middle age such as tuberculosis, nor improvements in diagnosis provide a completely satisfactory explanation for periods of increase in cancer and circulatory-disease death rates. The 'M-shaped' trend in the age-standardised death rate for circulatory disease since the mid nineteenth century is likely to reflect in part changes in behaviour, living conditions and the effects of wartime circumstances, while cigarette-smoking undoubtedly caused much of the increase in heart-disease mortality among males in the mid twentieth century.

The death rate from circulatory disease for women as well as that from cancer has in fact generally fallen in the twentieth century, and this runs counter to any suggestion that these are diseases of an industrial way of life *per se*. The decline in cancer death rates among cohorts of females born after the mid nineteenth century may be a genuine reflection of some improvement in childhood experience, carrying lasting benefit throughout life with regard to coping with risks from carcinogens and somatic mutation.[122] Despite increases in death rates for cancer of the lung and bronchus, the rate of increase in cancer death rates for successive cohorts of males declined after the mid nineteenth century. It might be that reductions in transmission rates of air-borne infectious diseases, and hence in severity of illness,[123] resulted in more efficient cellular-immunological processes throughout life for successive cohorts. Any such benefit for males could have been partially offset by a greater exposure to industrial hazards combined with a greater indulgence in cigarette-smoking in the twentieth century, compared with females. Some combination of industrially related environmental changes, such as increasing exposure to dust, chemicals and air pollution, may in part explain increasing age-specific death rates from cancer, bronchitis and other respiratory and circulatory diseases in the nineteenth century,[124] since increasing recognition and sophistication of diagnosis while contributing, seem unlikely to explain all the increases.[125]

The multifactorial aetiology of non-communicable diseases involves many well established environmental agents and risk factors, such as dust, smoke, industrial pollution and the adverse effects of damaging behaviour and diet. Such influences often inter-relate and combine to exacerbate underlying disorders, and are known to correlate with high adult death rates from the major non-communicable causes of death, heart disease, stroke, cancer and bronchitis. This implies a high potential for preventing early death and this has been confirmed for those avoiding health hazards such as lack of exercise, being overweight, having poor eating and sleeping habits, and consuming cigarettes or too much alcohol.[126] However, no convincing case has emerged that the recent downturn in age-standardised death rates in the general population of many industrialised countries – after a slowing down of decline in the mid twentieth century – has been the result of changes in relevant behaviour, the application of curative medicine, or socio-economic advances.[127] In the past many non-communicable diseases were in fact thought of as diseases of the modern industrial way of life and increasing affluence, but clearly this is a simplistic view of the relationship with the economic standard of living. Death rates from circulatory disease or cancer are as high in some countries with a lower economic standard of living and with much less heavy industry than Western populations. Also, within England and Wales most categories of disease now cause higher death rates in middle age among the lower socio-economic groups. However, the best-known risk factors associated with socio-behavioural characteristics can only explain part of the social-class differentials in mortality – from circulatory disease for example – while changes in these variables do not provide a satisfactory explanation of the recent decline in death rates in many national populations. It has been emphasised here that there are other significant biological and statistical indications that changes in circulatory-disease death rates might be causally linked with the changing incidence of common air-borne infectious diseases, since certain viruses produce immune reactions repeatedly throughout life and these may have adverse consequences contributing to circulatory disorders such as atherosclerosis and embolism. Adverse effects of micro-organisms or immune reactions to them have in fact been implicated in diseases as varied as circulatory disease, cancer, diabetes, nephritis and cirrhosis of the liver. The challenge of non-communicable diseases continues to be exposed in a global transition in mortality and cause-of-death structure, but micro-organisms and infectious diseases still directly cause high mortality in many parts of the world. Any further evidence that the continuing prevalence of certain infectious diseases also contributes to some of the underlying processes in non-communicable disease, and affects death rates from these diseases, could have implications for health programmes worldwide.

7 A global transition in disease and mortality

The emergence of a radically new pattern of cause of death is illustrated by the evidence from England and Wales, and such changes have affected industrialised countries more than elsewhere. However, the growing predominance of non-communicable diseases as they replace communicable diseases as major killers, can also be seen as part of a global phenomenon affecting less industrialised developing countries as well. Many of the chronic non-communicable diseases are a serious problem throughout the world, and less industrialised countries which have not yet controlled infectious-disease mortality face an increasing threat. Health strategies are being formulated in a World Health Organisation programme to prevent and control non-communicable diseases at the community level.[1] Types of chronic disorder being addressed include circulatory diseases, cancer, occupational diseases, diabetes, gastro-intestinal diseases such as ulcers, cirrhosis of the liver, respiratory diseases, allergies, dental disease and accidents. Only the major cause-groups have been considered in this study partly because of limitations in the early data,[2] but trends have been outlined in the context of a changing and inter-related pattern of communicable and non-communicable disease. The experience of a decline in mortality attributable to infectious diseases in England since the eighteenth century will be summarised here with regard for some of the problems facing developing countries today as they undergo the transition in disease and mortality.

Trends in cause-specific mortality and differentials between socio-economic groups in populations of the North, and levels of mortality in the less industrial countries of the South, suggest that the major non-communicable diseases cannot be understood simply as a consequence of an affluent and industrial way of life, and rural populations in developing countries are affected as well.[3] Many of the less industrialised countries of the South now have a high proportion of deaths in 'middle age' recorded as due to circulatory disease and cancer, at the same time as having high mortality from infectious diseases among adults as well as children. Infectious diseases such as malaria and tuberculosis which have been controlled in Europe still cause morbidity and high mortality at all ages in many parts of the world. About one-third of all deaths in India, for example, are recorded as due to some specified infectious, parasitic or respiratory cause.[4] Changes in recording accuracy, differential levels of recording, and bias towards particular sections of the population in urban areas, have all to be borne in mind when comparing cause-of-death data from different countries. Even so, records from all parts of the world reflect different stages in a transition from communicable to non-communicable causes of death in which the differential application of public-health measures continues to be significant.[5]

The importation of public-health techniques into many countries of the South has meant that death rates are lower than they were in industrialised countries at a similar stage of economic development.[6] Sri Lanka experienced one of the most rapid falls in mortality, largely attributable to the postwar programme of malaria control using insecticides.[7] Even more rapid increases in average life expectancy were found to have occurred in Venezuela between 1920 and 1960.[8] A historical and comparative analysis of Latin-American mortality change, supported the view that in recent decades public-health measures exercised a strong influence on death rates, independently of economic development.[9] A study of data from Guyana for the period 1911–40, when there was economic stagnation, showed that despite this there had been a decline in the crude death rate.[10] After World War II, the death rate declined even further in spite of economic circumstances rather than as a result of them, and malaria control with DDT was important in this phase. The decline in infectious-disease mortality in Mexico differed between different regions, and differential application of public-health measures was probably involved.[11] Data from Cuba give an indication of the transition in cause of death in that country and – as in more industrial countries – the proportion of deaths from circulatory diseases increased from 27% in 1901 to 38% in 1953, although the death rate for this group fell as infectious-disease mortality declined.[12]

It is now feasible to initiate policies aimed at eradicating most of the main infectious diseases that can be immunised against, and this cuts across regional, international and socio-economic class differences in mortality. The objective of seeking to immunise on a worldwide scale against diseases such as tuberculosis, measles, poliomyelitis, diphtheria and whooping cough, has been supported by the World Health Organisation. Such a programme might also have implications for industrialised countries, if some immuno-cellular reactions are implicated in adult mortality from major non-communicable diseases. Even if such links are not substantiated, immunisation can benefit people in developing countries where there may be little immediate prospect of economic growth to improve their standard of living. Such intervention might be particularly effective if immunisation, health and family-limitation programmes are linked, and readily accessible. Locally-based initiatives can be effective and dispensaries useful – as in

England in the past.[13] The distribution of simple treatment products such as those for infant diarrhoea can be organised, and health information disseminated to encourage self-administered hygiene. Trained health workers are often the requirement in many parts of the world, rather than expensive medical care and high technology which anyway have not been significant in reducing death rates in the past.

A recent study of mortality changes in South India found that improvements had been made without any great input of medical technology, as elsewhere.[14] Changes in social attitudes towards health initiatives and behaviour had been extremely important, although it was pointed out that there would be a limit to improvements in life expectancy that could be achieved without considerable improvements in the standard of living and nutrition. Levels of undernutrition may be worse in many countries of the South than in England in the nineteenth century, and this is likely to be a major contributing factor in continuingly high child mortality. The two-way interaction between nutrition and infectious illness means that an under-nourished child is both more at risk and infective for longer, while infection itself can preciptitate malnutrition and kwashiorkor. However, one general conclusion of this study is that the decline in infectious-disease mortality in England was linked more with preventive and public-health measures and other factors affecting transmission, than with nutrition-related resistance, and there may be more universality and continuity in a global process of change than has been suggested in previous studies.

The initial reduction in the death rate in the eighteenth century does not appear to have coincided with any well-documented increase in average income that might have been translated into an improvement in regular levels of food consumption. In relation to mortality levels, the recession of famine was probably important as much because of the associated living conditions which had given rise to epidemics of certain diseases. In the eighteenth century increased supplies of food may only have kept pace with demand, although at the beginning of the nineteenth century and again after the 1870s, there appear to have been periods of a few decades in which prices fell. Even so, there is little firm evidence that the average diet improved dramatically when mortality declined quite sharply and changes in normal levels of food consumption were probably not a key factor in the mortality transition in Europe. On the other hand, the unprecedented increases in numbers and the now steady but larger population, could not have been sustained without a rapid increase in food supply. This was in part possible because of the advantages of exploitative colonialism and relatively cheap imports. The resulting disruption of food production for local consumption in many countries of the South weighs against the advantages of contact with more economically developed countries. For many countries, improving the availability of food per head or even just maintaining it, can become impossible where severe climatic conditions and even higher population growth rates prevail.

In Europe, limitation of family size has led to a new balance between the birth rate and a vastly reduced death rate, and again this is likely to have contributed significantly to mortality decline through reduced transmission rates and also reduced severity of childhood infectious diseases. There was a downturn in the birth rate coinciding with the final phase of mortality decline from the 1870s in England, when child mortality at ages 1–4 years fell. Higher wages do indicate an improvement in the standard of living for those in work, but this is not necessarily the only reason for the coincident decline in fertility and child mortality at this time. Physiological factors may have played some deterministic role as increased child survival brought longer periods of infertility associated with suckling. There may also have been a boost to confidence in the ability of children to survive, particularly as vaccination proved reliable. The limitation of family size became a less risky option, even for the less well-off sections of the population, while the introduction of compulsory education at this time contributed to the spread of ideas among different sections of society. The dissemination of ideas about limiting family size was particularly important, and the Besant–Bradlaugh trial of 1877 which challenged their right to do this, probably focused attention on the issue and in fact promoted their informative pamphlet on birth control.[15] Whatever the effect on the use of birth-control methods or attitudes at this time, the birth rate did begin to fall again, and continued to do so in the twentieth century.

The net effect on the birth rate of a relaxation of the impact of infectious diseases at any time may have depended on whether morbidity and mortality among young adults, or among children under five, was the more significant. There is some evidence of a resurgence in the birth rate in England in the 1850s and 1860s, when there was a sharp fall in the death rate among young adults of reproductive ages, while the final decline did not occur until the 1870s when mortality at ages 1–4 years began to fall continuously. Generally birth rates were falling in Europe in the nineteenth century, though not as rapidly as death rates and there was an upturn before the final long-term decline in some countries – as in England. The national records that are available for Denmark and Sweden for example, indicate that this was only a resurgence, and fertility had been falling in the early stages of mortality decline.[16]

A period of fertility increase prior to the final downturn has also been identified in non-Western populations in the twentieth century, and particularly in the 1940s and 1950s – in many countries of Latin America and the Caribbean, for example.[17] Although this phase of fertility increase was again probably not right at the beginning of the mortality transition, the likelihood of a comparable trend in developing countries is certainly an important consideration, and efforts to integrate family-limitation advice into health-education programmes may be considered an appropriate response. Changes in socio-economic circumstances can obviously be important for changes in behaviour, and in the case of developing countries in recent decades it has been suggested that possible influences in increasing birth rates just prior to the final long-term decline might include breast-feeding practices, changes in behaviour with regard to sexual abstinence following birth, and changes in the incidence of sterility that could be linked with infection,[18] while the changed impact of other infectious diseases among young adults could have affected fertility in other ways.

If there was increasing fertility in England in the second half of the eighteenth century,[19] at the very beginning of the mortality transition when the standard of living does not appear to have been improving, it may be that the changing impact of infectious diseases was the significant factor as it was for increased life expectancy. Declining morbidity among adolescents and young adults as a result of the reduced impact of smallpox among the inoculated would seem to be a plausible explanation which might be investigated further in local-area studies. If the increase in birth rates did in fact occur throughout the eighteenth century, as the Cambridge study has suggested, the absence of plague after the seventeenth century might have contributed in a similar way through its effect on marriage patterns. Later, the preventive measure of inoculation against smallpox reduced the impact of a disease which almost certainly interfered with marriage patterns. This seems particularly likely in rural areas where adolescents and young adults had contracted the disease,[20] so there could have been a lower age at marriage as epidemics receded from the mid eighteenth century. It is also possible that there was a reduction in the incidence of male sterility, known to have been linked with smallpox infection, and this would have tended to increase fertility levels in the population. From the beginning of the nineteenth century – when vaccination had a dramatic impact on smallpox mortality in towns – the improved survival of young children might have had an opposite effect, tending to reduce fertility because of the associated deterministic and voluntaristic effects mentioned.

The impact of smallpox control on mortality decline in the early stages can really only be assessed in relation to total mortality, since few data on both age- and cause-specific mortality exist before the registration period. Evidence from different studies has indicated that smallpox epidemics occurred largely independently of changing economic or agricultural circumstances in the eighteenth century. Epidemic years were also peak years for overall mortality, characterised by an excess of deaths over births, indicating the frequent check on population growth which the disease produced. Deaths attributed directly to smallpox were between 8–20% of those recorded in different parts of Europe. Many more deaths, particularly among infants, were probably not recognised as due to the disease and were classified under vague categories such as fevers and convulsions, while many deaths from sequelae and intercurrent infections were probably classified under other headings.

Evidence from many sets of records and studies has been drawn together here, and this indicates that smallpox was almost under control in much of Europe by the time the Germ Theory of contagion was accepted. The development of preventive measures was based on truly 'grass-roots' initiatives with the folk practices of inoculation from Asia, and vaccination, the modified method of immunisation used in farming communities in England and eventually taken up by all sections of society. A more rapid and sustained population growth in China in fact pre-dated that in Europe,[21] and may in part have been associated with the use of inoculation, but unfortunately there are no data with which to examine its impact on mortality in that country. In Europe, and particularly in England, the measure initially became popular in rural areas rather than in towns, while control of smallpox was really achieved because of the boost to the credibility of immunisation provided by the successful tests with vaccination reported by Jenner. Although the material used may in fact still have been smallpox rather than cowpox matter, this if anything might add to the case that inoculation had been capable of making a significant contribution to mortality decline in the second half of the eighteenth century. Vaccination was anyway an adaptation of inoculation which farmers began using in south-west England in the second half of the eighteenth century. Jenner's publication in 1798 appears to have persuaded the medical profession that the practice could be successful, and certainly within a decade immunisation based on the idea of vaccination was in use throughout Europe, and the impact on mortality was quite dramatic.

Rapid reductions in epidemic mortality from smallpox were recorded in the first few decades of the nineteenth century, regardless of likely differences in economic circumstances, in Sweden, Denmark, Norway, and many towns in Germany and England. By the end of the century there was probably no pool of 'new susceptibles' large enough to sustain the disease in England, Germany and Scandinavia. Various measures – including the adoption of re-vaccination, compulsory vaccination, monitoring for cases and isolation of the infected – were particularly important in this after a resurgence of smallpox in an epidemic in 1870–2. A downturn in overall mortality occurred after this in most of Europe, as it had done at the beginning of the century when vaccination was first introduced. The resurgence of smallpox, and increases in mortality recorded in different industrial towns in England, Germany and the Netherlands in the middle decades of the nineteenth century, may in part have been due to a lapse in vaccination coverage. However, even then there was no return to the kind of peaks in annual mortality that had been experienced in the eighteenth century, despite public-health problems in the rapidly growing towns. In the eighteenth century, the use of inoculation in rural England in particular probably contributed to mortality decline and population growth from the 1740s, but immunisation based on the idea of vaccination produced an unprecedented growth in the population of Europe at the beginning of the nineteenth century as mortality declined sharply when there was still high fertility.

The control and virtual eradication of smallpox during the course of the nineteenth century opened up possibilities for sustained improvements in health and living standards. There were clearly fewer extreme peaks in mortality as smallpox epidemics came under increasing control, but the disease had been only one of a series of infections to which people were regularly exposed. Various records from the eighteenth century have given some indication of the other main causes of death, such as tuberculosis, different fevers, and gastro-intestinal diseases including dysentery. The fevers probably included the childhood disease of scarlet fever, known from the later registration records to cause very high mortality between the ages of one and eight years. Many other fevers and gastro-intestinal diseases were prevalent with typhoid and dysentery being linked with the faecal contamination of food, water and hands. Among the fevers, typhus may have been the biggest killer of adults, and this lice-borne disease was known to spread from places where living conditions were crowded and filthy, and was first recognised in England in jails. However, it had long been associated with famine conditions in Europe and with people living or searching for food in close proximity to rats which could be carriers of infected lice.

Typhus appears often to have run its course of destruction along with plague, which had a similar mode of transmission and original source among the rat population. Crowded conditions in army camps and ships were known to be sources of epidemics, and it is possible that observations on this in the eighteenth century led to some efforts to prevent the disease from spreading to the crowded towns where it flourished among the poverty-stricken inhabitants. Even so, epidemics in the mid nineteenth century could have been associated with the influx of immigrants from famine-stricken Ireland, and with soldiers returning from the Crimea. After these epidemics in the 1850s and 1860s the disease became separated from typhoid in the registration records, and it does not appear to have caused much further mortality in the country as a whole. With the decreasing frequency of famine within Britain, conditions in which typhus epidemics flourished were gradually reduced, while action to contain the spread of the disease from known foci such as crowded jails, could have further limited internal sources of epidemics. At the end of the nineteenth century, the clearance of refuse from the crowded inner areas of cities may also have contributed to a reduced risk of the disease remaining endemic if it was introduced from sources outside the country.

Overcrowding in living conditions and at work also contributed to the spread of respiratory tuberculosis which had become endemic in the towns of England by the eighteenth century. However, such conditions and associated poverty were not necessarily prerequisites for contracting the disease, and it seems likely that many people from rural areas contracted tuberculosis for the first time through increasing contacts with a nearby town. Closeness of contact with the infected and under-nutrition probably affected the risk of clinical disease on first contact, while other living conditions affected the risk of mortality on re-activation of the disease later in life. The recording of deaths under the vague term 'consumption' appears to have reached its peak in the eighteenth century on the evidence from the London Bills of Mortality which also suggest a downturn at the beginning of the nineteenth century. Registration data from England and Wales as a whole suggest that adult death rates from respiratory tuberculosis fell over successive cohorts born in the nineteenth century. Further evidence from other countries indicates reductions in the tuberculosis death rate among children at the beginning of the nineteenth century, although period death rates for adults were still increasing. Together, these sets of evidence suggest that in England respiratory-tuberculosis death rates could have been falling at all ages over successive birth cohorts in the nineteenth century. By the second half of the century, period death rates were declining at all ages in England, while the lack of decline in some other countries may have been due to a later process of urbanisation, or to the spread of the disease with migration from famine-stricken areas with a higher incidence of clinical disease.

Some of the decline in mortality from respiratory tuberculosis in England in the nineteenth century was probably the result of a transfer of recording to other categories of respiratory disease as distinctions became more accurately observed. However, the rate of decline in the second half of the century suggests there was some genuine reduction in the death rate from the disease, although the population almost certainly continued to have 100% contact with tubercle bacillus. In view of this, there was either improved resistance to the disease, a postponement of serious infection to older ages, or some reduction in the incidence of clinical cases in the population. Continuingly high death rates from other air-borne infectious diseases do not suggest there had been improvements in resistance to infectious diseases generally as a result of a better standard of living and nutrition. There does not appear to have been any effective treatment for tuberculosis in the nineteenth century, and although provision of suitable care for the sick may eventually have improved survival chances, sanitoria were still only used by a minority even when they became more widespread in England towards the end of the century. There had been some efforts to promote better ventilation from the eighteenth century onwards, but before the end of the nineteenth century these were directed mainly at public buildings. If there was some genuine decline in tuberculosis death rates when living conditions in towns were under pressure from rapid population growth at the beginning of the nineteenth century, this required some rather exceptional change. A possible explanation is that there were indirect benefits of vaccination against smallpox, since the disease had probably re-activated latent infection or weakened the resistance of survivors. Children in particular would have been the initial beneficiaries, although the risk of mortality from tuberculosis later in life could also have been reduced.

After the discovery of the causal agent in tuberculosis which lent support to the contagion theory, preventive-health measures against the disease had a firmer scientific basis. Views about the need for ventilation of crowded buildings, and the need to restrict the social contacts of the infected became more widely accepted, and in the twentieth century the efforts of anti-tuberculosis movements probably led to a reduction in the dosage of bacillus contracted, and hence to a reduction in the risk of clinical infection. Influences specific to the respiratory form of the disease do seem to have been important before this, since the death rate from non-respiratory tuberculosis did not decline much in the second half of the nineteenth century. This lack of decline suggests that the organism remained virulent, and even in the 1940s tuberculosis cases only had a 50% chance of recovery. After this time BCG vaccination and chemotherapy became important both for the individual and for the further interruption of the transmission process. Other aspects of the programme to control the spread of the disease, and further improvements in housing conditions, probably continued to contribute to the declining death rate. Improvements in milk and food quality seem likely to have become significant in the decline in mortality from non-respiratory forms of the disease in the twentieth century.

The decline of respiratory-tuberculosis mortality made the most significant contribution to overall mortality decline in the second half of the nineteenth century, as McKeown emphasised. On the basis of registration classification it contributed 0.33 towards each unit of decline in the overall age- and sex-standardised death rate. Unfortunately data for the second half of the nineteenth century for other countries are not so complete, so it is difficult to assess just how typical the case of England and Wales was before the twentieth century. However, in the period 1901–71 respiratory tuberculosis contributed about 0.11 to each unit of decline in the overall death rate, which was much the same as in a model based on international data mainly from the twentieth century.[22] McKeown and others based analyses of overall mortality decline on the arithmetic contribution made by different recorded causes, but many qualifications have been made here in a re-interpretation of events, while the main diseases involved were very different in the earlier phase of the mortality transition not considered by McKeown. For example, the control of smallpox in England between the mid eighteenth century and the end of the nineteenth century, almost certainly contributed even more than the 0.1–0.2 towards each unit of decline in the death rate implied by records from the eighteenth century, and the 0.05 in the second half of the nineteenth century. However, the contribution made by the prevention of unrecognised smallpox and sequelae of the disease is really unquantifiable.

A decline in the death rate from scarlet fever in the second half of the nineteenth century contributed 0.12 towards each unit of decline in the overall death rate, but there are no data with which to investigate whether it was declining before this. It has been suggested that there were periods in the past when scarlet fever was a more mild disease, but there is no firm evidence of any change in the virulence of the organism even after the 1870s when case-fatality appears to have fallen, according to records from some European countries. The fall in the death rate from scarlet fever from the 1870s in England and Wales was particularly significant for child mortality, since the disease had accounted for about 15% of deaths in the age group 1–4 years in the 1860s. It might be that more severe forms of infection spread from Ireland in the mid nineteenth century, so that the death rate declined as famine and associated migration ended. The combined effect of intercurrent or prior infections such as typhus and smallpox, and confusion with other diseases including diphtheria when it first arrived, may have boosted mortality attributed to scarlet fever in the mid nineteenth century. From the 1880s, increasing hospitalisation could have had some effect on the transmission rate from severe cases of the disease as well as on case-fatality.

At about the same time, in the last few decades of the nineteenth century, there were many public-health initiatives to control the spread of infectious disease, and again arithmetic analysis may obscure the true role of preventive measures in the mortality decline indicated by the registration records. For example, the threat of cholera becoming a regular and major killer in Britain, seems to have led to investigation of possible sources of gastro-intestinal diseases generally, and eventually to efforts to improve water supplies and sewerage and to monitor potential outbreaks. Asiatic cholera first appeared in Britain in the 1830s, and threatened to become the cause of at least 10% of overall annual mortality in regular epidemics, but the last major epidemic was recorded in 1866. The monitoring of shipping and ports where the disease could be introduced was a major development following efforts to control the sources of transmission within the country, which were also important in relation to other diseases which spread in similar ways.

Typhoid was transmitted in milk and food as well as water and had been endemic in the eighteenth century, although it was not distinguished from typhus for the purposes of registration until 1869. The decline in mortality recorded as due to typhus and typhoid contributed 0.17 towards each unit of decline in the overall age-standardised death rate in the second half of the nineteenth century in England and Wales. Of this about 0.07 occurred from 1871–1901, when typhoid mortality decline contributed 0.043 and the final recession of typhus 0.025, although the death rate from the disease had probably been much higher before this. Long before concerted efforts to improve water supplies and sanitation, the 'fevers' which included these diseases, and probably scarlet fever, made a major contribution of 0.19 to the mortality decline in London between the 1720s and the 1820s. The reduction of famine conditions affecting the transmission of typhus may have been particularly important, as mentioned, along with any changes in the death rate from scarlet fever.

The fall in the death rate from typhoid was more rapid and continuous from the beginning of the twentieth century, by which time specific control measures were in operation. It is unlikely that domestic sanitary provision was involved in the initial stages of the decline in the death rate when only a small proportion of the population had water closets, and anyway these may themselves have been sources of infection. The monitoring of water supplies had been encouraged because of the threat of cholera even before sanitary legislation was fully implemented. The inspection of water and food supplies, the monitoring of outbreaks of infectious disease, and the isolation of cases in fever hospitals, seem likely to have helped to reduce the spread of infection. The actual provision of pure water supplies and sewerage became even more effective from the end of the century and, together with purer milk supplies, this probably contributed to a more rapid fall in mortality from the gastro-intestinal diseases generally in the twentieth century. Gastro-intestinal causes of death other than typhoid contributed arithmetic-ally about 0.12 towards each unit of decline in the overall age-standardised death rate in the second half of the nineteenth century, but the importance of the control of the new disease cholera in preventing additional deaths should not be underestimated. The contribution to mortality decline made by gastro-intestinal diseases from 1901–71 was again about 0.10, which was the same as the proportion in the international model, while the final elimination of typhoid mortality in this period only contributed a further 0.01.

The decline in the death rate from gastro-intestinal disease in the second half of the nineteenth century did not reflect any improvement among infants. Total infant mortality levelled off in mid-century after what appears to have been a significant fall in the second half of the eighteenth century, but the parish records indicating this give little information about the diseases which had contributed. The data from the London Bills of Mortality suggest that the reduction in deaths attributed to 'convulsions', which were symptoms associated with the terminal stages of illness in infants, contributed 0.29 towards each unit of decline in the total burial rate in the period from the 1720s to the 1820s, while a decline in other categories of infancy mortality contributed a further 0.10. Death was probably recorded under convulsions when diarrhoeal diseases or some specific infection was the cause of death which in very young infants had not produced other recognisable symptoms. The overall burial rate in fact fell by 60% in this period, and reductions in deaths classified under the categories of convulsions, infancy and smallpox alone led to a fall of over 30% and much of this was probably a direct result of immunisation.

A lapse in vaccination coverage after the first few decades of the nineteenth century, probably contributed to the setback in infant mortality decline until the 1870s when there was some improvement. The resurgence of infant mortality from about 1881 coincided with the second major epidemic wave of diphtheria, although it involved increasing death rates recorded as due to respiratory disease and prematurity. Almost one in five infants died each year throughout the second half of the nineteenth century, and the main categories of specified disease involved were diarrhoeal disease, bronchitis, pneumonia, tuberculosis, whooping cough and measles. These diseases contributed arithmetically about 0.6 to each unit of decline in the overall infant mortality rate in the period 1901 to 1971, but the contribution of diarrhoeal desease of 0.22, and that of respiratory disease of 0.16 should be viewed with caution because of the inter-relationships between all these cause groups. Many of the childhood epidemic diseases resulted in diarrhoeal and respiratory complications, and some deaths in these categories were probably due basically to air-borne infections such as measles and whooping cough. However, there was almost certainly a large component of water- and food-borne diarrhoeal disease, particularly when increased infant mortality occurred in the 1890s with unusually hot summers exacerbating the problems of water- and fly-borne disease transmission.

Unhygienic substitutes for breast-feeding meant that infants were more at risk than the rest of the population, but efforts in the towns to promote the education of mothers concerning infant care may have begun to have an impact on mortality risk in the early decades of the twentieth century. Improvements in water and sanitary provision ensured that reductions in infant mortality could be sustained because such sources of infection were increasingly restricted. Also, infant mortality from measles and diphtheria both peaked in the 1890s. Although mortality attributed to them was much lower than that for the major cause groups, this change in the impact of epidemic infections together with the absence of smallpox altogether, was significant in the sustained decline in total infant mortality in the twentieth century. The decline in mortality in the diarrhoeal, respiratory and convulsions categories was arithmetically far more significant, but the last two in particular may to some extent have reflected a decline in severe cases of the air-borne epidemic diseases which were still prevalent.

The failure of infant mortality to fall in the second half of the nineteenth century, meant that increased survival rates among children were due largely to reductions in the death rate at ages over 5 years, and from the 1870s to the decline at ages 1–4 years. Falling child mortality in part reflected the recession of typhus and smallpox epidemics, but most of the decline was in deaths attributed to scarlet fever. In the three decades before the 1870s, a lapse in vaccination coverage and the spread of epidemics arising in severe famine conditions in Ireland, could have contributed to the particularly high child death rate in England. However, the delay in the decline of the total death rate at ages 1–4 years until the 1870s, compared with that for older children, also reflects the much greater component of respiratory-disease mortality at these ages. The death rate from respiratory diseases continued to increase until the 1890s, as did that for diphtheria before antitoxin became exceptional as a treatment measure which contributed significantly to mortality decline.

The death rate from measles also continued to be high throughout the nineteenth century such that the trend was quite distinct from that for respiratory tuberculosis which declined among adolescents and young adults long before the end of the nineteenth century. The failure of the death rate from measles to fall much before the twentieth century, might be taken as an indication of continuingly inadequate nutrition among large sections of the population in continuingly adverse living conditions. There was probably little significant improvement in housing conditions or diet among the poor in the nineteenth century, and about half the children of working-class people did not live to the age of five in the Victorian era. There was, however, a consistent decline in the death rate from measles after 1910, following a downturn in the 1890s, and evidence from other countries suggests that case-fatality fell from this time.

Many aspects of living conditions and child care are known to be important in relation to both incidence and case-fatality from measles, while the virus does not appear to vary in virulence. Evidence from historical data and from contemporary studies indicates that declining family size in the twentieth century could have led to a later age at infection and less severe forms of illness because of the effect on the transmission of the disease. This could have reduced the risk of fatality even where nutrition was not improving much, although the economic advantages for families with fewer children might have been significant in this respect. Apart from any improvement in nutrition that might have occurred for some income groups at this late stage in the general mortality transition, isolation of severe cases of infection and better care for the sick could also have begun to affect the death rate from measles and the other childhood infectious diseases. Reduced overcrowding may also have had some effect on the transmission rates, and hence the severity of infections, as municipal and voluntary housing schemes developed from the end of the nineteenth century. In the second half of the twentieth century, the immunisation of children has dramatically reduced the incidence of measles, whooping cough, diphtheria and poliomyelitis, although low coverage rates have recently caused concern – particularly in the case of measles and whooping cough.

The downturn in mortality from whooping cough also occurred at the end of the nineteenth century, and again changes in transmission rates seem a plausible explanation. As mentioned, both measles and whooping cough were probably more important than indicated by the registered deaths from the diseases which suggest a contribution of 0.04 towards each unit of decline in the overall death rate in the second half of the nineteenth century, and 0.05 in the period 1901–71. As emphasised, they frequently gave rise to secondary complications such as diarrhoea and respiratory problems so that deaths could have been recorded under these categories. Whooping cough was probably also a major contributing factor in the risk of clinical tuberculosis in children, and in the re-activation of latent infection among adolescents and even adults. The constant coughing caused by the infection would have been disruptive of the lungs in a way that smallpox had been earlier, so that reduced severity of infection may have been linked with the continuing decline in the death rate from respiratory tuberculosis.

The death rates for bronchitis and broncho-pneumonia declined from about the same time as that for whooping cough, and the inflammatory reaction with this infection could have been involved in respiratory disorders among children and possibly adults as well. However for adults, changes in the pattern of influenza, pneumonococcal and other respiratory infections were probably more significant for the death rate attributed to respiratory disease. Again changes in family size may have been of major significance in reducing the risk of severe respiratory illness, since children may be the most likely to spread respiratory infections to other members of a household, while severity of infection may also be lower among children with fewer siblings. The reduction in respiratory-disease mortality in the period 1901 to 1971 was particularly significant, contributing arithmetically 0.19 towards each unit of decline in the overall age-standardised death rate. The proportion compares with that found in the international model, of 0.24 for males and 0.28 for females, and differences in the way that air-borne and respiratory diseases were distinguished as primary cause of death might account for some of this difference in the contribution to overall mortality decline.

These trends in respiratory-disease death rates among adults and children, and the downturn in air-borne infectious-disease death rates at the end of the nineteenth century, contrast with other aspects of adult mortality change. In addition to the increasing death rate for respiratory diseases, there were increases in age-standardised death rates for circulatory diseases and cancer in the second half of the nineteenth century, so there were negative contributions of 0.10, 0.18 and 0.11 towards a unit of decline in the overall death rate. A small part of this adverse trend was offset by reductions in the cerebrovascular-disease death rate which contributed 0.02 towards each unit of decline in the overall death rate in the periods 1848–54 to 1901 and 1901 to 1971. The total death rate from circulatory disease also declined from the end of the nineteenth century, which reflected reductions in cerebrovascular disease and rheumatic heart-disease death rates in particular, but this fall only lasted until the 1920s. There followed a resurgence until the 1950s, which may be seen as exceptional, together with death rates from cancer among males which continued to increase into the twentieth century. Although cigarette-smoking was probably the most important factor in this, along with other aspects of behaviour, environment and socio-economic conditions, such factors do not satisfactorily explain the earlier increases in the nineteenth century which occurred for females as well. Increased air pollution and industrial hazards could have been involved, affecting bronchitis death rates as well, but improved diagnosis and more specific certification might account for much of the increase in this earlier period.

Despite these adverse trends in adult death rates from non-communicable diseases, the overall age- and sex-standardised death rate fell by 4.9 in the second half of the nineteenth century to reach an actual level of 17.0 per 1,000 in 1901.[23] Reductions in infectious-disease death rates contributed 4.6 to the decline and nearly all of this was the result of falling death rates among children and young adults, with improvements in mortality at ages 1–34 years being responsible for a fall of 4.1 in the overall age-standardised death rate per 1,000. Reductions in child mortality at ages 1–14 contributed 0.53 towards each unit of decline in the overall death rate in the second half of the nineteenth century (see Appendix 6a). Most of the remaining fall in overall mortality was the result of declining death rates among young adults aged 15–34 years who had earlier been particularly affected by tuberculosis mortality.

In the period 1901 and 1971, the fall in the overall death rate resulting from mortality changes at ages 1–34 years was again about 4 per 1,000, as in the second half of the nineteenth century, with a further reduction of 4 following the resumption of infant mortality decline. Mortality at ages over 35 years also declined (see Appendix 6b), contributing 5.4 to the total fall of 13.4 in the age- and sex-standardised death rate. There was a marked contrast with the second half of the nineteenth century, when the death rate among infants did not decline as it had done earlier when smallpox immunisation was being enthusiastically adopted. Also all age groups were affected by increasing respiratory-disease death rates, and middle-aged and older adults by increasing death rates from non-communicable diseases. Much of the decline in the death rate among older adults from the 1890s was the result of the falling death rate from respiratory disease which was also highly significant in the resumption of infant mortality decline. In addition there were the reductions in death rates from some non-communicable diseases, such as cerebrovascular disease, and from circulatory disease in general among females. Reductions in death rates for most diseases contributed to an even more rapid fall in the age-standardised death rate in the first half of the twentieth century compared with the earlier decline. This occurred despite the resurgence of the circulatory-disease death rate and the continued increase in the cancer death rate among males, and despite the economic depression of the inter-war period.

Whereas average life expectancy in England increased from just under thirty years in the 1740s to about forty-seven years in 1901, it then improved dramatically to reach three score years and ten by 1971, with female life expectancy now being almost eighty years. Disease-specific preventive measure, such as the anti-tuberculosis programmes and the isolation of severe cases of childhood infectious disease, continued to be important as they had been earlier for the control of plague and smallpox. Public-health measures earlier introduced under the threat of cholera, continued to be effective in restricting the transmission of other diseases, and it was recognised in the United States that the maintenance of standards with regard to water, food protection and sewage had been crucially important in the depression of the 1930s, when the overall death rate might have been expected to rise.[24] In England the overall age-standardised death rate in fact continued to fall between the wars, and although the decline was not as rapid as at other times this century, it does indicate the importance of factors other than those determined by people's own economic standard of living and nutrition.

Death rates declined for all infectious diseases in England in the twentieth century, regardless of the extent to which undernutrition is known to contribute to the risk of dying.[25] Many factors discussed here seem likely to have been involved, while improvements in quality could have been at least as important as increased consumption of food up to World War II, particularly in relation to the decline in the death rate among infants and from non-respiratory tuberculosis. The decline in the death rate from respiratory tuberculosis and from respiratory diseases contributed most to adult mortality decline which appears to have been at least as rapid among the higher socio-economic groups, in the period 1921–71 for example.[26] In addition to preventive measures against tuberculosis, changes in family size initially among the middle classes, and in housing conditions among the less well-off, could have been involved with a reduction in transmission rates and severity of air-borne infectious diseases. This might account for much of the decline in related respiratory-disease death rates in the first three or four decades of this century before the introduction of sulphonamides and the new era of cheomotherapy with antibiotics. After World War II further preventive measures became available to fight infectious diseases with new vaccines as well as the new curative treatments. There was also a growing recognition of the need to investigate the causal agents and risk factors in the chronic non-infectious diseases which were becoming predominant. Many risk factors associated with the major causes of death – heart disease and lung cancer – have become increasingly recognised, but differential changes in behaviour such as avoiding cigarette-smoking, and taking care over diet and exercise have probably contributed to the maintenance of socio-economic class differentials in mortality risk at different ages.[27]

Summary and conclusions

In the two-hundred-year period up to the mid twentieth century, there was a shift from communicable to non-communicable causes of death and a great reduction in the death rate with consequences for population growth in an epidemiological-demographic transition which is now a global phenomenon. Most adult deaths in 'middle age', and 90% of all deaths from disease in England, are now attributed to the three main groups of non-communicable diseases: circulatory disease, bronchitis, and cancer. Industrialised countries have higher death rates from non-communicable disease than developing countries, although some exceptions indicate that these cannot be described simply as diseases of the affluent, industrial way of life. Death rates are also higher among those with a lower standard of living within industrialised populations. Many controllable risks have been identified in recent decades, and increased cigarette-smoking – particularly among males during and after World War II – has probably been the most significant factor in adverse trends in adult death rates. Many other behavioural and environmental factors affect death rates at all ages and, together with structural inequalities and socio-economic differences in society, they contribute to differentials in health and in the risk of dying before the expected seventy or eighty years of life.

Generally, combinations of known risk factors are more readily linked with differentials in non-communicable disease mortality between areas, socio-economic groups and between the sexes, than they are with changes in death rates over time, and not all the identified risk factors could have contributed to increasing death rates in the nineteenth century. Some aspects of the trends in death rates from non-communicable diseases over successive cohorts are also difficult to explain in terms of life-long risk factors and these probably relate to circumstances in childhood. Death rates for cancer and peptic ulcer reveal reduced death rates among those born after the 1860s, and the 1880s respectively. This might be linked with the changing impact of infectious diseases in childhood. There are also links between communicable diseases and non-communicable diseases involving immunological-cellular processes which could be important throughout life given other exacerbating environmental circumstances and behavioural risks. The aetiology of circulatory disease, cancer and other non-communicable diseases is multifactorial with many external agents being capable of similar effects on the cellular processes of the body. There are many possibilities for preventive measures to reduce the risk of debilitating morbidity and mortality from non-communicable disease, both through individual and community action on pollution, sedentary work with a lack of exercise and, above all, cigarette-smoking.

It has been argued that today no other industry kills people on the scale that the tobacco industry does, and unlike other industries which are made to curb their activities when the health of workers and consumers is threatened, this industry has actually been allowed to increase its efforts to persuade people to consume its products.[28] Historically, financial advantage for a small minority has often been put before human health, and one response to this was the accusation of social murder which Engels made against the Victorian middle classes in England. Today, tobacco companies refuse to acknowledge publicly that cigarettes contribute to the risk of dying from lung cancer and other diseases. Whether or not this amounts to social murder or social manslaughter, any legal issue would involve a consideration of relevant scientific evidence by those without a vested interest. Despite the evidence that possibly one smoker in four dies prematurely through smoking, tobacco companies and advertisers have initiated a massive sales drive towards new markets in developing countries. In the USSR also, there have been regular increases in the production of cigarettes, despite the recognition there that they are causally linked with cancer. Many other governments throughout the world have to decide whether legislation is the best means of dealing with what is a social problem affecting everyone in some way.[29]

In the past there have been interventions to reduce the risk from the most feared diseases and a process of adaptation to an urban and later to an industrial way of life. The transmission of infectious diseases has been affected by human action throughout the history of human settlement and migration, while recently the products of industrial life have impinged on micro-biological processes in ways which threaten health. Preventive health measures have often been introduced in spite of opposition from powerful conservative elements in society, and smallpox immunisation, for example, was opposed for misguided religious and 'moral' reasons. Later, sanitary reforms were seen as a threat to the self-interest of certain groups who favoured a *laissez-faire* approach in political, social and economic matters. A Malthusian perspective had provided a justification for avoiding the often exaggerated expense of measures to overcome social and health problems which weighed most heavily on the poor who were least able to help themselves. Wars and epidemics were described as 'necessary' checks on population growth. In the eighteenth century it had been known that at least 8–20% of the population of Europe died early in life as a direct result of smallpox, which was also conspicuous with severe sequelae and maiming. In these circumstances, the success of the folk practice of immunisation became recognised as offering some hope that smallpox at least, might not be 'necessary'. Smallpox vaccination became particularly important as people moved into already crowded towns where there was inadequate provision for housing, sanitation and water supply.

The general social upheaval and change in social structure concomitant with urbanisation, has had other consequences for health relating to work, unemployment, and the break up of kinship and community relationships.[30] Urbanisation itself has had global implications for the types of disease which have affected human health and longevity throughout history. Increasing contacts between populations throughout the world led to the spread of plague, smallpox, and later cholera, from Asia to Europe.[31] In the late nineteenth century, measles could still devastate whole communities when they first contacted the disease, for example with colonisation from Europe. New susceptibles were mainly children by then because immunity was gained by survivors in universal contact. Nevertheless, the disease continued to cause high mortality among children in Europe because of poverty and large families with inadequate food and crowded living conditions, all of which contributed to more severe forms of infection. Both typhus and tuberculosis were also major causes of death among adults under such living conditions which favoured rapid transmission and high dosage of infection. The rate of transmission of infectious diseases is linked with migration, overcrowding, numbers of children in a household and social contacts, which means there is an important socio-cultural component of disease aetiology which has implications for control.

Although many controllable air-borne infectious diseases are still prevalent and threaten health, the major epidemic diseases of the seventeenth and eighteenth centuries no longer occur at all in Europe, and the recession of plague, smallpox, cholera and typhus epidemics constitutes a revolutionary change in the human condition. The extent to which the recession of infectious diseases and mortality decline have involved human intervention in the deleterious relationship between micro-organisms and man is more than just an interesting historical question, since there is no evidence that the virulence of the micro-organisms has declined. Studies of the impact of more recent health programmes on mortality have often adopted a categorical approach to disease, reflecting the specificity of programmes themselves.[32] In considering changes in mortality in the past, it is often more difficult to apply quantitative analysis to the data that are available and to distinguish between the effects of possible contributing factors. The inter-related role of diseases contributing to the risk of death and the more diffuse or secondary effects of interventions and changes in living conditions give rise to complications for evaluation. Even so, for different phases in the mortality transition it is possible to distinguish between the disease-specific health measures which could have contributed and the various other changes affecting disease patterns.

Long before the transmission process of insect-borne diseases such as plague and typhus was understood, they had been associated with certain adverse circumstances such as wars, while plague was known to spread from Asia, and from medieval times its pattern of spread through Europe had been linked with famine. The course of typhus epidemics in Europe had been linked with famine and with plague, but epidemics recurred in the eighteenth century long after the last plague outbreak, and it was recognised that there were particular foci of infection such as jails and ships. In times of famine the disease spread in the terrible living conditions exacerbated by a desperate search for the means to survive. The reduced incidence of famine in Europe after the seventeenth century probably contributed to the decline in fevers mortality from the very high levels partly attributable to typhus. However, ideas about the spread of typhus from known foci of infection and the importance of hygiene may have been translated into effective preventive action directed specifically against this disease. The most plausible explanation for the earlier recession of plague seems to be that it was the result of preventive interventions directed at controlling its spread, such as the cordon sanitaire, isolation measures and quarantine for ships.

Smallpox and cholera receded when disease-specific preventive measures were effectively applied, and these were crucial in the process of man's adaptation to living in densely populated towns. By the eighteenth century many towns had become large enough for major infectious diseases to be endemic, while living conditions there probably deteriorated at the beginning of the nineteenth century. The recognition by radical social reformers and philanthropists at the end of the nineteenth century, of the conditions in which endemic infectious diseases caused high mortality provided a further impetus for intervention over the next hundred years. Community action to provide for basic needs – such as pure water, sewerage and less overcrowded housing – also affected the transmission of infectious diseases which were still prevalent, and helped reduce incidence. However, the limitation of family size also seems likely to have contributed significantly to a reduction in severity of infection, so that factors affecting transmission probably caused much of the decline in death rates in the first half of the twentieth century.

Many efforts to control the spread of other major infectious diseases, and changes affecting transmission, severity and immunity to infection have been highly significant for mortality decline since the eighteenth century in Europe, and since the nineteenth century in developing countries. In the period of urbanisation and industrialisation in the eighteenth and nineteenth centuries. it was probably disease-specific preventive health measures which made the most significant contribution in bringing down mortality from eignteenth-century levels with the control of smallpox. In addition, cholera, which also had a high case-fatality regardless of economic standard of living, was prevented from taking over as a regularly recurring epidemic killer. Although improvements in sanitation and water supply had a diffuse effect in reducing the risk of other infectious diseases, there were disease-specific measures to monitor outbreaks and prevent importation from abroad. Later, from the end of the nineteenth century, there was more specific identification of the organisms involved in infectious diseases. Better knowledge about transmission, of tuberculosis for example, supported long-prevalent ideas concerning appropriate interventions such as isolation of the infected.

In the early stages of the mortality transition in England, and in the second half of the nineteenth century, human intervention in, or directly affecting, the disease-transmission processes, appears to have been the significant factor in a minimum of 10–20% but quite possible most of the mortality decline. This often occurred when there was no discernible improvement in the economic standard of living for most people, and the interpretation of events presented here provides an alternative to explanations of sustained mortality decline as a consequence of advances in the standard of living and associated improvements in nutrition and resistance to infectious disease. Death rates had been high among all socio-economic groups in the eighteenth century, and would not have declined without recession of the more virulent infectious diseases such as plague, smallpox, typhus and cholera, which required preventive measures and other interventions. It is unlikely that economic advance by itself could have led to such a rate of decline in death rates, particularly from smallpox and cholera which were not famine-related diseases. Indeed, economic advance itself may not have occurred at quite the same pace if these diseases had not been controlled by the end of the nineteenth century.

There is little evidence from indicators of economic standard of living or food consumption per head that improvements in general levels of nutrition occurred in conjunction with the early phases of the mortality transition in England, or in Europe generally. Without the later socio-demographic changes affecting the transmission and severity of the remaining air-borne infectious diseases among large families in the crowded centres of expanding towns, it is by no means certain whether any improvement in nutrition that occurred in the first half of the twentieth century would have been sufficient to bring down child mortality. In developing countries in the twentieth century, increased life expectancy has also been achieved even in periods of economic stagnation when it is unlikely that resistance to infectious disease could have improved through better nutrition. Other studies have shown that hospitals could not have played a major part in the decline in mortality in England, since this began before they became effective, while there were few effective treatment measures or curative medicines until chemotherapy was developed in the 1940s. However, many preventive and public-health measures had been introduced, even before the Germ Theory brought a more scientific understanding of transmission processes, and these were later applied in developing countries.

The historical perspective of this study suggests that there has been more universality and continuity in a global process of mortality transition than has been implied by many previous studies which have provided a rather fragmented view of the phenomenon. Much of the early decline in death rates in other parts of the world, such as India, was the result of controlling epidemics of smallpox, cholera and plague, using preventive measures which had been effective against these diseases in Europe in earlier times.[33] Historical evidence concerning the decline in mortality from other infectious diseases in Europe, can still have implications for health programmes in the less industrialised populations today, where child mortality from other infectious diseases – such as measles, tuberculosis, respiratory and diarrhoeal diseases – is continuingly high and treatment measures are often beyond the means of the poor, or are difficult to administer effectively. Apart from isolation measures and immunisation, many factors can affect the transmission rates of infectious diseases, and smaller families and reduced overcrowding are likely to delay age at infection and reduce severity of illness as well as the risk of intercurrent infections.

Socio-economic circumstances in countries of the South are obviously different from those in Europe in the past, as well as environmental conditions and problems associated with urbanisation without rapid industrialisation. An equitable distribution of resources which can affect the health of both rural and urban communities requires the political and social will to co-ordinate policies on education, housing, food, public health and primary care. The experience of Kerala State in the postwar period has shown how the pursuit of strategies based on considerations of equity has brought its people higher literacy rates, wages and life expectancy than elsewhere in India, despite having been among the poorest of the states, with the fewest resources to invest.[34] Equity in education for the sexes and opportunities for women to pursue alternatives to constant child-bearing were clearly major factors in the more rapid fall in fertility levels concomitant with improved survival chances. The benefits of socio-economic development in terms of health and other aspects of living do not as a matter of course 'trickle down' to all sections of society in a way that is consistent with social justice, and equity cannot even be approached without the political will and the policies aimed at achieving it. There are many social and environmental aspects of disease which make a commitment to social change important, as well as a political commitment to health reforms. Nevertheless for international organisations, the 'vertical' health interventions such as immunisation programmes have a strong appeal by cutting across existing social and regional divisions in societies with differing prospects for social and political change.

As with other ecological problems, the control of communicable disease should be a global concern, whether or not the continued prevalence of air-borne infectious diseases and other viruses is a significant factor in non-communicable disease. Infectious diseases still directly cause high mortality in many parts of the world, despite the transition to a new cause-of-death structure. Any further evidence that their continuing prevalence in fact contributes to morbidity and mortality risk from non-communicable diseases might suggest hitherto unsuspected benefits from more effective control strategies. Micro-organisms and immune reactions to them have been implicated in the processes underlying many non-communicable diseases including circulatory disorders, cancers, diabetes, nephritis and cirrhosis of the liver. The role of viral agents in cancer may prove to be limited to a few specific associations such as that between cancer of the liver and viral hepatitis which has also been linked with cirrhosis of the liver. However, more sensitive techniques of investigation may reveal a more widespread influence on cancer incidence, and lead to substantiation of the suspected involvement of immunological-cellular reactions to viruses in other non-communicable disorders such as diabetes and nephritis.

The role of viral agents and immune reactions in respiratory disorders also requires further substantiation, but damage to the tracheo-bronchial system is known to occur with the immune reaction to many air-borne viruses including those responsible for common childhood infections such as measles and whooping cough in particular. The important viral hypothesis of circulatory disease could be further investigated with laboratory testing of the effect on the blood of antigen-antibody reactions to a wider range of viruses including measles. It might also be feasible to test for raised antibody levels among stroke patients, for example, which could indicate any specific micro-organisms that might have precipitated an immune reaction resulting in embolism. The virtual eradication of many childhood infectious diseases in some populations can also be considered in relation to reductions in circulatory-disease death rates which cannot be satsifactorily explained in terms of changes in health-related behaviour.

For the less industrialised countries of the South where conditions of poverty and overcrowding still contribute in making air-borne and other infectious diseases major killers of children, it has been recognised that in addition to 'vertical' health interventions such as immunisation, supportive primary health-care services and other social initiatives have to be developed, not least because of the difficulties of eradication of some diseases such as measles. Many areas of the world have additional tropical diseases and particularly malaria to contend with, although this disease was also prevalent in Europe until relatively recently. Many infectious diseases which produced high mortality in Europe in the past, are still of great importance worldwide, but well-tried public-health measures can be adapted to particular local needs everywhere. Immunisation, malaria control, the provision of locally accessible education in child care and feeding, measures to increase energy intake,[35] and the use of simple oral rehydration preparations for diarrhoea, can play a major role in reducing child mortality. Important as this is in itself, further perceived improvements in child survival, particularly in the 1–4 age group, may be necessary for further changes in attitudes to child-bearing which might lead to the kind of sustained decline in fertility which in Europe led to demographically-stable populations.

Despite this stability in the populations of the industrialised world there is an increasing demand for natural resources, and economic growth continues to be the politically and commercially expedient objective pursued in most countries. The Industrial Revolution has clearly brought dramatic changes in the material conditions of life, but economic pressures and the exploitation of natural resources have given rise to environmental problems which now demand an 'Ecological Revolution' in attitudes and socio-economic activity at all levels of society. The environmental problems affecting many of the less industrialised countries of the South are not always the consequence of their own mismanagement of resources, and they may have little influence on the economic activities which generate them. In addition, rapid population growth in some circumstances puts a greater strain on the environment and on the limited resources available for social and development policies including health programmes.

There is now a growing awareness of the environmental consequences of economic and demographic change, while the concept of disease as an ecological process has developed throughout this century. The idea that social, cultural and economic factors affect the risk of incidence and mortality, gained acceptance with regard to infectious diseases and extended to non-communicable diseases with the growing awareness that these were becoming more significant as infectious-disease death rates declined. In the more industrialised countries, the debate over the relative importance of deterministic or behaviour-related risk factors in non-communicable disease is political as well as epidemiological, since it relates to questions of private responsibility and public intervention in health matters. Socio-economic factors which are largely outside the control of most people, and environmental factors which include micro-organisms, have been found to be associated with the incidence and risk of dying, before the expected lifespan is complete, from diseases such as cancer, circulatory disease and bronchitis. Many of the factors contributing to the risk of dying from the non-communicable diseases, suggest that changes in individual behaviour would be beneficial, but preventive public-health action and structural economic change are required if environmental hazards and inequity in life chances are to be effectively counteracted. Adult mortality from such causes in 'middle age' is socially disruptive and is a social problem linked with relative levels of economic deprivation in the industrialised world. In the far worse conditions of deprivation and poverty in the Third World, communicable diseases continue to cause high mortality as well as morbidity. Public-health and preventive measures against disease cannot by themselves redress inequity in life chances and in living conditions which contribute to the risk of severe illness but, as in the past, they provide a means of improving survival chances and quality of life worldwide. Structural sources of economic inequality both within countries and between those of the North and South, remain to exacerbate differences in health and life expectancy between rich and poor.

Notes

Chapter 1

1. See for example, P. M. Newberne and G. Williams (1970). Nutritional influences on the course of infections. In *Resistance to Infectious Disease*, R. H. Dunlop and H. W. Moon, eds (Saskatoon Modern Press), p. 93.
2. P. Townsend and N. Davidson (1982) *Inequalities in Health, The Black Report* (Harmondsworth: Penguin) discuss data on social-class differentials in death rates. M. Alderson (1981) *International Mortality Statistics* (London: Mac-Millan) gives age-standardised mortality indices with which to compare non-communicable disease mortality in different countries.
3. E. A. Wrigley and R. Schofield (1981) *The Population History of England 1541–1871: A Reconstruction* (London: Edward Arnold), pp. 531–535.
4. Early series of estimated birth rates suggested a rise between 1700 and 1800, but the major increase took place before 1750. On reconstruction of these series it has been suggested that birth rates may even have declined in the second half of the eighteenth century in every decade, and in both urban and rural areas. G. T. Griffith (1926). *Population Problems in the Age of Malthus* (Cambridge University Press); J. Brownlee (1916). History of birth and death rates in England and Wales taken as a whole, from 1570 to the present time. *Public Health* **29**, pp. 228–238. D. J. Loschky (1969) Urbanisation and England's eighteenth-century crude birth and death rate. *Journal of European Economic History* **1**(3), pp. 697–712.
5. Data presented in Figure 2.3.
6. J. D. Chambers (1957). The Vale of Trent, 1670–1800. *Economic History Review, Supplement 3*, pp. 29–57. G. Ütterstrom (1954). Some population problems in pre-industrial Sweden. *Scandinavian Economic History Review* **2**, pp. 103–165.
7. W. H. McNeill (1979). *Plagues and Peoples* (Harmondsworth: Penguin).
8. Two early studies of the mortality transition suggested that medical innovations might have been important: G. T. Griffith, *op. cit.* in note 4; and M. C. Buer (1926). *Health, Wealth and Population in the Early Days of the Industrial Revolution* (London: Routledge).

9. T. McKeown and R. G. Record (1962). Reasons for the decline in mortality in England and Wales during the nineteenth century. *Population Studies* **26**, pp. 345–382. T. McKeown (1976). *The Modern Rise of Population* (London: Edward Arnold). A. R. Omran (1977). A century of epidemiologic transition in the United States. *Preventive Medicine* **6**, pp. 30–51. Other publications will be referred to elsewhere.

10. T. McKeown, *op. cit.* in note 9, p. 82.

11. J. C. Riley (1987). *The 18th-Century Campaign to Avoid Disease* (London: MacMillan) p. 114.

12. T. McKeown, *op. cit.* in note 9, p. 128.

13. See, for example, E. Van de Walle (1978). Accounting for population growth. *Science* **197**, p. 653. McKeown acknowledged that there was no evidence of an actual improvement in diet: T. McKeown (1978). Fertility, mortality and causes of death. *Population Studies* **32**, p. 541.

14. A. J. Taylor, ed. (1975). *The Standard of Living in Britain in the Industrial Revolution* (London: Methuen): see for example, R. S. Tucker, Real wages of artisans in London, 1729–1935, pp. 21–35; E. J. Hobsbawm, The British standard of living, 1790–1850, pp. 58–92. Also P. H. Lindert and J. G. Williamson (1983). English workers' living standards during the industrial revolution: a new look. *Economic History Review* **36**, pp. 1–25.

15. R. Woods and J. Woodward (1984). Mortality, poverty and the environment. In *Urban Disease and Mortality in Nineteenth-Century England* (London: Batsford) p. 31.

16. A recent study of the mortality transition in Cuba followed the approach to component cause-specific mortality trends used by McKeown and came to similar conclusions about the importance of advances in standard of living. S. Diaz-Briquets (1981). Determinants of mortality transition in developing countries before and after the 2nd World War. *Population Studies* **35**, pp. 399–411.

17. A. R. Omran, *loc. cit.* in note 9.

18. S. J. Kunitz (1984). Mortality change in America, 1620–1920. *Human Biology* **56**(3), pp. 559–582.

19. S. H. Preston (1975). The changing relationship between mortality and level of economic development. *Population Studies* **29** (2), pp. 231–245.

20. See also T.McKeown (1976). *The Role of Medicine: Dream, Mirage or Nemesis?* (London: Nuffield Provincial Hospitals Trust).

21. T. McKeown and R. G. Brown (1955). Medical evidence related to English population changes in the eighteenth century. *Population Studies* **9** , pp. 119–141.

22. J. Woodward (1984). Medicine and the city: the nineteenth-century experi-ence. In R. Woods and J. Woodward, *op. cit.* in note 15, p. 72. S. Cherry (1980). The hospitals and population growth: the voluntary general hospitals, mortality and local populations in the English provinces in the eighteenth and nineteenth centuries, Part II. *Population Studies* **34**(2), pp. 251–265, p. 261.

23. S. Cherry, *loc. cit.* in note 22, pp. 252 and 265.

24. Figures on hospitalisation of infectious-disease cases are given in R. Woods (1984). Mortality and sanitary conditions in late nineteenth-century Birming-ham. In R. Woods and J. Woodward *op. cit.* in note 15, p. 179.

25. See note 8.

26. P. E. Razzell (1974). An interpretation of the modern rise of population in Europe: a critique. *Population Studies* **28**, pp. 5–17.

27. J. C. Riley, *op. cit.* in note 11, p. 133.

28. P. E. Razzell, *loc. cit.* in note 26.

29. T. McKeown and R. G. Brown, *loc. cit.* in note 21.

30. J. Marshall (1832) *Mortality in the Metropolis* (London) gives a summary of the London Bills of Mortality up to 1830.

31 *Northampton Bills of Mortality, 1738–1856: Bills of Mortality for All Saints Parish* (held in the British Library, London). J. Heysham (1794). Abridged observations on the Bills of Mortality for Carlise for 1779–1787. In *The History of Cumberland* (W. Hutchinson ed.) (Carlisle); J. Heysham (1782). *Observations on the Bills of Mortality in Carlisle for the Year 1779* (Carlisle: Mililieu).

32. The Royal Commission on Vaccination (1889–96) referred to many secondary complications and sequelae of smallpox: *Report of the Royal Commission on Vaccination* (London), *Appendix*, p. 90.

33. J. C. Riley, *op. cit.* in note 11, p. 114.

34. E. A. Wrigley and R. Schofield, *op. cit.* in note 3, and R. Woods and J. Woodward, *op. cit.* in note 15.

35. See, for example, Figure 3.12.

36. See T. McKeown, for example, *op. cit.* in note 9, pp. 8–10.

37. D. V. Glass (1973) *Numbering the People* (Farnborough: Saxon House) considered the early observations on the Bills from Graunt onwards, the eighteenth-century population controversy, and the development of census and vital statistics in Britain. See pp. 190–191.

38. J. M. Eyler (1979). *Victorian Social Medicine: The Ideas and Methods of William Farr* (Baltimore: Johns Hopkins University Press), pp. 37–65.

39. *ibid.*

40. D. V. Glass, *op. cit.* in note 37, p. 188.

41. See, for example, F. F. Cartwright (1977) *A Social History of Medicine* (London: Longman), p. 140, on the work of Pasteur and Koch.

42. J. C. Riley, *op. cit.* in note 11, p. 29.

43. F. F. Cartwright, *op. cit.* in note 41, pp. 138–139.

44. The Royal Commission on Vaccination (1889–96). *Report of the Royal Commission on Vaccination* (London).

45. G. M. Howe (1972). *Man, Environment and Disease in Britain: A Medical Geography through the Ages* (Harmondsworth: Penguin), p. 20.

46. See, for example, R. M. Anderson and R. M. May (1982). *Population Biology of Infectious Diseases* (Dahlem Konferenzen, Springer-Verlag).

47. T. McKeown, *op. cit.* in note 9, p. 53.

48. Data will be referred to in Chapter 6 from a study of post-mortem investigations: H. A. Waldron and L. Vickerstaff *Intimations of Quality: Ante-Mortem and Post-Mortem Diagnoses* (London: Nuffield Provincial Hospitals Trust). 1977.

49. See, for example, the editorial in the *British Medical Journal* 1973 (1), p. 29: Pathogenesis of measles.

50. F. M. Burnet (1969) *Cellular Immunology* (Carlton: Melbourne University Press), pp. 21–29.

51. F. M. Burnet (1970) *Immunological Surveillance* (Oxford: Pergammon).

52. For example, J. F. Mustard (1970) Platelets and thromboembolic disease. *Advances in Cardiology* **4**, pp. 131–142; J. F. Mustard, E. A. Murphy, H. C. Rowsell and H. G. Downie (1964) Platelets and atherosclerosis. *Journal of Atherosclerosis Research* **4**, pp. 1–28.

53. A. T. Cockburn (1963) *The Evolution and Eradication of Infectious Diseases* (London and Baltimore).

54. T. P. Magill (1955). The immunologist and the evil spirits. *Journal of Immunology* **74**, pp. 1–8; M. Greenwood, W. W. C. Topley and G. S. Wilson

(1936) *Experimental Epidemiology*. Medical Research Council, Special Report Series No. 209. (London: MRC).

55. W. H. McNeill, *op. cit.* in note 7.
56. *Ibid.*; M. Burnet and D. O. White (1972) *Natural History of Infectious Disease* (London: Cambridge University Press).
57. R. Dubos and J. Dubos (1952) *The White Plague* (London: Gollanz).
58. T. McKeown, *op. cit.* in note 9, has been the main exponent of this hypothesis.
59. C. M. Fletcher (1976) The natural history of chronic bronchitis. *British Medical Journal* 1976(1), pp. 1529–1593; C. M. Fletcher, R. Peto, C. M. Tinker and F. S. Speizer (1978) *The Natural History of Chronic Bronchitis and Emphysema* (London: Oxford University Press).
60. M. Susser and Z. Stein (1962) Civilisation and peptic ulcer. *Lancet* 20 January, pp. 115–119.
61. A. J. Mercer (1981) Risk of dying from tuberculosis and cancer: further aspects of a possible association. *International Journal of Epidemiology* **10** (4), pp. 377–380.
62. F. M. Burnet (1971) *Cellular Immunology* (Carlton: Melbourne University Press), p. 249.
63. Morris discussed some of the results of the national necropsy survey in J. N. Morris (1964) *Uses of Epidemiology* (London: Livingstone): see, for example, p. 146.
64. J. F. Mustard (1970) Platelets and thromboembolic disease. *Advances in Cardiology* **4**, pp. 131–142. J. F. Mustard, E. A. Murphy, H. C. Rowsell and H. G. Downie (1964) Platelets and atherosclerosis. *Journal of Atherosclerosis Research* **4**, pp. 1–28, and other studies referred to in Chapter 6. A general correlation between the decline in circulatory-disease mortality and general mortality levels was reported by S. H. Preston and V. Nelson (1974) Structure and change in cause of death. *Population Studies* **28** (2), pp. 19–52.

Chapter 2

1. The burials in London (the City, Out-parishes and distant parishes) in 1665, amounted to 97,306, of which 68,596 were attributed to plague. Glass suggested that total deaths were almost certainly underestimated, and Graunt showed a sizeable number of deaths from plague were recorded under other categories. Glass suggested that the total population of London before the 1665 plague may have been between 5–600,000, so that possibly one-fifth of the population died in the plague year. D. V. Glass (1973) *Numbering the People* (Farnborough: Saxon House), p. 9.
2. T. McKeown (1976) *The Modern Rise of Population* (London: Edward Arnold), pp. 128–142.
3. E. A. Wrigley and R. Schofield (1981) *The Population History of England 1541–1871: A Reconstruction* (London: Edward Arnold), p. 403–429.
4. In F. M. Burnet and D. O. White (1972) *Natural History of Infectious Disease* (Cambridge: Cambridge University Press), pp. 1–21.
5. W. H. McNeill (1979) *Plagues and Peoples* (Harmondsworth: Penguin), pp. 23–77.
6. M. S. Bartlett (1957) Measles periodicity and community size. *Journal of the Royal Statistical Society* **120**, pp. 48–62.
7. See F. M. Burnet and D. O. White, *op. cit.* in note 4, p. 16.
8. S. J. Kunitz (1984) Mortality change in America, 1620–1920. *Human Biology* **56**(3), pp. 559–582.
9. *Ibid.*, p. 563.

10. A. R. Omran (1977) A century of epidemiologic transition in the United States. *Preventive Medicine* **6**, pp. 30–51.
11. S. J. Kunitz, *loc. cit.* in note 8.
12. M. Flinn (1981) *The European Demographic System, 1500–1820* (Brighton: Harvester), pp. 95–101.
13. W. H. McNeill, *op. cit.* in note 5, p. 227.
14. J. D. Chambers (1972) *Population, Economy and Society in Pre-Industrial England* (London: Oxford University Press), p. 98.
15. J. P. Goubert (1974) *Malades et Médicines en Bretagne, 1770–1970* (Paris), pp. 318–380.
16. S. J. Kunitz (1983) Speculations on the European mortality decline. *Economic History Review* **36**(3), pp. 349–364.
17. *Ibid.*
18. M. Flinn, *op. cit.* in note 12, p. 92.
19. S. Sosner (undated) *Folkevekst og Flytting, I–II.* Diss. Stensiltrykk (University of Oslo), referred to in: I. Larsen (1979) *Eighteenth-Century Diseases, Diagnostic Trends and Mortality* (Oslo: University of Oslo).
20. *Ibid.*
21. J. P. Goubert, *op. cit.* in note 15. See also other records from north-west Europe, in C. Bruneel (1977) *La Mortalité dans les Camapgnes: Le Duché de Brabant aux XVIIe et XVIIIe Siècles* (Louvain), p. 452; W. R. Lee (1977) *Population Growth, Economic Development and Social Change in Bavaria, 1750–1850* (New York: Arno), p. 100.
22. Biraben pointed out that there are three main varieties of virus responsible for the plague, in Asia for example, which come under the genus *Yersinia*. There is a close relationship with the bacillus *Yersinia pseudotuberculosis* which has antigens in common with plague bacillus, such that one may transform itself into the other by some as yet unknown mechanism. The plague bacillus is also very closely related to a third micro-organism of the same genus, *Yersinia enterocolitica* which has appeared recently and spread rapidly. *Yersinia pseudotuberculosis* is relatively inocuous to man and produces a mild disease, especially in children, with fever and abdominal pain. Biraben pointed out that there is considerable interest in the cross-immunity with plague bacillus, since even if *Yersinia pseudotuberculosis* produces no clinical symptoms, it gives both man and rats total immunity against plague. He suggested that a hypothesis could be advanced that the appearance of such a new form of bacillus might have caused the disappearance of the plague after the seventeenth century in Europe. A change in the immune status of the population might have resulted from this kind of cross-immunity, although *Yersinia pseudotuberculosis* itself could not have played such a role as it has only recently become widespread. See J.-N. Biraben (1977) Current medical and epidemiological views on the plague. In *The Plague Reconsidered. Local Population Studies, Supplement* (Stafford: Hourdsprint).
23. N. L. Tranter (1985) *Population and Society 1750–1940* (London: Longman), p. 66.
24. R. Pollitzer (1954) *Plague* (Geneva: World Health Organization), pp. 282–299; A. A. Appleby (1977). Famine, mortality and epidemic diseases: a comment. *Economic History Review* **30**(3), pp. 508–510.
25. See M. Flinn, *op. cit.* in note 12, pp. 58–64; J. D. Post (1976). Famine, mortality and epidemic disease in the process of modernisation. *Economic History Review* **29**(1), pp. 14–37.
26. *Ibid.*, p. 58–61.
27. P. Slack (1985) *The Impact of Plague in Tudor and Stuart England* (London:

Routledge), p. 313. Figures for Marseilles and Hong Kong given by F. F. Cartwright (1977) *A Social History of Medicine* (London: Longman), p. 71; figure for Moscow given by W. H. McNeill, *op. cit.* in note 5, p. 225.

28. A. Hardy (1983) Smallpox in London: factors in the decline of the disease in the nineteenth century. *Medical History* **27**, pp. 111–138.

29. P. Slack, *loc. cit.* in note 27; see penultimate chapter for a discussion of the final epidemic in England in the 1660s.

30. J. Hatcher (1977) *Plague, Population and the English Economy 1348–1530* (London: Macmillan): see pp. 68–73.

31. W. H. McNeill, *op. cit.* in note 5, p. 221.

32. C. Creighton (1894) *A History of Epidemics in Britain* (Cambridge: Cambridge University Press), p. 775.

33. J. Heysham (1782) *Observations on the Bills of Mortality in Carlise for the Year 1779* (Carlisle: Mililieu). Abridged observations on the Bills of Mortality for Carlisle for 1779–1787, in W. Hutchinson (1794) *The History of Cumberland*.

34. A. Perrenoud (1979) *La Population de Genève du Seiziéme au debut du Dix-neuvième Siècle* (Geneva), pp. 458–479.

35. L. Widen (1975) *Mortality and Causes of Death in Sweden during the 18th Century.* Statistisk Tidskrift (Stockholm).

36. B. I. Lindskos (1978) Mortalitaetsdiagnosen in Suedschweden 1749–1801. In *Medizinische Diagnostik in Geschichte und Gesenwart*, C. Habrick *et al.*, eds (Munich: Fritsh), pp. 583–606.

37. O. Turpeinen (1980) Les causes des fluctuations annuelles du taux de mortalité finalandaise entre 1750 et 1806. *Annales de Demographie Historique* (Paris), pp. 287–296.

38. See T. McKeown, R. G. Record and R. G. Brown (1972) An interpretation of the modern rise of population in Europe. *Population Studies* **26**, pp. 345–382. The role of medicine was further discussed in T. McKeown (1976) *The Modern Rise of Population* (London: Edward Arnold) and in T. McKeown (1976) *The Role of Medicine: Dream, Mirage or Nemesis?* (London: Nuffield Provincial Hospitals Trust).

39. See P. E. Razzell (1974) An interpretation of the modern rise of population in Europe: a critique. *Population Studies* **28**, pp. 5–17, p. 5.

40. E. A. Wrigley and R. Schofield, *op. cit.* in note 3, p. 244.

41. M. Flinn, *op. cit.* in note 12, pp. 92–95.

42. E. A. Wrigley and R. Schofield, *op. cit.* in note 3, p. 332.

43. *Ibid.*, pp. 332–355.

44. *Ibid.*, pp. 416–417.

45. B. Appleby (1975) Nutrition and disease: the case of London, 1550–1750. *Journal of Interdisciplinary History* **6**, pp. 1–22.

46. *Ibid.*

47. See P. M. Newberne and G. Williams (1970) Nutritional influences on the course of infections. In *Resistance to Infectious Disease*, R. H. Dunlop and H. W. Moon, eds (Saskatoon Modern Press), p. 93.

48. J. C. Riley (1987) *The Eighteenth-Century Campaign to Avoid Disease* (London: Macmillan), p. 114.

49. Scandinavian studies in particular have considered the evidence, for example G. Ütterström (1954) Some population problems in pre-industrial Sweden. *Scandinavian Economic History Review* **2**, pp. 103–165.

50. See the studies by T. McKeown referred to in note 38, particularly *The Modern Rise of Population*, p. 128. Also T. McKeown and R. G. Brown (1955) Medical evidence related to English population change in the eighteenth century. *Population Studies* **9**, pp. 119–141; E. Van de Walle (1978)

Accounting for population growth. *Science* **197**, p. 653.

51. M. Flinn, *op. cit.* in note 12, p. 50.

52. *Ibid.*, p. 72.

53. *Ibid.*, p. 96

54. *Ibid.*, p. 97.

55. *Ibid.*, p. 96.

56. P. E. Razzell, *loc. cit.* in note 39, p. 8. See also E. J. Hobsbawm (1975) The British standard of living, 1790–1850. In *The Standard of Living in Britain in the Industrial Revolution*, A. J. Taylor ed. (London), pp. 58–92.

57. J. T. Krause (1958) Changes in English fertility and mortality, 1781–1850. *Economic History Review* **11**, pp. 52–70.

58. J. D. Chambers (1957) The Vale of Trent, 1670–1800. *Economic History Review, Supplement 3*, pp. 29–57.

59. R. Pickard (1947) *Population and Epidemics of Exeter* (Exeter: Exeter University Press), p. 47.

60. P. H. Lindert and J. G. Williamson (1983) English workers' living standards during the industrial revolution: a new look. *Economic History Review* **36**, pp. 1–25, p. 12.

61. P. E. Razzell, *loc. cit.* in note 39, p. 7, referred to these data. See also A. J. Taylor, *op. cit.* in note 56, pp. 11–13.

62. G. N. Von Tunzelmann (1979) Trends in real wages, 1750–1850, revisisted. *Economic History Review* **32**, pp. 33–49; M. Flinn (1974) Trends in real wages, 1750–1850, *Economic History Review* **27**, pp. 395–413. Trends in food prices in London are given in R. S. Tucker (1975) Real wages of artisans in London, 1729–1935, in A. J. Taylor ed., *op. cit.* in note 56, pp. 21–35.

63. A.J. Taylor, *op. cit.* in note 56, pp. 1–20.

64 R. Floud and K. W. Wachter (1982) Poverty and physical stature. *Social Science History* **4**, pp. 422–452: see graphs on p. 435.

65. R. W. Fogel, S. L. Engerman and J. Trussel (1982) Exploring the uses of data on height: the analysis of long-term trends in nutrition, labour welfare, and labour productivity. *Social Science History* **4**, pp. 401–421. Data from the National Child Development Study has also indicated that mother's height, length of gestation and birthweight were associated with height at age 7 years, while earlier studies of children under 5 years, found that maternal care was particularly important in social-class differences in the impact of infectious diseases on health. See H. Goldstein (1971) Factors influencing the height of seven-year old children: results from the National Child Development Study. *Human Biology* **43**, pp. 92–111; J. W. B. Douglas and J. M. Blomfield (1958) *Children Under 5* (London: Allen and Unwin), p. 141.

66. J. N. Morris (1964) *Uses of Epidemilogy* (London: Livingstone), p. 62, referring to the study by J. Clay (1844) *Report of the Commission for Enquiry into the State of Large Towns and Populous Districts* (London) Appendix, p. 41.

67. W. A. Armstrong (1981) The trend of mortality in Carlisle between the 1780s and the 1840s: a demographic contribution to the standard-of-living debate. *Economic History Review* **34**, pp. 94–114, p. 94.

68. F. Engels (1845/1982) *The Condition of the Working Class in England* (London: Granada), pp. 137–140.

69. J. Burnett (1979) *Plenty and Want: A Social History of Diet in England from 1815 to the Present Day* (London: Scolar Press).

70. See J. Burnett, *op. cit.* in note 69; C. Booth (1902–4) *Life and Labour of the People in London* (London); B. S. Rowntree (1901) *Poverty: A Study of Town Life* (London: Macmillan).

71. J. D. Oddy (1982) The health of the people. In *Population and Society in Britain*, T. Barker and M. Drake eds (1964) (London: Batsford), pp. 121–139.

72. T. H. Hollingsworth (1964) The demography of the British peerage. *Population Studies, Supplement* **18**(2), p. 57.

73. E. A. Wrigley and R. Schofield, *op. cit.* in note 3, p. 231 and p. 243.

74. M. Flinn (1970) *British Population Growth, 1700–1850* (London: Macmillan), pp. 45–50; K. F. Helleiner (1965) The vital revolution reconsidered. In *Population in History: Essays in Historical Demography*, D. V. Glass and D. E. V. Eversley, eds (London: Edward Arnold), pp. 79–86. Both studies emphasised this point about the population growth in the eighteenth century returning to sixteenth-century levels. Much of the decline was thought to have been in the first half of the century until the work by Wrigley and Schofield. Early series of birth rates suggested a rise between 1700 and 1800, but with most of the increase in the first half of the century: G. T. Griffith (1926) *Population Problems in the Age of Malthus* (Cambridge); J. Brownlee (1916) History of birth and death rates in England and Wales taken as a whole, from 1570 to the present time. *Public Health* **29**, pp. 228–238. On reconstruction of these data it has been found that birth rates may have declined in the second half of the eighteenth century in every decade in both rural and urban areas: D. J. Loschky (1969) Urbanisation and England's eigtheenth-century crude birth rate and death rate. *Journal of European Economic History* **1**(3), pp.697–712.

75. Data given in E. A. Wrigley and R. Schofield, *op. cit.* in note 3, pp. 531–535.

76. M. Flinn, *op. cit.* in note 12, pp. 47–64, p. 80.

77. C. McEvedy and R. Jones (1978) *Atlas of World Population History* (Harmondsworth: Penguin), p. 18.

78. E.A. Wrigley and R. Schfield, *op. cit.* in note 3, pp. 403–412.

79. *Ibid.*, p. 412. T. R. Malthus (1798/1970) *An Essay on the Principle of Population, 1798*. A. Flew, ed. (Harmondsworth: Penguin) see for example p. 77.

80. *Ibid.*, p. 417.

81. Ibid., p. 420.

82. E. A. Wrigley and R. Schofield, *op. cit.* in note 3, data on pp. 528–529; Phelps-Brown and Hopkins index of prices based on evidence that 80% of household expenditure was on food, and index of real wages for building craftsmen. E. H. Phelps-Brown and S. V. Hopkins, Seven centuries of the prices of consumables compared with builders' wage rates. In *Essays in Economic History, II*. Carus-Wilson, ed., pp. 179–196.

83. *Ibid.*, p. 453.

84. J. A. Goldstone (1986). The demographic revolution in England: a re-examination. *Population Studies* **49**, pp. 5–33, pp. 13–14.

85. E. A Wrigley and R. Schofield, *op. cit.* in note 3, pp. 350–355.

86. *Ibid.*, p. 324.

87. *Ibid.*, p. 363.

88. *Ibid.*, p. 355.

89. P. E. Razzell (1977) *The Conquest of Smallpox* (Firle, Sussex: Caliban), pp. 108–110.

90. W. T. Councilman *et al.*, (1909) The pathological anatomy and histology of variola. In *Studies in the Pathology and the Etiology of Variola and Vaccination*, pp. 69–70; A. M. Phadke *et al.*, (1973) Smallpox as an etiologic factor in male infertility. *Fertility and Sterility* **24**, pp. 802–804.

91. T. H. Hollingsworth, *op. cit.* in note 72, pp. 29–31.

92. Recent work at the MRC Unit of Reproductive Biology and Edinburgh has

indicated that the main variables involved in post-partum infertility are suckling frequency and suckling duration. See S. W. Howie, A. S. McNeilly, M. J. Houston, A. Cook and H. Boyle (1981) Effect of supplementary food on suckling patterns and ovarian activity during lactation. *British Medical Journal* 19 Sept., **283**, p. 757.

This period of natural infertility not only enables a mother to regain her physical and emotional strength between pregnancies, but confers advantages on the child with regard to better health and development. The mechanism itself is regarded as being neural, with an increased hypothalmic sensitivity to the negative feedback effect of ovarian steroids, leading to a failure of adequate gonadotrophin production from the pituitary which is required for ovulation. See A. S. McNeilly (1979) Effects of lactation on fertility. *British Medical Bulletin* **35**, pp. 151–154.

A further study pointed out the prolonged birth-spacing of up to four years associated with frequent short bursts of suckling during the first three years of life, among the !Kung, which may relate to certain aspects of the way-of-life of these gatherer-hunters in the Kalahari Desert. A further study stressed that breast-feeding could not be relied on by individual mothers as a guarantee against pregnancy, but the aggregate effects in a population mean that it can be regarded as an important component of fertility control, and certainly where alternative methods are used infrequently. Further to this, any abandonment of prolonged breast-feeding is likely to influence not only suckling frequency and duration but also, through this, to contribute to the resumption of ovulation at an earlier stage. See M. Konner and C. Worthman (1980) Nursing frequency, gonadal function and birth spacing among !Kung hunter-gatherers. *Science* **207**, pp. 788–791. P. W. Howie and A. S. McNeilly (1982) Effect of breast-feeding patterns on human birth intervals. *Journal of Reproductive Fertility* **65**, pp. 559–569, and *loc. cit.* above under P. W. Howie *et al.*

93. See S. H. Preston, ed., (1977) *The Effects of Infant and Child Mortality on Fertility.* (New York: Academic Press).

94. See notes 74 and 84; Razzell also quesioned the assumed proportion marrying: P. E. Razzell (1982) Neo-Malthusianism. *New Society*, 4 February, p. 201. Estimates of mean age of women at first marriage given by Flinn, although only based on a small number of parish records, did not suggest a dramatic reduction in the eighteenth century: Flinn, *op. cit.* in note 12, pp. 124–125.

95. Schofield examined the question of change in population growth rates in the period 1750–1850, and the relative mathematical contribution of fertility and mortality change. Changes in Sweden were more consistently due to falling mortality than indicated by estimates for England. He suggested that population growth rates in this period were more attributable to increases in the birth rate in England, despite the decline in Gross Reproduction Rate estimated to have occurred after 1816. In France, GRR declined consistently over the period as a whole while average expectation of life at birth increased: R. Schofield (1985) Population growth in the century after 1750: the role of mortality decline. In *Pre-Industrial Population Change: The Mortality Decline and Short-term Population Movements*, T. Bengtsson, G. Fridlizius and R. Ohlsson, eds (Stockholm: Almquist and Wiksell International), pp. 17–40.

96. M. Flinn, *op. cit.* in note 12, pp. 100–101.

97. See, for example, the estimates given by Brownlee, *loc. cit.* in note 74.

98. Fridlizius, for example, rejected the view that improved nutritional resistance to infectious disease occurred in Scandinavia, because of the lack of evidence that per capita food consumption improved before the mid nineteenth century. He also noted that the decline in mortality began at about the same time and

followed a similar pattern in regions which differed socio-economically as well as geographically. G. Fridlizius (1985). The mortality decline in the first phase of the demographic transition: Swedish experiences. In *op. cit.* in note 95, pp. 71–114. Perrenoud pointed out the simultaneity and similarity of patterns of mortality decline in areas of France with quite different economic and social development: A. Perrenoud (1985) Mortality decline in its secular setting. In *op. cit.* in note 95, pp. 41–70.

99. P. R. Galloway (1988) Basic patterns in annual variations in fertility, nuptiality, mortality and prices in pre-industrial Europe. *Population Studies* **42**, pp. 275–303.

100. M. W. Flinn (1970) *British Population Growth, 1700–1850* (London: Macmillan), p. 47.

101. P. R. Galloway, *loc. cit.* in note 99.

102. N. L. Tranter, *op. cit.* in note 23, p. 83.

103. M. W. Flinn, *op. cit.* in note 12, p. 97; and data from the London Bills of Mortality shown in Figure 3.7.

104. This has been suggested, for example, by G. Fridlizius, *loc. cit.* in note 98, and G. Fridlizius and R, Ohlsson (1985) Mortality patterns in Sweden, 1751–1802: a regional analysis. In *op. cit.* in note 95. Fridlizius doubted that inoculation had been used widely enough in Sweden after it was introduced in the 1780s, or that vaccination had been sufficiently effective to have caused the mortality decline, but the evidence was not examined in detail.

Chapter 3

1. P. E. Razzell (1965) Population change in 18th-century England: a reinterpretation. *Economic History Reivew* **18**, pp. 312–332.

2. T. McKeown (1976) *The Modern Rise of Population* (London: Edward Arnold), p. 107; T. McKeown, R. G. Record and R. G. Brown (1972) An interpretation of the modern rise of population in Europe. *Population Studies* **26**, pp. 345–383.

3. The Royal Commission on Vaccination (1889–96) *Report of the Royal Commission on Vaccination, Final Report*, (London), p. 18. Creighton also gave evidence of a much lower number of deaths in smallpox epidemics in the small rural town of Blandford, when about one in seven of the population had been recorded as receiving inoculation: C. Creighton (1894) *A History of Epidemics in Britain* (Cambridge: Cambridge University Press), p. 513.

4. P. E. Razzell (1977) *The Conquest of Smallpox* (Firle, Sussex: Caliban), p. 143.

5. P. E. Razzell (1977) *Edward Jenner's Cowpox Vaccine: the History of a Medical Myth* (Firle, Sussex: Caliban). See also W. Luckin (1977) The decline of smallpox and the demographic revolution of the eighteenth century. *Social History* **6**, pp. 793–797; F. F. Cartwright (1977) *A Short History of Medicine* (London: Longmans), pp. 90–91.

6. See K. Chimin Wong and Wu Lien-Teh (1932) *History of Chinese Medicine* (China: Tientsin Press), p. 140.

7. W. H. McNeill (1976) *Plagues and Peoples* (Harmondsworth: Penguin), pp. 230–236. G. Miller (1957) *The Adoption of Inoculation for Smallpox in England and France* (London: Oxford University Press) considered the social and political context.

8. L. Henry and Y. Blayo (1975) La population de la France de 1740 à 1860. *Population*, Numéro special, November 1975, pp. 71–122. The data from

France suggest that there may have been an exceptional decline in the birth rate in that country, from about the same time. McKeown also referred to this in a comparison with Sweden and England, in *op. cit.* in note 2, p. 30.

9. The Royal Commission on Vaccination, *op. cit.* in note 3, *First Report, Appendix*, pp. 112–113.
10. *Ibid.* Data taken from *First Report*, pp. 107–111.
11. Data from censuses in different European countries are summarised in B.R. Mitchell (1971) *European Historical Statistics, 1750–1850* (London: Macmillan), pp. 19–24.
12. See also H. O. Hansen (1981) Some age-structural consequences of mortality variations in pre-transitional Iceland and Sweden. In *The Great Mortalities: Methodological Studies of Demographic Crises in the Past*, H. Charbonneau and A. Larose, ed. (Liège: Ordna).
13. The Royal Commission on Vaccination, *op. cit.* in note 3, *First Report, Appendix*, pp. 112–113.
14. G. Fridlizius and R. Ohlsson (1985) Mortality patterns in Sweden, 1751–1802: a regional analysis; G. Fridlizius (1985). The mortality decline in the first phase of the demographic transition: Swedish experiences. In *Pre-Industrial Population Change: The Mortality Decline and Short-term Population Movements*, T. Bengtsson, G. Fridlizius and R. Ohlsson, eds (Stockholm: Almquist and Wiksell International).
15. P. E. Siljeström (1885) *En Studie i Sjukdomsstatististik* (Stockholm). Data given to the author by Dr Roger Schofield of the Cambridge Group for the History of Population and Social Structure.
16. E. Hofsten and H. Lundström (1977) *Swedish Population History: Main Trends from 1750–1970*, Urval No. 8 (Stockholm: Statistiska Centralbyran), pp. 55–59.
17. L. Widen (1975) Mortality and causes of death in Sweden during the 18th century. *Statistisk Tidskrift* (Stockholm), pp. 89–104.
18. G. Ütterstrom (1954) Some population problems in pre-industrial Sweden, *Scandinavian Economic History Review* **2**, pp. 103–165, considered the relationship between smallpox epidemics and poor harvests.
19. Hedrich showed that epidemics of measles for example, corresponded with peaks in the proportion of non-immune new susceptibles in the population: A. W. Hedrich (1930) The corrected average attack rate for measles among city children. *American Journal of Hygiene* **11**, pp. 576–600.
20. G. Üttestrom, *loc, cit.* in note 18.
21. O. Turpeinen (1980) Les causes des fluctuations annuelles du taux de mortalité Finlandaise entre 1750 et 1806. *Annales de Demographie Historique* (Paris), pp. 287–296.
22. O. Turpeinen (1978) Finnish death rates 1749–1773. *Population Studies* **32**, p. 528. Separate figures for smallpox and measles mortality in Finland as a whole for the period 1776–1800 show that about 87% of the combined death rate was due to smallpox. Data from O. Turpeinen, *loc. cit.* in note 21; and data from O. Turpeinen (1979) Fertility and mortality in Finland since 1750. *Population Studies* **33**(1), pp. 101–114.
23. See O. Turpeinen (1979), *loc. cit.* in note 22, pp. 108–109.
24. *Ibid.*, p. 104.
25. *Ibid.*, p. 105. Infant mortality declined most in districts where breast-feeding had not been practiced in mid eighteenth century, but had probably become more widespread following campaigns to encourage the practice and promote better infant care and hygiene.
26. K. J. Pitkanen, J. H. Mielke and L. B. Jorde (1989) Smallpox and its eradication in Finland: implications for disease control. *Population Studies*

43, pp. 95–111.

27. A. Perrenoud (1978) La mortalié à Genève de 1625 à 1825. *Annales de Demographie Historique* pp. 209–233.

28. Data from Norway were illustrated by M. Drake (1969) *Population and Society in Norway 1735–1865* (Cambridge: Cambridge University Press), 1969, p. 44 and pp. 52–54. Data taken from B. R. Mitchell, *op. cit.* in note 11, pp. 104–107, and this volume also contains data from Finland.

29. C. M. Cipolla (1965) Four centuries of Italian demographic development. In D. V. Glass and D. E. C. Eversley, eds *Population in History: Essays in Historical Demography* (London: Edward Arnold), pp. 577–587, data on pp. 576–577.

30. The Royal Commission on Vaccination, *op. cit.* in note 3, *Final Report*, p. 65.

31. E. J. Edwardes (1902) *A Concise History of Smallpox and Vaccination in Europe* (London: Lewis), pp. 12, 18–19, 48 and 50.

32. A graph of data from Austria, where vaccination was less widely used, shows that peaks in the death rate regularly exceeded the level of the birth rate in that country until the late nineteenth century, unlike in many other European countries, with the exception of Ireland, where diseases other than smallpox may have been involved: H. Helczmanovski (1979) Austria–Hungary. In *European Demography and Economic Growth* , W. R. Lee, ed. (London: Croom Helm).

33. T. McKeown, *op. cit.* in note 2, p. 108, pp. 6–10 and p. 59.

34. P. E. Razzell, *op. cit.* in note 4; *loc. cit.* in note 1, pp. 312–332.

35. *Ibid.*; D. W. Zwanenberg (1978) The Suttons and the business of inoculation. *Medical History* **22**.

36. P. E. Razzell (1974) The smallpox controversy. *Local Population Studies* **12**, pp. 42–44. Bradley disputed the contention that smallpox was universal in eighteenth-century England, and challenged the idea that mortality from smallpox was very high anyway before inoculation was used on a large scale. See L. Bradley in his reply to a review in *Local Population Studies* 1973, **10**, pp. 67–68, and in the introduction to *Smallpox Inoculation: an 18th-Century Mathematical Controversy*, with translation and critical commentary, L. Bradley, ed. (Nottingham: University of Nottingham Adult Education Department, 1971). T. Short (1749). *A History of the Air, Weather, Seasons, etc.* (London), p. 518, gives data from the smallpox censuses.

37. J. Landers (1987) Mortality and metropolis: the case of London 1675–1825. *Population Studies* **41**, pp. 59–76, 66 and 73.

38. *Ibid.*

39. C. Creighton, *op. cit.* in note 3, pp. 525–526, 540. A continuous series of data for Boston, Lincs., reveals a similar pattern to that for Chester, while epidemics in the smaller town of Banbury were less frequent, and data from the larger town of Edinburgh show the disease was endemic there (p. 526).

40. *Ibid.*, p. 526.

41. W. H. McNeill, *op. cit.* in note 7, p. 230.

42. *The Census of Great Britain, Parish Register Abstracts* (London, 1801) included examples of parishes with excess baptisms over burials during the second half of the eighteenth century, although only data at ten-year intervals are given.

43. Watt was the first to make a detailed study of deaths from smallpox in relation to other diseases, in Glasgow: R. Watt (1813) *Treatise on the History, Nature and Treatment of Chincough* (Glasgow). See also W. A. Guy (1882) 250 years of smallpox in London. *Journal of the Royal Statistical Society* **45**, pp. 399–443.

44. Most of the data from the Bills were extracted by Marshall who gave a summary of the Bills: J. Marshall (1832) *Mortality in the Metropolis* (London).

Any data from the Bills after 1830, used in this study have been extracted from the original Bills held in the Guildhall Library, London.

45. A reasonably firm figure for the population within the area of the Bills, comes from the census of 1801, when it was about 750,000. Although the Bills show that the population was not increasing naturally before this time – and in fact there was quite a deficit of baptisms compared with burials throughout the eighteenth century – it seems likely that the population did not decrease because of in-migration. If in fact the population of 1700 had been above the 1801 level, the baptism rate would have been very low at under 21.0 per 1,000. Even allowing for under-registration this seems rather low for the period. Gregory King estimated the population of the whole of London at about 528,000 for 1695. (See D. V. Glass (1969) Socio-economic status and occupation in the City of London at the end of the 17th century. In *Studies in Local History*, A. E. J. Hollaender and W. Kellerway, eds. (London: Hodder and Stoughton), pp. 373–389). The proportion of the population of London in 1801 that was within the parishes covered by the Bills was 85%, and assuming a similar ratio in 1695, the population would have been about 450,000 on King's estimate. This figure may be too low, and the method he used – based on household numbers and an estimate of the density according to national figures – has been criticised as somewhat obscure and dubious. (See P. E. Jones and A. V. Judges (1935) London population in the late 17th century. *Economic History Review* 6, pp. 45–63). Glass suggested that the population of London at the time of the plague was probably between 500,000–600,000 and a figure of 575,000 was estimated by E. A. Wrigley (1967) A simple model of London's importance in changing English society and economy, 1650–1750. *Past and Present* 37, p. 45. Using the above ratio of 85%, the population within the area of the Bills at 1700 was probably between 450,000 and 550,000. A working figure of 500,000 has been used in Appendix 3d for the calculation of some very crude cause-specific death rates.

46. P. E. Razzell, *op. cit.* in note 4, p. 105.

47. During these nine years, smallpox deaths accounted for 13.1% of all deaths, a figure comparable with the 13.8% found in Manchester for the longer period, 1754–74, by T. Percival (1973) Essays on the Smallpox and Measles. In *Population and Diseases in Early Industrial England*, B. Benjamin, ed. (Gregg International) p. 82. The burial records for the period after the Bills were sent to Joshua Milne. The totals are given by Lonsdale, and indicate a fall of about 3 per 1,000 population in the crude death rate after vaccination, on the basis of population figures given by Heysham: H. Lonsdale (1970) *The Life of John Heysham MD* (London: Longman's Green) see pp. 52–53 and Table VIII which summarises cause-of-death statistics from the Bills. (See also D. V. Glass (1973) *The Development of Population Statistics* (Farnborough: Saxon House), (no page numbers), for reproductions of the Bills.

48. See P.E. Razzell, *op. cit.* in note 4, pp. 145–146. J. Heysham (1782) *Observations on the Bills of Mortality in Carlisle for the Year 1779* (Carlisle: Mililieu); J. Heysham (1794) Abridged observations on the Bills of Mortality for Carlisle for 1779–1787. In *The History of Cumberland*, W. Hutchinson ed.

49. *The Parish Register of St John's Chester* is held at the County Records Office, Chester. The term natural increase in population is used to refer to the difference between births and deaths only, that is excluding migration.

50. P.E. Razzell, *op. cit.* in note 4, p. 73.

51. W.A. Armstrong (1981) The trend of mortality in Carlisle between the 1780s and the 1840s: a demographic contribution to the standard of living debate. *Economic History Review* 34, pp. 99–114, pp. 107–108.

52. E. J. Edwardes, *op. cit.* in note 31.

53. S. Cherry (1979) The hospitals and population growth: voluntary hospitals, mortality and local population in the English provinces in the 18th and 19th centuries, Part I. *Population Studies* **34**, pp. 59–74, p.69.

54. Data from Warrington are given in *op. cit.* in note 3, *Final Report, Appendix IV*, p. 41.

55. Cherry presented many of these data which were extracted from parish registers, and suggested that it was more likely that the figures for the early decades of the nineteenth century reflected a low point in the accuracy of the registers, rather than a reduction in the death rate. However, no evidence or reason for this was given, and the fact that some kind of change occurred in several towns might be taken to reflect some common influence. S. Cherry, *loc.cit.* in note 53. See also M. W. Flinn (1981) *The European Demographic System 1500–1820* (Brighton: Harvester), p. 99.

56. A. Hardy (1983) Smallpox in London: Factors in the decline of the disease in the nineteenth century. *Medical History* **27**, pp. 111–138.

57. H. J. Parish (1968) Victory With Vaccines (Edinburgh: Livingstone), pp. 57–58.

58. Registrar-General (1962) *Annual Statistical Review for England and Wales* (London: HMSO), Part I Medical, p. 14 and p. 351.

Chapter 4

1. A. Hardy (1988) Diagnosis, death and diet: the case of London, 1750–1909. *Journal of Interdisciplinary History* **18**, pp. 387–401, p. 390.

2. V. A. Fildes (1986) *Breasts, Bottles and Babies* (Edinburgh: Edinburgh University Press), p. 253 and p. 390.

3. A. Hardy, *loc, cit.* in note 1, p. 390.

4. V. A. Fildes, *loc. cit.* in note 2, p. 390.

5. W. Black (1788) *A Comparative View of the Mortality of the Human Species at all Ages* (London: Printed for C. Dilly). W. Heberden (1801/1973) *Observations on the Increase and Decrease of Different Diseases*, reprinted in *Population and Disease in Early Industrial England*, B. Benjamin, ed. (West Germany: Gregg International).

6. P. E. Razzell (1979) *The Conquest of Smallpox* (Firle, Sussex: Caliban), p. 105.

7. Pearsons product-moment correlation coefficients based on detrended series of quinquennial data for the period after the plague, 1671/75 to 1831/35, smallpox: infancy +0.59 ($p < 0.0005$), smallpox: fevers +0.64 ($p < 0.0005$), smallpox: total burials + 0.49 ($p < 0.0005$). The use of annual deaths – rather than data with epidemic fluctuations removed – for the computation of z scores to assess the correlation between short-term variations in mortality for different cause-groups resulted in a lower correlation between smallpox deaths and those from other causes, than between the other causes of death themselves: J. Landers (1987) Mortality and metropolis: the case of London 1675–1825. *Population Studies* **41**, pp. 59–76, p. 73.

8. E. A. Wrigley and R. Schofield (1983) English population history from family reconstitution. *Population Studies* **37**, p. 157.

9. E. A. Wrigley (1977) Births and baptisms: the use of Anglican baptism registers as a source of information about the numbers of births in England before the beginning of civil registration. *Population Studies* **31**(2), pp. 281–312, p. 286 and p. 292.

10. J. Landers, *loc. cit.* in note 7, p. 66.
11. T. H. Hollingsworth (1964) A demographic study of the British ducal families. *Population Studies, Supplement,* **18**(2).
12. R. E. Jones (1980) Further evidence on the decline in infant mortality in North Shropshire 1561–1810. *Population Studies* **34**(2), pp. 239–250.
13. *Ibid.*
14. V. A. Fildes, *op. cit.* in note 2, p. 81.
15. See evidence on maternal mortality in E. A. Wrigley and R. Schofield (1981) *The Population History of England 1541–1871: A Reconstruction* (London: Edward Arnold), pp. 157–184.
16. F. B. Smith (1979) *The People's Health, 1830–1910* (London: Croom Helm), p. 87.
17. See, for example, the discussion by B. Thompson (1984) Infant mortality in Bradford. In *Urban Disease and Mortality in 19th-Century England* R. Woods and J. Woodward, eds. (London: Batsford), p. 143.
18. *Ibid.*
19. See Registrar-General's Reports and Commentary for these years, which discuss this aspect of diarrhoeal-disease mortality, and also the graphs of temperature and diarrhoeal deaths in A. H. Gale (1959) *Epidemic Diseases* (Harmondsworth: Penguin), p. 85.
20. S. H. Preston and E. Van de Walle (1978) Urban French mortality in the 19th century. *Population Studies* **32**(2), pp. 275–291.
21 S. H. Preston (1976) *Mortality Patterns in National Populations* (New York: Academic Press), p. 44.
22. B. Thompson, *loc. cit.* in note 17, p. 129.
23. A. K. Chalmers (1905) Infant mortality. *Public Health* **18**(7), pp. 209–438.
24. P. Watterson (1984) Environmental factors in infant and early-childhood mortality decline in England and Wales, 1895–1910. *Bulletin of the Society for the Social History of Medicine* **35**, December, pp. 37–40.
25. B. Thompson, *loc. cit.* in note 17, p. 143.
26. N. L. Tranter (1985) *Population and Society 1750–1940* (London: Longman), pp. 80–81, questioned whether the use of sterilised milk could have made any significant impact as suggested by M. W. Beaver (1973) Population, infant mortality and milk. *Population Studies* **27**, pp. 243–254. Evidence from St Helens given in *Lancet* 16 August, 1902, p. 478, and referred to by F. B. Smith, *op. cit.* in note 16.
27. See Chapter 2, note 92.
28. V. A. Fildes, *op. cit.* in note 2, p. 81 and p. 88.
29. *Ibid.*, p. 91.
30. R. I. Woods, P. A. Watterson and J. H. Woodward (1988) The causes of rapid infant mortality decline in England and Wales, 1861–1921, Part I. *Population Studies* **42**, pp. 343–366, p. 356.
31. R. I. Woods (1987) The fertility transition in Victorian England. *Population Studies* **41**, pp. 283–311, p. 295. S. H. Preston (1985) Mortality in childhood: lessons from the WFS. In *Reproductive Change in Developing Countries*, J. Cleland and J. Hobcraft, eds. (Oxford: Oxford University Press), pp. 253–272. R. I. Woods, P. A. Watterson and J. H. Woodward (1984) The causes of rapid infant mortality decline in England and Wales, 1861–1921, Part II. *Population Studies* **43**, pp. 113–132, p. 125 and p. 126.
32. J. M. Winter (1982) Aspects of the impact of the First World War on infant mortality in Britain. *Journal of European Economic History* **11**, pp. 713–738. P. A. Watterson (1988) Infant mortality by father's occupation from the 1911 census of England and Wales. *Demography* **25**(2), pp. 289–306, p. 295.

33. P. A. Watterson, *loc. cit.* in note 32, pp. 298–302.
34. P. A. Watterson (1984) Environmental factors in infant and early childhood mortality decline in England and Wales, 1895–1910. *Bulletin of the Society for the Social History of Medicine,* **35**, December, pp. 37–40.
35. R. Reeves (1985) Declining fertility in England and Wales as a major cause of the twentieth-century decline in mortality. *American Journal of Epidemiology* **122**(1), pp. 112–126.
36. R. I. Woods, P. A. Watterson and J. H. Woodward, *loc. cit.* in note 31, p. 122.
37. See, for example, D. Dwork (1987) *War is Good for Babies and other Young Children* (London).
38. F. B. Smith, *op. cit.* in note 16.
39. C. Creighton (1894) A History of Epidemics in Britain (Cambridge: Cambridge University Press), pp. 82–84 and p. 133.
40. H. Zinsser (1934) *Rats, Lice and History* reprinted 1985 (Basingstoke: MacMillan), p. 217. Typhus was labelled as 'purples and spotted fever' in 1629, but was merged with the general fevers category in 1729. See A. B. Appleby (1975) Nutrition and disease: the case of London, 1550–1750. *Journal of Interdisciplinary History* **6**, pp. 1–22.
41. H. Zinsser, *op. cit.* in note 40, p. 221.
42. A. B. Appleby, *loc. cit.* in note 40.
43. J. C. Riley (1987) *The Eighteenth-Century Campaign to Avoid Disease* (London: Macmillan) discussed the impact of the ideas of Pringle particularly on the ventilation of prisons.
44. C. Creighton, *op. cit.* in note 39, p. 82.
45. See R. Porter (1987) *Disease, Medicine and Society in England 1550–1860* (London: Macmillan), p. 55–56; and J. C. Riley, *op. cit.* in note 43, who considered a variety of improvements suggested by environmentalists, pp. 132–137.
46. R. Porter, *op. cit.* in note 45, p. 37.
47. P. E. Razzell (1974) An interpretation of the modern rise of population in Europe: a critique. *Population Studies* **28**, pp. 5–17. N. L. Tranter (1985) *Population and Society 1750–1940* (London: Longman), p. 78.
48. B. Luckin (1984) Evaluating the sanitary revolution: typhus and typhoid in London, 1851–1900. In R. I. Woods and J. H. Woodward, *op. cit.* in note 17, pp. 102–119.
49. *Ibid.*, p. 114.
50. The exact role of under-nutrition, as distinct from the general conditions prevalent in a famine area or concomitant with extreme poverty, is difficult to ascertain. See, for example, B. Appleby (1975) Nutrition and disease: the case of London, 1550–1750. *Journal of Interdisciplinary History* **6**, pp. 1–22.
51. See, for example, W. H. Parry (1969) *Infectious Diseases* (London: English Universities Press), p. 166.
52. This was suggested by A. R. Omran (1977) A century of epidemiologic transition in the United States. *Preventive Medicine* **6**, pp. 30–51.
53. *Ibid.*, p. 103; and F. F. Cartwright (1977) *A Social History of Medicine* (London: Longmans), pp. 105–107.
54. F. F. Cartwright, *op. cit.* in note 53, p. 103.
55. E. Chadwick (1842) Report on the Sanitary Condition of the Labouring Population of Great Britain reprinted 1965 (Edinburgh: Edinburgh University Press).
56. F. F. Cartwright, *op. cit.* in note 53, pp. 110–114. W. H. McNeill (1976) *Plagues and Peoples* (Harmondsworth: Penguin), pp. 250–252.
57. W. H. McNeill, *op. cit.* in note 56, p. 250.

58. See a discussion of this in A. S. Wohl (1983) *Endangered Lives: Public Health in Victorian Times* (London: Dart), pp. 110–112.

59. *Ibid.*

60. G. Rosen (1973) Disease, debility and death. In *The Victorian City*, H. J. Dyos and M. Wolff, eds. (London: Routledge and Kegan Paul), pp. 625–667.

61. See for example B. Luckin (1984) Evaluating the sanitary revolution: Typhus and typhoid in London, 1851–1900. In R. I. Woods and J. H. Woodward, *op. cit.* in note 17, pp. 102–119; and A. S. Wohl, *op. cit.* in note 58.

62. R. Porter, *op. cit.* in note 45, p. 57; and F. F. Cartwright, *op. cit.* in note 53, pp. 101–107.

63. A. Hardy (1983) Smallpox in London: factors in the decline of the disease in the nineteenth century. *Medical History* **27**, pp. 111–138, p. 125.

64. N. Longmate (1966) *King Cholera* (London: Hamish Hamilton).

65. See the collection of studies edited by R. I. Woods and J. H. Woodward, *op. cit.* in note 17.

66. M. E. Pooley and C. G. Pooley (1984) Health, society and environment in Victorian Manchester. In *op. cit.* in note 17, pp. 148–175.

67. G. Howe (1976) *Man, Environment and Disease in Britain* (Harmondsworth: Penguin), p. 201.

68. F. Engels (1845) *The Condition of the Working Class in England* reprinted 1982 (London: Grenada), for example pp. 60–61, 69–77, 83–88. C. Dickens *Bleak House* (1838), *Oliver Twist* (1838) and *Hard Times* (1854) reprinted 1983 (Harmondsworth: Penguin).

69. M. E. Pooley and C. G. Pooley, *loc. cit.* in note 66, p. 174.

70. B. Luckin, *loc. cit.* in note 61, p. 112.

71. *Ibid.*, p. 118.

72. R. Woods (1984) Mortality and sanitary conditions in late nineteenth-century Birmingham. In R. I. Woods and J. H. Woodward, *op. cit.* in note 17, pp. 176–202, pp. 200–201.

73. B. Thompson, *loc. cit.* in note 17, pp. 120–147, pp. 140–142.

74. *Ibid.*, pp. 132–133.

75. G. A. Condran and R. A. Cheney (1982) Mortality trends in Philadelphia: age- and cause-specific death rates 1870–1930. *Demography* **19**(1), pp. 97–123.

76. N. Longmate, *op. cit.* in note 64, pp. 222–232.

77. B. Luckin, *loc. cit.* in note 61, p. 118.

78. See R. Woods and J. Woodward (1984) Mortality, poverty and the environment. In *op. cit.* in note 17, pp. 19–36; and T. McKeown and R. G. Record (1975) Reasons for the decline in mortality in England and Wales during the nineteenth century. *Population Studies* **29**, pp. 94–122, p. 120.

79. R. Reeves, *loc. cit.* in note 35.

Chapter 5

1. T. McKeown (1976) *The Modern Rise of Population* (London: Edward Arnold), pp. 137–138.

2. A. Hardy (1988) Diagnosis, death and diet: the case of London, 1750–1909. *Journal of Interdisciplinary History* **18**, pp. 387–401, p. 392.

3. W. Black (1788) *A Comparative View of the Mortality of the Human Species at all Ages* (London).

4. A. Hardy, *loc. cit.* in note 2.

5. *Ibid.*, p. 394.

6. The cycle of epidemics relates to the changes in the proportion of newly susceptible infants and young children in the population, which builds up after an epidemic to the point where transmission of the disease again becomes possible. See A. W. Hedrich (1930) The corrected average attack rate for measles among city children. *American Journal of Hygience* **11**, pp. 576–600.

7. Age-specific data on childhood infectious diseases became available in the Registrar-General's records towards the end of the nineteenth century. Heysham's data for Carlisle in the eighteenth century suggest that most deaths from scarlet fever at that time may have been under the age of five years: J. Heysham (1782) *Observations on the Bills of Mortality in Carlisle for the Year 1779* (Carlisle: Mililieu).

8. M. Behar (1974) A deadly combination. *World Health*, February-March, pp. 28–33.

9. A. T. Cockburn (1963) *The Evolution and Eradication of Infectious Diseases* (Baltimore and London).

10. R. Schofield (1977) Book review: The modern rise of population. *Population Studies* **31**, pp. 179–181.

11. R. Dubos and J. Dubos (1952) *The White Plague* (London: Gollancz), p. 231. Data from Massachusetts show a decline in tuberculosis mortality from at least 1863: see *Historical Statistics in the United States, Part 1, Colonial Times to 1970* (Washington DC: US Department of Commerce, Bureau of Census, 1975). Increases in some southern states were recorded in *Census of the United States, 1860–* : those in New York were mentioned by E. Van de Walle (1978) Accounting for population growth. *Science* **197**, p. 653.

12. R. Dubos and J. Dubos, *op. cit.* in note 11, p. 232.

13. M. B. Lurie (1964) *Resistance to Tuberculosis: Experimental Studies in Natural and Acquired Defence Mechanism* (Cambridge: Harvard University Press).

14. M. Daniels, F. Ridealgh, V. H. Springett and I. M. Hall (1948) *Tuberculosis in Young Adults: Report on the Prophit Tuberculosis Survey, 1935–44* (London: Lewis).

15. A. W. Anderson, B. Benjamin, R. Grenville-Mathers and H. J. Trenchard (1957) Control of tuberculosis: importance of heredity and environment. *British Journal of Preventive and Social Medicine* **11**, pp. 1–6.

16. F. J. Kallman and D. Reisner (1943) Twin studies of the significance of genetic factors in tuberculosis. *American Review of Tuberculosis* **47**, pp. 549–574.

17. See R. Dubos and J. Dubos, *op. cit.* in note 11, pp. 115–118.

18. W. W. Stead (1967) Pathogenesis of a first episode of chronic pulmonary tuberculosis in man. *American Review of Respiratory Diseases* **95**, pp. 729–745.

19. V. H. Springett (1950) A comparative study of tuberculosis mortality rates. *Journal of Hygiene* **48**(3), pp. 361–395.

20. See, for example, J. W. Bentzon (1953) Effect of certain infectious diseases on tuberculin allergy. *Tubercle* **34**, pp. 34–41; S. Starr and S. Berkovich (1964) Effects of measles: gamma-globulin modified measles on the tuberculin test. *New England Journal of Medicine* **270**(8), pp. 386–391.

21. R. L. Nemir (1972) Disorders of the respiratory tract in children. In *Pulmonary Disorders, Vol. II*, E. L. Kendig Jnr. ed. (Philadelphia: Saunders).

22. W. Black, *op.cit.* in note 3, p. 102.

23. See P. E. Razzell (1977) *The Conquest of Smallpox* (Firle, Sussex: Caliban), pp. 107–109.

24. The Royal Commission on Vaccination (1889–96) *Report of the Royal Commission on Vaccination, First Report, Appendix*, p. 90.

25 C. W. Dixon (1962) *Smallpox* (London: Churchill).

26. Data from Paris given in S. H. Preston and E. Van de Walle (1978) Urban French mortality in the nineteenth century. *Population Studies* **32**, p. 284. Data from Sweden: G. Sundbärg, *Dodligheten af Lungtuberculos i Sverige åren 1751–1830* (Uppsala).

27. Circumstances obviously varied between different working-class contexts. For example, women worked in the factories, where there was high risk of severe infection in the crowded conditions, but not in the mining communities.

28. See M. W. Beaver (1973) Population, infant mortality and milk. *Population Studies* **27**, pp. 243–254. The boiling of milk could also have been beneficial, but no clear evidence has been reported of this becoming more widespread among users.

29. G. Cronje (1984) Tuberculosis and mortality decline in England and Wales, 1851–1910. In *Urban Disease and Mortality in Nineteenth-Century England*, R. Woods and J. Woodward, eds. (London: Batsford), pp. 79–101.

30. *Ibid.*, pp. 91 and 98.

31. J. C. Riley (1987) *The Eighteenth-Century Campaign to Avoid Disease* (London: Macmillan), p. 29 and p. 132, considered the places in which ventilation might have been improved. G. Rosen (1973) Disease, debility and death. In *The Victorian City*, H. J. Dyos and M. Wolff, eds. (London), pp. 625–667, suggested that it was well-known early in the nineteenth century that tuberculosis was associated with poor working conditions.

32. R. Dubos and J. Dubos, *op. cit.* in note 11, pp. 201–206.

33. F. Engels (1845) *The Condition of the Working Class in England* reprinted 1982 (London: Grenada). See, for example, pp. 179–194.

34. C. Dickens (1854) *Hard Times*, p. 102. For descriptions of living and working conditions see also *Bleak House* (1838) and *Oliver Twist* (1838). See also F. Engels, *op. cit.* in note 33, for example pp. 60–61.

35. See, for example, M. E. Pooley and C. G. Pooley (1984) Health society and environment in Victorian Manchester, in *op. cit.* in note 29, pp. 148–175, p. 173.

36. D. J. Oddy (1982) The health of the people. In *Population and Society in Britain, 1850–1980* T. Barker and M. Drake, eds (London: Batsford), pp. 121–139. The standard of living of some working people may have improved in the 1880s, but Burnett for example has pointed out that there was still appalling poverty and under-nutrition up to the First World War: J. Burnett (1979) *Plenty and Want: A Social History of Diet in England from 1815 to the Present Day* (London: Scolar).

37. A. Hardy, *loc. cit.* in note 2, p. 399.

38. Data taken from *Statistical Summaries of the Change in Population of Japan* (Tokyo: Department of Census).

39. The case-fatality rate in the period 1923 to 1940, for example, was about 50% of all clinical cases of tuberculosis: P. Stocks and Lewis-Faning (1944) Wartime incidence and mortality from respiratory tuberculosis. *British Medical Journal*, 1944(1), pp. 581–583.

40. T. McKeown, *op. cit.* in note 1, p. 93.

41. Dahlberg found evidence which suggested that most of the population in Western countries before BCG was introduced, would have become sensitised to tuberculin before the age of thirty: G. Dahlberg (1949) Mortality from tuberculosis in some countries. *British Journal of Social Medicine* **4**, pp. 220–227.

42. R. Dubos and J. Dubos, *op. cit.* in note 11, p. 210.

43. S. H. Preston (1976) *Mortality Patterns in National Populations* (New York: Academic).

44. See, for example, S. W. Tromp (1963) *Medical Biometeorology* (New York:

Elsevier); and R. H. Daw (1954) Some statistical aspects of mortality from degenerative heart disease. *Journal of the Institute of Actuaries*, **354** (1), pp. 69–100.

45. Respiratory diseases appear to have been treated in the early hospitals at the end of the eighteenth century, but the majority of patients were the sick poor in towns, and the more direct casualties of the industrial system through accidents. S. Cherry (1980) The hospitals and population growth: voluntary hospitals, mortality and local population in the English provinces in the 18th and 19th centuries. *Population Studies* **35**(2), pp. 251–265. With regard to the effects of air pollution, see for example the discussion of historical aspects by G. Howe (1972) *Man, Environment and Disease in Britain: A Medical Geography through the Ages* (Harmondsworth: Penguin), p. 240. In the worst episode of mortality from bronchitis during the great London smog of December 1952, huge increases in deaths from bronchitis, pneumonia and heart disease occurred, and pointed to the deleterious effects of air pollution. See also studies by: A. T. Gore and C. W. Shaddick (1958) Atmospheric pollution and mortality in the County of London. *British Journal of Preventive and Social Medicine* **12**, pp. 104–113; A. S. Fairbairn and D. D. Reid (1958) Air pollution and other local factors in respiratory disease. *British Journal of Preventive and Social Medicine* **12**, pp. 94–103; C. Daley (1959) Air pollution and causes of death. *British Journal of Preventive and Social Medicine* **13**, pp. 14–27; R. J. W. Melia, C. du V. Florey and A. V. Swan (1981) Respiratory illness in British schoolchildren and atmospheric smoke and sulphur dioxide 1973–7. *Journal of Epidemiology and Community Health* **35**, pp. 161–167.

46. The great smog in London in 1952 was probably significant in galvanising action, such as the introduction of the Clean Air Act in 1956. Fletcher pointed out that improvements came far too late to have been involved in the long-term decline in mortality from respiratory diseases: C. M. Fletcher (1976) The natural history of chronic bronchitis. *British Medical Journal*, 1976(1), pp. 1592–1593.

47. C. M. Fletcher, R. Peto, C. M. Tinker and F. S. Speizer (1978) *The Natural History of Chronic Bronchitis and Emphysema* (London: Oxford University Press).

48. J. R. T. Colley and D. D. Reid (1970) Urban and social origins of childhood bronchitis in England and Wales. *British Medical Journal*, 1970(2), pp. 213–218.

49. J. R. T. Colley, J. W. B. Douglas and D. D. Reid (1973) Respiratory diseases in young adults: influences of early childhood respiratory tract illness, social class, air pollution and smoking. *British Medical Journal*, 1973(3), pp. 195–198.

50. F. M. Burnet and D. D. White (1972) *Natural History of Infectious Disease* (Cambridge: Cambridge University Press), pp. 1–21. Pneumonia has a pattern of infection determined by one bacterial antigen and a corresponding antibody. There are, however, many different types of pneumonococci all relating to one major antigen, SSS, or specific soluble substance.

51. G. Howe, *op. cit.* in note 45, p. 197. Such a mutation led to infection among people who would have escaped before alteration, but in the absence of specific immunity, the resistance of the population was unusually low. The pandemic of 1918–19 was one of the most globally destructive of any kind in history, and it is likely that under-nourishment and food shortages following World War I contributed to high mortality from influenza and pneumonia, as provisions for an adequate diet in Britain were nothing like those in World War II.

52. A summary of known causes was given in *British Medical Journal*, 1976, Editorial: Natural history of chronic bronchitis, pp. 181–188.

53. C. M. Fletcher, R. Peto, C. M. Tinker and F. S. Speizer, *op. cit.* in note 47.

54. Further inter-relationships include bacterial infection in the presence of organisms such as *Hemophilus influenzae, Staphylococcus,* and *Streptococcus,* while pneumonia may also be a secondary complication of bronchitis associated with viral infection. Other common agents that have been isolated include myxoviruses, respiratory synctial viruses and the adenoviruses.

55. G. F. Badger, J. H. Dingle, A. E. Feller *et al.* (1953) A study of illness in a group of Cleveland families, II. Incidence of the common respiratory diseases. *American Journal of Hygiene* **58**, pp. 31–40.

56. C. J. Watkins, S. R. Leeder and R. T. Corkhill (1979) The relationship between breast and bottle feeding and respiratory illness in the first year of life. *Journal of Epidemiology and Community Health* **33**, pp. 180–182.

57. I. M. Longini, J. S. Koopman, A. S. Monto *et al.* (1982) Estimating household and community transmission parameters for influenza. *American Journal of Epidemiology* **115**, pp. 736–751.

58. F. S. W. Brimblecombe, R. Cruikshank, P. L. Masters *et al.* (1958) Family studies of respiratory infections. *British Medical Journal*, 1958(1), pp. 119–128.

59. R. Reeves (1985) Declining fertility in England and Wales as a major cause of the twentieth-century decline in mortality. *American Journal of Epidemiology* **122**(1), pp. 112–128, p. 121.

60. R. L. Nemir, *loc. cit.* in note 21.

61. T. L. Kurt, A. S. Yeager, S. Guerette, S. Dunlop (1972) Spread of pertussis by hospital staff. *Journal of the American Medical Association* **221**, pp. 264–267.

62. *Ibid.* See also C. C. Linnemann Jnr. *et al.* (1975) Use of pertusis vaccine in an epidemic involving hospital staff. *Lancet*, 1975(2), pp. 540–545; H. J. Lambert (1965) Epidemiology of a small pertussis outbreak in Kent County, Michigan. *Public Health Report* **80**, pp. 365–369.

63. T. McKeown, *op. cit.* in note 1, p. 95, referred to this.

64. N. C. Oswald (1947). Collapse of the lower lobes of the lungs in children. *Proceedings of the Royal Society of Medicine* **40**, pp. 736–737.

65. J. Fawcett and H. E. Parry (1957) Lung changes in pertussis and measles in childhood. *British Journal of Radiology* **30**(350), pp. 76–83.

66. G. N. Wilson (1905) Measles: its prevalence and mortality in Aberdeen. *Public Health* **18**, pp. 65–82.

67. J. O. Warner and W. C. Marshall (1976) Crippling lung disease after measles and adenovirus infection. *British Journal of Diseases of the Chest* **70**, pp. 89–94.

68. N. Bwibo (1970) Measles in Uganda: an analysis of children with measles admitted to Mulago Hospital. *Tropical Geographical Medicine* **22**, pp. 167–172.

69. D. Morley (1969) Severe measles in the tropics. *British Medical Journal*, 1969(1), pp. 297–301 and pp. 363–365.

70. H. C. Whittle, A. Bradley-Moore, A. Fleming and B. M. Greenwood (1973) Effects of measles on the immune response in Nigerian children. *Archives of the Diseases of Childhood* **48**, pp. 753–756.

71. M. E. Pooley and C. G. Pooley, *loc. cit.* in note 35, p. 157.

72. F. M. Burnet and D. D. White (1972) *Natural History of Infectious Disease* (Cambridge: Cambridge University Press), p. 200.

73. See G. Rosen, *loc. cit.* in note 31, and T. McKeown, *op. cit.* in note 1, p. 82.

74. A. H. Gale (1959) *Epidemic Diseases* (Harmondsworth: Penguin), pp. 90–91; and T. McKeown, *op. cit.* in note 1, p. 82.
75. A. H. Gale, *op. cit.* in note 74, pp. 90–91; and C. Creighton (1894) *The History of Epidemics in Britain* (Cambridge: Cambridge University Press), p. 706 and p. 719.
76. G. Rosen, *loc. cit.* in note 31, pp. 625–667; and M. E. Pooley and C. G. Pooley, *loc. cit.* in note 35, pp. 165–166.
77. A. H. Gale, *op. cit.* in note 74, p. 90.
78. M. E. Pooley and C. G. Pooley, *loc. cit.* in note 35, p. 173.
79. R. Woods, Mortality and sanitary conditions in late nineteenth-century Birmingham. In *op. cit.* in note 29, pp. 176–202, p. 179 and p. 189.
80. A. H. Gale, *op. cit.* in note 74, p. 89. The Registrar-General noted that deaths before the 1850s epidemic would probably have been recorded as cynanche maligne, or putrid throat, and that there was confusion with scarlet fever, while croup was a general term for obstructed breathing.
81. F. M. Burnet and D. D. White (1972) *Natural History of Infectious Disease* (Cambridge: Cambridge University Press), p. 193.
82. T. McKeown, *op. cit.* in note 1, p. 98. Magill suggested that a decline in the death rate may have occurred before the 1890s in the United States, but epidemic variations could account for the downturn in the graph to which he referred. This does in fact show a long-term decline from about 1895, when antitoxin was first used: T. P. Magill (1955) The immunologist and the evil spirits. *Journal of Immunology* **74**, pp. 1–8. See also evidence from Philadelphia which shows reduced incidence and case-fatality from that time: G. A. Condran and R. A. Cheney (1982) Mortality trends in Philadelphia: age- and cause-specific death rates 1870–1930. *Demography* **19** (1), pp. 97–123, pp. 110–111.
83. F. F. Cartwright (1977) *A Social History of Medicine* (London: Longman), p. 91.
84. M. S. Bartlett (1957) Measles periodicity and community size. *Journal of the Royal Statistical Society* **120**, pp. 48–62.
85. See, for example, P. E. M. Fine and J. A. Clarkson (1980) Measles in England and Wales, III. Assessing published predictions of the impact of vaccination on incidence. *International Journal of Epidemiology* **12**(3), pp. 332–339.
86. S. H. Preston and E. Van de Walle (1978) Urban French mortality in the nineteenth century. *Population Studies* **32**, p. 283.
87. Figures on school places and attendance given in N. Middleton and S. Weitzman (1976) *A Place for Everyone: A History of State Education from the 18th Century to the 1970s* (London: Victor Gollancz).
88. R. Woods, *loc. cit.* in note 79, p. 200.
89. J. A. Yelling (1986) *Slums and Slum Clearance in Victorian London* (London: Allen and Unwin), p. 10.
90. M. E. Poley and C. G. Pooley, *loc. cit.* in note 35.
91. A. S. Wohl (1966) *The Housing of the Artisans and Labourers in Nineteenth-Century London, 1815–1914*. Brown University, PhD thesis, p. 458.
92. See R. Reeves, *loc. cit.* in note 59, for example.
93. P. Aaby, J. Bukh, I. M. Lisse and A. J. Smits (1986) Severe measles in Sunderland, 1885: a European–African comparison of causes of severe infection. *International Journal of Epidemiology* **15**(1), pp. 101–107.
94. P. Aaby, J. Bukh, I. M. Lisse and A. J. Smits (1984) Overcrowding and intensive exposure as determinants of measles mortality. *American Journal of Epidemiology* **120**, pp. 49–63. P. Aaby, J. Bukh, I. M. Lisse, A. J. Smits, J. Gomes, M. A. Fernandes, I. Francisco and M. Soares (1984) Determinants of

measles mortality in a rural area of Guinea–Bissau: crowding, age and malnutrition. *Journal of Tropical Paediatrics* **30**, pp. 164–167.

95. P. Aaby, J. Bukh, I. M. Lisse and A. J. Smits, *loc. cit.* in note 93.
96. R. Reeves, *loc. cit.* in note 59.
97. Data on births from Registrar-General's *Statistical Reviews for England and Wales, 1900–* (London: HMSO).
98. P. E. M. Fine (1982) The control of infectious disease; C. E. G. Smith (1982) Practical problems in the control of infectious disease; and R. M. Anderson (1982) Transmission dynamics and control of infectious disease agents. In *Population Biology of Infectious Diseases*, R. M. Anderson and R. M. May, eds (Berlin: Springer-Verlag, Dahlem Konferenz), pp. 121–143; 182–184; and 149–176. Many factors determine Ro, such as duration of latent period, duration of infectiousness and lifespan of a parasite in a host, density of susceptibles, and behaviour patterns in the community. There are many important demographic implications, and birth rates, death rates and recovery rates all affect the transmission process. R. M. Anderson and R. M. May (1979) Population biology of infectious diseases; Part I. *Nature* **280**, pp. 361–367.
99. W. Brass and M. Kabir (1977) Regional variations in fertility and child mortality during the demographic transition in England and Wales. In *Regional Demographic Development*, J. Hobcraft and P. Rees, eds. (London: Croom Helm), pp. 71–88.
100. See Chapter 2, note 92, concerning the link between suckling and infertility.
101. J. M. Winter (1982) Aspects of the impact of the First World War on infant mortality in Britain. *Journal of European Economic History* **11**, pp. 713–738.
102. See J. W. Tanner (1968) Earlier maturation in man. *Scientific American* **218**, pp. 21–27.
103. McKeown referred to the experience of those working in developing countries which suggests that malnutrition does not have the same effect with every infectious disease, being marked in the case of diarrhoeal disease, measles and tuberculosis, but less so with whooping cough: T. McKeown (1978) Fertility, mortality and cause of death. *Population Studies* **32**(3), pp. 535–542. D. Morley (1973) *Paediatric Priorities in the Developing World* (London: Butterworth), pp. 184, 217, 238, 259.
104. T. McKeown and R. G. Record (1962) Reasons for the decline of mortality in England and Wales during the nineteenth century. *Population Studies* **16**, pp. 94–122; and criticisms in R. Woods and J. Woodward (1984) Mortality, poverty and the environment. In *op. cit.* in note 29, pp. 19–36, especially pp. 29–32.
105. *Ibid.*
106. For example by T. McKeown, *op. cit.* in note 1, p. 55.
107. Apart from the increased contribution of circulatory disease to declining overall mortality, other non-infectious diseases became more significant in the declining mortality of the twentieth century in England and Wales. McKeown pointed out that the largest fall was associated with the heterogenous category 'prematurity, immaturity and other diseases of infancy', much of which probably resulted from transfers to more specific categories, as well as improved maternal health. The category of 'other diseases' included alcoholism, rickets and non-infectious respiratory conditions. There was also some reduction in mortality under the category of 'other diseases of the nervous system', including brain tumours, diseases of the cord and neuritis. Improved treatment of epilepsy may have had some effect on this category of causes. See T. McKeown (1979) *The Role of Medicine* (Oxford: Blackwell), p. 66.

Chapter 6

1. O. R. Omran (1971) The epidemiological transition. *Millbank Memorial Quarterly* **49**(4), pp. 509–538; O. R. Omran (1977). Epidemiological transition in the United States. *Population Studies* **32**, pp. 3–42.

2. J. H. de Haas (1976) *Changing Mortality Pattern of Cardiovascular Disease* (Haarlem: De Erven, F. Bohn).

3. S. H. Preston (1976) *Mortality Patterns in National Populations* (New York: Academic Press), p. 157.

4. S. H. Preston (1970) International comparisons of excessive adult mortality. *Population Studies* **24**, pp. 5–20. R. D. Retherford (1975) *The Changing Sex Differential in Mortality*, Studies in Population and Urban Demography No. 1 (Connecticut: Greenwood).

5. See, for example, G. Gilliam (1955) Trends in mortality attributed to carcinoma of the lung: possible effects of faulty certification of deaths to other respiratory diseases. *Cancer* **8**, pp. 1130–1136. Registrar–General (1917). *Statistical Review of England and Wales* also considered changes in mortality among males and females separately for 'accessible' and 'inaccessible' sites of cancer, but with inconclusive results.

6. Digestive diseases as a group account for between 2–3% of all deaths, but the proportion of deaths caused in some other European countries is higher, such as in France where it is about 7%. The other two small groups considered separately here, diabetes and nephritis/nephrosis, may be more significant in terms of incidence, because treatment measures have made the risk of mortality much lower in recent decades. Data from OPCS (1981). *Mortality Statistics: Cause, Series DH2* (London: HMSO).

7. H. A. Waldron and L. Vickerstaff (1977) *Intimations of Quality: Ante Mortem and Post Mortem Diagnoses* (London: Nuffield Provincial Hospitals Trust), p. 6 and p. 14. This is also about the level of error found in an earlier study of data from England and Wales by M. A. Heasman and L. Lipworth (1966) *Accuracy of Certification of Cause of Death*, Medical and Population Subjects, No. 20 (London: HMSO).

8. M. Britton (1974) Diagnostic errors discovered at autospy. *Acta Medica Scandinavica* **196**, pp. 203–219.

9. *Population Bulletin of the United Nations, No. 6* (New York: United Nations, 1962).

10. See A. M. Lillienfeld (1976) *Foundations of Epidemiology* (New York: Oxford University Press), p. 53; A. Adelstein (1977) Certification of cause of death. *Health Trends* **9**(4), pp. 78–79. For example, in the heart disease category, undefined, ICD 90–99, in 1926, to which about one fifth of all deaths were ascribed, respiratory disease – and mainly bronchitis – was given as an associated cause of death in 19.5% of cases according to the Registrar-General's Supplement for 1931. See also K. G. Manton and S. S. Poss (1979) Effects of dependency among causes of death for cause-elimination life-table strategies. *Demography* **16**(2), pp. 313–326.

11. W. Black (1788) *A Comparative View of the Mortality of the Human Species at all Ages* (London).

12. W. Heberden (1801) *Observations on the Increase and Decrease of Different Diseases*. Reprinted in *Population and Diseases in Early Industrial England*, B. Benjamin, ed. (West Germany: Gregg International, 1973).

13. M. Campbell (1963) The main cause of increased death rate from diseases of the heart, 1920–1959. *British Medical Journal*, 1963(2), pp. 712–715.

14. A. H. T. Robb-Smith (1967) *The Enigma of Coronary Heart Disease* (Chicago:

Year Book of Medical Publishers, 1967).

15. W. J. Walker (1977) Changing United States life style and the declining vascular mortality: cause of coincidence? *New England Journal of Medicine* **297**, pp. 163–165. T. Gordon and T. Thom (1975) The recent decrease in CHD mortality. *Preventive Medicine* 1975, **4**, p. 115.

16. T. W. Anderson and W. H. Le Riche (1970) Ischaemic heart disease and sudden death, 1960–61. *British Journal of Preventive and Social Medicine* **24**, pp. 1–9.

17. D. G. Clayton, D. Taylor and A. G. Shaper (1977) Trends in heart disease in England and Wales, 1950–73. *Health Trends* **9**, pp. 1–6.

18. W. J. Walker; and T. Gordon and T. Thom: *loc. cit.* in note 15.

19. C. Duv Florey, R. J. Melia and S. C. Darby (1978) Changing mortality from ischaemic heart disease in Great Britain, 1968–76. *British Medical Journal*, 1978(1), pp. 635–637.

20. D. G. Clayton, D. Taylor and A. G. Shaper, *loc. cit.* in note 17.

21. Wylie suggested that there had probably been a transfer of 'sudden deaths' to more specific categories of heart disease: C. M. Wylie (1961) Recent trends in mortality from cerebrovascular accidents in the United States. *Journal of Chronic Diseases* **14**, pp. 213–220.

22. P. O. Yates (1964) A change in the pattern of cerebrovascular disease. *Lancet*, 1964(1), pp. 65–69.

23. L. Kuller, R. Seltser, R. Paffenberger and D. Kruger (1966) Trends in death rates from hypertensive disease in Memphis, Tennessee, 1920–1960. *Journal of Chronic Diseases* **19**, p. 847.

24. S. Wing (1984) The role of medicine in the decline of hypertension-related mortality. *International Journal of Health Services* **14**(4), pp. 649–666.

25. R. Cooper, J. Stammler, A. Dyer and D. Garside (1978) The decline in mortality from coronary heart disease. *Journal of Chronic Diseases* **31**, pp. 709–720.

26. E. Guberan (1979) Surprising decline in cardiovascular mortality in Switzerland, 1951–76. *Journal of Epidemiology and Community Health* **33**, pp. 114–120.

27. A. J. Mercer (1983) Trends in circulatory-disease mortality in western populations: evidence of similarities in the pattern of measles epidemics. *International Journal of Epidemiology* **12**(3), pp. 366–371.

28. Central Institute of Statistics (1956–74) *Cause di Morte: 1887–1955, Annuaria di Statistiche Sanitarie* (Roma: Republica Italiana).

29. W. I. B. Onuigbo (1975) Some 19th-century ideas on links between tuberculosis and cancerous diseases of the lung. *British Journal of Diseases of the Chest* **169**, pp. 207–210.

30. R. Pearl (1929) Cancer and tuberculosis. *American Journal of Hygiene* **9**, pp. 97–159.

31. T. A. Coglan (1902) *International Medical Congress of Australasia, Transactions of the 6th Session* (Hobart), p. 203.

32. T. Cherry, Cancer and acquired resistance to tuberculosis, Part I, *Medical Journal of Australia*, 1924(2), pp. 372–378; Part II, *Medical Journal of Australia*, 1925(1), pp. 581–598; Cancer and tuberculosis: the development of malignancy, *Lancet*, 7 February 1931, pp. 285–288; Cancer and tuberculosis, *Medical Journal of Australia*, 1933(2), pp. 197–217; *Cancer and Tuberculosis* (Melbourne: Patterson, 1935); *Cancer and Tubercle Bacillus* (Melbourne: Melbourne Cancer Causation Committee, 1945). See later studies by A. H. Campbell (1961) The relationship between cancer and tuberculosis mortality rates, *British Journal of Cancer* **15**, pp. 10–18; A. H. Campbell and P. Guilfoyle (1970) Pulmonary tuberculosis, isoniazid and

cancer, *British Journal of Diseases of the Chest* 64(3), pp. 141–149; D. B. Cruickshank (1939) The association of tuberculosis and cancer. *Papworth Research Bulletin* 2(1) (Papworth: Pendragon); D. B. Cruickshank (1940) The topography of the relative distribution of cancer and tuberculosis, *Tubercule*, 1940, pp. 281–291; J. L. Haybittle (1962 and 1963) Mortality rates from cancer and tuberculosis *British Journal of Preventive and Social Medicine* 16, pp. 93–104; and 17, pp. 23–28; T. G. Paxon (1956) A study of tuberculosis and cancer mortality rates with special reference to lung cancer rates, *British Journal of Cancer* 10, pp. 623–633. A. J. Mercer (1981) Risk of dying from tuberculosis and cancer: further aspects of a possible association, *International Journal of Epidemiology* 10(4), pp. 377–380 gives further references.

33. Summary of data for census years given in S. H. Preston, N. Keyfitz and R. Schoen (1972) *Causes of Death, Life Tables for National Populations* (New York: Seminar Press).

34. Studies in the past have indicated a general tendency for each generation to carry its own levels of overall mortality with it. One study found that for England and Wales, trends in mortality from all causes, for different age groups, ran roughly in parallel when plotted against year of birth: V. P. A. Derrick (1927) Changes in generation mortality: England and Wales. *Journal of the Institute of Actuaries* 58, pp. 117–159. Another analysis in the 1930s showed the possibility of a cohort influence on mortality and suggested that the health of an individual with respect to fatal illness, was greatly influenced by experience and environment in childhood: M. A. Kermack, A. G. McKendrick and P. L. McKinlay (1934) Death rates in Great Britain and Sweden; some general regularities and their significance. *Lancet* 1934, pp. 698–703. Period increases in death rates from cancer and circulatory disease since then indicate that influences in adult life are also highly significant and have disrupted the former parallelism of age-specific death rates by year of birth.

35. See S. H. Preston, *loc. cit.* in note 4. R. D. Retherford (1975) *The Changing Sex Differential in Mortality*. Studies in Population and Urban Demography, No. 1 (Connecticut: Greenwood).

36. R. A. M. Case (1956) Cohort analysis of cancer mortality in England and Wales, 1911–54, by site and sex. *British Journal of Preventive and Social Medicine* 10, pp. 172–199.

37. Data from Institute of Cancer Research (1976) *Serial Mortality Tables* (London: ICR).

38. S. H. Preston and V. Nelson (1974) Structure and change in cause of death. *Population Studies* 28(2), pp. 19–52.

39. R. Cooper and A. Schatzkin (1982) The pattern of mass disease in the USSR. *International Journal of Health Services* 12, pp. 459–480; R. Cooper (1981) Rising death rates in the Soviet Union. *New England Journal of Medicine* 304, 21, pp. 1259–1265.

40. P. A. Compton (1985) Rising mortality in Hungary. *Population Studies* 39, pp. 71–86.

41. Data on Gross Domestic Product and Net Material Product from *United Nations* (1985) *Statistical Yearbook, 1982* (New York: UN); population data from *United Nations* (1983) *Demographic Yearbook, 1983* (New York: UN). Estimates of GDP were available for the following nineteen countries and were compared with death rates per 100,000 at ages 45–54 in 1981 except where otherwise stated: Australia, Austria, Belgium (1979), Canada, Denmark, Finland, France, German FR, Greece, Iceland, Ireland, Italy (1980), Netherlands, New Zealand, Norway, Portugal, Spain (1979), Sweden,

USA. England and Wales was not included in the regression analysis because estimates of GDP were for England only.

42. Data from *World Health Statistics Annual* (Geneva: WHO, 1982–5). Death rates from CD at ages 45–54 in England and Wales in 1981 were 314.6 for males and 97.7 for females, while rates for cancer were 165.4 and 190.7 respectively. Data from many countries of the South are published by the WHO and in the UN Demographic Year Books. See also United Nations (1982). *Levels and Trends in Mortality since 1950* (New York: UN), pp. 111–112.

43. I. Tauber (1958) *The Population of Japan* (Princeton: Princeton University Press), pp. 284–309.

44. J. E. Gordon, S. Singh and J. B Wyon (1965) Causes of death at different ages, by sex, and by season, in a rural population of the Punjab, 1957–1959, *Indian Journal of Medical Research* **53**, pp. 906–917; J. B. Wyon and J. E. Gordon (1971) *The Khanna Study: Population Problems in the Rural Punjab* (Cambridge: Harvard Press), pp. 172–207.

45. K. Veda (1983) *Recent Trends of Mortality in Asian Countries* (Tokyo: SEAMIC), pp. 93–119.

46. L. Rui-Zhu, A brief account of 30 years mortality of the Chinese population, *World Health Organisation, Quarterly Report* **34**(2), pp. 127–134.

47. See, for example, the collection of studies edited by N. F. Stanley and R. A. J. Joschke: *Changing Disease Patterns and Human Behaviour* (London: Academic Press, 1980), including that by I. Maddocks: The impoverishment of community life and the need for community health. This considers stress-related city problems, including unemployment, overcrowding and social isolation. Articles on specific disease patterns are also included in *Disease and Urbanisation*, E. J. Clegg and J. P. Garlick, eds. (London: Taylor Francis, 1980).

48. O. M. Jensen, International and urban-rural variation in cancer. In *op. cit.* in note 47, pp. 107–126.

49. See, for example, one of his later studies: P. Stocks (1947) *Regional and Local Differences in Cancer Death Rates*, Studies in Medical and Population Subjects, No. 1 (London: HMSO).

50. Data on England and Wales in G. Howe (1970) *A National Atlas of Disease Mortality in the United Kingdom* (London: Nelson) and M. J. Gardiner, P. D. Winter and D. J. P. Barker (1984) *Atlas of Mortality from Selected Diseases in England and Wales: 1968–79* (Chichester: Wiley).

51. See Chapter 5, notes 45 and 46.

52. See G. Howe, *op. cit.* in note 50.

53. M. G. Marmot (1980) Affluence, urbanisation and coronary heart disease, in Clegg and Garlick, *op. cit.* in note 47, pp. 127–143.

54. J. N. Morris, M. D. Crawford and J. A. Heady (1961) Hardness of local water supplies and mortality from cardiovascular disease in the county boroughs of England and Wales. *Lancet* 1961(1), pp. 860–862. Also, P. Townsend and N. Davidson (1982) *Inequalities in Health* (Harmondsworth: Penguin), pp. 65–70.

55. See also M. G. Marmot, A. M. Adelstein, N. Robinson and G. A. Rose (1978) Changing social-class distribution of heart disease. *British Medical Journal* 1978(2), pp. 1109–1112; and M. L. Halliday and T. W. Anderson (1979) The sex differential in ischaemic heart disease: trends by social class, 1931–1971. *Journal of Epidemiology and Community Health* **35**, pp. 73–77.

56. P. Townsend and N. Davidson, *op. cit.* in note 54, p. 69.

57. J. Le Grande (1986) Inequalities in health: some international comparisons, *London School of Economics and Political Science, paper*, September;

R. Illsley and J. Le Grande (1987) Measurement of inequality in health, *LSE paper*, February.

58. R. Illsey (1986 and 1987) Occupational class, selection and the production of inequalities. *Quarterly Journal of Social Affairs* 1986(2), pp. 151–161; 1987(3), pp. 213–223.

59. P. O. Goldblatt (1990) Social class mortality differences. In *The Biology of Class*, N. Mascie-Taylor, ed. (Oxford: Oxford University Press), pp. 24–57. K. A. Moser, H. S. Pugh and P. O. Goldblatt (1988) Inequalities in women's health: looking at mortality differentials using an alternative approach. *British Medical Journal* **296**, pp. 1221–1224.

60. P. O. Goldblatt, *loc. cit.* in note 59, p. 55.

61. *Ibid.*, p. 31.

62. *Ibid.*, p. 31. See W. P. D. Logan (1982) Cancer mortality by occupation and social class 1851–1971, IARC SP No. 36/OPCS SMPS No. 44 (Lyon/London: HMSO); R. O. Cummins, A. G. Shaper, M. Walker and C. J. Wale (1981) Smoking and drinking by middle-aged British men: effects of social class and town of residence, *British Medical Journal* **283**, pp. 1497–1502; G. Rose and M. G. Marmot (1981) Social class and coronary heart disease, *British Heart Journal* **45**, pp. 13–19; M. G. Marmot, A. M. Adelstein, N. Robinson and G. Rose (1978) The changing social-class distribution of heart disease, *British Medical Journal* 1978(2), pp. 1109–1112.

63. In seven large prospective studies, age-adjusted mortality ratios of cigarette smokers compared with non-smokers, were significantly greater than 1. See S. H. Preston, *loc. cit.* in note 4; and United States Surgeon-General (1964) *Smoking and Health* (Washington DC: US Department of Health Education and Welfare, Advisory Committee to the Surgeon-General of the Public Health Service); also the comprehensive evidence set out in successive reports on the harmful effects of smoking, eg. Royal College of Physicians (1977). *Smoking or Health*, Third Report (London: Pitman Medical).

64. S. H. Preston, *op. cit.* in note 3, and *loc. cit.* in note 4.

65. Evidence from G. F. Todd (1963) *Tobacco Consumption in Various Countries*, Research Paper No. 6 (Tobacco Research Council).

66. R. D. Retherford, *op. cit.* in note 4.

67. H. M. Marks (1960) Influence of obesity on morbidity and mortality. *Bulletin of the New York Academy of Medicine, Series 2*, **36**, pp. 296–312.

68. T. R. Tauber (1980) *The Framingham Study, The Epidemiology of Arteriosclerotic Diseases*. (Cambridge Massachusetts: Harvard Press).

69. The following review found inconclusive evidence about the relationship: S.M. Fox and J. S. Skinner (1964) Physical activity and cardiovascular health, *American Journal of Cardiology* **14**, pp. 731–746.

70. See discussion of this in J. N. Morris (1964). *Uses of Epidemilogy* (London: Livingstone) pp. 178–182 and 143–146. J. N. Morris, A. Kagan, D. C. Pattison, M. J. Gardner and P. Raffle (1966) Incidence and prediction of ischaemic heart diseases in London busmen, *Lancet*, pp. 553–559. Recent study in the United States: D. R. Ragland, M. A. Winkleby, J. Schwalbe, B. L. Holman, L. Morse, S. L. Sym and J. M. Fisher (1987) Prevalence of hypertension in busdrivers, *International Journal of Epidemiology* **16**, pp. 208–214.

71. R. Doll and R. Peto (1976) Mortality in relation to smoking: 20 years observations on male British doctors. *British Medical Journal* 1976(2), pp. 1525–1536.

72. M. G. Marmot, *loc. cit.* in note 53.

73. M.G. Marmot, G. Rose, M. Shipley and P.J.S. Hamilton (1978) Employment grade and coronary heart disease in British civil servants. *Journal of*

Epidemiology and Community Health 32, pp. 244–249.

74. E. Guberan, *loc. cit.* in note 26.

75. J. T. Salonen and I. Valonen (1985) Longitudinal cross-national analysis of coronary mortality. *International Journal of Epidemiology* 11, pp. 229–238.

76. R. Byington, A. Dyer, D. Garside *et al.*, (1979). Recent trends of major coronary risk factors and CHD mortality in the United States and other industrialised countries. In *Proceedings on the Decline in Coronary Heart Disease Mortality*, J. R. Havlick and M. Fenleib, eds (Washington DC: US Department of Health Education and Welfare, NIH Publications No. 79), p.1110.

77. The possibility of a stress-related link has been suggested by M. H. Brenner: (1971) Economic changes and heart disease mortality, *American Journal of Public Health* 61(3), pp. 606–610; (1979) Mortality and the national economy, a review, and the experience of England and Wales, 1936–76, *Lancet*, 2, 15 September, pp. 568–573; (1973) Fetal, infant and maternal mortality during periods of economic instability, *International Journal of Health Services* 3(2), p. 145.

78. J. Eyer: (1975) Hypertension as a disease of modern society, *International Journal of Health Services* 5(4), p. 539; (1977) Prosperity as a cause of death, *International Journal of Health Services* 7(1), p. 125; (1977) Does employment cause the death rate peak in each business cycle? *International Journal of Health Services* 7(4), p. 625.

79. See P. Townsend and N. Davidson, *op. cit.* in note 54, pp. 116–118.

80. S. H. Preston and V. Nelson, *loc. cit.* in note 38.

81. Some of the main studies are: Z. Jerushalmy, A. Kohn and A. de Vries (1961) Interaction of myxovirus with human blood platelets in vitro, *Proceedings of the Society of Experimental Biology* 106, pp. 462–466; H. Morat, J. F. Mustard, N. S. Taichman and T. Uriuhara (1965) Platelet aggregation and release of ADP, serontinin and histamine associated with phagocytosis of antigen-antibody complexes, *Proceedings of the Royal Society for Experimental Biology* 120, pp. 232–237; Wan Ching Lu (1958) Agglutination of human blood platelets by influenza PR8 strain virus and mumps virus, *Federation Proceedings* 17, p. 446; H. Terada, M. Baldini, S. Ebbe and M. A. Madoff (1966) Interaction of influenza virus with human blood platelets, *Blood* 28, pp. 213–228; M. A. Packham, W. E. Nishizawa and J. F. Mustard (1968) Response of platelets to tissue injury, *Biochemical Pharmacology, Supplement* 17, pp. 171–184.

82. J. F. Mustard (1970) Platelets and throboembolic disease, *Advances in Cardiology* 4, pp. 131–142; J.F. Mustard, E.A. Murphy, H.C. Rowsell and H. G. Downie (1964) Platelets and atherosclerosis, *Journal of Atherosclerosis Research* 4, pp. 1–28.

83. E. P. Benditt and J. M. Benditt (1973) Evidence for a monoclonal origin of human atherosclerotic plaques. *Proceedings of the National Academy of Science in the USA* 70, pp. 1753–1756.

84. D. Bainton, G. R. Jones and D. Hole (1978) Influenza and ischaemic heart disease – a possible trigger for acute myocardial infarction? *International Journal of Epidemiology* 7, pp. 231–239.

85. A. J. Mercer, *loc. cit.* in note 27.

86. General association with mortality levels pointed out by S. H. Preston and V. Nelson, *loc. cit.* in note 38. R. Reeves (1985) Declining fertility in England and Wales as a major cause of the twentieth-century decline in mortality. *American Journal of Epidemiology* 122(1), pp. 112–128.

87. W. Cramer (1936) On antagonism in development of malignancy in two

different organisms, *Journal of Pathological Bacteriology* **43**, pp. 73–89.

88. See F. M. Burnet (1970) *Immunology, Aging and Cancer* (San Francisco: Freeman) pp. 358–360; An immunological approach to aging, *Lancet* 1970(2), pp. 358–360.

89. R. Doll and R. Peto (1981) Avoidable risks in cancer in the United States. *Journal of the National Cancer Insitute* **66**(6), pp. 1191–1265.

90. Epstein concurred with Peto about the disaster that tobacco-smoking has caused: S. S. Epstein (1979) *The Politics of Cancer* (New York: Anchor Doubleday). He replied to a review of this work by R. Peto (1980) Distorting the epidemiology of cancer: the need for a more balanced overview, *Nature* **289**, pp. 297–301, in the paper by S. S. Epstein and J. B. Schwarz (1981) Fallacies of lifestyle cancer theories, *Nature* **289**, pp. 127–130.

91. S. S. Epstein and J. B. Schwarz, *loc. cit.* in note 90.

92. *Ibid.*; L. J. Kinlen (1987) Fat and breast cancer, *Cancer Surveys* **6**, pp. 585–599.

93. R. Doll and R. Peto, *loc. cit.* in note 89.

94. S. H. Preston and V. Nelson, *loc. cit.* in note 38.

95. P. Maupas and J. L. Malnick, eds (1981) Hepatitis B and primary hepato-cellular carcinoma, *Prog. Medical Virology* **27**, pp. 1–210; D.W.M. Millan, J.A. Davis, T.E. Torbet and M. S. Campo (1986) DNA sequences of human papillomavirus types 11, 16 and 18 in lesions of uterine cervix in the west of Scotland, *British Medical Journal* **293**, pp. 93–96; A. M. Al-Sumidae, C. A. Hart, S. J. Levisher, C. D. Green and K. McCarthy (1988) Particles with properties of retroviruses in monocytes from patients with breast cancer, *Lancet* 1988(1), pp. 5–9.

96. R. Doll and R. Peto, *loc. cit.* in note 89.

97. F. M. Burnet (1967) Immunological aspects of malignant disease, *Lancet* 1967(2), pp. 1171–1174; (1970) *Immunological Surveillance* (Oxford: Pergammon). In a study of epidemiological evidence it was found that there was little to suggest that clinical cancer is generally the result of a breakdown of immune surveillance. Only some cancers have been found to be closely associated with immunological disorders: see, for example, R. Doll and L. Kinlen (1970) Immunosurveillance and cancer – epidemiological evidence, *British Medical Journal* 1970(4), pp. 420–422; L. J. Kinlen (1982) Immuno-suppressive therapy and cancer, *Cancer Surveys* 1982 **4**(1), pp. 565–583.

98. M. D. Waterfield, G. T. Scrace, N. Whittle, P. Strobant, A. Johnsson, A. Wasteson, B. B. Westermark, C. H. Heldin, S. S. Huang and T. F. Deuel (1983) Platelet-derived growth factor is structurally related to the putative transforming protein p28^{sis} of simian sarcoma virus, *Nature* **304**, pp. 35–39.

99. R. Doll (1967) *Prevention of Cancer – Pointers from Epidemiology* (London: Nuffield Provincial Hospitals Trust), pp. 90–92.

100. F. M. Burnet (1971) *Cellular Immunology* (Carlton: Melbourne University Press), p. 249; and evidence of a constant proportion of cohort mortality attributed to tuberculosis or cancer in A. J. Mercer, *loc. cit.* in note 32.

101. M. Susser and Z. Stein (1962) Civilisation and peptic ulcer. *Lancet* 1962(1), pp. 116–120.

102. M. Alderson (1981) *International Mortality Statistics* (London: Macmillan).

103. M. Susser and Z. Stein, *loc. cit.* in note 101.

104. M. Alderson, *op. cit.* in note 102.

105. H. Trowell (1974) Diabetes mellitus death rates in England and Wales 1920–70 and food supplies. *Lancet* 26 October, pp. 998–1002.

106. A. L. Notkins (1979) The causes of diabetes. *Scientific American* **241** (5), pp. 59–67.

107. R. E. Gleason, C. B. Kahn, I. B. Funk and J. E. Craighhead (1982) Seasonal incidence of insulin-dependent diabetes (IDDM) in Massachusetts, 1964–1973. *International Journal of Epidemiology* 11(1), pp. 39–45.
108. D. R. Gamble (1980) The epidemiology of insulin-dependent diabetes, with particular reference to the relationship of virus infection to its aetiology. *Epidemiological Review*, 1980(2), pp. 49–70.
109. M. Alderson, *op. cit.* in note 102, see Appendix 6h.
110. See, for example, a recent study which found frequent incidence of late manifestations of HBV infection, such as non-alcholic cirrhosis and cancer of the liver in Tonga: R. B. Wainwright, B. J. McMahon, T. R. Bucher, W. L. Hayward, S. Nakaviski, K. Y. Wainwright, S. Foliaki, S. L. Erickson and H. A. Fields (1986) Prevalence of Hepatitis B virus infection in Tonga: identifying high-risk groups for immunisation with hepatitis B vaccine, *International Journal of Epidemiology* 15(4), pp. 567–571. P. A. Compton, *loc. cit.* in note 40, p. 79, referred to the rising death rate from cirrhosis of the liver in Hungary.
111. Data for this group as a whole are given in S. H. Preston, N. Keyfitz and R. Schoen, *op. cit.* in note 33.
112. D. M. Kessner and C. Du Florey (1967) Mortality trends for acute and chronic nephritis and infections of the kidney. *Lancet* 4 November, pp. 979–983.
113. S. H. Preston and V. Nelson, *loc. cit.* in note 38, p. 30. Death rates for circulatory disease among children and young adults in fact declined from slightly earlier than the downturn for older adults among whom most deaths now occur. The proportion of all circulatory-disease deaths which occurred at ages over 55 years was 69.1% in 1901 and 94.6% in 1981.
114. O. Auerbach (1965) Smoking in relation to atherosclerosis of the coronary arteries. *New England Journal of Medicine* **268**, pp. 569–574. See also, J. F. Mustard, E. A. Murphy, H. C. Rowsell and H. G. Downie, *loc. cit.* in note 82.
115. R. Doll and R. Peto, *loc. cit.* in note 89.
116. A. J. Mercer, *loc. cit.* in note 27, and in Chapter 5 the discussion of related respiratory and air-borne infectious diseases. Jones suggested a more general role of childhood infection as 'trauma', which probably had lasting consequences for adult health: H. B. Jones (1956) Aging, disease and life expectancy. *Advances in Biological and Medical Physics* 1956(4), pp. 281–337.
117. Statistical studies include P. Armitage and R. Doll (1957) A two-stage theory of carcinogenesis in relation to the age distribution of human cancer. *British Journal of Cancer* **11**, pp. 161–169.
118. P. R. J. Burch (1968) *An Enquiry Concerning Growth, Disease and Aging* (Edinburgh: Oliver and Boyd).
119. F. M. Burnet discussed this phenomenon in *loc. cit.* and *op. cit.* in note 88, p. 95.
120. The role of different agents and risk factors in chronic non-infectious disease is discussed in relation to mutation theory in G. M. Lower and M. S. Kanarak (1982) The mutation theory of chronic, non-infectious disease: relevance to epidemiologic theory, *American Journal of Epidemiology* **115**(6), pp. 803–817.
121. *Ibid.*
122. It has also been suggested that factors operating in early life might influence adult death rates from heart disease and some other non-communicable diseases, but in a rather different way. A strong geographical correlation between current IHD death rates and earlier neonatal mortality has been taken to suggest that poor living standards in childhood and particularly the influence of maternal nutrition and lactation, could increase susceptibility to

other influences associated with greater affluence in later life. However, it was also suggested that the effect of factors affecting health in the post-neonatal period might influence future susceptibility to other non-communicable diseases in other ways: D.J.P. Barker and C. Osmond (1986) Infant mortality, childhood nutrition, and ischaemic heart disease in England and Wales. *Lancet* 10 May, pp. 1077–1081.

123. See Chapter 5 notes 93–96.
124. See Chapter 5 notes 45 and 46.
125. G. Gilliam, *loc, cit.* in note 5, for study of this effect on long-term trends in mortality from lung cancer.
126. L. Breslow and J.E. Enstrom (1980) Persistence of health habits and their relationship to mortality, *Preventive Medicine* **9**, pp. 469–483; B. Junge and H. Hoffmeister (1982) Civilisation-associated diseases in Europe and industrial countries outside Europe: regional differences and trends in mortality, *Preventive Medicine* **11**, pp. 117–130.
127. The decline in death rates in the United States since the 1960s has been attributed in one study to advances in medical technology, health-care programmes targetted at the poor, and changes in behaviour with regard to smoking, diet and excercise: S. J. Olshansky and A. B. Ault (1986) The four stages of the epidemiologic transition: the age of degenerative diseases, *Millbank Memorial Quarterly* **64**(3), pp. 355–391.

Chapter 7

1. I. S. Glasunov, V. Grabanskas, W. W. Holland and F. H. Epstein (1983) WHO: An integrated programme for the prevention and control of non-communicable diseases. A Kaunas report for a meeting of 16–20 November 1981. *Journal of Chronic Diseases* **36**(5), pp. 419–426.
2. The 10% of mortality in England and Wales that is attributed to diseases other than circulatory, respiratory and neoplastic, relates mainly to diabetes, digestive diseases, diseases of the nervous system, genito-urinary and rheumatic diseases. Some of these have been considered as part of a group of degenerative diseases, but none of the component groups accounts for more than about 1% of all deaths. Digestive diseases as a group account for between 2–3% of all deaths, and both ulcers and cirrhosis of the liver have been briefly considered separately. The proportion of deaths caused in some other European countries is higher, such as in France where it is about 7%. The other two small groups considered separately here, diabetes and nephritis/nephrosis, may be more significant in terms of incidence, because treatment measures have made the risk of mortality much lower in recent decades. Data from OPCS (1978) *Mortality Statistics: Cause.* Series DH2 (London: HMSO).
3. See, for example, L. Rui-Zhu, A brief account of 30 years mortality of the Chinese population. *World Health Organisation, Quarterly Report* **34**(2), pp. 127–132.
4. K. Ueda (1983) *Recent Trends of Mortality in Asian Countries* (Tokyo: SEAMIC), pp. 93–119. R. H. Cassen (1978) *India: Population, Economy, Society* (London: Macmillan). J. E. Gordon, S. Singh and J. B. Wyon (1965) Causes of death at different ages, by sex, and by season, in a rural population of the Punjab, 1957–1959, *Indian Journal of Medical Research* **53**, pp. 906–917. J. B. Wyon and J. E. Gordon (1971) *The Khanna Study: Population Problems in the Rural Punjab* (Cambridge: Harvard Press), pp. 172–207.
5. Data from many countries of the South are now available and published by the

WHO and in the UN Demographic Year Books. Uncertainties about recording coverage and certification differences between countries really preclude international comparisons with much of these data at this time. See also, United Nations (1982) *Levels and Trends in Mortality since 1950* (New York: UN), pp. 111–112. The decline in infectious diseases, including those not found in Europe, has been considered in K.D. Patterson (1977) The impact of medicine on population growth in twentieth-century Ghana: a tentative assessment. In *African Historical Demography, Proceedings of a Seminar held in the Centre of African Studies, University of Edinburgh*, (Edinburgh: University of Edinburgh), pp. 437–452.

6.   See, for example, J. B. Wyon and J. E. Gordon, *op. cit.* in note 4, p. 190.
7.   R. H. Gray (1974) The decline of mortality in Ceylon and the demographic effects of malaria control. *Population Studies* **28**(2), pp. 205–229.
8.   E. E. Ariaga and K. Davis (1969) The pattern of mortality change in Latin America. *Demography* **6**(3), pp. 223–242.
9.   Preston estimated that factors exogenous to a country's level of income probably accounted for 75–90% of the growth in life expectancy for the world as a whole, between the 1930s and the 1960s: S.H. Preston (1975) The changing relation between mortality and level of economic development. *Population Studies* **29**(2), pp. 231–246.
10. J. R. Mandle (1970) The decline in mortality in British Guyana, 1911–1960. *Demography* **7**(3), pp. 301–315.
11. S. F. Cook and W. Borah (1974) *Mexico and the Caribbean, Vol. 2* (Berkeley: University of California), pp. 409–435. Deaths recorded as due to infections and fevers accounted for about three-quarters of the total in Jalisco and Oaxaca in 1872, but this had fallen to 41% in Jalisco by 1952 while remaining about the same in Oaxaca where malaria was more prevalent. Both malaria and dysentery accounted for an increasing proportion of deaths in Oaxaca in the first half of the twentieth century.
12. S. Diaz-Briquets (1981) Determinants of mortality transition in developing countries before and after the 2nd World War: some evidence from Cuba. *Population Studies* **35**(3), pp. 399–411.
13. The role of dispensaries and other local health services in reducing mortality in one village in Nigeria compared with another, has been examined in: I. O. Orubuloye and J. C. Caldwell (1975) The impact of public health services on mortality: a study of mortality differentials in a rural area of Nigeria. *Population Studies* **29** (2), pp. 259–272.
14. J. C. Caldwell, P. H. Reddy and P. Caldwell (1983) The social component of mortality decline: an investigation in South India employing alternative methodologies. *Population Studies* **37**, pp. 185–205.
15. See, for example, E. Draper (1972) *Birth Control in the Modern World* (Harmondsworth: Penguin), p. 317.
16. See trends for these countries in Figure 2.3. A fall in age-specific marital fertility rates for all five-year age groups of women in Sweden and Denmark in the period from the 1750s to the 1830s was followed by an upsurge between the 1840s and 1870s, and then the long-term decline, according to data presented by P. R. A. Hinde and R. I. Woods (1984) Variations in historical natural fertility patterns and the measurement of fertility control. *Journal of Biosocial Science* **16**, pp. 309–321.
17. T. Dyson and M. Murphy (1985) The onset of fertility transition. *Population and Development Review* **11**(3), pp. 399–440.
18. *Ibid.*
19. The basis for the estimates of vital rates used in the study by Wrigley and

Schofield has not been examined here, but other studies have challenged this and also the relationship between fertility changes and changes in wage indices. See, for example, P. E. Razzell (1982) Neo-Malthusianism. *Neww Society* 4 February, p. 201; and J. A. Goldstone (1986) the demographic revolution in England: a re-examination. *Population Studies* **49**, pp. 5–33.

20. W. H. McNeill (1976) *Plagues and Peoples* (Harmondsworth: Penguin), p. 221. The study by Goldstone, *ibid.*, indicates the importance of changes in age at marriage for fertility changes in the crucial period 1750–1816, when increases were most important for population growth according to the data presented by Wrigley and Schofield. While changes in wages may have been related to these changes, it remains a possibility that a relaxation of the infectious-disease environment affecting adolescents could have been highly significant for both marriage and fertility patterns, as smallpox inoculation became more widespread in rural areas.

21. C. McEvedy and R. Jones (1978) *Atlas of World Population History* (Harmondsworth: Penguin), pp. 170–173.

22. S. H. Preston and V. Nelson (1974) Structure and change in cause of death. *Population Studies* **28**(2), pp. 19–52. Few data on component causes of death exist for other countries for the second half of the nineteenth century, so it is difficult to assess how typical the case of England and Wales was in that period. Varying proportions of ill-defined and unknown causes, and causes for which death rates actually increased, make comparison between countries difficult even for the twentieth century. In the international study it was found that respiratory tuberculosis contributed 0.10 and 0.12 towards each unit of decline in the overall death rate for females and males respectively, while McKeown suggested that 17.5% of mortality decline between the mid nineteenth century and 1971 was the result of a reduction in the death rate from this disease. As mentioned, this is misleading since the contributions made by component disease groups for which mortality declined, add up to more than 100% to offset increasing death rates for some non-communicable diseases. Variations in this, between populations, make comparisons with international data difficult to interpret in these terms, but anyway these may be somewhat more meaningful when data from England for the twentieth century are used. The contribution to each unit of decline in the overall death rate made by other infectious and parasitic diseases in the whole period 1848–54 to 1971 in England and Wales was also higher at 0.47, compared with about 0.14 in the international model, but the contribution was 0.27 in the period 1901–1971. A far larger component of 'other and unknown' causes of death probably distorts some of the cause-specific components of mortality decline in the international model.

23. Death rates for the mid nineteenth century were based on age- and sex-specific death rates for 1848–54 applied to the 1901 population, while the death rate for 1971 was also age- and sex-standardised to the 1901 population.

24. T. Smith (1928) The decline of infectious disease in its relation to modern medicine. *Preventive Medicine* **11**, pp. 345–363.

25. McKeown referred to the experience of those working in developing countries which suggests that malnutrition does not have the same effect with every infectious disease being marked in the case of diarrhoeal disease, measles and tuberculosis but less so in whooping cough: T. McKeown (1978) Fertility, mortality and causes of death. *Population Studies* **32**(3), pp. 535–542, p. 541. D. Morley (1973) *Paediatric Priorities in the Developing World* (London: Butterworth), pp. 184, 217, 238, 259.

26. S. H. Preston, M. R. Haines and E. R. Pamuk (1981) Effects of industrialisa-

tion and urbanisation on mortality in developed countries. *Solicited Papers 2, Proceedings of the 19th International Population Conference, Manila.* (Liege: IUSSP).

27. P. O. Goldblatt (1990) Social-class differences in mortality. In *The Biology of Class* N. Mascie-Taylor, ed. (Oxford: Oxford University Press), p. 31.

28. R. Peto (1980) Distorting the epidemiology of cancer: the need for a more balanced overview. *Nature* **284**, pp. 297–301.

29. R. Roemer (1982) *Legislative Action to Combat the World Smoking Epidemic.* (Geneva: WHO). It was suggested that legislation was the cornerstone for a comprehensive programme against smoking.

30. See, for example, several chapters in N. F. Stanley and R. A. Joshke (1980) *Changing Disease Patterns and Human Behaviour* (London: Academic Press).

31. W. H. McNeill, *op. cit.* in note 20, pp. 78–140.

32. F. H. Epstein and W. W. Holland (1983) Prevention of chronic diseases in the community—one disease versus multiple disease strategies. *International Journal of Epidemiology*, **12**(2), pp. 135–137.

33. K. Davis (1951) *The Population of India and Pakistan* (Princeton: Princeton University Press), p. 46.

34. J. Ratcliffe (1978) Social justice and the demographic transition: lessons from India's Kerala State. *International Journal of Health Services* **18**(1), pp. 123–144.

35. D. C. Morley (1980) Nutrition and infectious diseases. In *Disease and Urbanisation*, E. J. Clegg and J. P. Garlick, eds (London: Taylor Francis), pp. 37–43.

Bibliography

Aaby, P., Bukh, J., Lisse, I.M. and Smits, A.J. (1984). Overcrowding and intensive exposure as determinants of measles mortality. *American Journal of Epidemiology* **120**, pp. 49–63.

Aaby, P., Bukh, J., Lisse, I.M. and Smits, A.J. (1986). Severe measles in Sunderland, 1885: A European–African comparison of causes of severe infection. *International Journal of Epidemiology* **15**(1), pp. 101–107.

A.J. Aaby, P., Bukh, J., Lisse, I.M., Smits, A.J., Gomes, J., Fernandes, M.A., Francisco, I. and Soares, M. (1984). Determinants of measles mortality in a rural area of Guinea–Bissau: crowding, age and malnutrition. *Journal of Tropical Paediatrics* **30**, pp. 164–167.

Adelstein, A. (1977). Mortality from tuberculosis: a generation effect. *Population Studies* **8**, pp. 20–23.

Adelstein, A. and White, G. (1976). Leukaemia 1911–1973: a cohort analysis. *Population Trends* **6**, Winter, pp. 7–14.

Al-Sumidae, A.M., Hart, C.A., Levisher, S.J., Green, C.D. and McCarthy, K. (1988). Particles with properties of retroviruses in monocytes from patients with breast cancer. *Lancet* 1988 (1), pp. 5–9.

Alderson, M. (1981) *International Mortality Statistics* (London: Macmillan).

American Review of Respiratory Diseases (1976). Does measles really predispose to tuberculosis. Editorial. **114**, pp. 257–265.

Anderson, A.W., Benjamin, B., Grenville-Mathers, R. and Trenchard, H.J. (1957). Control of tuberculosis: importance of heredity and environment, *British Journal of Preventive and Social Medicine* **11**, pp. 1–6.

Anderson, R.M. and May, R.M. (1979). Population biology of infectious diseases: Part I. *Nature* **280**, pp. 361–367.

Anderson, R.M. and May, R.M. (1982). *Population Biology of Infectious Diseases*. (West Germany: Dahlem Konferenzen, Springer-Verlag).

Anderson, T.W. and Le Riche, W.H. (1970). Ischaemic heart disease and sudden death: 1960–1. *British Journal of Preventive and Social Medicine* **24**, pp. 1–9.

Appleby, A.B. (1975). Nutrition and disease: the case of London, 1550–1750. *Journal of Interdisciplinary History* **6**, pp. 1–22.

Appleby, A.V. (1977). Famine, mortality and epidemic disease—a comment. *Economic History Review* **30** (3), pp. 508–510.

Armitage, P. and Doll, R. (1957). A two-stage theory of carcinogenesis in relation to the age distribution of human cancer. *British Journal of Cancer* **11**, pp. 161–169.

Armstrong, W.A. (1981). The trend of mortality in Carlisle between the 1780s and the 1840s: a demographic contribution to the standard-of-living debate. *Economic History Review* **34** (1), pp. 94–114.

Arriaga, E.E. and Davis, K. (1969). The pattern of mortality change in Latin America. *Demography* **6** (3), pp. 223–242.

Auerbach, O. (1965). Smoking in relation to atherosclerosis of the coronary arteries. *New England Journal of Medicine* **268**, pp. 569–574.

Badger, F.F., Dingle, J.H., Feller, A.E. *et al.* (1953). A study of illness in a group of Cleveland families: II, Incidence of the common respiratory diseases. *American Journal of Hygiene* **58**, pp. 31–40.

Baillie, M. (1793). *The Morbid Anatomy of Some of the Most Important Parts of the Human Body.* (London: Johnson and Nicol).

Bainton, D., Jones, G.R. and Hole, D. (1978). Influenza and ischaemic heart disease—a possible trigger for acute myocardial infarction? *International Journal of Epidemiology* **7** (3), pp. 231–239.

Barker, T. and Drake, M. (1982). *Population and Society in Britain, 1850–1980.* (London: Batsford).

Bartlett, M.S. (1957). Measles periodicity and community size. *Journal of the Royal Statistical Society* **120**, pp. 48–62.

Beaver, M.W. (1973). Population, infant mortality and milk. *Population Studies* **27**, pp. 243–254.

Behar, M. (1974). A deadly combination. *World Health* February-March, pp. 28–33.

Benditt, E.P. and Benditt, J.M. (1973). Evidence for a monoclonal origin of human atherosclerotic plaques. *Proceedings of the National Academy of Science in the USA* **70** pp. 1753–1756.

Bengtsson, T., Fridlizius, G. and Ohlsson, R., eds (1985). *Pre-industrial Population Change: The Mortality Decline and Short-term Population Movements.* (Stockholm: Almquist and Wiksell International).

Benjamin, B. and Carrier, N.H. (1954). An evaluation of the quality of demographic statistics in England and Wales. *Proceedings of the World Population Conference*, Vol. 4. (New York: United Nations).

Bentzon, J.W. (1953). The effect of certain infectious diseases on tuberculin allergy. *Tubercle* **34**, pp. 34–41.

Berkson, J. (1958). Smoking and lung cancer: some observations on two recent reports. *Journal of the American Statistical Association* **53**, pp. 28–38.

Biraben, J.N. (1977). Current medical and epidemiological views on plague. *Local Population Studies, Supplement, The Plague Reconsidered.* (Stafford: Hourdsprint).

Black, F.L. (1962). Measles antibody prevalence in diverse populations. *American Journal of Diseases of Children* **103**, pp. 242–249.

Black, W. (1788). *A Comparative View of the Mortality of the Human Species at all Ages.* (London).

Black, W. (1789). *An Arithmetical and Medical Analysis of the Disease and Mortality of the Human Species.* Reprinted by Gregg International, West Germany, 1973.

Bradley, L. (1973). Reply to a review in *Local Population Studies* **10**, pp. 67–69 of *Smallpox Inoculation: an 18th-Century Mathematical Controversy*, L. Bradley ed., (Nottingham: University of Nottingham Adult Education Department, 1971).

Brass, W. and Kabir, M. (1977). Regional variations in fertility and child mortality during the demographic transition in England and Wales. In *Regional Demographic Development*, J. Hobcraft and P. Rees eds (London: Croom Helm), pp. 71–88.

Brenner, M.H. (1975). Economic changes and heart disease mortality. *American Journal of Public Health* **61** (3), pp. 606–610.

Brenner, M.H. (1973). Fetal, infant and maternal mortality during periods of economic instability. *International Journal of Health Services* **3** (2), p. 145.

Brenner, M.H. (1979). Mortality and the national economy, a review and the experience of England and Wales, 1936–76. *Lancet* 15 September, pp. 568–573.

Breslow, L. and Enstrom, J.E. (1980). Persistence of health habits and their relationship to mortality. *Preventive Medicine* **9**, pp. 469–483.

Brimblecombe, F.S.W., Cruikshank, R., Masters, P.L. *et al.* (1958). Family studies of respiratory infections. *British Medical Journal* 1958 (1). pp. 119–128.

British Medical Journal (1973). Pathogenesis of measles. Editorial, p. 29.

British Medical Journal (1976). Natural history of chronic bronchitis. Editorial, pp. 181–188.

Britton, M. (1974). Diagnostic errors discovered at autopsy. *Acta Medica Scandinavica* **196**, pp. 203–219.

Brownlee, J. (1916). History of birth and death rates in England and Wales taken as a whole, from 1750 to the present time. *Public Health*, **29**.

Brownlee, J. (1918). *An investigation into the Epidemiology of Phthisis in Great Britain and Ireland*. Medical Research Committee. (London: HMSO).

Bruneel, C. (1977). *La Mortalité dans les Campagnes, Le Duché de Brabant aux XVII et XVIII Siècles*. (Louvain).

Buer, M.C. (1926). *Health, Wealth and Population in the Early Days of the Industrial Revolution*, (London).

Bull, G.M. (1973). Meterological correlates with myocardial and cerebral infarction and respiratory diseases. *British Journal of Preventive and Social Medicine*, **27**, pp. 108–113.

Burch, P.R.J. (1968). *An Enquiry Concerning Growth Disease and Aging*. (Edinburgh: Oliver and Boyd).

Burch, P.R.J. (1976). *The Biology of Cancer – A New Approach*, (Lancaster: MTP).

Burnet, F.M. (1967). Immunological aspects of malignant disease. *Lancet* 1967 (2), pp. 1171–1174.

Burnet, F.M. (1969). *Cellular Immunology*. (Carlton: Melbourne University Press).

Burnet, F.M. (1970). *Immunology, Aging and Cancer*. (San Francisco: Freeman).

Burnet, F.M. (1970). An immunological approach to aging. *Lancet* 1970 (2) 2, pp. 358–360.

Burnet, F.M. (1970). *Immunological Surveillance*. (Oxford: Pergammon).

Burnet, F.M. and White, D.O. (1972). *Natural History of Infectious Diseases*. (Cambridge: Cambridge University Press).

Burnett, J. (1979) *Plenty and Want: A Social History of Diet in England from 1815 to the Present Day*. (London: Scolar Press).

Bwibo, N. (1970). Measles in Uganda: an analysis of children with measles admitted to Mulago Hospital. *Tropical Geographical Medicine* **22**, pp. 167–171.

Byington, R., Dyer, A., Garside, D. *et al.* (1979). Recent trends of major coronary risk factors and CHD mortality in the United States and other industrialised countries. In *Proceedings of the Conference on the Decline in Coronary Heart Disease Mortality*, J.R. Havlick and M. Fenleib eds

(Washington DC: US Department of Health Education and Welfare, NIH Publication), No. 79, p. 1110.

Cambell, A.H. (1961). The relationship between cancer and tuberculosis mortality rates. *British Journal of Cancer* **15**, pp. 10–18.

Cambell, A.H. and Guilfoyle (1970). Pulmonary tuberculosis, isoniazid and cancer. *British Journal of Diseases of the Chest* **64** (3). pp. 141–149.

Campbell, M. (1963). Death rates from diseases of the heart: 1876–1959. *British Medical Journal* 1963 (2), pp. 528–535.

Cambell, M. (1963). The main cause of increased death rate from diseases of the heart 1920–1959. *British Medical Journal* 1963 (2), pp. 712–717.

Cartwright, F.F. (1977). *A Social History of Medicine*. (London: Longman).

Case, R.A.M. (1956). Cohort analysis of cancer mortality in England and Wales, 1911–54, by site and sex. *British Journal of Preventive and Social Medicine* **10**, pp. 172–199.

Cassen, R.H. (1978). *India: Population, Economy, Society*. (London: Macmillan).

Census of Great Britain (1801). *Parish Register Abstracts*. (London).

Census of the United States (1860–). *Mortality and Vital Statistics: Population Volumes*. (Washington: Secretary of Interior).

Central Institute of Statistics (1956–). *Annuaria di Statistiche Sanitaria*. (Roma: Republica Italiana).

Central Institue of Statistics (1887–1955). *Causi di Morte*. (Roma: Republica Italiana).

Chadwick, E. (1842). *Report on the Sanitary Condition of the Labouring Population of Great Britain*. (Reprinted Edinburgh: Edinburgh University Press, 1965).

Chalmers, A.K. (1905). Infant mortality. *Public Health* **18**, pp. 409–438.

Chambers, J.D. (1957). The Vale of Trent, 1670–1800. *Economic History Review, Supplement 3*, pp. 33–57.

Cherry, S. (1980). The hospitals and population growth: voluntary hospitals, mortality and local population in the English provinces in the 18th and 19th centuries, Part I. *Population Studies* **34** (1), pp. 59–75.

Cherry, S. (1980). The hospitals and population growth, Part II. *Population Studies* **35** (2). pp. 251–265.

Cherry, T. (1924). Cancer and acquired resistance to tuberculosis, I. *Medical Journal of Australia* 1924 (2), pp. 372–378.

Cherry, T. (1925). Cancer and acquired resistance to tuberculosis, II. *Medical Journal of Australia* 1925 (1), pp. 581–598.

Cherry, T. (1931). Cancer and tuberculosis: the development of malignancy. *Lancet*, 7 Febraury, pp. 285–288.

Cherry, T. (1933). Cancer and tuberculosis. *Medical Journal of Australia* 1933 (2), pp. 197–217.

Cherry, T. (1935). *Cancer and tuberculosis*. (Melbourne: Patterson).

Cherry, T. (1945). *Cancer and Tubercle Bacillus*. (Melbourne: Melbourne Cancer Causation Research Committee).

Cipolla, C.M. (1965). Four centuries of Italian demographic development. In *Population in History: Essays in Historical Demography*, D.V. Glass and D.E.C. Eversley eds (London: Edward Arnold).

Clay, J. (1844). *Report of the Commission for Enquiry into the State of Large Towns and Population Districts, Appendix*. (London).

Clayton, D.G., Taylor, D. and Shaper, A.G. (1977). Trends in heart disease in England and Wales, 1950–73, *Health Trends* **9**, pp. 1–6.

Cockburn, A.T. (1963). *The Evolution and Eradication of Infectious Diseases*. (Baltimore: Johns Hopkins University Press).

Coglan, T.A. (1902). *International Medical Congress of Australasia, Transactions of the 6th Session.* (Hobart: IMCA), p. 263.

Colley, J.R.T., Douglas, J.W.B. and Reid, D.D. (1973). Respiratory disease in young adults: influences of early childhood respiratory-tract illness, social class, air pollution and smoking. *British Medical Journal* 1973 (3), pp. 195–198.

Colley, J.R.T. and Reid, D.D. (1970). Urban social origins of childhood bronchitis in England and Wales. *British Medical Journal* 1970 (2), pp. 213–218.

Commonwealth of Massachusetts (1916). *Vital Statistics, 75th Annual Report on Births Marriages and Deaths.* (Connecticut).

Condran, G.A. and Cheney, R.A. (1982). Mortality trends in Philadelphia: age- and cause-specific death rates 1870–1930. *Demography* 19 (1). pp. 97–123.

Condran, G.A. and Crimmins-Gardner, E. (1978). Public health measures and mortality in US cities in the late 19th century, *Human Ecology* 6 (2), pp. 27–54.

Cook, S.E. and Borah, W. (1974). *Mexico and the Caribbean, Volume 2.* (Berkeley: University of California Press, pp. 409–435.

Cooper, R. (1981). Rising death rates in the Soviet Union. *New England Journal of Medicine* 304, 21, pp. 1259–1265.

Cooper, R. and Schatzkin, A. (1982). The pattern of mass disease in the USSR. *Interntional Journal of Health Services* 12. pp. 459–480.

Cooper, R., Stamler, J., Dyer, A. and Garside, D. (1978). The decline in mortality from coronary heart diseases. *Journal of Chronic Diseases* 31, pp. 709–720.

Cramer, W. (1936). On antagonism in development of malignancy in two different organisms. *Journal of Pathological Bacteriology* 43, pp. 73–89.

Creighton, C. (1894). *The History of Epidemics in Britain.* (Cambridge: Cambridge University Press).

Cruikshank, D.B. (1939). The association of tuberculosis and cancer. *Papworth Research Bulletin* 2 (1), (Papworth: Pendragon).

Cruikshank, D.B. (1940). The topography of the relative distribution of cancer and tuberculosis. *Tubercle* 1940, pp. 281–291.

Cummins, R.O., Shaper, A.G., Walker, M. and Wale, C.J. (1981). Smoking and drinking by middle-aged British men: effects of social class and town residence. *British Medical Journal* 283, pp. 1497–1502.

Dahlberg, G. (1949). Mortality from tuberculosis in some countries. *British Journal of Preventive and Social Medicine* 4, pp. 220–227.

Daly, C. (1959). Air pollution and causes of death. *British Journal of Preventive and Social Medicine* 13, pp. 14–27.

Daniels, M., Ridehalgh, F., Springett, V.H. and Hall, I.M. (1948). *Tuberculosis in Young Adults: Report on the Prophit Tuberculosis Survey 1935–44.* (London: Lewis).

Davis, K. (1951). *The Population of India and Pakistan.* (Princeton: Princeton University Press).

Daw, R.H. (1954). Some statistical aspects of mortality from degenerative heart disease. *Journal of the Institute of Actuaries* Part I, 1954, 354, pp. 69–100.

Deane, P. and Coale, W.A. (1962). *British Economic Growth 1688–1959.* Cambridge: Cambridge University Press).

Department of Health and Social Security (1954). *Reports on Public Health and Medical Subjects, No. 95.* (London: HMSO).

Derrick, V.P.A. (1927). Changes in generation mortality: England and Wales. *Journal of the Institute of Actuaries* 58, pp. 117–159.

Diaz-Briquets (1981). Determinants of mortality transition in developing countries before and after the 2nd World War: some evidence from Cuba. *Population Studies* 35 (3), pp. 399–411.

Dickens, C. (1983). *Hard Times.* (Harmondsworth: Penguin).

Dixon, C.W. (1962). *Smallpox*. (London: Churchill).

Doll, R. (1967). *Prevention of Cancer – Pointers from Epidemiology*. (London: Nuffield Provincial Hospitals Trust).

Doll, R. and Kinlen, L. (1970). Immunosurveillance and cancer – epidemiological evidence. *British Medical Journal* 1970 (4), pp. 420–422.

Doll, R. and Peto, R. (1981). Avoidable risks of cancer in the United States. *Journal of the National Cancer Institute* **66** (6), pp. 1191–1265.

Dominion Bureau of Statistics (1920–). *Vital Statistics, 1920–1960, Annual Report of Notifiable Diseases*. (Ottawa).

Douglas, J.W.B. and Blomfield, D. (1958). *Children Under 5*. (London: Allen and Unwin).

Drake, M. (1969). *Population and Society in Norway, 1735–1865*. (Cambridge: Cambridge University Press).

Draper, E. (1972). *Birth Control in the Modern World*. (Harmondsworth: Penguin).

Dubos, R. and Dubos, J. (1952). *The White Plague*. (London: Gollanz).

Dwork, D. (1987). *War is Good for Babies and Other Young Children*. (London).

Dyson, T. and Murphy, M. (1985). The onset of fertility transition. *Population and Development Review* **11** (3), pp. 399–440.

Edwardes, E.J. (1902). *A Concise History of Smallpox and Vaccination in Europe*. (London: Lewis).

Engels, F. (1845). *The Conditions of the Working Class in England*. (Reprinted London: Grenada, 1982).

Epstein, F.H. and Holland, W.A. (1983). Prevention of chronic diseases in the community – one disease versus multiple disease strategies. *International Journal of Epidemiology* **12** (2), pp. 135–137.

Epstein, S.S. (1979). *The Politics of Cancer*. (New York: Anchor Doubleday).

Epstein, S.S. and Swartz, J.B. (1981). Fallacies of lifestyle cancer theories. *Nature* **289**, pp. 127–130.

Eyer, J. (1975). Hypertension as a disease of modern society. *International Journal of Health Services* **5** (4), p. 539.

Eyer, J. (1977). Prosperity as a cause of death. *International Journal of Health Services* **7** (1), p. 125.

Eyer, J. (1977). Does employment cause the death rate peak in each business cycle? *International Journal of Health Services* **7** (4), p. 625.

Eyler, J.M. (1979). *Victorian Social Medicine: The Ideas and Methods of William Farr*. (Baltimore).

Fairbairn, A.S. and Reid, D.O. (1958). Air pollution and other local factors in respiratory disease. *British Journal of Preventive and Social Medicine* **12**, pp. 94–103.

Farr, W. (1837). *Vital Statistics or the Statistics of Health, Sickness and Death*. Reprinted in *Mortality in Mid 19th-Century Britain*, R. Wall ed. (West Germany: Gregg International).

Fawcett, J. and Parry, H.E. (1957). Lung changes in pertussis and measles in childhood. *British Journal of Radiology* **30**, 350, pp. 76–82.

Fildes, V.A. (1986). *Breasts, Bottles and Babies*. (Edinburgh: Edinburgh University Press).

Fletcher, C.M. (1976). The natural history of chronic bronchitis. *British Medical Journal* 1976 (1), pp. 1592–1593.

Fletcher, C.M., Peto, R., Tinker, C.M. and Speizer, F.S. (1976). *The Natural History of Chronic Bronchitis and Emphysema*. (London: Oxford University Press).

Flinn, M. (1970). *British Population Growth 1700–1850*. (London: MacMillan).

Flinn, M. (1977). *Scottish Population History from the 17th Century to the 1920s*. (Cambridge: Cambridge University Press).

Florey, C. du V., Melia, R.J.W. and Darby, S.C. (1978). Changing mortality from ischaemic heart disease in Great Britain, 1968–76. *British Medical Journal* (1), pp. 635–637.

Floud, R. and Wachter, K.W. (1982). Poverty and physical stature. *Social Science History* **4**, pp. 422–452.

Fogel, R.W., Engerman, S.L. and Trussell, J. (1982). Exploring the uses of data on height: the analysis of long-term trends in nutrition, labour welfare, and labour productivity. *Social Science History* **4**, pp. 401–421.

Fox, S.M. and Skinner, J.S. (1964). Physical activity and cardiovascular health. *American Journal of Cardiology* **14**, pp. 731–746.

Gale, A.H. (1959). *Epidemic Diseases*. (Harmondsworth: Penguin).

Galloway, P.R. (1988). Basic patterns in annual variations in fertility, nuptiality, mortality and prices in pre-industrial Europe. *Population Studies* **42**, pp. 275–303.

Gamble, D.R. (1980). The epidemiology of insulin-dependent diabetes, with particular reference to the relationship of virus infection to its aetiology. *Epidemilogic Review* **2**, pp. 49–70.

Gardner, M.J., Winter, P.D. and Barker, D.J.P. (1984). *Atlas of Mortality from Selected Diseases in England and Wales: 1968–1978*. (Chichester: Wiley).

Genton, E., Weily, H.S. and Steck, P.P. (1973). Platelets, thrombosis and coronary diseases. *Advances in Cardiology* **9**, p. 29.

Gilliam, G. (1955). Trends in mortality attributed to carcinoma of the lung: possible effects of faulty certification of deaths to other respiratory diseases. *Cancer* **8**, pp. 1130–1136.

Glass, D.V. (1965). Population Movements 1700–1850. In *Population in History – Essays in Historical Demography*, D.V. Glass and D.E.C. Eversley eds (London: Edward Arnold).

Glass, D.V. (1969). Socio-economic status and occupation in the city of London at the end of the 17th century. In *Studies in London History*, A.E.J. Hollaender and W. Kellerway eds (London: Hodder and Stoughton).

Glass, D.V. (1973). *Numbering the People*. (Farnborough: Saxon House).

Gleason, R.E., Kahn, C.B., Funk, I.B. and Craighead, J.E. (1982). Seasonal incidence of insulin-dependent diabetes (IDDM) in Massachusetts, 1964–1973. *International Journal of Epidemiology* **11** (1), pp. 39–45.

Goldblatt, P.O. (1990). Social class mortality differences. In *The Biology of Class*, N. Mascie-Taylor ed. (Oxford: Oxford University Press).

Goldstein, H. (1978). Factors influencing the height of seven year old children – results from the National Child Development Study. *Human Ecology* **6** (2), pp. 27–54.

Goldstone, J.A. (1986). The demographic revolution in England: a re-examination. *Population Studies* **49**, pp. 5–33.

Goodhart, C.B. (1959). Cancer process and lung cancer. *Practitioner* **182**, pp. 578–584.

Gordon, J.E., Singh, S. and Wyon, J.B. (1965). Causes of death at different ages, by sex, and by season, in a rural population of the Punjab, 1957–1959: a field study. *Indian Journal of Medical Research* **53**, pp. 906–917.

Gore, A.T. and Shaddick, C.W. (1958). Atmospheric pollution and mortality in the county of London. *British Journal of Preventive and Social Medicine* **12**, pp. 104–113.

Goubert, J.P. (1974). *Malades et Médicines en Bretagne, 1770–1970*. (Paris).

Gray, R.H. (1974). The decline of mortality in Ceylon and the demographic effects of malaria control. *Population Studies* **28** (2), pp. 205–229.

Greenwood, M., Topley, W.W.C. and Wilson, G.S. (1936). *Experimental Epidemiology*. Medical Research Council, Special Report Series No. 29. (London: MRC).

Griffith, G.T. (1926). *Population Problems in the Age of Malthus*. (Cambridge).

Gruver, R.H. and Freis, E.D. (1957). A study of diagnostic error. *Annals of Internal Medicine* **47**, p. 108.

Guberan, E. (1979). Surprising decline in cardiovascular mortality in Switzerland 1951–76. *Journal of Epidemiology and Community Health* **33**, pp. 114–120.

Guy, W.A. (1882). 250 years of smallpox in London. *Journal of the Royal Statistical Society* **45**, pp. 399–443.

Haas, J.H. de (1964). *Changing Mortality Pattern of Cardiovascular Disease*. (Haarlem De Erven: F. Bohn).

Halliday, M.L. and Anderson, T.W. (1979). The sex differential in ischaemic heart disease: trends by social class 1931 to 1971. *Journal of Epidemiology and Community Health* **33**, pp. 74–77.

Hansen, H.O. (1981). Some age-structural consequences of mortality variation in pre-transitional Iceland and Sweden. In *The Great Mortalities: Methodological Studies of Demographic Crises in the Past*, H. Charbonneau and A. Larose eds (Liege: Ordina).

Hardy, A. (1983). Smallpox in London: Factors in the decline of the disease in the nineteenth century. *Medical History* **27**, pp. 111–138.

Hardy, A. (1988). Diagnosis, death and diet: the case of London, 1750–1909. *Journal of Interdisciplinary History* **18**, 387–401.

Hatcher, J. (1977). *Plague, Populations and the English Economy 1348–1530*. (London: MacMillan).

Haybittle, J.L. (1962 and 1963). Mortality rates from cancer and tuberculosis. *British Journal of Preventive and Social Medicine* **16**, pp. 93–104; **17**, pp. 23–28.

Hayflick, L. (1965). The limited in vitro lifetime of human diploid cell strains. *Experimental Cell Research* **37**, pp. 614–636.

Haygarth, J. (1777). Observations on the Population and Disease of Chester in the Year, 1774. A paper given to the Royal Society. *Philosophical Transactions and Observations, Royal Society*, January 1777. (Original in Chester Town Hall).

Heasman, M.A. and Lipworth, L. (1966). Accuracy of certification of cause of death. *Medical and Population Subjects No. 20* pp. 110–128 (London: HMSO).

Herberden, W. (1801). Observations on the Increase and Decline of Different Diseases. (Reprinted in *Population and Disease in Early Industrial England*, B. Benjamin ed. (West Germany: Gregg International)).

Hedrich, A.W. (1930). The corrected average attack rate for measles among city children. *American Journal of Hygiene* **11**, pp. 576–600.

Helczmanovski, H. (1979). Austria-Hungary. In *European Demography and Economic Growth*, W.R. Lee ed. (London: Croom Helm).

Henry, L. (1975). The population of France in the 18th century. In *Population*, Numéro Special, Novembre 1975, pp. 71–122.

Heysham, J. (1782). *Observations on the Bills of Mortality in Carlisle for the Year 1779*. (Carlisle: Mililieu). Abridged observations on the Bills for 1779–1787, in *The History of Cumberland* (Hutchinson, 1794).

Hinde, P.R.A. and Wood, R.I. (1984). Variations in historical natural fertility patterns and the measurement of fertility control. *Journal of Biosocial Science* **16**, pp. 309–321.

Hofsten, E. and Lundström, G. (1977). *Swedish Population History: Main Trends from 1750–1970*. Urval No. 8 (Stockholm: Statistiska Centralbyran).

Hollingsworth, T.H. (1965). A demographic study of the British ducal families. *Population Studies* Supplement, **18** (2).

Howe, G.M. (1970). *A National Atlas of Disease Mortality in the UK*. (London: Nelson).

Howe, G.M. (1972). *Man, Environment and Disease in Britain, A Medical Geography through the Ages*. (Harmondsworth: Penguin).

Howie, P. and McNeilly, A.S. (1982). Effect of breast-feeding patterns on human birth intervals. *Journal of Reproduction and Ferility*, 65.

Howie, P., McNeilly, A.S., Huston, M.J., Cook, A. and Boyle, H. (1981). Effect of supplementary food on suckling patterns and ovarian activity during lactation. *British Medical Journal* **283**, pp. 757–759.

Jerushalmy, Z., Kohn, A. and de Vries (1961). Interaction of myxoviruses with human blood platelets in vitro. *Proceeding of the Royal Society for Experimental Biology* **106**, pp. 462–466.

Jones, H.B. (1956). Aging, disease and life expectancy. *Advances in Biological and Medical Physics*. **4**, pp. 281–337.

Jones, P.E. and Judges, A.V. (1935). London Population in the late 17th century. *Economic History Review* **6**, pp. 45–63.

Jones, R.E. (1980). Further evidence on the decline in infant mortality in North Shropshire 1561–1810. *Population Studies*. **34** (2), pp. 239–250.

Junge, B. and Hoffmeister, H. (1982). Civilisation-associated disease in Europe and industrial countries outside Europe: regional differences and trends in mortality. *Preventive Medicine* **11**, pp. 117–130.

Kallman, F.J. and Reisner, D. (1943). Twin studies on the significance of genetic factors in tuberculosis. *American Review of Tuberculosis* **47**, pp. 549–574.

Kermack, M.A., McKendrick, A.G. and McKinlay, P.L. (1934). Death rates in Great Britain and Sweden: some general regularities and their significance. *Lancet* 1934 (2), pp. 698–703.

Kessner, D.M. and Florey, C. du V. (1967). Mortality trends for acute and chronic nephritis and infections of the kidney. *Lancet* 1967 (2), pp. 979–982.

Keys, A. (1954). Obesity and degenerative heart disease. *American Journal of Public Health* **44**, pp. 864–871.

Kinlen, L.J. (1982). Immunosuppressive therapy and cancer. *Cancer Surveys* **1** (4), pp. 565–583.

Konner, M. and Worthman, C. (1980). Nursing frequency, gonadal function and birth spacing among !Kung hunter-gatherers. *Science* **207**, pp. 788–791.

Krause, J.T. (1958). Changes in English fertility and mortality, 1781–1850. *Economic History Review* **11**, pp. 52–70.

Kuller, L., Seltser, R., Paffenberger, R. and Krueger, D. (1966). Trends in death rates from hypertensive disease in Memphis Tennessee, 1920–1960. *Journal of Chronic Diseases* **19**, p. 847.

Kunitz, S.J. (1983). Speculations on the European mortality decline. *Economic History Review* **36** (3), pp. 349–364.

Kunitz, S.J. (1984). Mortality change in America, 1620–1920. *Human Biology*, **56** (3), pp. 559–582.

Kurt, T.L., Yeager, A.S., Guerette, S. and Dunlop, S. (1972). Spread of pertussis by hospital staff. *Journal of the American Medical Association* **221**, pp. 264–267.

Lambert, H.J. (1965). Epidemiology of a small pertussis outbreak in Kent County, Michigan. *Public Health Report* **80**, pp. 365–369.

Landers, J. (1987). Mortality and metropolis: the case of London 1675–1825. *Population Studies* **41**, pp. 59–76.

Larsen, I. (1979). *Eighteenth-Century Disease, Diagnostic Trends and Mortality*.

(Oslo: University of Oslo Press).

Laurence, J.Z. (1855). *The Diagnosis of Surgical Cancer*. (London: Churchill).

Lee, W.R. (1977). *Population Growth, Economic Development and Social Change in Bavaria, 1750–1850*. (New York: Arno).

Lew, E.A. (1957). Some implications of mortality statistics relating to coronary artery disease. *Journal of Chronic Disease* **6**. pp. 192–209.

Lillienfeld, A.M. (1976). *Foundations of Epidemiology*. (New York: Oxford University Press).

Lillienfeld, A.M., Pederson, E. and Dowd, J.E. (1967). *Cancer Epidemiology: Methods of Study*. (Baltimore: John Hopkins University Press).

Lindert, P.H. and Williamson, J.G. (1983). English workers' living standards during the industrial revolution: a new look. *Economic History Review* **36**, pp. 1–25.

Lindskos, B.I. (1978). Mortalitaetsdiagnosen in Suedschweden 1749–1801. In *Medizinische Diagnostik in Geschichte und Gesenwart*, C. Habrick *et al.* eds (Munich: Fritsch), pp. 583–606.

Linnemann, C.C. *et al.* (1975). Use of pertussis vaccine in an epidemic involving hospital staff. *Lancet* 1975 (2), pp. 540–545.

Logan, W.P.D. (1950). Mortality in England and Wales from 1848–1947. *Population Studies* **4**, pp. 132–178.

Logan, W.P.D. (1982). Cancer mortality by occupation and social class 1851–1971. *IARC SP No. 36/OPCS SMPS No. 44* (Lyon/London: HMSO).

Longini, I.M., Koopman, J.S., Monto, A.S. *et al.* (1982). Estimating household and community transmission parameters for influenza. *American Journal of Epidemiology* **115**, pp. 736–751.

Longmate, N. (1966). *King Cholera*. (London: Hamish Hamilton).

Lonsdale, H. (1970). *The Life of John Heysham MD*. (London: Longmans Green).

Loschky, D.J. (1972). Urbanisation and England's eighteenth-century crude birth and death rates. *Journal of European Economic History* 1972 (1), pp. 697–712.

Lower, G.M. and Kanarak, M.S. (1982). The mutation theory of chronic infectious disease: relevance to epidemiologic theory. *American Journal of Epidemiology* **115** (6), pp. 803–817.

Lu, Wan Ching (1958). Agglutination of human platelets by influenza PR8 strain virus and mumps virus. *Federation Proceedings* **17**, p. 446.

Luckin, W. (1977). The decline of smallpox and the demographic revolution of the 18th century. *Social History* **6**, pp. 793–797.

Lurie, M.B. (1964). *Resistance to Tuberculosis: Experimental Studies in Natural and Acquired Defence Mechanism*. (Cambridge, Massachusetts: Harvard University Press).

Magill, T.P. (1955). The immunologist and the evil spirits. *Journal of Immunology* **74**, pp. 1–8.

Malthus, T.R. (1798). *An Essay on the Principle of Population*. (Reprinted Harmondsworth: Penguin, 1970, A. Flew ed.).

Mandle, J.R. (1970). The decline in mortality in British Guyana, 1911–1960. *Demography* **7** (3), pp. 301–315.

Manton, K.G. and Poss, S.S. (1979). Effects of dependency among causes of death for cause-elimination life-table strategies. *Demography* **16** (2). pp. 313–326.

Marks, H.M. (1960). Influence of obesity on morbidity and mortlity. *Bulletin of the New York Academy of Medicine* Series 2, **36**, pp. 296–312.

Marmot, M.G. (1980). Affluence, urbanisation and coronary heart disease. In *Disease and Urbanisation*, E.J. Clegg and J.P. Garlick eds (London: Taylor Francis), pp. 127–143.

Marmot, M.G., Adelstein, A.M., Robinson, N. and Rose, G.A. (1978). Changing social-class distribution of heart diseases. *British Medical Journal* 1978 (2), pp. 1109–1112.

Marmot, M.G., Rose, G., Shipley, M. and Hamilton, P.J.S. (1978). Employment grade and coronary heart disease in British civil servants. *Journal of Epidemiology and Community Health* **32**, pp. 244–249.

Marshall, J. (1832). *Mortality in the Metropolis*, (London).

Maupas, P. and Melnick, J.L. eds (1981). Hepatitis B and primary hepatocellular carcinoma. *Prog. Medical Virology* **27**, p. 1–210.

McEvedy, C. and Jones, R. (1978). *Atlas of the World Population History*. (Harmondsworth: Penguin).

McKeown, T. (1976). *The Modern Rise of Population*. (London: Edward Arnold).

McKeown, T. (1976). *The Role of Medicine: Dream, Mirage or Nemesis?* (London: Nuffield Provincial Hospitals Trust).

McKeown, T. (1978). Fertility, mortality and cause of death. *Population Studies* **32** (3), pp. 535–542.

McKeown, T. and Brown R.G. (1955). Medical evidence related to English population changes in the eighteenth century. *Population Studies* **9**, pp. 119–141.

McKeown, T. and Record, R.G. (1962). Reasons for the decline in mortality in England and Wales during the nineteenth century. *Population Studies* **16**, pp. 94–122.

McKeown, T., Record, R.G. and Brown, R.G. (1972). An Interpretation of the modern rise of population in Europe. *Population Studies* **26** (3), pp. 345–382.

McKeown, T., Record, R.G. and Turner, R.D. (1975). An interpretation of the decline in mortality in England and Wales during the 20th century. *Population Studies* **29**, pp 391–422.

McNeill, W.H. (1976). *Plagues and Peoples*. (Harmondsworth: Penguin).

McNeilly, A.S. (1979). Effects of lactation on fertility. *British Medical Bulletin* **35**, pp. 151–154.

Medical Research Council (1972). BCG and vole bacillus in the prevention of tuberculosis in early adult life. *Bulletin WHO* **46**, pp. 371–385.

Melia, R.J.W., Florey, C. du V. and Swan, A.V. (1981). Respiratory illness in British schoolchildren and atmospheric smoke and sulphur dioxide, 1973–7. *Journal of Epidemiology and Community Health* **35**, pp. 161–167.

Mercer, A.J. (1981). Risk of dying from tuberculosis and cancer: further aspects of a possible association. *International Journal of Epidemiology* **10** (4), pp. 377–380.

Mercer, A.J. (1983). Trends in circulatory-disease mortality in western populations: evidence of similarities in the pattern of measles epidemics. *International Journal of Epidemiology* **12** (3). pp. 366–371.

Mercer, A.J. (1985). Smallpox and epidemiological-demographic change in Europe in the 18th and 19th centuries: the importance of vaccination. *Population Studies* **39** (2), pp. 287–307.

Mercer, A.J. (1986). Relative trends in mortality from related respiratory and airborne infectious diseases. *Population Studies* **40** (1), pp. 129–145.

Middleton, N. and Weitzman, S. (1976). *A Place for Everyone – A History of State Education from the 18th Century to the 1970s*. (London: Gollanz).

Millan, D.W.M., Davis, J.A., Torbet, T.E. and Campo, M.S. (1986). DNA sequences of human papillomavirus types 11, 16 and 18 in lesions of uterine cervix in the west of Scotland, *British Medical Journal* **293**, pp. 93–96.

Mitchell, B.R. (1971). *European Historical Statistics 1750–1970*. (London: MacMillan).

Morat, H.Z., Mustard, J.E., Taichman, N.S. and Uriuhara, T. (1966). Platelet aggregation and release of ADP, serontinin and histamine associated with phagocytosis of antigen-antibody complexes. *Proceedings of the Society for Experimental Biology* **120**. pp. 232–237.

Moriyama, I.M., Dawber, T.R. and Kammel, W.B. (1966). Evolution of diagnostic information supporting medical certification of deaths from cardio-vascular disease. In *Epidemiological Approaches to the Study of Cancer and Other Chronic Diseases*, W. Haenzel ed., *National Cancer Institute Monograph* 19.

Morley, D. (1969). Severe measles in the tropics. *British Medical Journal* 1969 (1), pp. 297–301 and 363–365.

Morley, D. (1980). Nutrition and infectious disease. In *Diseases and Urbanisation* E.J. Clegg and J.P. Garlick eds (London: Taylor Francis), pp. 37–43.

Morris, N. (1964). *Uses of Epidemiology*. (London: Livingstone).

Moser, K.A., Pugh, H.S. and Goldblatt, P.O. (1988). Inequalities in women's health: looking at mortality differentials using an alternative approach. *British Medical Journal* **296**, pp. 1221–1224.

Mustard, J.F, (1970). Platelets and thromboembolic disease. *Advances in Cardiology* **4**, pp. 131–142.

Mustard, J.F., Murphy, E.A., Rowsell, H.C. and Downie, H.G. (1964). Platelets and atherosclerosis. *Journal of Atherosclerosis Research* **4**, pp. 1–28.

National Diet Heart Study (1968). Final Report. *Circulation* **37**, Supplement 1.

Neill, W.A., Duncan, D.A., Kloster, F. and Mahler, D.J. (1974). Response of coronary circulation to cutaneous cold. *American Journal of Medicine* **56**, pp. 471–476.

Nemin, R.L. (1972). Disorders of the respiratory tract in children. In *Pulmonary Disorders, Vol. I*, E.L. Kendig Jnr. ed. (Philadelphia: Saunders).

Newberne, P.M. and Williams, G. (1970). Nutritional influences on the course of infections. In *Resistance to Infectious Disease*, R.H. Dunlop and H.W. Moon, eds (Saskatoon Modern Press).

Northampton Bills of Mortality. *Bills of Mortality for All Saints Parish*. (Held in the British Library, London).

Notkins, A.L. (1979). The causes of diabetes. *Scientific American* **241** (5), pp. 59–67.

Office of Population Censuses and Surveys (1974–). *Mortality Statistics: Cause. Series DH2*. (London: HMSO).

Office of Population Censuses and Surveys (1975). *Cancer Mortality in England and Wales, 1911–70. Studies in Medical and Population Subjects, No. 29* (London: HMSO).

Office of Population Censuses and Surveys (1978). Ischaemic and related heart diseases in middle age: Trends in mortality 1951–75, England and Wales. *Series DH1, No. 3*, pp. 13–17. (London: HMSO).

Olshansky, S.J. and Ault, A.B. (1986). The fourth stage of the epidemiologic transition: the age of degenerative diseases. *Millbank Memorial Quarterly* **64** (3), pp. 355–391.

Omran, O.R. (1971). The epidemiologic transition. *Millbank Memorial Fund Quarterly*. **49** (4i), pp. 509–538.

Omran, O.R. (1977). Epidemiologic transition in the United States. *Population Bulletin 32*, pp. 3–42.

Omran, D.R. (1977). A century of epidemiologic transition in the United States. *Preventive Medicine* **6**, pp. 30–51.

Onuigbo, W.I.B. (1975). Some 19th-century ideas on links between tuberculosis and cancerous diseases of the lung. *British Journal of Diseases of the Chest* **169**, pp. 207–210.

Orubuloye, I.O. and Caldwell, J.C. (1975). The impact of public health services on mortality: a study of mortality differentials in a rural area of Nigeria. *Population Studies* **29** (2), pp. 259–272.

Osmond, C., Gardner, M J and Acheson E D. (1982). Analysis of trends in cancer mortality in England and Wales during 1951–80, separating changes associated with period of birth and period of death. *British Medical Journal* **284**, pp. 1005–1008.

Oswald, N.C. (1947). Collapse of the lower lobes of the lungs in children. *Proceedings of the Royal Society of Medicine* **40**, pp. 736–737.

Packham, M.A., Nishizawa, E.E. and Mustard, J.F. (1968). Response of platelets to tissue injury. *Biochemical Pharmacology* **17**, Supplement, pp. 171–184.

Parish, H.J. (1968). *Victory with Vaccines*. (Edinburgh: Livingstone).

Parry, W.H. (1969). *Infectious Diseases*. (London: English Universities Press).

Patterson, K.D. (1977). The impact of modern medicine on population growth in 20th-century Ghana: a tentative assessment. In *African Historical Demography, Proceedings of a Seminar held in the Centre of African Studies*, pp. 437–452. (Edinburgh: University of Edinburgh Press).

Paxton, T.G. (1956). A study of tuberculosis and cancer mortality rates with special reference to lung cancer rates. *British Journal of Cancer* **10**, pp. 623–633.

Pearl, R. (1929). Cancer and tuberculosis. *American Journal of Hygiene* **9**, pp. 97–159.

Percival, T. (1798). *Essays on the Smallpox and Measles*. Reprinted in *Population and Disease in early Industrial England*, B. Benjamin ed (West Germany: Gregg International, 1973).

Perrenoud, A. (1978). La mortalité à Genève de 1625 à 1825. *Annales de Demographie Historique* (Paris), pp. 209–233.

Perrenoud, A. (1979). *La population de Genève du Seizième au début du Dix-neuvième Siècle*. (Genève), pp. 458–479.

Peto, R. (1980). Distorting the epidemiology of cancer: the need for a more balanced overview. *Nature* **284**, pp. 297–301.

Peto, R. and Stott, H. (1978). Cancer epidemiology and clinical trials report. In *Imperial Cancer Research Fund, Scientific Report, 1978*.

Pickard, R. (1947). *Population and Epidemics of Exeter*. (Exeter).

Pitkanen, K.J., Mielke, J.H. and Jorde, L.B. (1989). Smallpox and its eradication in Finland: implications for disease control. *Population Studies* **43**, pp. 95–111.

Poitou, C. (1978). La mortalité en Sologne Orleanes de 1670 à 1870. *Annales de Demographie Historique* (Paris).

Pollitzer, R. (1954). *Plague*. (Geneva).

Porter, R. (1987). *Disease, Medicine and Society in England 1550–1860*. (London: MacMillan).

Post, J.D. (1976). Famine mortality and epidemic diseases in the process of modernisation. *Economic History Review* **29**, pp. 14–37.

Preston, S.H. (1975). The changing relation between mortality and level of economic development. *Population Studies* **29** (2), pp. 231–245.

Preston, S.H. (1976). *Mortality Patterns in National Populations*. (New York: Academic Press).

Preston, S.H., ed. (1977). *The Effects of Infant and Child Mortality on Fertility*. (New York: Academic Press).

Preston, S.H., Haines, M.R. and Pamuk, E.R. (1981). Effects of industrialisation and urbanisation on mortality in developed countries. *Solicited Papers, 2, Proceedings of the 19th International Population Conference, Manila*. (Liege: IUSSP).

Preston, S.H., Keyfitz, N. and Schoen, R. (1972). *Causes of Death. Life Tables for National Populations.* (New York: Seminar Press).

Preston, S.H. and Nelson, V. (1974). Structure and change in cause of death. *Population Studies* **28** (2), pp. 19–52.

Preston, S.H. and Van de Walle, E. (1978). Urban French mortality in the 19th century. *Population Studies* **32** (2), pp. 275–291.

Ratcliffe, J. (1978). Social justice and the demographic transition: lessons from India's Kerala State. *International Journal of Health Services* **18** (1), pp. 123–144.

Razzell, P.E. (1965). Population change in 18th-century England – a reinterpretation. *Economic History Review* **18**, pp. 312–332.

Razzell, P.E. (1973). Smallpox a difference of opinion. *Local Population Studies* **10**, pp. 65–69.

Razzell, P.E. (1974). An interpretation of the modern rise of population in Europe – a critique. *Population Studies* **28**, pp. 5–17.

Razzell, P.E. (1974). The smallpox controversy. *Local Population Studies* **12**, pp. 42–44.

Razzell, P.E. (1977). *Edward Jenner's Cowpox Vaccine: the History of a Medical Myth.* (Firle, Sussex: Caliban).

Razzell, P.E. (1977). *The Conquest of Smallpox.* (Firle, Sussex: Caliban).

Razzell, P.E. (1982). Neo-Malthusianism. *New Society,* 4 February.

Reeves, R. (1985). Declining fertility in England and Wales as a major cause of the twentieth-century decline in mortality. *American Journal of Epidemiology* **122** (1), pp. 112–126.

Registrar-General (1838–). *Annual Reports for England and Wales.* (London: HMSO).

Registrar-General (1900–). *Annual Statistical Review for England and Wales.* (London: HMSO).

Registrar-General of Eire (1864–1954). *Annual Report* (Dublin: Stationary Office).

Registrar-General of Eire (1955). *Report on Vital Statistics* Dublin: Stationary Office).

Registar-General of Scotland (1855–). *Annual Report* (Edinburgh: HMSO).

Retherford, R.D. (1975). *The Changing Sex Differential in Mortality.* Studies in Population and Urban Demography No. 1 (Connecticut: Greenwood).

Riley, J.C. (1987). *The Eighteenth-Century Campaign to Avoid Disease* (London: MacMillan).

Rinzler, S.H. (1957). *The Clincal Aspects of Arteriosclerosis* (Springfield, Illinois: Charles C. Thomas).

Robb-Smith, A.H.T. (1967). *The Enigma of Coronary Heart Disease.* Year Book of Medical Publishers, 1967 (Chicago).

Rose, G. (1966). Cold weather and ischaemic heart disease. *British Journal of Preventive and Social Medicine* **20**, pp. 92–100.

Rosen, G. (1973). Disease debility and death. In *The Victorian City*, H.J. Dyos and M. Wolff eds, pp. 625–667. (London).

Royal College of Physicians (1970). *Air Pollution and Health.* (London: Pitman).

Royal College of Physicians (1977). *Smoking or Health.* (London: Pitman).

Royal Commission on Vaccination (1889–96). *Report of the Royal Commission on Vaccination.* 5 volumes and appendices. (London).

Salonen, J.T. and Valonen, I. (1983). Longitudinal cross-national analysis of coronary mortality. *International Journal of Epidemiology* **11**, pp. 229–238.

Schofield, R. (1977). Book reviews: The modern rise of population. *Population Studies* **31**, pp. 179–181.

Service de la Statistique Municipal (1888–). *Annuaire Statistique de la Ville de Paris*. (Paris: Préfecture de la Seine).

Service de la Statistique Municipal (1889). *Population Parisiènne: Fréquences des Principals Maladies à Paris 1865–1889*. (Paris: Envoyés à l'éxposition universelle de 1889).

Short, T. (1749). *A History of the Air, Weather, Seasons, etc.* (London).

Siljeström, P.E. (1885). *En studie i Sjukdomsstatististik*, (Stockholm).

Smith, F.B. (1979). *The People's Health 1830–1910*. (London: Croom Helm).

Smith, T. (1928). The decline of infectious diseases in its relation to modern medicine. *Preventive Medicine* **11**, pp. 345–363.

Sosner, S. (undated). Folkevekst og Flytting, I–II, Diss, Stensiltrykk, University of Oslo. Referred to in I. Larsen, (1979). Eighteenth-Century Diseases, Diagnostic Trends and Mortality, (Oslo: University of Oslo Press).

Springett, V.H. (1950). A comparative study of tuberculosis mortality rates. *Journal of Hygiene* **48** (3), pp. 361–395.

Stanley, N.F. and Joshke, R.A. (1980). *Changing Disease Patterns and Human Behaviour*. (London: Academic Press).

Starr, S. and Berkovich, S. (1967). Effects of measles: gama-globulin modified measles, on the tuberculin test. *New England Journal of Medicine* **95**, pp. 729–745.

Steinitz, R. (1965). Pulmonary tuberculosis and carcinoma of the lung. *American Review of Respiratory Diseases* **92**, pp. 758–766.

Stewart, G.T. (1981). Whooping cough in relation to other childhood infections in 1977–79 in the United Kingdom. *Journal of Epidemiology and Community Health* **35**, pp. 139–145.

Stocks, P. (1935). The effect of influenza epidemics on the certified causes of death. *Lancet*, 1935 (2), pp. 386–396.

Stocks, P. (1953). A study of the age curve for cancer of the stomach in connection with a theory of the cancer-producing mechanism. *British Journal of Cancer* **7**, pp. 407–417.

Stocks, P. and Lewis-Faning, E. (1944). Wartime incidence and mortality from respiratory tuberculosis. *British Medical Journal* 1944 (1), pp. 581–583.

Stolnitz, G. (1955 and 1956). A century of international mortality trends, Part I. *Population Studies* **9**, pp. 24–55; Part II, Vol **10**, pp. 17–42.

Sundbärg, G. (1905). *Dodlighteten af Lungtuberculos i Sverige åren 1751–1830*. (Uppsala).

Susser, M. and Stein, Z. (1962). Civilisation and peptic ulcer. *Lancet* 1962 (1), pp. 115–119.

Tanner, J.M. (1968). Earlier maturation in Man. *Scientific American* **218** (1), pp. 21–27.

Tanner, J.M. (1986). Physical development. *British Medical Bulletin* **42**, pp. 131–138.

Tauber, I. (1958). *The Population of Japan*. (Princeton).

Taylor, A.J., ed. (1975). *The Standard of Living in Britain in the Industrial Revolution*. (London).

Terada, H., Baldini, M., Ebbe, S. and Madoff, M.A. (1966). Interaction of influenza virus with blood platelets. *Blood* **28**, pp. 213–228.

Tobacco Research Council (1963). *Tobacco Consumption in Various Countries, Reasearch Paper No. 6.*

Townsend, P. and Davidson, N. (1982). *Inequalities in Health: The Black Report*. (Harmondsworth: Penguin).

Tranter, N.L. (1985). *Population and Society 1750–1940*. (London: Longman).

Tromp, S.W. (1963). *Medical Biometereorology*. (New York: Elsevier).

Trowell, H. (1974). Diabetes mellitus death rates in England and Wales 1920–70 and food supplies. *Lancet* 1974 (2), pp. 998–1002.

Tudor, V. and Strati, T. (1977). *Smallpox: Cholera.* (Tonbridge Wells: Abacus).

Turner, J.A.P. (1972). Chapter in *Pulmonary Disorders, Vol. I*, E.L. Kendig Jnr. ed. (Philadelphia: Saunders).

Turpeinen, O. (1978). Finnish death rates 1749–1773. *Population Studies* **32** (3), pp. 523–542.

Turpeinen, O. (1979). Fertility and mortality in Finland since 1750. *Population Studies* **33** (1), pp. 101–114.

Turpeinen, O. (1980). Les causes des fluctuations annuelles du taux de mortalité finlandaise entre 1750 et 1806. *Annales de Demographie Historique*, pp. 287–296.

Ueda, K. (1983). *Recent Trends of Mortality in Asian Countries.* (Tokyo: SEAMIC).

United Nations (1948–) *Demographic Yearbook.* (New York: UN).

United Nations (1962). *Population Bulletin of the United Nations, No. 6.* (New York: UN).

United Nations (1982). *Levels and Trends of Mortality since 1950.* (New York: UN).

United States Department of Commerce (1921–). *Annual Statistical Reviews for the United States.* (Washington DC: Bureau of Census).

United States Department of Health Education and Welfare (1920–). *Vital Statistics of the United States.* (Washington DC).

United States Department of Health Education and Welfare, *Reported Incidence of Selected Notifiable Diseases, United States, Each Division and State, 1920–1950. Vital Statistics Special Reports*, 37, 9. (Washington DC).

United States Department of Health Education and Welfare (1950–). *Annual Supplement to the Morbidity Weekly Reports.* Washington DC: Centre for Disease Control).

United States Surgeon-General (1964). *Smoking and Health.* (Washington DC: United States Department of Health Education and Welfare, Advisory Committee to the Surgeon-General of the Public Health Service).

Ütterström, G. (1954). Some population problems in pre-industrial Sweden. *Scandivian Economic History Review* **2**, pp. 103–165.

Van de Walle, E. (1978). Accounting for population growth. *Science* **197**, p. 653.

Waldron, H.A. and Vickerstaff, L. (1977). *Intimations of Quality: Ante Mortem and Post Mortem Diagnoses.* (London: Nuffield Provincial Hospitals Trust).

Walker, W.J. (1977). Changing United States life styles and the declining vascular mortality: cause or coincidence? *New England Journal of Medicine* **297**, pp. 163–165.

Warner, J.O. and Marshall, W.C. (1976). Crippling lung disease after measles and adenovirus infection. *British Journal of Diseases of the Chest* **70**, pp. 89–94.

Warren, J.C. (1837). *Surgical Observations on Tumours.* (Boston: Crocker and Brewster).

Waterfield, M.D., Scrace, G.T., Whittle, N., Strobant, P., Johnsson, A., Wasteson, A., Westermark, B., Heldin, C.-H., Huang, S.S. and Devel, T.F. (1983). Platelet-derived growth factor is structually related to the putative transforming protein p 28^{sis} of simian sarcoma virus. *Nature* **304**. pp. 35–39.

Watkins, C.J., Leeder, S.R., Corkhill, R.T. (1979). The relationship between breast- and bottle-feeding and respiratory illness in the first year of life. *Journal of Epidemiology and Community Health* **33**, pp. 180–182.

Watt, R. (1813). *Treatise on the History, Nature and Treatment of Chincough.* (Glasgow).

Watterson, P. (1984). Environmental factors in infant and early childhood mortality decline in England and Wales, 1895–1910. *The Society for the Social History of Medicine, Bulletin* **35**, December, pp. 37–40.

Watterson, P.A. (1988). Infant mortality by father's occupation from the 1911 census of England and Wales. *Demography* **25** (2), pp. 289–306.

West, R.R., Lloyd, S. and Roberts, C.J. (1973). Mortality from ischaemic heart diseases: association with the weather. *British Journal of Preventive and Social Medicine* **27**, pp. 36–40.

West, R.R. and Lowe, C.R. (1976). Mortality from ischaemic heart diseases, inter-town variation and its association with climate in England and Wales. *International Journal of Epidemiology* **6** (2), pp. 195–201.

Whittle, H.C., Bradley-Moore, A., Fleming, A. and Greenwood, B.M. (1973). Effects of measles on the immune response on Nigerian children. *Archives of the Diseases of Childhood* **48**, pp. 753–756.

Widen, L. (1975). Mortality and Causes of Death in Sweden during the 18th Century. *Statistisk Tidskrift*, (Stockholm: Government of Sweden).

Wilson, G.N. (1905). Measles: its prevalence and mortality in Aberdeen. *Public Health* **18**, pp. 65–82.

Wing, S. (1984). The role of medicine in the decline of hypertension-related mortality. *International Journal of Health Services* **14**, pp. 649–666.

Winter, J.M. (1982). The decline of mortality in Britain 1870–1950. In *Population and Society in Britain, 1850–1980*, T. Barker and M. Drake eds, (London: Batsford).

Winter, J.M. (1982). Aspects of the impact of the First World War on infant mortality in Britain. *Journal of European Economic History* **11**, pp. 713–738.

Wohl, A.S. (1966). *The Housing of the Artisans and Labourers in Nineteenth-Century London, 1815–1914*. PhD thesis, Brown University.

Wohl, A.S. (1983). *Endangered Lives: Public Health in Victorian Times*. (London: Dart).

Wong, Chimin K. and Wu, Lien Teh (1932). *History of Chinese Medicine*. (Tientsin: Tientsin Press).

Woods, R.I. (1987). Approaches to the fertility transition in Victorian England. *Population Studies* **41**, pp. 283–311.

Woods, R., Watterson, P.A. and Woodward, J.H. (1988 and 1989). The causes of rapid infant mortality decline in England and Wales, 1861–1921, Part I. *Population Studies* **42**, pp. 343–366; Part II, **43**, pp. 113–132.

Woods, R. and Woodward, J. (1984). *Urban Disease and Mortality in 19th-Century England*. (London: Batsford).

Woolsey, T.D. and Moriyama, I,M, (1948). Statistical studies of heart disease, II: Important factors in heart disease mortality trends. *Public Health Reports, United States Department of Health Education and Welfare* **63**, 39, pp. 1247–1273.

World Health Organisation (1947–). *Annual Epidemiological and Vital Statistics*. (Geneva: WHO).

World Health Organisation (1948–). *World Health Statistics, Annual*. (Geneva: WHO).

World Health Organisation (1969). *International Classification of Diseases, 8th Revision*. 2 volumes, and earlier revisions. (Geneva: WHO).

World Health Organisation (1983). An integrated programme for the prevention and control of non-communicable diseases, a Kaunas report of meeting on 16–20 November, 1981. *Journal of Chronic Diseases* **36** (5), pp. 281–312.

Wrigley, E.A. (1977). Births and baptisms: The use of Anglican baptism registers as a source of information about the numbers of births in England before the beginning of civil registration. *Population Studies* **31** (2), pp. 281–312.

Wrigley, E.A. and Schofield, R. (1981). *The Population History of England 1541–1871 – a Reconstruction*. (London: Edward Arnold).

Wrigley, E.A. and Schofield, R.S. (1983). English population history from family reconstitution. *Population Studies* **37**, p. 157.

Wylie, C.M. (1961). Recent trends in mortality from cerebrovascular accidents in the United States. *Journal of Chronic Diseases* **14**, pp. 213–220.

Wyon, J.B. and Gordon, J.E. (1971). *The Khanna Study: Population Problems in the Rural Punjab*. (Cambridge Mass: Harvard University Press).

Yelling, J.A. (1986). *Slums and Slum Clearance in Victorian London*. (London: Allen and Unwin).

Zinsser, H. (1934). *Rats, Lice and History*. (Reprinted Basingstoke: MacMillan, 1985).

Appendix 2a Percentage of deaths attributed to different causes in the London Bills of Mortality, 1650s to 1830s

Decade	Convulsions	Teething	Abortion and stillborn	Rickets	Consumption	Fevers	Smallpox	Measles	Whooping cough	Apoplexy and sudden death	Dropsy	Old age	Inflammation (intestinal)**	Asthma and tissick	Total causes shown here
1650s	5.6	6.8	3.6	3.1	20.9	8.9	6.0	0.4		0.8	5.0	8.8	(5.5)		75.4*
1660s	5.1	4.8	2.1	1.5	13.8	9.0	3.6	0.4		0.3	4.1	4.4	(8.5)	(28.5)	86.1
1670s	11.2	6.2	3.4	2.1	15.6	10.4	7.1	0.8		0.4	4.4	5.0	(17.0)	(Plague)	83.6
1680s	16.5	5.3	3.0	1.8	16.2	14.2	7.4	–		0.5	3.5	5.5	(13.8)		87.7
1690s	19.2	5.6	2.4	1.5	15.7	13.5	4.7	–		0.5	3.2	5.4	(7.6)		79.3
1700s	27.7	6.9	2.8	1.7	15.0	16.0	5.6	0.5		0.7	4.1	8.7	(5.5)	1.6	96.8
1710s	28.3	5.3	2.6	0.7	12.0	14.9	8.9	1.1		0.7	3.3	8.4	(3.1)	1.5	90.8
1720s	25.2	5.9	2.3	0.4	11.1	13.1	7.5	0.5		0.6	3.5	8.1	(2.5)	1.9	82.6
1730s	30.4	5.4	2.4	0.3	15.9	13.4	7.6	0.7		0.8	3.9	7.0	(1.4)	2.2	91.4
1740s	25.9	4.8	1.7	0.1	17.4	16.6	8.2	0.6	0.5	0.9	4.2	8.3	0.2	2.3	91.7
1750s	26.3	4.2	2.8		19.3	13.4	9.4	1.1	1.4	1.0	4.1	7.6	0.3	1.7	92.6
1760s	26.0	3.6	3.0		21.0	14.8	10.5	1.1	1.2	1.0	4.0	6.7	0.4	1.7	94.0
1770s	26.5	3.5	3.1		21.4	12.4	10.2	0.9	1.5	1.0	4.3	6.1	0.5	1.7	93.1
1780s	24.2	2.4	3.2		24.5	12.7	8.8	1.2	1.5	1.2	4.6	6.6	1.2	1.7	93.8
1790s	21.9	2.1	3.7		23.0	10.1	9.2	1.3	2.0	1.1	4.5	6.3	1.8	2.5	89.5
1800s	19.5	2.0	2.8		23.4	9.4	7.3	2.7	3.1	1.6	4.4	7.9	3.2	3.0	90.3
1810s	17.7	2.1	3.5		23.8	5.6	4.4	3.7	3.3	1.9	4.1	8.9	4.7	3.9	87.6
1820s	13.8	2.1	4.0		22.9	4.5	3.5	3.3	3.3	2.3	4.6	9.2	9.6	4.0	87.1
1830s	9.0	1.8	3.9		17.2	3.0	2.8	2.4	3.5	1.8	3.6	10.6	8.8	3.8	72.2*

* The much lower proportion of deaths in these two decades reflects transfers, e.g. 'chrisomes and infant deaths' (8.9%), and in the 1830s new categories: cholera (3.1%), scarlet fever (1.4%) and a separate category for head dropsy (3.0%).

** The gastro-intestinal group before the 1740s includes surfeit, twisting and griping of the guts, and bloody flux, while there were probably other smaller categories also reflecting mortality from diarrhoea and dysentery and other gastro-intestinal diseases.

Sources: London Bills of Mortality, held in the Guildhall Library, London; J. Marshall (1832) *Mortality in the Metropolis* (London) summarised the Bills up to 1830.

Appendix 2b   Dr Heysham's table of deaths at different.ages and for different causes in Carlisle, 1779–87*

	(0–4)	(5–9)	(10–14)	(15–19)	(20–9)	(30–9)	(40–9)	(50 +)	All Ages
FEVERS									
Inflammatory fever	3	–	–	–	1	–	–	1	5
Nervous fever	2	3	1	4	3	9	15	22	59
Putrid fever	5	4	1	2	8	5	8	10	43
Jail fever	4	2	1	2	–	2	3	–	14
Mortification	–	–	–	–	–	–	–	3	3
Sore throat	3	–	–	–	–	–	–	–	3
Pleurisy	3	2	1	1	–	1	2	9	9
Stone and Gravel	–	–	–	–	1	–	1	7	9
Rheumatism	–	–	–	–	–	–	–	6	6
Gout	–	–	–	–	–	–	1	3	4
Smallpox	225	8	2	–	3	–	–	–	238
Measles	28	2	1	–	–	–	–	–	31
Scarlet fever	31	4	2	1	1	–	–	–	39
Thrush	63	2	–	–	–	–	–	–	65
Consumption	34	15	10	15	45	34	31	30	214
Worm fever	19	8	–	–	–	–	–	–	27
Flooding	–	–	–	–	–	–	3	–	3
Teething	3	–	–	–	–	–	–	–	3
Other diseases (5)	–	–	–	1	1	–	1	2	5
NERVOUS									
Apoplexy		–	–	1	–	2	5	24	32
Palsy		–	–	–	–	–	1	13	14
Fainting		1	–	–	–	1	2	2	6
Indigestion		–	–	–	–	1	6	14	21
Convulsions	10	–	–	–	–	–	–	–	10
Epilepsy	–	–	–	1	1	1	–	1	4
Asthma	1	–	–	–	–	–	2	24	27
Chincough	18	1	–	–	–	–	–	–	19
Looseness	7	1	1	1	1	1	2	5	18
Other diseases (4)	–	–	–	1	–	2	–	1	5
Weakness of infancy	204	–	–	–	–	–	–	–	204
Decay of age	–	–	–	–	–	–	–	226	226
Dropsy	1	1	2	3	3	5	5	29	49
Dropsy of the brain	2	2	1	–	–	–	–	–	5
King's Evil	–	2	–	–	–	–	–	1	3
Venereal disease	–	–	–	–	1	–	1	–	2
Jaundice	3	–	–	–	1	–	5	4	13
LOCAL DISEASES									
Cancer	–	–	–	–	–	–	–	5	5
Difficult delivery	–	–	–	–	4	4	1	–	9
Unknown diseases	32	11	5	–	2	8	9	41	115
Other diseases (8)	1	–	–	1	–	1	2	4	9
Accidents	7	5	2	4	3	4	2	2	29
GRAND TOTAL	709	74	30	38	79	81	108	496	1,615

*   Lonsdale notes that the year 1780 was not included and that the data were either lost or not accurate enough.

Source: H. Lonsdale (1870) *The Life of John Heysham MD*. (London: Longmans Green).

Appendix 2c Percentage decennial population growth before and after 1800: a comparison of England with other European countries

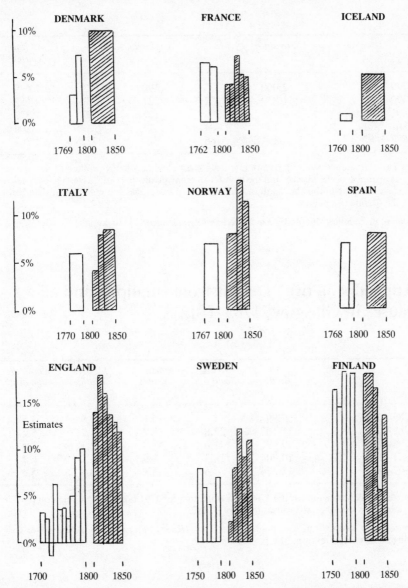

Sources: Census data only from B.R. Mitchell (1971) *European Historical Statistics, 1750–1970* (London, MacMillan); Estimates for England from E.A. Wrigley and R. Schofield (1981) *The Population History of England 1541–1871 – A Reconstruction* (London: Edward Arnold); Census data are for England and Wales, for 1800–50.

Appendix 3a (i)   Annual average death rate per million from some infectious diseases in Sweden for the period 1779–89 to 1872–82

	Smallpox	Measles	Diptheria	Scarlet fever	All four causes
1779–1789	2,060	347	190	(52)	2,649
1790–1800	1,879	452	221	(80)	2,633
1801–1811	797	399	127	(50)	1,373
1861–1871	198	404	511	690*	1,804
1872–1882	194	166	715	732	1,807

* The tenfold increase in the death rate from scarlet fever probably resulted from improved recognition of the disease and the transfer of many deaths previously classified vaguely as 'fevers'. Despite this the death rate for the four diseases was still much lower than before the decline of smallpox.

Source: P. E. Siljeström (1885) En Studie i Sjukdomsstatististik (Stockholm).

Appendix 3a (ii)   Deaths from smallpox and all causes in Glasgow, 1783–1812

	All deaths	Crude death rate	Smallpox deaths %	Measles deaths %	Whooping cough deaths %
1783–1788	9,994	*	19.6	0.9	4.5
1789–1794	11,103	27.8	18.2	1.2	5.1
1795–1800	9,991	21.6	18.7	2.1	5.4
1801–1806	10,304	18.3	8.9	3.9	6.1
1807–1812	13,354	20.6	3.9	10.8	5.6

* No population figure for the 1780s available; that for 1791 taken from Creighton (66,578) compares with the 1801 census figure of 84,122.

Source: data taken from C. Creighton (1894) A History of Epidemics, (Cambridge: Cambridge University Press), p. 513, p. 635.

Appendix 3b (i) Finland: crude death rates per 1,000 for smallpox and typhus/typhoid, 1751–1806

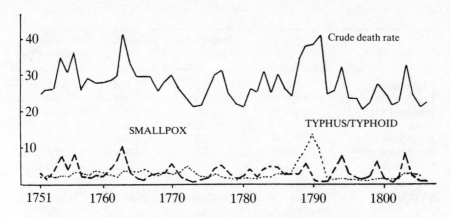

Source: O. Turpeinen (1980) Les causes des fluctuations annuelles du taux de mortalité Finlandaise entre 1750 et 1806. *Annales de Demographie Historique* (Paris), p. 288.

Appendix 3b (ii) Geneva: mortality quotients per 1,000 at ages 1–4, 1620/9 – 1790/9

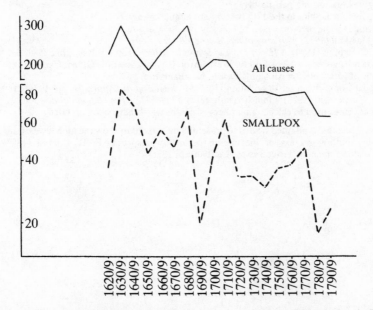

Source: A. Perrenoud (1978), La Mortalité à Géneve de 1625 à 1825. Annales de Demographie Historique (Paris), 1978, pp. 209–233.

Appendix 3c   Proportion of deaths due to smallpox in different parts of Europe in the 18th century

		Smallpox deaths	All deaths	Deaths due to smallpox (%)
Kilmarnock	1728–62	621	4,514	13.8
London[1]	1710–39	63,579	772,751	8.2
Boston, Lincs.[2]	1749–57	106	691	15.3
Maidstone	1752–61	252	1,462	17.2
Whitehaven*[3]	1752–80	570	2,969	19.2
Northampton*[4]	1740–74	377	3,536	10.7
Edinburgh*[2]	1744–63	2,441	24,322	10.0
26 Towns	Smallpox	(Case-fatality rate)		(16.9)
6 Villages	Census	(Case-fatality rate)		(24.1)
Dublin	1661–90	(472)[†]	(2,236)[†]	21.1
	1715–46	13,759	74,585	18.4
Copenhagen[5]	1750–69	6,267	71,170	8.8
Sweden[5]	1749–73	171,058[†]	1,382,834	12.4[‡]
Finland[6]				
Rural parishes	1749–73	2,730[‡]	18,920	14.4[‡]
Urban parishes	1749–73	1,640[‡]	12,390	13.2[‡]

* Figures are for one parish only.
[†] Figures for Dublin in the 17th century are annual averages.
[‡] Includes some measles cases, but mostly smallpox deaths.
[1] J. Marshall (1832) *Mortality in the Metropolis* (London).
[2] C. Creighton (1894) *A History of Epidemics in Britain* (Cambridge), pp. 525–6, p. 540.
[3] Parish Register for Holy Trinity, Whitehaven (County Records Office, Carlisle).
[4] Bills of Mortality for All Saints Parish, Northampton.
[5] Royal Commission on Vaccination (1889–96) *First Report, Appendix*, pp. 107–113.
[6] O. Turpeinen (1978) Finnish death rates 1749–1773. *Population Studies*, **32**, p. 528. Death rates used to calculate numbers of deaths which have been rounded.

Source: The table is adapted from one presented by Razzell to show the high level of smallpox mortality before the use of inoculation became widespread, P. E. Razzell (1977) *The Conquest of Smallpox* (Firle, Sussex: Caliban), p. 133.

Appendix 3d Average annual death rate per 100,000 for the main causes recorded in the London Bills of Mortality

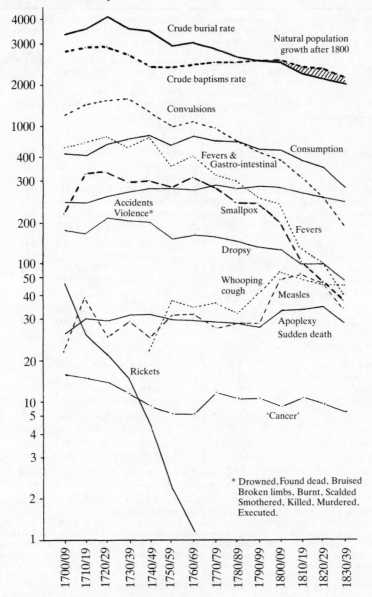

Source: J. Marshall (1838) *Mortality in the Metropolis* (London). Population base discussed in Chapter 3, note 45. Gastro-intestinal group includes surfeit, griping of the guts, bloody flux and, later, inflammation.

Appendix 4a   Change in the overall death rate attributed to different cause-groups in England

Cause-groups	Percentage change in total death rate attributed to cause-groups			Contribution to a unit change in the death rate			Death rates per million		
	London	*England & Wales*		*London*	*England & Wales*		*England & Wales*		
	1720s to 1820s	*1848–54 to 1901*	*1901 to 1971*	*1720s to 1820s*	*1848–54 to 1901*	*1901 to 1971*	*1848–54*	*1901*	*1971*
Abortion/Stillbirth	− 0.7			−0.012					
Dropsy	− 1.7			−0.028					
Fevers	−11.3			−0.188					
Convulsions/Infancy[1]	−23.8	−2.5	−10.0	−0.396	−0.113	−0.147	2,571	2,018	319
Smallpox	− 6.1	−1.2	− 0.1	−0.102	−0.052	−0.001	263	10	0
Respiratory TB	− 1.9	−7.5	− 7.4	−0.032	−0.333	−0.108	2,901	1,268	13
'Old age'	− 4.4	−2.4	− 5.4	−0.074	−0.105	−0.079	1,447	930	16
Childbirth/Pregnancy	− 0.5	−0.3	− 0.4	−0.008	−0.012	−0.006	130	71	3
Accidents/Violence	+ 0.1	−0.6	− 1.7	+0.002	−0.025	−0.025	761	640	345
Other	− 9.7	−5.6	− 8.28	−0.164	−0.252	−0.120	2,886	1,653	264
Respiratory		+2.3	−12.6		+0.104	−0.185	2,239	2,747	603
Whooping cough		−0.5	− 1.8		−0.023	−0.027	423	312	1
Measles		−0.3	− 1.6		−0.013	−0.024	342	278	0
Scarlet fever and Diphtheria		−2.8	− 2.4		−0.124	−0.035	1016	407	0
Other TB		−1.0	− 3.2		−0.043	−0.047	753	544	2
Typhoid and Typhus		−3.8	− 0.9		−0.170	−0.013	990	155	0
Cholera, Diarrhoea and Dysentery		−2.7	− 7.1		−0.120	−0.104	1,819	1,232	33
Digestive diseases		−0.5	− 2.8		−0.024	−0.042	706	586	105
Nervous system		−0.1	− 1.4		−0.002	−0.021	316	305	63
Nephritis		+0.5	− 2.0		+0.020	−0.030	291[3]	391	46
Urinary diseases		−0.1	− 0.4		−0.003	−0.006	107	91	23
Cerebrovascular		−0.4	− 1.2		−0.018	−0.017	890	803	603
Rheumatic HD		+1.9	− 2.4		+0.086	−0.034	64	487	88
Other circulatory		+2.5	+ 3.0		+0.113	−0.043	634	1,186	1,688
Cancer		+2.5	+ 1.9		+0.110	+0.028	307	844	1,169
TOTAL	−60.2[2]	−22.4	−68.3	−1.002	−0.999	−1.000	21,856	16,958	5,384

[1] Teething accounted for 17.1% of infancy deaths in the 1720s and convulsions 72.8%. The registration data include mainly convulsions, teething, prematurity and congenital disease.

[2] Based on burial rates for the area of the London Bills for the 1720s and 1820s of 47.3 and 19.0. The latter figure is rather low, but is based on the census population and probably reflects the fact that many deaths were not included. The burial rate for the earlier period is based on a figure of 600,000 for the whole of London in 1700, and assumes that the same proportion of 85% were within the area of the Bills as at the 1801 census. These data only give very rough estimates, but the relative changes probably adequately reflect the contribution of the main recording groups.

[3] This figure has been revised from that of 615 given by McKeown.

Source: London Bills of Mortality; J. Marshall (1832) *Mortality in the Metropolis* (London); data from the Register-General, age-standardised to 1901 population by T. McKeown (1976) *The Modern Rise of Population* (London: Edward Arnold), pp. 55–62.

Appendix 4b Cause-specific infant mortality rates for England and Wales and their contribution to decline in IMR

Cause	Infant mortality rate per 1,000 births and (%)			Contribution to unit of decline in IMR 1901–71
	1848–54	1901–10	1971	
Whooping cough	5.88 (3.8)	4.89 (3.8)	0.03 (0.2)	0.04
Measles	2.10 (1.4)	2.56 (2.0)	0.01 (0.1)	0.02
Smallpox	2.18 (1.4)	0.01 (–)	– (–)	–
Scarlet fever	1.79 (1.2)	0.16 (0.1)	– (–)	–
Meningitis	n/a	1.99 (1.6)	0.18 (1.0)	0.02
Diarrhoea and dysentery	13.32 (8.6)	15.20 (11.9)	0.42 (2.3)	0.13
Digestive diseases	7.34 (4.7)	8.38 (6.6)	0.36 (2.0)	0.07
Non-respiratory tuberculosis	7.55 (4.9)	4.77 (3.7)	– (–)	0.05
Respiratory TB	2.72 (1.8)	0.40 (0.3)	– (–)	
Respiratory diseases	19.96 (12.9)	22.36 (17.5)	3.17 (17.7)	0.18
Congenital anomaly	1.21 (0.8)	4.63 (3.6)	3.77 (21.1)	0.01
Convulsions	33.12 (21.3)	12.50 (9.8)	– (–)	0.11
Teething	3.49 (2.2)	1.64 (1.3)	– (–)	0.01
Prematurity	27.76 (17.9)	20.09 (15.8)	1.83 (10.2)	0.17
Debility		16.37 (12.8)	– (–)	0.15
Atrophy	9.86 (6.3)			
Other and ill-defined	14.33 (9.2)	9.21 (7.2)	7.06 (39.4) (6.03 Perinatal other than immaturity)	0.02
Accidents and violence	2.68 (1.7)	2.39 (1.9)	1.07 (6.0)	0.01
TOTAL	155.29 (100.0)	127.55 (100.0)	17.90 (100.0)	1.00

Sources: Data from Register-General, *Annual Review for 1855*; *Decennial Supplement 1901–10*; *Annual Report for England and Wales*, 1971.

Appendix 4c   Male infant mortality rate per 1000 live births in England and Wales

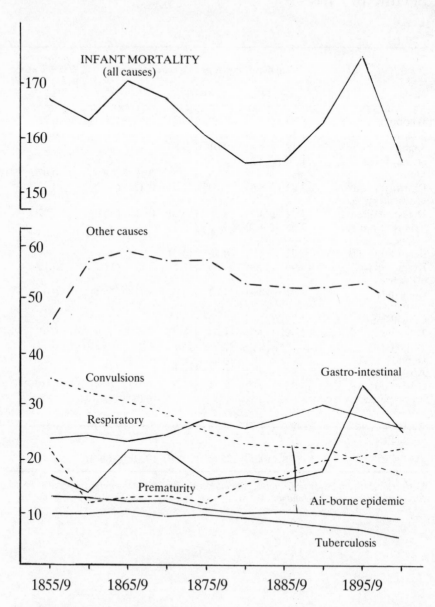

Note: Air-borne epidemic disease group: measles, scarlet fever, whooping cough, diphtheria, croup and smallpox.

Source: Registrar-General, *Annual Reports for England and Wales.*

Appendix 5a Death rates per million from bronchitis in England and Wales

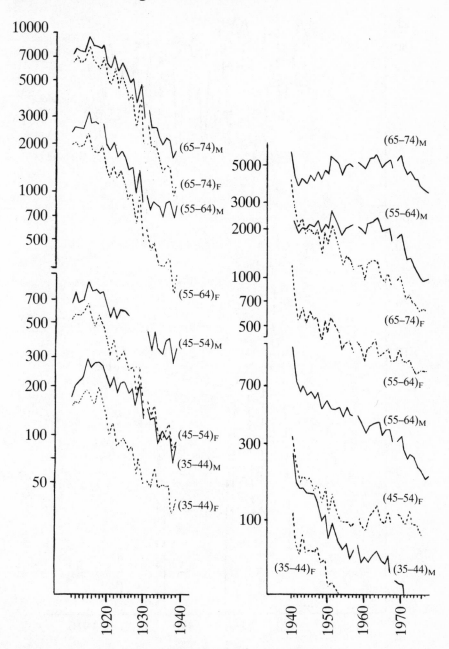

Sources: Registrar-General, *Annual Reports*, *Annual Statistical Reviews*.

Appendix 5b   Crude death rates per 100,000 in Ireland 1866–1910

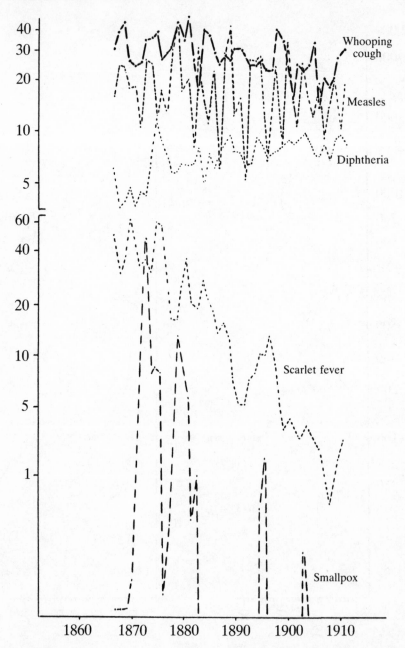

Source: Annual Reports of the Registrar-General for Ireland.

Appendix 5c Triennial death rates per million in London at ages 0–9 years for air-borne infectious diseases

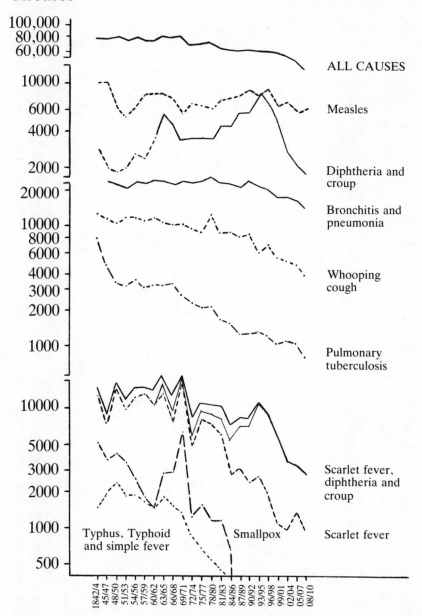

Source: Registrar-General (1838–) *Annual Reports for England and Wales* (London: HMSO)

Appendix 6a Contribution of falling mortality at different ages to decline in the age- and sex-standardised death rate for England and Wales, 1848–54 to 1971

	Contribution to ASDR by mortality at different ages and (%)			Contribution to change in ASDR at different ages		Contribution made to a unit decline in the overall age-standardised death rate	
	1848–54	1901	1971	1848–54 to 1901	1901 to 1971	1848–54 to 1901	1901 to 1971
0–	3.96 (18.4)	4.31 (25.5)	0.29 (8.2)	+0.35	-4.03	-0.08	0.30
1–4	3.44 (16.0)	1.87 (11.1)	0.04 (1.1)	-1.57	-1.83	0.34	0.14
5–14	1.56 (7.2)	0.67 (4.0)	0.05 (1.4)	-0.89	-0.63	0.19	0.05
15–24	1.65 (7.7)	0.74 (4.4)	0.09 (2.6)	-0.91	-0.65	0.20	0.05
25–34	1.70 (7.9)	0.93 (5.5)	0.08 (2.3)	-0.77	-0.85	0.17	0.06
35–44	1.62 (7.5)	1.18 (7.0)	0.16 (4.5)	-0.44	-1.02	0.10	0.08
45–54	1.57 (7.3)	1.42 (8.4)	0.34 (9.7)	-0.15	-1.08	0.03	0.08
55–64	1.79 (8.3)	1.78 (10.5)	0.59 (16.8)	-0.01	-1.19	0.00	0.09
65–74	2.07 (9.6)	2.04 (12.1)	0.83 (23.6)	-0.03	-1.21	0.01	0.09
75+	2.18 (10.1)	1.96 (11.6)	1.05 (29.8)	-0.22	-0.90	0.05	0.07
All Ages ASDR	21.53 (100.0)	16.91 (100.0)	3.52 (100.0)	-4.62	-13.39	1.00	1.00

Note: Age-specific death rates for 1848–54 and 1971 were applied to the male and female population of 1901. Deaths at different ages were then divided by the total population at 1901 to calculate the contribution to the overall death rate made by mortality changes at these different ages.

Source: Data from Register-General, *Annual Reports* and *Annual Statistical Reviews* for England and Wales.

Appendix 6b   Average annual death rates per 1,000 in England and Wales for quinquennial periods, 1841/5 to 1946/50

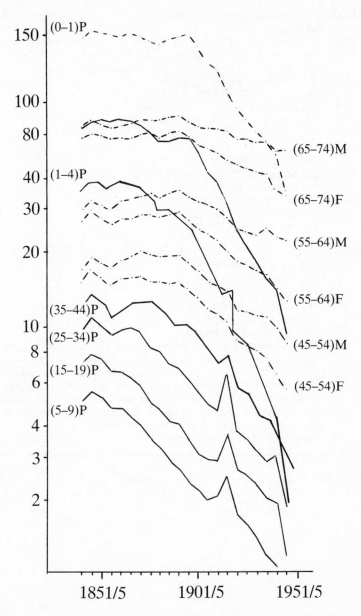

Source: Registrar-General, *Annual Report for England and Wales, 1950* (London: HMSO)

Appendix 6c   *Disease classification changes*

Circulatory diseases:

1882–1900	: Group VI, 3, Circulatory diseases and apoplexy, hemiplegia, brain paralysis.
1901–1910	: Group B, III and IV, Diseases of heart and blood vessels.
1911	: 2nd revision ICD, 47, 64–66, 77–85, 142.
1921	: 3rd revision ICD, 51, 74, 75, 83, 87–90, 91b, c.
1931	: 4th revision ICD, 56, 82, 90–95, 97–103.
1940	: 5th revision ICD, 58, 83, 90–103.
1950–1955	: 6th and 7th revs., 330–334, 400–468.
1968–1975	: 8th and 9th revs., 393–398, 400–438.

All Neoplasm:

1911	: 2nd revision ICD, 39–46, 53, 129, 131.
1921	: 3rd revision ICD, 43–50, 65, 137, 139.
1931	: 4th revision ICD, 56, 82, 90–95, 97–103.
1940	: 5th revision ICD, 58, 83, 90–103.
1950	: 6th and 7th revs., 140–239.
1968	: 8th and 9th revs., 140–239.

Respiratory diseases:

1911	: 2nd revision ICD, 10, 89–92.
1921	: 3rd revision ICD, 11, 99–101.
1931	: 4th revision ICD, 11, 106–109.
1940	: 5th revision ICD, 33, 106–109.
1950	: 6th and 7th revs., 480–502.
1968	: 8th and 9th revs., 470–493.
1940	: Method changed for assignment of the primary cause of death, which affected mainly the respiratory group. The removal of specially defined procedures for assigning primary cause when more than one cause was mentioned on the certificate, resulted in more deaths being given as bronchitis when the underlying cause was inferred from the statement made by the certifier. The change coincided with the 5th revision, and although the effect was considerable, the trends in mortality can still be interpreted with reasonable certainty.

Source: World Health Organisation (1969) *International Classification of Diseases* 8th revision.

Appendix 6d Age-specific death rates per 1,000,000 for some non-communicable diseases in England and Wales

Age group	Period	MALES			FEMALES		
		Diabetes	Nephritis	Liver cirrhosis	Diabetes	Nephritis	Liver cirrhosis
Under 1 year	1848–72	1	32	–	2	21	–
	1901–10	2	259	–	1	191	5
	1921	–	101	–	–	85	5
1–4 years	1848–72	3	51	–	17	35	–
	1901–10	5	118	–	30	104	2
	1921	8	71	–	30	52	3
5–14 years	1848–72	7	30	–	6	21	–
	1901–10	14	57	2	15	52	2
	1921	16	43	1	21	41	2
15–24 years	1848–72	13	43	–	13	34	–
	1901–10	31	79	3	31	81	2
	1921	37	58	1	37	80	1
25–44 years	1848–72	46	121	–	23	79	–
	1901–10	68	253	84	56	246	72
	1921	66	172	26	59	143	14
45–64 years	1848–72	92	263	–	39	149	–
	1901–10	260	1,195	505	221	846	–
	1921	206	772	228	208	575	93
65 and over	1848–72	145	395	–	44	212	–
	1901–10	728	2,980	604	544	1,897	349
	1921	649	2,448	349	636	1,685	143

Source: W. P. D. Logan (1950) Mortality in England and Wales from 1848–1947. *Population Studies*, **4**, pp. 132–178.

Appendix 6e   Death rates per 1,000,000 persons in England and Wales, age- and sex-standardised to 1901 population

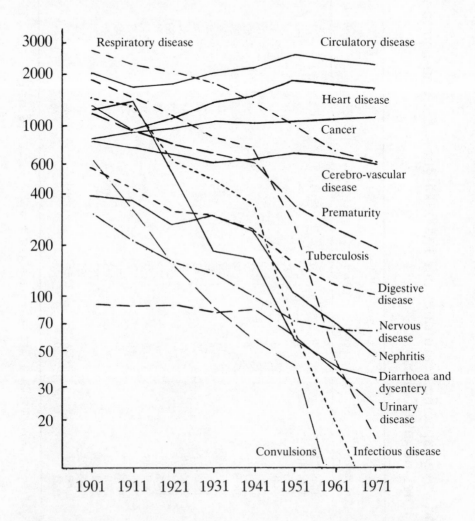

Source: Data taken from T. McKeown, R.G. Record and R. Turner (1975) An interpretation of the decline in mortality in England and Wales during the 20th century, *Population Studies* **29**, p. 391.

Appendix 6f A comparison of death rates per 100,000 at ages 45–54 years in 1981, for CD and Cancer in selected Western populations

Country*		Neoplasms		Circulatory disease		Ill-defined	Total
		Death rate	Percentage of total	Death rate	Percentage of total	Percentage of total	Death rate
Australia	(M)	167.9	26.8	273.8	43.6	(0.4)	659.9
	(F)	144.7	44.8	90.5	28.0	(0.3)	323.3
Austria	(M)	206.1	25.0	264.9	32.1	(0.4)	825.3
	(F)	159.3	45.3	76.6	21.8	(0.3)	351.3
Belgium	(M)	201.6	29.4	228.4	33.4	(5.3)	684.7
	(F)	165.8	44.7	80.4	21.7	(4.3)	371.1
Canada	(M)	159.5	25.8	249.4	40.3	(1.1)	618.3
	(F)	158.9	47.4	74.6	22.4	(1.0)	335.3
Denmark	(M)	154.6	24.3	249.8	39.2	(4.5)	637.5
	(F)	222.8	50.7	80.2	18.2	(3.2)	439.5
Finland	(M)	164.8	19.3	394.4	46.3	(0.4)	852.6
	(F)	117.0	42.5	79.5	28.8	(0.1)	275.6
France	(M)	277.7	35.5	154.6	19.7	(5.1)	782.8
	(F)	127.3	41.3	45.8	14.9	(4.3)	308.2
Germany FR	(M)	177.5	25.4	245.4	35.1	(3.3)	698.3
	(F)	155.0	44.6	74.6	21.6	(2.2)	347.7
Greece	(M)	141.9	31.9	161.5	36.3	(1.4)	445.5
	(F)	125.4	51.3	56.2	23.0	(1.9)	244.5
Iceland	(M)	118.2	23.2	218.2	42.9	(3.6)	509.1
	(F)	110.1	54.6	27.5	13.6	(–)	201.8
Ireland	(M)	169.2	25.5	325.3	49.1	(0.1)	663.0
	(F)	189.2	46.7	117.8	29.1	(–)	405.4
Italy (1980)	(M)	232.1	35.0	201.6	30.4	(0.6)	664.0
	(F)	140.6	47.2	71.2	23.9	(0.6)	297.6
Netherlands	(M)	164.2	31.9	217.4	42.3	(5.6)	514.1
	(F)	159.8	53.7	66.3	22.3	(4.1)	297.6
New Zealand	(M)	191.8	29.1	304.6	46.3	(–)	658.5
	(F)	189.0	48.3	109.4	27.9	(0.2)	391.6
Norway	(M)	125.7	21.9	235.6	41.1	(5.6)	573.8
	(F)	142.8	51.9	59.4	21.6	(1.8)	275.1
Portugal	(M)	169.2	20.8	204.6	26.0	(6.0)	788.1
	(F)	129.6	36.6	96.1	27.1	(3.6)	354.3
Spain (1979)	(M)	163.0	27.7	179.9	30.6	(2.3)	587.6
	(F)	118.0	42.5	75.4	27.2	(2.1)	277.7
Sweden	(M)	116.7	21.3	214.0	39.1	(0.8)	548.0
	(F)	144.6	51.1	54.3	19.2	(0.2)	282.7
USA	(M)	187.3	24.9	314.3	41.8	(1.6)	751.7
	(F)	169.6	41.7	113.0	27.8	(1.5)	406.9
England and and Wales	(M)	165.4	27.3	314.6	51.9	(0.1)	606.0
	(F)	190.7	50.6	97.7	25.9	(0.1)	376.7

* The 19 countries have estimates available for GDP. England and Wales was not included in the regression analysis because estimates of GDP relate to England only.

Source: World Health Organisation (1985) *World Health Statistics, Annual* (Geneva).

Appendix 6g (i) A comparison of circulatory-disease death rates and measles incidence rates per 100,000 in several populations

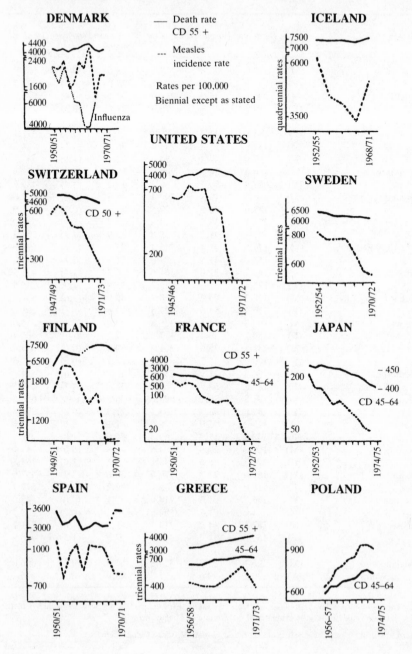

DENMARK

—— Death rate
CD 55 +

... Measles
incidence rate

Rates per 100,000
Biennial except as stated

ICELAND

SWITZERLAND

UNITED STATES

SWEDEN

FINLAND

FRANCE

JAPAN

SPAIN

GREECE

POLAND

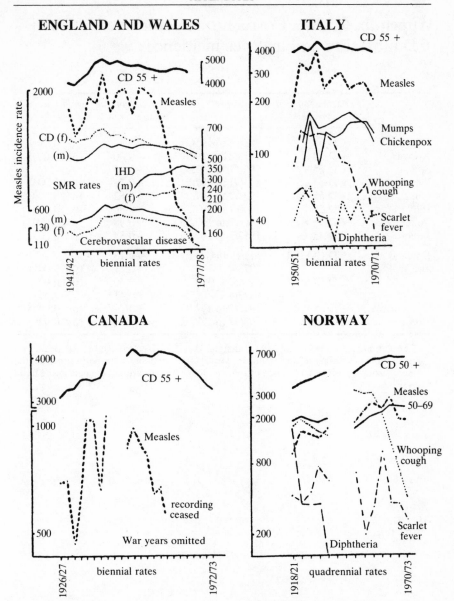

ENGLAND AND WALES

ITALY

CANADA

NORWAY

Note: Within each graph the same semilogarithmic scale has been used for each trend. Group VII ICD codes used: 390–458 (8th revision); 330–334, 400–468 (6th, 7th); 58, 83, 90–103 (5th); 56, 82, 90–95, 97–103 (4th); 51, 74, 75, 83, 87–90, 91b, c (3rd); 47, 64–66, 77–85, 142 (detailed 2nd).

Sources: Registrar-General (1900–); OPCS (1974–); WHO (1948–) *Epidemiological and Vital Statistics*; *World Health Statistics* Annual (Geneva); Dominion Bureau of Statistics, *Vital Statistics*; (1920–) *Annual Report of Notifiable Diseases* (Ottawa); Central Bureau of Statistics (1880–) *Health Statistics* (Oslo).

Appendix 6g (ii)   Correlation coefficients between CD mortality and measles incidence

	CD trend and period		Correlation with measles trend	Significance level
Canada	CD 55+	1926/7 to 1956/7	+0.32	
Norway	CD 50+	1918/21 to 1970/3	+0.80	(p< 0.0005)
Spain	CD 55+	1950/1 to 1972/3	+0.45	
Denmark	CD 55+	1950/1 to 1970/1	+0.78	(p< 0.005)
United States	CD 65–74	1921/2 to 1973/4	+0.82	(p< 0.0001)
Italy	CD 55–64	1900/1 to 1972/3	+0.80	(p< 0.0001)
Poland	CD 45–64	1956/7 to 1972/3	+0.98	(p< 0.0005)
Japan	CD 45–64	1952/3 to 1974/5	+0.84	(p< 0.005)
England and Wales	CD (ASDR)	Males 1941/2 to 1973/4	+0.13 +0.71*	(p< 0.001)
	CD (ASDR)	Females 1941/2 to 1973/4	+0.60 +0.41*	(p< 0.005)
South-west Wales	CD 65+	1946/7 to 1972/3	+0.79	(p< 0.0005)
Wales	CD 65+	1946/7 to 1972/3	+0.57	(p< 0.025)

* Correlation coefficients calculated for detrended series. Even though the CD death rate trend for males was particularly influenced by cigarette-smoking in the postwar period, the more strongly positive correlation of short-term fluctuations around the underlying trend is significant.

Appendix 6h   Age-standardised death rates per million for certain non-communicable diseases in England and Wales

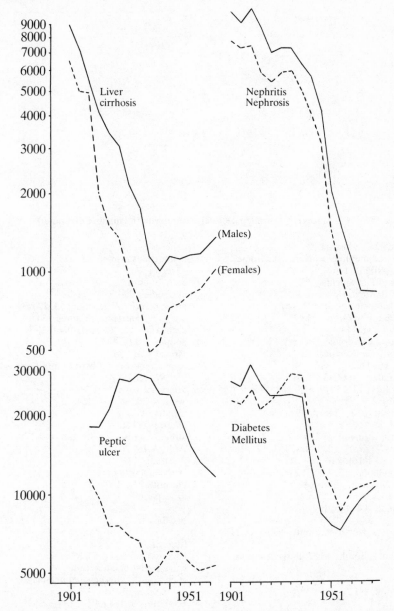

Source: Data from M. Alderson (1981) *International Mortality Statistics* (London: MacMillan).

Index